Sisters of Fortune

5/94

NANCY COFFEY HEFFERNAN

&

ANN PAGE STECKER

Sisters of Fortune

Being the true story of how three motherless sisters

saved their home in New England and raised

their younger brother while their father went fortune

hunting in the California Gold Rush.

✳

UNIVERSITY PRESS OF NEW ENGLAND

HANOVER & LONDON

University Press of New England, Hanover, NH 03755

© 1993 by University Press of New England

All rights reserved

Printed in the United States of America 5 4 3 2 1

CIP data appear at the end of the book

In Memory of Lizzie, Annie, and Charlotte Wilson

Contents

PART THREE

"Where Is Father?"

(1 8 5 5 – 1 8 6 4)

Illustrations follow page 194

Introduction: "The Feeling Passes the Letter Remains"

I n 1858, Mary Elizabeth Wilson Sherwood wrote to her father to apologize for a fit of pique "The feeling passes the letter remains." Diaries, account books, inventories of household goods, wills, and letters—private artifacts that remain long after their immediate significance or usefulness has passed—are revolutionizing historians' understanding of those fleeting feelings and activities that inform the texture of daily life. Social historians interested in family life and particularly in the experience of women, children, workers, racial and ethnic minorities, and other classes excluded from the more traditional concerns of political and economic historians now rely on these valuable new sources to flesh out information gathered from public records.

Consider the family of James Wilson, Jr., of Keene, New Hampshire. Wilson's public life sounds a note, if minor, in the political history of the nineteenth century. Political historians might include him in a footnote to a history of the Whig party in New Hampshire. He appears in records and histories of the U.S. Congress of 1848–1850. He was occasionally the subject of fiery denunciations in the public press. There is a handsome portrait of him in the Cheshire County Historical Society.

His oldest daughter, Lizzie, would appear in accounts of nineteenth-century society and etiquette books, for instance, Appleton's *Cyclopedia of American Biography* (New York 1888):

Sherwood, Mary E., author, b. in Keene, N.H. about 1830. She is the daughter of James Wilson, member of Congress from New Hampshire, and married to John Sherwood, a lawyer of New York city [*sic*]. She is well known as a society leader, and has devoted special attention to the advancement of literary and artistic pursuits. One of her sons married, in 1887, Rosina Emmet, the artist. Mrs. Sherwood has given in New York city and elsewhere, for several seasons, readings that have been exceedingly successful, has written for various periodicals, and is author of

"The Sarcasm of Destiny" (New York, 1877); "Home Amusements" (1881); "Amenities of Home" (1881); "A Transplanted Rose" (1882); and "Manners and Social Usages" (1884).

But Lizzie had two younger sisters whose distinctive voices would be lost to us without the letters they wrote to their father. Lizzie never mentions Annie and Charlotte in her memoirs, and they never wrote their autobiographies. There are no accounts in any newspapers of their political stands. Their portraits do not hang in historical societies. And still their voices are as polished and nuanced as their sister's, their passions as compelling, their stories as interesting. Without their voices we would not be able to understand the Wilsons as a family that was both typical and, as Lizzie says, eccentric. As Carl Degler has proposed, these letters allow us to construct "a synthesis of the history of women and the history of the family."

Often, what matters to Lizzie, Annie, and Charlotte has been creatively exegeted by historians using similar documents. Laurel Ulrich calls on the same material for her brilliant study of seventeenth-century New England women in *Good Wives* (1980) and *A Midwife's Tale: The Diary of Martha Ballard* (1991). Passages in letters from Lizzie to her friend Susan Colby echo the easy intimacy and touching passion described by Carroll Smith-Rosenberg in "The Female World of Love and Ritual: Relations between Women in Nineteenth-Century America" (1975). The cultural and emotional "bonds of womanhood" described by Nancy Cott implied for the Wilson sisters both the reality of shared burdens and the possibility of sympathetic connection. Throughout their letters it is clear that they not only share each other's trials but also find solace in the sense of solidarity created by their father's absence. Their sentimentalized treatment of the death of friends—particularly that of a young Keene neighbor, Sarah Adams—parallels similar accounts elaborately and elegantly analyzed in Ann Douglas's *Feminization of American Culture* (1988). So too, like many young women and girls of their class, do they draw immense imaginative pleasure from their reading of the popular English novels of their day. As they enjoin their father to participate in the pleasures of Dickens, Thackeray, and Gaskell, it is easy to suspect, with Rachel Brownstein (*Becoming a Heroine: Reading about Women in Novels* (1982), that the novels provide the daughters with effective ways to rehearse possible life plots for themselves.

Nevertheless, these women and this family persist in remaining eccentric. Their lives and their letters refuse to fit into any theoretical prescription for women's lives or family life in the nineteenth century. It is the peculiarity of the Wilsons' story, as well as the charm of their style, that makes the correspondence interesting as both literature and history.

Letters have long been considered an ideal vehicle for domestic narrative. Samuel Richardson recognized that in 1739 when he wrote the wildly popular epistolary novel *Pamela*. A. S. Byatt paid tribute to that tradition as late as 1990, when she used the form in her novel *Possession*. Writers like Madame de Sévigné in the seventeenth century and J. Hector St. John de Crèvecoeur in the eighteenth chose the form of the letter in which to write engaging essays—more public than private—without adopting the fictional voice. Somewhat less public are the private letters of famous people, which were written perhaps with only half an eye to publication. For example, Joseph Conrad's voluminous letters are being exhaustively collected and edited by Frederick Karl and Laurence Davies. Besides adding significantly to the canon of interpretation of this novelist's work and life, they also may be treated as another product of his creative genius.

Valuable as letters by these public figures are, letters of private people are also creating a niche for themselves as literary texts. What is perhaps surprising is how clearly the Wilson family concerns—debts, private ambitions, education, religious practices, treatment of servants, friendship, marriage, childbirth and illness—intersected with major public events like the gold rush, the slavery issue, the Civil War, the search for land in the West, and the transition from an agrarian to an industrial society. At this junction of public and private events, they observed, judged, participated in, and even influenced the course of public history. Out of this experience they produced three hundred letters that, taken together, create a personal narrative that borders on autobiography.

The aim of these letters written to their father (who had gone to California) was not, after all, to record history, personal or public, but to save their family from dissolution, a remarkable achievement for the language of three unprofessional writers. In fact, they deployed the language and form of the letter with extraordinary effectiveness to record and manipulate their experience. No doubt this ability helped them manage their affairs. But in their skilled hands, letter writing also became a tool, even a weapon, to get what they wanted from their father. In the final analysis, the three women constructed in their letters the father they needed and did not have. The writers accomplished this remarkable feat in the conventional form of the letter; but as Richardson recognized, this form can bear a heavy emotional weight.

Familiar as it is in this lengthy correspondence, the form emerges afresh, like the form of any other literary work. The writers establish in the dateline the place and the time of compositions, which in letter writing acts as a kind of reverse foreshadowing. Instead of suggesting what might happen next, the dateline reminds us that what follows is valid only to that date and location. Unfolding events remind us again and again how vital this warning is. In letters there are no promises or predictions of closure.

The salutation, in which these women identify and address their father, often seems to summon his spirit into their presence. Put in the context of the opening lines of the letter, the salutation absorbs a tone of love, anxiety, gratitude, anger, boredom, happiness—whatever emotion informs the body of the letter.

Though the body of the letter is less formulaic, it too has its conventions, beginning with thanks for letters or presents and talk about the weather and everybody's health. Even in letters carrying important news, the writers often spend a page or two discussing minor matters before moving on to important subjects like money, an engagement, a new baby, a serious illness, or a death. However intense, anxious, elated, resentful, or even desperate they sound on these matters, the writers end with pleasantries: bits of gossip, entreaties that the father take care of his health, God's blessing, and a wish for his return. These pleasantries merge with the complimentary close, which is often less formulaic and more effusive than those employed by contemporary writers. Here they reaffirm some specific emotional and filial relationship with their father and validate their work with the signature. In the closing they reaffirm him as their father, the head of the family, and themselves as his daughters, loving and dutiful.

The form of the letter is not, perhaps, more distinctive to the nature of the letter than what happens once the letter leaves the writer's hand. Unlike writers of novels, poems, essays, and the like, these women not only knew precisely who would read their letters, but they had in mind a general notion of how long it should take for their father to receive their letters and how long before they could expect a reply.

Since the writers' perception of that one reader controlled the selection and shape of the material, other readers are nudged out of the direct line of communication. We are not the designated audience and cannot possibly know the hundreds of friends and acquaintances they mention or understand all of the family jokes and allusions. Nearly 150 years have elapsed since these letters were written. Although writers who direct their work to a public readership may anticipate such a time lapse, may even long for this kind of immortality, these women's time frame has long since collapsed.

They did not expect us to be reading their correspondence. In fact, private letter writers often seek to control the readership of their letters, in postscripts ranging from the businesslike "copy to" to the dramatic "Burn this letter!" The first courtesy suggests that the recipients of letters expect them to be intended for their eyes only. If they are not, then politeness requires that the addressee be informed that that writer does not consider the correspondence confidential. The injunction "Burn this letter!" suggests just the opposite. The writer wishes to protect the confidentiality of the communication and fears that other eyes besides the addressee's might fall on information the writer considers confidential. We are those other eyes—intruders and eavesdroppers. We may be curious, titillated, or a little embarrassed at reading someone else's mail, but in any case we can never fit ourselves into the direct line of communication. At first glance our situation seems thoroughly disadvantageous, but we may find that it evokes an interesting and different response to the text. Because the writers did not expect to be read by strangers 150 years after their letters left their hands, we may credit the letters with a kind of integrity we would hesitate to accord public writers. After all, when peering through a keyhole, we don't expect the action we witness to be staged. Better yet, the intense emotions that inform the correspondence don't threaten us but simply engage us in the story. Unlike James Wilson, we don't need to resist the women's blandishments or defend ourselves against their accusations.

From our first reading of the Wilson letters in the dignified calm of the New Hampshire Historical Society, we were impressed with the pace of the narrative the sisters unfold. Our fascination with the narrative's twists and turns persisted as our study progressed from passing original white and blue stationery back and forth to each other, through detailed study of photocopies of the originals, to the more systematic study of typescripts.

In the development of the present manuscript we have thus endeavored to preserve the letters' pace and to liberate the remarkable voices of the letter writers by making certain editorial decisions regarding the scope of material cited from the letters. We have also made changes, dictated by concern for readability, in the original spellings and formats.

As indicated by ellipsis dots, we have deleted material from the letters to avoid slowing down the pace of the narrative with needless repetition. Often this repetition results from the natural courtesies, obeisances, or coy comments that characterize the openings and closings of correspondence. For instance, we have eliminated repeated references to the weather, which commonly follow the salutation. At other times deleted material consists of idiosyncratic family talk, such as repeated references to minor characters and events in family life. In this and other instances deletions allow us to emphasize important events without the distraction of "small talk." Similarly, nearly as many people as are identified and mentioned have been deleted from the letters either because they have little relation to the texture of the narrative or because extensive research has failed to reveal reliable identification. When possible, we have also identified political, literary, and social figures of the Wilsons' day in summary so that they will be familiar when they reappear in the correspondence. Histories of the town of Keene, New Hampshire, and periodicals and newspapers from New York and New England have been particularly valuable sources for understanding the wide web of relationships that sustained the Wilson children.

Finally, in a pragmatic effort to enhance the manuscript's readability,

we have regularized capitalizations, eliminated the excessive use of amper-
sands, and added apostrophes in contractions and the possessive. We believe that these relatively minor and systematic changes avoid unnecessary
imposition of current usage to allow the reader to experience the individual voices of the Wilson correspondents as they unfold their particular
family story.

The correspondence between James Wilson, Jr. (1797–1881), and his four
children may be found lodged in a collection of Wilson's papers (1835–1873)
that occupies twenty-four archival boxes in the permanent collection of the
New Hampshire Historical Society. Of the twenty-four boxes, letters from
his children during his extended stay in California occupy two. From his
oldest daughter, Mary Elizabeth (1826–1903), there are eighty-nine letters
written from 1848 to 1861. The box containing Lizzie's letters also includes
forty letters from her husband, attorney John Sherwood, as well as letters
from several of her sons. Annie Wilson Fiske's (1832–1916) letters to her
father number ninety-nine, written between 1848 and 1861. Letters from
Charlotte Wilson Taintor (1835–1901) to her father, the last of which closes
the family correspondence, number 110, written between 1849 and 1864.
The collection also includes ninety-one letters and items concerning the
education of James Henry Wilson's (1837–1892), some from his own hand
and some from the hand of his admiring and vigilant sisters.

The letters' value to us as history and their charm as literature cannot
compare to their significance for the women who wrote them. Obsessed
as these women are with their father and convinced as they were that only
a patriarchal family could provide them with security and identity, clearly
they created in their letters a father who substituted for the real thing.
While they declare directly or indirectly in every letter that he is the cornerstone of the family, without him they establish a family that functions
extraordinarily well.

PART ONE

"An Eccentric and Curious Thing"

(1 8 4 7 - 1 8 5 1)

"Dear and Sacred Charges"

Once upon a time in New England there lived a poor man who had three daughters. When his wife died, he left his children to go west and seek his fortune. He traveled over land and sea, through mountains and jungles and deserts. He finally arrived at a wild and golden land where he had many adventures. He fought many glorious battles, won a great estate, and found gold. Years passed. Then fortune turned against him: His gold ran out. He lost his great estate. And poorer than ever, he journeyed back to live in the house his daughters had saved for him.

James Wilson, Jr., of Keene, New Hampshire, is the hero of this old tale. In 1850, when he was fifty-three, he left New Hampshire for California, seeking his fortune in land and gold, both of which he found and then lost. Wilson himself, however, would probably have cast himself not as the hero of an old tale but as the dashing protagonist of one of the western adventure stories popular in eastern journals.

However, a different story is to be told about the three daughters Wilson left behind:

Once upon a time there was a poor widower who had three daughters. The eldest was charming and clever and ambitious. The middle one was beautiful and passionate and dutiful. The youngest was sympathetic and observant and thoughtful. When their father abandoned them, they put their wits together to save the family and take care of their young brother . . .

What kind of story would these three women, Lizzie, Annie, and Charlotte Wilson, tell about themselves? Rather than heroines in a fairy story, these three women might have cast themselves in one of the elegant melodramas they saw and admired in New York. In fact, they might have seen something of themselves in even the most outrageous parodies of old melodramas where the villianous mustachioed landlord leers at the heroine, declaring, "You must pay the rent!" or the rich banker threatens to foreclose on the mortgage and put the destitute family out on the street, for the three Wilson sisters faced similar situations so often that their story is inextricably tied to that of their home in New Hampshire. But Mary Elizabeth, Charlotte, and Annie Wilson wrote neither fairy stories nor melodramas. Instead, they created their story and the story of their family in a collection of three hundred vital and articulate letters to their father.

A passionate letter from Lizzie written eight years after their father had left them dramatizes and summarizes the difficulties his children endured during the long years of his absence.

✳ [LIZZIE]   New York Nov 5th 1858

My dear Father,

Eight years ago on the twelfth of Sept. I stood on the wharf at New York (as the carriage was conveying us on our way to the depot) and saw you leaving the port on the Steamship *Georgia* (was it not?). The feeling of gloom and despondency which settled down on my heart *then* comes on me again tonight as I remember it. What power could have sustained me had I seen how long that separation was to be? As it was I felt it enough. One poor girl, with three younger sisters and brother to sustain and counsel and our only support and hope gone gone on that terrible journey. Eight long years away from your young and unprotected daughters. Does it not strike you as an unparalleled fact. What should we think of it, if Mr. Sumner Wheeler or any other man should do so? Does it not strike you, looking at it from a *common* point of view as an eccentric and curious thing?

Since then a veil has fallen between you and me. Before we were intimate. I used to know something of what you meant, what motives activated you, but now I know nothing of you. I write to you begging for a reply. You never make it. I ask for an explanation. You never give it. I entreat it of you. It does not move you. You write of everything else, your farm, your reading, the climate, etc. All very fine letters, but not what I want to know. I want ten minutes *confidence* from you such as your daughter should receive, such as you ought to give her, such as you used to give her. . . .

Then I am astonished at the way you seem to feel toward Annie and Charlotte. The tone of your last letters to them was that of a person writing to some enemy, some hated enemy who had tried to injure him. You not only hint at their probable destitution, which one would think a sufficiently sad thing but you *taunt them* with their inability to work, and their idea of its disgrace. When that letter arrived Annie and Charlotte had been turned out of their own room by my illness. They had had company unexpectedly arrive. Roxana as usual had refused to do anything and they had been working night and day. Annie's hands and face were red with the exertions she had been making. Charlotte was looking over the week's mending. I went in to their crowded room and found them both crying over your letter. "Now Lizzie," said Annie, "won't you read this letter and tell me what I can do. What does Father *mean* by treating me so. I, who am slaving my life out to please him, to manage this place, to economize to work, to think, to worry, until my life has no pleasure in it." I could only tell her I did not know, that you seemed changed most radically since you went away, that you were always kind and lovely to me. Never did Father treat daughter better, but why you feel so toward these poor dear girls who are much better than ever I was, I don't know. *I should like to know* I assure you.

If you were to ask any man in Keene from Mr. Crossfield the carpenter up to Mr. White the clergyman who was the best girl in Keene, they would both tell you Annie Wilson. If you were to ask the poor Irish woman who would have starved but for her who was the best girl in Keene she would say the same. If you want to see a model housekeeper, neat, energetic, economical, you have only to look at her, and yet what an opinion you seem to have of her! If the public could know what *you* seem to think of her they would say there was a new chapter in this most eccentric history of the Wilson family. But God forbid. Let this sad secret be always locked within our own hearts. Now as to the question of spending too much, do you not see that if anyone is to blame, I am the one? The housekeeping of those two girls would not be very expensive if they had not us there all summer. Therefore you should have written to me that it would not be convenient and agreeable for you to have me there this summer, and I should not have taken it amiss. . . . Annie has to be responsible for all these [bills] and really gets the advantage of none of it except the gratification of having her nephews with her. I can offer her the shelter of my roof in return, and that she shall have as long as I have one. God bless her for all her unselfish devotion to me! Poor girl. She has had trouble enough without having her Father turn against her. If she had been a bad undutiful daughter I would not say a word, but she is religious, hard working loving soul devoting her life like a sister of charity to the poor, to my children and to you, and I cannot stand it. I must speak.

Now Father, do if you can raise money enough to pay your passage, come home, don't stay any longer. You said in a letter of June . . . that you would certainly come to attend to that business of Uncle Roberts, and honor demands that you should. Have you no yearnings to see us? Do you not love us better than any one. Don't you want to see your *four grandsons*? Oh do come dear Father. We have not many years to be together on this earth. Do let us have the rest of your life, no matter for fortune. . . . We will economize, only let us have our Father within our grasp. . . .

If by any horrible necessity or determination you don't intend to come home write to the girls what you want to spend and they will conform.

They can give up housekeeping, which with them involves some hospitality and I can refrain from going there. That you will find makes all the difference.

As for Jamie, he is one of the noblest and most satisfactory of young men. Every one speaks well of him. If he gives way to some temptations they are nothing to what he resists. He is not perfect, but he is very good. Surrounded by every temptation I believe he makes a pretty good fight and will make an admirable man. Don't be discouraged or disgusted with him. Let us all try to get him thro' college. He is as handsome as he can be, witty, manly modest and truthful. I dare say he has his little fun now and then, but what fellow that is worth anything don't, at 20? As Thackeray says, 'Glorious youth, it never comes again, let us be fools and enjoy ourselves once in our lives.' But Jimmy is no fool. He has no despicable amount of caution, I can tell you particularly with the young ladies who are all after him.

Charlotte has been miserably this summer but she is better. I felt very much alarmed about her. Charlotte has not much constitution.

You knew I have my fourth son. I am sorry for the other boys that he is not a girl. For my own sake I am glad and for his. I am quite well and strong. Came down to town less than five weeks, and have been quite well all the time. The baby looks exactly like you, has curling black hair, and is very fat and healthy.

. . . Wil and Sam are up at Keene, very splendid indeed, sucking sweet cider *thro' a straw*, and being very big and boyish. Charlotte teaches them to read and works very hard with them. . . .

My dear husband, than whom none more worthy ever lived, has an excellent business, works very hard, is very successful, but our expenses are enormous. I sometimes fear he will break down, but he is patient and courageous. Need I say that I love him dearly, try to make him happy, and to help him bear his burdens.

Do write me soon and tell me that you are coming home. Come to my little house and see how I manage an establishment. Let us read in the next letter, 'expect me by the next steamer.' Then face to face all misunderstandings will vanish away and we shall find that we love each other, all of us as well as ever. . . .

Farewell, dear Father. Don't be angry with me. You know I love you as well as a daughter can love a Father and as poor Queen Katherine wrote to Henry the Eighth, "mine eyes do desire you of all things."

Farewell. God bless you

Your loving daughter   Lizzie

The story they tell in their letters has major characters—Mary Elizabeth, Annie, Charlotte, and Jamie—and minor characters: Wilson's half-brother, Uncle Robert; servants, Roxana (nicknamed Ottie) and George; friends, Susan Colby and Lizzie Eldredge; neighbors, Sumner Wheeler and Hannah Newcomb; a business associate, Mr. Skinner; and several suitors. In fact, practically everyone in Keene, Whig politicians from all over the country, and much of New England society form a chorus in the narrative, adding consistency and historical perspective for both Wilson and the modern reader. Instead of "once upon a time" there are datelines starting in 1848 and ending in 1864, and the poor man who had three daughters is addressed with great intensity: "Dear Father."

Since Lizzie, Annie, and Charlotte created their letters so expressly for their father, our understanding of their story depends to a certain extent on what we can learn about him. Unfortunately, we have not one letter in his hand to them. What we do have is one revealing letter to Jamie, their young brother, written in 1854; records and newspaper accounts of some events in which he was involved; a few haphazard diary entries; some account books, speeches, pamphlets, military records, letters to constituents and political cohorts; and Lizzie's memoir titled *An Epistle to Posterity* (New York: Harper and Bros., 1897)—an interesting title considering the far more revealing letters she had written to her father. James Wilson was a player not totally forgotten in the public record of the bristling middle years of the nineteenth century—the Mexican War, the settlement of the West, the gold rush, the debate over the slavery question. He held the rank of general for his service in the state militia. He served on the Land Commission in California, was accused of corruption and removed from the commission, practiced law, made speeches, bought a farm, found gold at the Gold Bluff, and reveled in the raw excitement of unruly frontier life.

Before General Wilson moved west, he occupied a conspicuous place in politics in New Hampshire and the Northeast. After serving in the state legislature in the 1820s and 1830s, he was nominated for Congress in 1838 and for governor of New Hampshire in 1839. He developed a wide circle of political and personal friends, including Daniel Webster, to whom he lent money and for whom he named one of his sons. Declared by Webster to be "the first of the stump speakers" (*Epistle*, 5), Wilson spoke with great success for Whig causes and was rewarded in 1841, when President Tyler appointed him surveyor general in Iowa and Wisconsin. He traveled to the frontier, where his fortunes flourished. When he returned home in 1845, he won election to Congress. He won a second term in 1847 and a third in 1849 and seemed set for a career in Washington; yet before his third term was over, Wilson resigned his seat and went to California.

Why did he go? A revealing insight to this question comes not from the record of his public life but from the portrait drawn in the memoirs that his eldest daughter wrote in 1897, sixteen years after her father's death: "My recollections of childhood are very vivid, especially of my father, a tall and most picturesque man, with blue eyes and fine curling black hair, with a great laughing mouth full of white teeth and of eloquent voice, and a laugh which filled the whole county of Cheshire; a man who liked to dance and to march, . . . a man, in fact, who had the veriest charm for children—a tremendous vitality. [He] dressed in furs and moccasins in January, when he would go up to the White Mountains to hunt the moose with Anans, an Indian of the St. Francois tribe. . . . He was impulsive and lavish, imprudent and always in hot water. . . . The strange contradictions, which had pervaded his nature—the child and the giant—it was all there—noble, lovable, and youthful . . ." (*Epistle*, 1–17). She recalled that years later he "always sighed for a buffalo-hunt and a chase over the prairies" (*Epistle*, 1).

On his first trip west, when he went to Iowa and Wisconsin to parcel out public land for the government, Wilson left his wife, Mary, and the younger children in Keene but took with him sixteen-year-old Lizzie. She and her father endured a long and wearying trip by stagecoach from Harrisburg, Pennsylvania, to Wheeling (now West Virginia), with "nothing decent to eat for three days and nights" (*Epistle*, 24). Relief came when they traveled down the Mississippi and Ohio rivers by steamboat; she met engaging men and danced and flirted as though the trip were one long party. But life on the prairie was something else. Waking up one morning in a log cabin, she opened her eyes to see a black snake "wriggling his dreadful head" through one of the crevices. After that she "determined never to undertake frontier life" (*Epistle*, 29). No such sights could frighten Wilson. Undaunted by snakes, fatigue, and hunger, he spent four years as surveyor for the U.S. government. Investing in land near Dubuque and copper mines in Wisconsin, he made a small fortune. The experience prepared him for his move to California.

Keene, New Hampshire, November 1850—the dateline for the first letters the three women wrote after their father's departure. Lizzie was twenty-four, Annie was eighteen, Charlotte was sixteen, Jamie was thirteen. Their mother was dead. Their father was on his way to California. For months and even years the three women perceived that date as the beginning of waiting, uncertainty, and hoping that eventually their father would return to Keene and the family would come together, secure again in their own home.

Although the Wilsons, like most prosperous Keene families, spent winters away in Washington, Boston, New York, or Hartford, Keene was home. In the 1840s, James Jr., Mary, and their children lived on the corner of Main and Emerald streets in a large elegant brick house with white columns and four tall chimneys. Although they lived in town, they were remarkably self-sufficient. The house was built on several acres of land, with a large vegetable garden and a flower garden. A few blocks away, bordering the railroad, the Wilsons had several more acres of land, with a small orchard, a pasture, a hay field, a carriage house, and other outbuildings. From this land they harvested enough produce to provide for the family, with some left over to sell. The house itself had cavernous storage cellars for wine and food. The Wilsons were deeply attached to their house. Mary Elizabeth, Annie, Charlotte, and Jamie had been born there, as well as their three brothers who had died as young children—William at three, James at two and a half, and Webster at five. Their house and gardens provided them the continuity and security that children need and many adults seek. As they grew up, the children sometimes complained about provincial Keene, but they continued to find their house and garden almost as mystically peaceful and perfect as the garden of Eden.

James Wilson's family had originally emigrated from Ireland to Belfast, Maine, and thence to Peterborough, New Hampshire. In 1815 James Wilson, Sr., moved his family to Keene. He prospered in law and real estate and built the finest house in town. He married twice and had one son by each wife—James Jr. and Robert. Among the professional families in this remote town in northern New England—the doctors, mill and factory owners, bankers, clergymen, and attorneys—the Wilsons held themselves in high esteem.

On the Ashuelot River, ten miles east of the Connecticut River in southwest New Hampshire, the town of Keene settles comfortably at the foot of Mount Monadnock. The mountain casts its shadow over that small hilly region to which it gives its name. In the middle of the nineteenth century the Monadnock was dotted with farms, more or less self-sufficient. Keene itself was a farming center, with several flourishing industries as well. With a population of 3,392, the town manned two textile mills, two glass factories, and several inns. The Wilsons owned one of those inns, called The Emerald House, which was across the street from their own house. Mr. Sumner Wheeler, widely esteemed for his integrity, owned of one of the glass factories and lived next door to the Wilsons. Miss Catherine Fiske ran a girls' boarding school, of which the town was very proud and which Lizzie and Annie attended. The passenger station of the newly built Ashuelot Railroad, which had recently transfigured the town by providing access to Boston, New York, and Washington, was just two blocks from the Wilsons' house. The railroad facilitated their escape to warmer climates during winter months, when temperatures reached thirty below and snow piled up three feet overnight in northern New England.

Although they considered their family to be deeply involved in the town, separations from each other and from their home mark the story of the Wilsons. Before James Wilson, Jr., left for California, he had already spent months and years away from Keene and his family, in Washington and in

Iowa and Wisconsin. They had already suffered the deaths of three siblings and finally that of their mother.

While her husband was away, the beautiful Mary Lord Richardson Wilson managed her children and her bustling house, took care of the poor, and provided lavish hospitality for family friends and her husband's political cronies. Had she lived, she would probably have done the same thing while James was in California. But Mary Wilson was a woman broken in spirit and in body. She had watched three of her babies die. When her five-year-old son Webster died of the croup, she hadn't much emotional capital left to invest in her other four children. Retreating to a life of puritanical renunciation, she reared her children with many tears and few smiles or caresses (*Epistle*, 7).

Still, she was a dutiful wife, though she did not enjoy public life. When James Wilson was elected to Congress in 1847, she was too sick to join him in Washington and spent much of the winter of 1848 in her room. By March, when she was better, she promptly left her three younger children in boarding schools and took Lizzie to Washington.

In 1848, the year Susan B. Anthony and Elizabeth Cady Stanton led the first women's rights convention in Seneca Falls, New York, Mary Wilson lived with her family in Washington, D.C. Women's rights were not part of her agenda, but neither was social life in the capital. Although Mary's "charms excited national admiration" in Washington, she found no pleasure in the glittering society there (*Epistle*, 7). With a "soul made for renunciation," she enjoyed neither admiration, society, or frivolity.

On the other hand, twenty-one-year-old Lizzie, who had already sampled the pleasures of Washington when she was there at sixteen with her father, delighted in Washington society. Fifty years later she recalled in her memoir the fashions of the "belles of [the] ball . . . falling ringlets . . . a low-cut gown . . . a pearl necklace . . . white kid gloves. Madame Bodisco . . . with a Russian head-dress full of diamonds" (*Epistle*, 49). She met John C. Calhoun, Dolley Madison, Abraham Lincoln, Henry Clay, and Presidents Polk, Taylor, Tyler, and John Quincy Adams, as well as almost everybody else of note—and Lizzie noted them all (*Epistle*, 50). She was smuggled into one of Mrs. Polk's last state dinners and recalled that state dinners were long, dreary, and tedious for a sixteen-year-old. (Her memory may have been faulty, for Lizzie would actually have been twenty-three when Polk left office—though state dinners probably still would have seemed long, dreary, and tedious.) Unlike her mother, Lizzie mostly loved the social life of Washington.

Poor health rather than temperament or grief drove Mary to leave Washington with Lizzie and return to Keene in 1848, while James Wilson remained to finish the session. In May, on a train trip, she became seriously ill. The telegraph line being down, Lizzie wrote a note to her father about the attack, in which she received generous assistance from Keene neighbors who were with her. It is with this note that James Wilson started saving family letters and thus began to preserve the narrative of his daughters' young adult years.

✳ [LIZZIE]   May 26 Friday

Dear Father

Mother has had a more violent attack than ever since she left home so Locomotion has been impossible. If she can be moved, we shall leave here tomorrow evening with Mr. and Mrs. Eastman and go the Fall river route. I fear she will not be able. I am very well attended too by Danl Trumbull and Mr. and Mrs. Eastman. Mother is made very Comfortable also. You will probably be here Monday if we stay. I delayed writing before because they said I could telegraph you but telegraphic wires are broken. . . .

M. E.

In Boston sixteen-year-old Annie, eager to come home from school, was unaware of her mother's deteriorating health. She did not plan to return to school, which she hated, referring to it ironically as "this *divine place!*" She especially looked forward to spending time with her father. "Oh! my dear father I do long to be with you, and talk to you, and have you talk to me. I have never lived with you much, but I trust next winter we shall get to knowing each other perfectly" (6-30-48).

In July, young Charlotte, studying Latin, French, and arithmetic at school in Boston, also longed to see her father. "I hope that Congress will soon adjourn for I wish to see you very much, indeed." By the time she got home, she felt optimistic about her mother's health. "Mother has been very sick, some of the time, since you have been away, and not able to leave her room, but she is much better now and is able to be down, and has been to ride with Uncle Robert several times, in the rockaway" (7-1-48). The invalid would benefit from the fresh air in this light, low open carriage while being protected from the sun by the roof.

Lizzie, older and more experienced than Charlotte, appreciated Uncle Robert's helpful offer of the carriage, but she knew he was an unstable support. She enclosed a letter with Charlotte's, describing a quarrel between George, the Wilsons' stalwart gardener and man-of-all-work, and Uncle Robert, in which he undermines Mary's authority with her servants.

✱ [LIZZIE] [July 1, 1848?]

My dear Father,

I received a severe scolding for having written to you, that you were not needed at home, but I thought I could bear it better than *you* could.

All is well except George. He wishes me to write that he does not want to stay. He says Uncle Robert damn's him if he does anything Mother tells him to. *Uncle Robert* came in and told Mother that George had treated him *very badly*, and Mother believes *him*.

She is very reasonable about it and asked George to stay until you came home, tho' I think Uncle Robert is entirely to blame. He told George that he was a fool for doing anything for a damn old crazy woman. . . . Mother don't know anything about it. She thinks Uncle is all right.

Uncle Robert is outwardly very kind, takes Mother to ride and if I make anything nice I send him down some and we have sent him strawberries etc at which he seems pleased.

Write to George, but don't write anything to me that cannot be seen. . . .

Yrs
M. E.

. . . don't ever say a word to any body about the epithets as perhaps George lies, but that is what he said. *Let us avoid difficulty.*

By September of 1848, Lizzie could see that disease was steadily overtaking her mother. Perhaps fearing that the sick woman might die without seeing her husband for the last time, Lizzie wrote a note to her father to hasten his return home.

✱ [LIZZIE] Tuesday noon

Mother is not as well, tho' not more dangerous. I hope you will come home Wednesday. M E

The note brought Wilson to Keene, where his children were watching their mother's decline. He and Lizzie sat at her bedside as Mary Wilson's condition grew worse until she died less than a month after Wilson got home.

On October 21, in reply to a letter of condolence sent by her dear friend Susan Colby, who lived in New London, New Hampshire, about fifty miles from Keene, Lizzie wrote a long letter on black-bordered mourning paper. As Lizzie tells the story of her mother's last days, hints of popular melodrama and the poetry of consolation tint her prose and her perceptions, soothing her grief. Perhaps she was influenced by the popular obituary poetry of people like Lydia Huntley Sigourney, though Lizzie claimed she "never admired her poetry much" (Lizzie to Susan Colby, 7-11-49). (See Ann Douglas, "Heaven Our Home: Consolation Literature in the Northern United States, 1830–1880" in *American Quarterly* 26 (1974): 496.) Here pain, fatigue, illness, grief, and death itself are swallowed up in duty and the promise of joy eternal. This letter is the only one in the correspondence in which we get a sense of the impact that their mother's death must have had on the children.

✳ [LIZZIE]   Keene Oct 21st 1848

You are happily not one of those my dear Susan, who with the best intentions, sink the knife still further into the lacerated heart, therefore your letter was one of the most grateful, most comforting of the many which have poured in upon me. . . . I ought to have been prepared for my mother's death and perhaps I was as much as one can be. For eight weeks she was scarcely ever from my sight—confined to the bed and with symptoms I knew were dangerous but I could do so much—my physical strength and anxiety enabled me to be [with] her always sixteen hours a day and often the entire twenty four—for [five] days and nights I watched her without taking off my clothes—only throwing myself on the bed for a few minutes during the day—it seemed as if such care must [save] her!—I should willingly have done so always but tho' 'the spirit is willing tho' the flesh was weak' I had to sleep—but I did it in her room and always prepared to jump up at a moments notice—think then of my loneliness when she was no longer there for me to serve—when the mainspring of my exertion was gone. I seemed to drop down as if my body were coming to pieces. Fatigue wiped me completely and bodily and mentally I should have been entirely inert had not her death been so beautiful, my faith so strong and my many ties to life so strong in my Brother and sisters.

Perhaps you will like to know how she has been for the past year. All last winter she was sick—unable to go out and most of the time confined to her room. Towards spring she became better and in the latter part of March able to go to Washington. She was very delicate and required constant care, but the beautiful climate, the change of scene, the interest with which every thing inspired her, helped her very much. I thought she was cured. During the summer she was very happy and quite well tho' not strong. We had several young ladies here and she enjoyed them exceedingly—took no care upon herself but came down when she felt inclined. I found whatever made her more cheerful in mind made her health better. In August she was taken down and was from the first very sick tho' she did not suffer much pain—yet she sank until she died.

During her sickness she did not think that she should die—she always said she wished to live, and she thought she should. Yet she should be resigned and happy if that was the will of God. But the last fortnight her nerves were very weak and she would shed tears often. We would ask her if she were distressed she always said no but that it 'did her good to cry.' She would sit up in the bed and lean forward on my shoulder supported by my arms for hours. The relation seemed changed between us—She was almost a child and I the support—yet always during this last fortnight she was in a lovely frame of mind. She could not find terms sufficiently affectionate in which to address us—On the Sabbath previous to her death she became delirious and continued so with short intervals of sanity until Wednesday morning when her soul seemed to be in Heaven tho' she was still here. She was endeavoring in her broken tho' sweet voice to sing hymns and prayers. Our minister prayed with her. I asked her if she would like to hear music. She said yes. and Chardie played the divine harmonies of [Le Desir?] the language of aspiration, of struggle, of Hope. She listened with great joy and peace. No pain or unhappiness darkened her soul at this moment. She did not seem to notice our tears, but one of us held her hand every moment. She would clasp fervently, and look at us with unspeakable love. But she made no farewells. Her soul seemed to be in a divine atmosphere of love and happiness. At noon she sank into a slumber in which she continued until she awoke in a brighter world. Showing no interval of consciousness meanwhile. Thus human love consigned her with many prayers into that Love Divine of which it is so poor a symbol.

. . . I have been wonderfully sustained, comforted and blessed. I have not suffered one morbid feeling nor has one . . . arisen in my heart. An intense thankfulness for her happy release—a joy that I was enabled to be with her has taken the sting from death. The happy spirit with which she left us has also given me a peace which passeth understanding. She gave the children long ago into my especial keeping. Dear and sacred charges they are to me enough to make life dear.

My dear Father has been very much tried but he has borne everything with the most beautiful spirit and given us reason for many thanks for such a parent. He will be *both* parents—for he unites to his manly qualities the tenderness of a woman.

Annie, Chardie, and Jamie are well and send much love to you whom they all remember with affection. They have born their mother's death with great composure tho' it is a grief which none of them will ever entirely recover from.

We all accompany Father to Washington the last of Nov. I am out of health so much that I cannot well bear the fatigue of housekeeping and as we cannot be separated we are all going. We shall pass a perfectly quiet winter with our books and music.   Love to dear Susie Colby,
                                                                        Lizzie

Since Lizzie was too out of health from caring for her mother to bear the fatigue of housekeeping, at the end of November the grieving children accompanied their father back to Washington. There they spent a winter of mourning though, with the high spirits of young people, they managed to enjoy some of the pleasures of the city, including the company of three Whig congressmen and the clever journalist Charlie March, with whom they shared their boardinghouse.

"We are living very pleasantly at a private boarding house with Hon. George Evans of Me. Hon. G. Ashmun of Mass. Hon. James Dixon of Conn. and a Mr. March of witty propensities. Mr. and Mrs. Dixon are my especial friends. They are a model couple, very handsome, distinguished learned and unpretending . . ." (Lizzie to Susan Colby, 1-4-49). The Dixons and Charlie March made an effort to entertain the children, and with their help the Wilsons managed to get through the winter.

Nearly fifty years later, Lizzie remembered the capital as "a small, straggling city, with very muddy streets in winter; plain living and high thinking; rather uncomfortable quarters in the hotels and boarding-houses; here and there a grand house, but not many of them; the White House, serene and squalid; a few large public buildings; the Capitol, with its splendid dome, like an architect's dream, overhanging and dominating the scene, as it does today, one of the most splendid public buildings in the civilized world. . . . Washington was cold and dreary in winter then. The houses were insufficiently heated . . ." (*Epistle*, 48–49).

Their social life in the capital city was far from the whirl that Lizzie had enjoyed the previous winter. "We have not been out, of course, except on the New Years day and to return some calls—on New Years we made our bow at the White House—Mrs. Polk receives very well and I fear we shall not see as elegant a mistress of the White House next administration. However the old hero [Zachary Taylor] will doubtless summon some worthy representative thither" (Lizzie to Susan Colby, 1-14-49). By January, Lizzie's spirits had improved, as she tells Susan, perhaps in part because of the glittering presence of Lady Bulwer, daughter of the first Duke of Wellington and wife of the British ambassador. "I went to a very splended ball the other night—the almacks of Washington—The Assemblies as they are called. I never saw so many well dressed people—Lady Bulwer was there with many diamonds and we had a very nice time—I danced myself quite lame—and forgot for a few hours that I was more than sixteen. I am glad to find I can enjoy as my sense of enjoyment generally is very much dimmed. . . .

"We have had New Years day excitement too since you were last informed of my movements and a very charming day it was too, I think a holiday is such a necessary thing in this work-a-day world and we have too few of them. Perhaps too much *eggnog* was drunk—but as I did not taste it I of course felt none of the evil effects—Every body was charming—well dressed and good natured. We have been going to some very pleasant little supper parties—What a nice meal a supper is. You meet people so agreeably and then every one's intellect is so freshened up by the contact. Come and see if we do not crowd life with sensation—and that too of the best kind" (Lizzie, 1-11-49). They attended the inauguration of Zachary Taylor and the ball following in a "large wooden barracks." It was a "cold, driving March day." Enthralled as she was, Lizzie later recalled that candles dripped on her bare shoulders and the cold would certainly have given her the flu "if grippe had been the fashion" (*Epistle*, 49).

Although these accounts may give the impression of an extravagant social life, the family was officially in mourning and led a quiet life except for these more or less official functions. Since they could do little visiting, which ordinarily occupied much of the daughters' days, they took advantage of the occupations that only Washington has to offer. "We spend the morning generally at the House or Senate tho' we have not yet heard much eloquence we have heard much fighting which is equally agreeable" (Lizzie to Susan Colby, 1-14-49).

The year of the Wilsons' mourning was an exciting year for the nation. The fighting Lizzie enjoyed was between some old and distinguished political lions. In the Senate, Daniel Webster, Henry Clay, and John C. Calhoun were still trying to hammer out a compromise on the slavery issue that would forestall hostilities between the North and the South. There were also problems stemming from the annexation of California. The treaty ending the Mexican War had been signed in February 1848, ceding California to the United States. All Mexican land grants, which Washington had promised to honor, had to be reviewed. Interest in those land grants had mushroomed since the news reached the eastern states that gold had been discovered at Sutter's Mill in California. When the full impact of the news struck a year later, gold fever swept the nation. The year gave its numerals to the '49ers who stampeded to prospect for treasure in California.

General Wilson was embroiled in a desperate campaign to save his congressional seat against the attacks of Isaac Hill, vitriolic editor of *The Patriot*, the Democratic paper in Concord, New Hampshire. In a series of corrosive editorials, Hill accused Wilson of being "governed by the animal passions and by selfish, mercenary and personal considerations" with a *"total want of correct moral principle"* (*The Patriot*, February 14, 1849, p. 2). Whatever Wilson did disgusted Hill. After Wilson changed his stand on the Mexican War, which he had opposed in Congress, he enthusiastically supported it in stump speeches around New Hampshire; and as an active member of the state militia, he even volunteered to lead a company of soldiers into battle. Though the war ended before his mettle was tested under fire, Wilson was promoted to the rank of general in the militia and was thereafter called "General" by almost everyone. Isaac Hill nicknamed him the "Awful Volunteer."

In the 1840s various congressional bills to regulate slavery sparked intense public debate. Though Wilson voted for a bill giving slaveholders the right to reclaim slaves who had escaped into free states, he opposed the spread of slavery into the territories. His actions suggest, however, that Wilson preferred not to take a stand on these issues at all. After he missed two votes on important slavery questions in the House, Hill changed his nickname to the "Artful Dodger."

Hill's nicknames were paper bullets. In spite of them and Hill's mudslinging, General Wilson's golden oratory, political savvy, and personal popularity won the day.

While Wilson was fighting and winning this political battle, the season changed. In Washington, as the winter thawed and turned to spring, the family's grief abated also. In June they returned in somewhat better spirits to the house they had left so mournfully eight months earlier. Annie kept house for Jamie and Charlotte back in Keene; Lizzie visited the Dixons from Washington, now living at their home in Connecticut. Under the influence of these amiable friends, she realized that she felt happier. She recovered "the enthusiasm of former and brighter days," and she was once again "open to agreeable influences" and aware "that fine people could excite [her] to as much admiration as of yore" (Lizzie to Susan Colby, 7-11-49). At their house she met Lydia Sigourney, whose work sentimentalizing the deaths of children and pure maidens was all the rage. Though Lizzie thought the poet "scribbled away her genius," in person Sigourney was "lovely and amiable," and Lizzie planned to spend a week with her at some future time.

She confessed to her friend Susan Colby a secret ambition: "I have one great ambition and it is to write well" (7-11-49). She began to show her writing to others and to submit some work—a critique of James Russell Lowell, who was a friend of the Wilsons, and one of *Jane Eyre*—to newspapers and magazines. Admitting that she had "written cartloads that will never see the light," Lizzie urged, "This is my *secret* don't reveal it" (Lizzie to Susan Colby, 7-11-49). Perhaps this reticence grew out of her mother's comment on the first story that she had published anonymously in the Keene paper. The Reverend Abiel Abbott Livermore, the family's beloved Unitarian minister, and others praised the story in Lizzie's presence, as did Mary Wilson herself before she knew her daughter had written it. When Lizzie confessed that she was the author, her mother pronounced the work *"a very poor story indeed"* (*Epistle*, 11). Although in later years Lizzie attributed her mother's disapproval to Mary Wilson's theory that "flattery of any kind was wicked," Lizzie kept her writing secret thereafter until her mother's death. She took up drawing as a hobby and thought she had a natural talent for it. In fact, she said if she ever had to earn her living it would be "taking likenesses"; but when she found, many years later, that she needed money, she earned it with her pen.

Lizzie's resolve to pursue her writing was only one of several plans that changed after Mary Wilson's death. During the improvised winter in Washington the family had established a new order, with father James Wilson as the head and Lizzie stepping into the role of mother with Annie as her helper. During the summer in Keene that new chain of command went into operation.

Lizzie and her father arranged satisfactory schools for the three children, who could not be cooped up in the boardinghouse another winter. Against her own wishes and despite her desire to spend time with her father, Annie went to Mrs. Adams's school in Boston in 1849. Charlotte returned to school with Mrs. Lowell in Boston; Jamie, to Mr. Abbot in Norwich, Connecticut. Lizzie mothered them. They sent their laundry home in valises, to be washed and returned by the servants, but Lizzie made and repaired most of their clothes. She found suitable boarding places for them, kept track of their studies, looked after their health. When they were unhappy or homesick or ill, she went to visit them and reported back to their father, who was in Keene.

"Jamie seems very pleased with every thing and will be very happy I hope. He is a very nice child, physically and mentally and I feel very much satisfied with Mr. Abbott. . . . James wishes his skates, which he forgot. They are in the office closet or in his box in the back chamber where he kept his clothes. Roxana will remember" (Lizzie, 10-31-49).

Since Charlotte was sickly and unhappy at Mrs. Lowell's, Lizzie went to assess the situation. Lizzie, who was ever aware of the social status of the company she kept, however accidentally, was pleased to arrive on the same train as Robert Waterston, a promising Unitarian clergyman; Josiah

Quincy, president of Harvard; and Mr. Albert Fearing, a well-known philanthropist and politician.

❋ [LIZZIE]   Oct 1 1849

My dear Father,
     I arrived here safely and found Chardie very impatient for my arrival.
She suffers considerably from severe headaches which come on in school
and have driven her home several times, more in consequence of excitement than study. Mrs. Lowell has shown herself very kind and considerate
on those occasions, and Chardie is getting over them. . . .
     Mrs. Lowell thinks it is Neuralgia and says she ought to take Valerian.
What do you say? . . . I think it is nothing but the excitement—which you
know she is keenly alive to. We went to Quincy Saturday and spent Sunday.
Mrs. Adams is a most whole hearted excellent woman—and made us very
happy. She begs of Chardie to come every Sunday—and seems to take a
genuine interest in her. Chardie was very happy and bright all the time. Her
boarding place is everything we could wish—in comfort, respectability and
happiness. . . . She loves Mrs. Lowell and feels very much interested in her
lessons.
     We had a very distinguished escort in, in the shape of Mr. Waterston,
President Quincey, and Mr. Albert Fearing, all of whom were very kind
and attentive, and complimentary to you. . . . I shall come in and see Charlotte every day. I am so glad I came with her as I don't know what she
would have done. . . .   Affy your daughter
                                                               M. E. W.

❋ [CHARLOTTE]   Quincy Oct. 14th 1849

My dear Father,
     . . . Lizzie has been in Dorchester all week, and I have been with her all
the time but Monday. Mary Basset goes to school with me. She asked me
from her mother to come out and spend Tuesday night, and as Lizzie was
making me a dress she found it was convenient for me to stay out there, till
she finished it, than to come in town herself every day.
     Every morning we rode in their carriage and it came for us after school.
Mary and I studied till dark or till we had learned our lessons so that none
of them suffered. I enjoyed the week very much and even the studying. . . .
     Mrs. Lowell continued very kind to me. She never requires too much of

me. She seems very anxious that I shall not be pressed beyond my strength, and seems quite interested in me. I think she is becoming more reasonable about the studies of the girls. Perhaps one reason is that one of her own daughters has studied so much, that she has been obliged to tell her, she shall not touch Latin or Italian. This daughter Anna is a very lovely girl and a very hard student also. She is reading Greek now.

. . . I love Mrs. Lowell *very* much. At first I was disappointed in her. I thought her very cold. But now I see nothing in her that is not ad*mir*able (as I used to pronounce it). I have not made any particular acquaintances in school yet, but I was really surprised to see the other morning how many girls I knew in school. . . .

I have heard the most melancholy thing about one of Mr. Sullivan's daughters. The youngest has been in the Insane Asylum all summer. She is only sixteen or seventeen, and the oldest, Lizzie, has been crazy a fortnight this summer. . . . This young lady is very pretty and Mrs. Lowell said she was one of the brightest girls she ever had in school, one of the most gifted. They are all remarkably bright. . . .

I remain your affectionate daughter,   Chardie J. Wilson

While the sisters concurred that the problem was nothing more than excitement, Charlotte's mixed accounts of her own struggles with poor health and the ill effects that study had had on other young women's mental health suggests she suspected that intellectual pursuits could drive her to join the bright Sullivan sisters in the insane asylum. In time she concluded that strenuous physical exercise would counteract the ill effects of mental exercise and adopted a regimen of vigorous walking.

Before her mother's death, Annie had not planned to return to school, so she made no apologies for being miserable there. Although in later years Annie professed that she would have liked to study law if she had been a man, at seventeen she showed no interest in pursuing any kind of studies.

✳   [ANNIE]   Boston Nov. 16th 1849

My dear Father,

I am so homesick today that I can do nothing else, and will therefore write to you. I don't know why I should be so either for my friends are all kindness and attention. Tonight Mrs. Adams is going to take us to the Museum and she has Charlotte here a great deal and seems very fond of her. But still there's an indescribable longing for home, and I can't help it. I want to see you so much, and Lizzie, and home, and every thing connected with it. I am rather more disheartened than usual from the fact that I lost some money yesterday, which is always provoking. My purse had only two and a half or three dollars in it, but it is provoking to *lose* even that. . . .

Love and devotion of your Daughter   Annie

Annie did not return to school in January 1850. At seventeen her formal education ended, and she fulfilled her heart's desire to stay with her father and Lizzie. They were not, however, at home in Keene but in a boarding-house in Washington.

Both socially and psychologically, the family's season of mourning was over with the beginning of the new decade. The wounds from their mother's death might never heal entirely, as Lizzie said, but the young women were ready to pursue the pleasures of society once again. When Annie joined her father and Lizzie in Washington, they no longer spent their days listening to the debates in the House and Senate. Lizzie did not mention in her letters to Susan Colby the debate and roll call on the historic Compromise of 1850, which strained to patch over the rift between North and South. Instead, the two sisters added their names to the list of belles who entertained themselves with balls and parties of the social season and enjoyed the attentions of many young men.

While enjoying the flirtation and frivolity of social occasions, wise young women made hardheaded evaluations of the young men who paid attention to them. Young Annie, less experienced and more impulsive than her sister, flung herself into the scene with enthusiasm but without much judgment. Of her myriad acquaintances Lizzie observed, "Miss Wright still entertains her 'army of generals.' Virginia still rails at the world. Adelaide still worships the English and Annie flirts with the fools" (Lizzie to Susan Colby, 2-3-50).

Lizzie's romances were the subject of considerable gossip. Lizzie understood the subtleties of courtship as she tartly commented to Susan Colby, ". . . you have heard the report which I have often heard—that I am endeavoring to make an *ambitious match*, but the public are not aware probably that an ambitious match is more easily made than a *love match*, and therefore I hope my remaining single may not accuse me in *your* eyes of any such intention" (1-11-49).

Even Henry Clay teased Lizzie about one of her suitors, a widower named Macalaster. "I seem to be the prominent person in everybody's mind here just now from Mr. Macalaster's preference. They are continually making me the subject of innuendoes and even Mr. Clay is very mischievious on the subject. Poor Mr. M. has gone tho' not without 'making a sign' and whenever anything of interest turns up I will acquaint you" (Lizzie to

Susan Colby, 2-3-50). Two dizzying weeks later she had not only rejected Mr. Macalaster but broken the heart of another young man. "I am very sorry to say that there are many things in [Mr. Macalaster] which are really desirable and admirable—so it is with a special regret that I reject a heart so . . . romantically devoted to me. There is something very touching in the love of a man so much older and so superior. . . . I am now really suffering under an affair which has long since driven the Macalaster matter entirely out of my head. There is a young gentleman here—handsome, fascinating, refined and good . . . we seem *born* for each other. I *cannot* marry him I hardly know why—and the poor fellow is miserable" (Lizzie to Susan Colby, 2-17-50).

Mr. Macalaster did not give up, however. When Lizzie and Annie stopped in Philadelphia as they traveled home from Washington, accompanied by Mrs. Sherwood, Mr. Macalaster appeared and showered Lizzie with attention. However, Lizzie had heard a devastating report from one of his relatives, which put an end to any reconsideration of his marriage proposal. "[Macalaster's relative] says he is not an honorable man—has failed repeatedly and put everything out of his creditors hands and made money by it! His houses etc are in his childrens hands. Isn't this a blow—and also that he makes love to every person who takes his fancy" (Lizzie to Susan Colby, 6-3-50).

By March the social season in Washington was over, and the winter in New England was waning. With Annie's head full of plans for a visit to West Point for the spring season at the military academy, she and Lizzie returned to Keene. Annie immediately got sick. "We have the stove up in Mother's room, and it has carried her back painfully to her illness. The weather is detestable two inches of snow and as cold as Greenland. I wish she were back in Washington or in some milder climate" (Lizzie, 4-14-50). But both the weather and Annie's health and spirits soon improved. Only the departure of the Rev. Mr. Livermore and Mrs. Livermore dampened her mood.

✳ [ANNIE]   Keene April 26th 1850

My dear Father,

Here we are very quietly seated in the back parlor, sewing, this beautiful Spring day, with windows open! and birds singing! wondering at a *fable* . . . that snow in Stoddard was, or rather *is* three feet, in drifts over the fences, and that the ground is every where covered. Our April has been a colder one than has been known for twenty years, at least so say our old gentlemen, who are kind of living Almanac. But now we have *sprung* from Winter to Summer, with out any Spring. I should say *perceptible* Spring. "Here we are," say the birds, with out ever telling us when, and how they came.

The genial weather has quite put new life in to me. . . .

Mr. and Mrs. Livermore leave us on Tuesday. Perhaps you heard of the proposed presents. They are sent from Boston today. A silver Pitcher and waiter for Mr. L. with the inscription

"To our beloved Pastor, the Rev. A. A. Livermore, this pitcher
is presented, as a testimonial of our gratitude and
affection."

"*We thank our God ever for thee.*"

To Mrs. L. a gold watch, "from the *ladies* of the society'
The pitcher and salver cost one hundred dollars, and the watch . . . fifty, although it is said to be worth seventy five.

. . . I don't know that there is any more news for you, except, perhaps you will be interested to know, that Roxana made some very nice soap yesterday! And that the violets in the garden are budding. . . .

accept the love of your
Annie

Charlotte joined the chorus of praise when Dr. Bowditch brought her home from Boston in June. "Keene is so *very* still that I have not yet accustomed myself to it. I could *hardly* persuade myself that I was not dreaming when I first reached home. Once in a *great while* I see a man. The birds take the place of the great lumber wagons in Boston, and the grass and flowers fully supply the places where bricks are *not*. All this is very lovely after a winter in town, and I am happy to be quiet again" (Charlotte, 6-9-50). Within a very few days she would be too sick to enjoy the springtime.

Lizzie postponed a visit to Susan Colby in New London—about fifty miles north—when Charlotte came down with a fever. General Wilson feared his daughter had erysipelas, a dangerous and contagious streptococcal infection that caused a rash, high fevers, an inflamed throat, and sometimes death. Dr. Bowditch assured Wilson his fears were exaggerated, that Charlotte's illness was nothing so dangerous. With that sanguine but erroneous diagnosis, he returned to Boston. Reassured, James Wilson returned to Washington; Annie departed on her long-anticipated trip to West Point. Fortunately, young Jamie was still in Providence.

Within a few days Charlotte became desperately ill. Buttressed by visits from Dr. Charles Adams, the family physician, Lizzie alone saw her sister through the raging fever and infected throat and the medical horrors. Fortunately, Lizzie was no novice at nursing the sick, having nursed her mother through her final illness the previous year and her two baby brothers as they perished with the croup in the cold New England winter years before. Now, like a knight going into battle, she marshaled all of her stamina and experience to save her sister.

✳ [LIZZIE]   June 18th 1850

My dear Father,

Lottie has been very dangerously ill with Erysipelas but is now better. Dr. Adams and I have conquered and she is out of danger. I did not think best to alarm you, as before a letter could reach you she would have been better probably. I now write to assure you of her safety.

She had leeches on her head and other extreme measures. Dr. A. has been very devoted and I feel we owe her restoration to him under God. . . . For five days and nights I fought single handed with this dreadful malignant disorder and conquered! . . .

All goes on well and I am as ever your aff/ate   Lizzie

✳ [CHARLOTTE]   Keene June 28th 1850

My dear Father,

I am delighted to be able . . . to tell you of my improved health. I have been to ride almost every day since Saturday. . . . I sit up all day and ride a good deal of the time as it is almost too warm to walk. I think I shall be *quite* strong and well by the time you come on. I am rather weak still, and find my hand inclined to *wander* over the paper. But of course you will excuse my writing. I do not engage much in literary pursuits as yet, for I *hull strawberries* and arrange the flowers most of the time. Lizzie has been *very very* devoted to me. I think *no* person was *ever* more self sacrificing than she is. . . .

Believe me your loving child   Charlie

It took many months for Charlotte to regain her strength, for her hair to grow back, and for her to look as pretty as she had. To celebrate and expedite her recovery, Chardie, wearing a pretty little frizette to cover her shaved head, went with Lizzie to visit to friends in Portland, Maine, stopping off to visit the Ladds, the Cutts, the Goodwins, and the Waldrons, a short list of who was who in Portsmouth, New Hampshire. If a social whirl was what Charlotte needed to get perfectly well, she must have returned in the pink of health. They were entertained with sailing and riding parties and "did not spend an evening at home" (Lizzie, 8-10-50).

Lizzie did not tell Annie about Charlotte's illness but allowed her to enjoy fully her visit to West Point. As Lizzie describes it, her visit was nearly as successful as the fictional visit of Zuleika Dobson to Oxford some seventy-five years later. "Annie has been . . . at West Point where she had the usual romantic accompaniments of music, epaulets and beaux. A certain Captain became quite "au despesori" I hear and any number of cadets went mad, but as they had not much brains to lose and since the army is getting every day more and more unnecessary I don't feel very much alarmed for the country" (Lizzie to Susan Colby, 6-3-50).

Back in Keene while her sisters were away, Annie kept house "perfectly well" though she was "dreadfully lonely" and alarmed at an outbreak of dysentery that killed many people.

By the end of the summer, nearly a year after their mother's death, the new family structure had been tested by some important decisions about Charlotte's and Annie's schooling, Annie's housekeeping, and the crisis of Charlotte's erysipelas. It seemed to be working. Although James Wilson participated little even in such life-or-death matters as Charlotte's illness, he was the source of their security. They loved him and idolized him. His money supported them, and his name, his position, his house stamped their identity as a family. In Keene that summer the family was peacefully unaware that without so much as a hint to them, their father, the cornerstone of their lives, was in Washington contriving to land a political appointment that would take him three thousand miles away from them, to California, for an indefinite period of time.

Annie gleaned from the newspapers something of what her father might be up to and timidly wished him well. Interestingly, John Anderson Collins, whom James Wilson may have known at Middlebury College, collaborated in 1852 in a mining operation with a John Wilson, whose success the children confused for a time with their father's.

* [ANNIE]
Home, Aug 31st 1850
Chardie's birthday

My dear Father,

Your very mysterious letter is on my desk. I shall obey kindly. Thinking that a letter might possibly reach the girls at Portland I have written them the contents of your letter.

I see by the papers that you are spoken of as a 'sucessor to Col. Collins, who is to be removed from the office of Collector of San Francisco.' The

New Hampshire papers all have it copied from the Boston, and they have it from the Wash/n correspondent. If you want it, I hope it is true. . . .

I must hurry for the mail.

As ever very affectionately and respectfully

Your daughter
Annie

The summer was nearly over, but Lizzie, having disposed of Charlotte's crisis, revived her plan to visit Susan Colby and sent Charlotte home to Keene without her. Before leaving Portland, however, she also was summoned home and once again sent her apologies to Susan.

* [LIZZIE] September 3.

Just as I was ready to start for New London an 'imperial mandate' sent me back to Keene. A letter from Father arrived and told me of affairs awaiting my immediate presence in Keene.

With hindsight, Annie might not have wished so courteously that her father receive an appointment that would take him away from his children for fourteen years and threaten the family with dissolution. From General Wilson's perspective, however, the situation was tailor-made for his inclination and experience. He was cut out for life in California and for distributing land. He had spent four years parceling out government land in Iowa and Wisconsin and evidently fancied himself chasing buffalo. Though he still owned land and copper mines on that frontier, the fortune he had made there was dissipated.

Wilson's financial situation looked bleak enough to conjure up dreams of gold mines. James and his half-brother Robert quarreled continually over their father's estate and other financial dealings so intricate and secret a Swiss banker might be hard-pressed to sort them out. Robert declared at various times that James owed him anywhere from $1,000 to $30,000. He claimed that he was the rightful owner of the house on the corner of Emerald and Main streets where James Wilson's family lived. Had Robert been more consistent in pressing his case, he might have taken the house away from them rather than simply worrying Wilson and his daughters with his demands. Certainly, James was improvident and often irresponsible, but Robert's erratic behavior toward James and Mary Wilson and his nieces cast doubt on his claims, which may be why they were never settled.

Banks and other debtors also were closing in on James Wilson. In April the holders of the mortgages on his house called the sheriff, who threatened foreclosure. Wilson managed to ward them off for the time being; but with everything he owned in Peterborough and Keene mortgaged, there was no way he could get the money he needed, and he rejected all suggestions that he sell off losing properties, pay his debts, and generally retrench. His salary as a congressman certainly would not get him out of debt. In fact, while he liked making speeches and electioneering, as Isaac Hill ruthlessly pointed out, Wilson did not like to vote on hard issues in Congress; nor, as his daughters observed, did he like dealing with the nitty-gritty of the legal profession. A tall, impressive man with a booming voice and a network of acquaintances, Wilson thrived on politics, the militia, prospecting, and speculating.

Daniel Webster, Wilson's friend and political crony, was Wilson's chit to California. This powerful friend, who was nearly as profligate as Wilson, owed him money and political favors. Webster promised him an appointment to the California Land Commission. In their father's absence he would repay to the children the money Wilson had loaned him. The lure of the frontier, the promise of gold, the prospect of an appointment that suited his experience—Wilson accepted the promise of a political appointment in San Francisco.

In fact, in September he had already resigned his seat in Congress. Without a hint to his family or a plan for their welfare, James Wilson was, in nine days time, to move three thousand miles away from his dependent and motherless children. Just how they received this news we cannot know because, of course, they were all summoned to Keene to hear it in person. In the nine days between Lizzie's return home and Wilson's departure he somehow managed to get ready to go and cobble together some instructions for them about how to manage while he was away.

Then the whole family went to New York to see him off on the steamship *Georgia*, which would take him south along the coast of the United States to Panama. Seeing Father off was a heart-sinking experience if we can believe Lizzie's recollection eight years later, though at the time she and Jamie strained to be dispassionate in the letters they sent immediately after his departure. "We . . . saw the Georgia off, from our boat and waved our handkerchiefs tho' those you could not see. May Providence carry you safely and pleasantly through" (Lizzie, 9-22-50).

"After you left us at New York, or rather after we left you we went up to the Astor House, thence to the Norwich steamboat from which we watched the Georgia, as she left the harbor, bearing you far away from us all" (Jamie, 12-23-50).

"God Bless You My Dear
and Only Parent"

·

The full weight of responsibility for the family fell on Lizzie's shoulders
—the chaotic finances; the house, garden, and livestock; the servants;
Uncle Robert's vagaries; Jamie's schooling; Charlotte's health; Annie's uncertain romances; and her own future. Although she had taken care of the
children and the house since her mother's death, she had never managed
the family's finances, and she had deferred to her father's judgment on
everything from allowing Annie to visit friends at West Point to choosing
a school for thirteen-year-old Jamie. His letters of advice and consent from
Washington took only two or three days to arrive by train. Now, at best,
her letters would take six weeks to get to him, and his advice and financial
support would take another six to get back to her. Moral support three
months old would hardly help in a crisis, and Wilson's financial support
was even more uncertain.

Besides a mortgaged house, he left them his vast network of friends
and acquaintances from Keene to Boston to New York to Washington
—Whigs, abolitionists, socialites, lawyers, business acquaintances. The
women moved easily in this fretwork of proper, liberal people with whom
they shared social and political values. These families graciously offered
the women the security of their houses for as long as they needed a place
to stay.

However, neither the children left behind nor the father who left them
viewed their separation by place and time as a dissolution of the family.
They maintained their relationship by communicating with each other as
well and as often as they could. James Wilson wrote voluminous letters,
sometimes sixteen pages long, when it was not too inconvenient, and his
daughters sent letters every two or three weeks on nearly every boat that
carried mail from Boston or New York to California. We can only infer
what he said to them; but they responded with the story of their family

during their late adolescence and young adulthood. Lizzie viewed the correspondence very seriously indeed. "I write to you every Sunday as part of my religion" (Lizzie, 9-29-50).

While their father sailed off to unknown adventures, the three women returned home to Keene to begin forging their own future—one step at a time. Autumn was well launched. Crops on their small farm were harvested and sold. Animals and bread were displayed and judged at the local fair. Wages were paid. They also planned for the winter. Jamie returned to Charles A. Abbott's Academy in Norwich, Connecticut, and Charlotte went back to Mrs. Lowell's in Boston, leaving Lizzie and Annie without a logical place to go. The problem was fraught with implications. The two women had to find a comfortable but economical place where they would be respectably chaperoned but one in which their identity would not be subsumed into another family. Something, in short, that did not make them look like poor orphans.

The house in Keene, which had the economical and social advantage of belonging to their father, was a summer place with minimal provisions against cold weather. No relatives from Keene or Peterborough tried hard to persuade them to take refuge with them, though doubtless the two women would have resisted staying in New Hampshire during the winter in any case. For November they decided to board with a family of their acquaintance in Dorchester, near Boston, where they could be close to Charlotte. In the winter they would stay with friends. This arrangement had the advantages of maintaining the unity and independence of the family unit—or what remained of it—and the family routine of leaving Keene for the season. It provided the respectability of a family setting, and it did not cost the earth.

Ten days after he left, they received their first letter from their father, which he had mailed en route, and Lizzie wrote to tell him about their arrangement, family business, and local news. Even without the *New Hampshire Sentinel*, the Keene paper, Lizzie typically mentioned everything from transfers of property to births and deaths. Lizzie's inquiry that her father might help Mr. Barrett find a job in California was combination request for political patronage and plea for a favor from a friend that occurs frequently in this correspondence. Because Wilson was generous and a politician, he probably got more requests for help than most people did, but friends and acquaintances and friends of friends often helped the Wilsons through their problems, too. Perhaps equally important, these friends served as a link between the children and their father.

Besides their own personal affairs, they wrote to him about whatever gossip and public events captured their imagination. Soprano Jenny Lind's American debut under the auspices of P. T. Barnum captivated the Wilsons.

Barnum had created a nearly hysterical audience for the Swedish Night-ingale in the United States with publicity describing her as "a lady whose vocal powers have never been approached by any other human being," gilded with a character that was "charity, simplicity, and goodness personi-fied" (Irving Wallace, *The Fabulous Showman* [New York: New American Library, 1959]). To an audience of five thousand in New York, Jenny Lind sang as her final number a song Barnum had commissioned for her, ending with "I greet with a full heart the Land of the West, / Whose Banner of Stars o'er a world is unrolled, / Whose empire o'ershadows Atlantic's wide breast / And opens to sunset its gateway to gold"—a less than earthshaking poem that seemed to capture the spirit that infected James Wilson.

Though the Wilsons proclaimed their disdain for Barnum, they were fascinated by him, and his advertizing blitz inspired them with longing to hear Jenny Lind. (Incidentally, seventy-five years later, in 1926, Lizzie's grandson, playwright Robert Sherwood, still fascinated by the great show-man who had engaged his grandmother, her sisters, and brother in 1850, observed, "I consider him the greatest genius that ever conducted an amusement enterprise in this country, a man of superlative imagination, indomitable pluck and artistic temperament" [Wallace, *Fabulous Showman*, Preface).

✳ [LIZZIE]   Keene Sept 22d 1850

My dear Father,

. . . I found the money ($229.89) at the bank as you said and have had no difficulty about my money matters. George and Roxana seemed satisfied with that you sent them.

We are to leave home the first of Nov. George thinks he shall get $50. for the potatoes and the other things in proportion. We hope now to board with Mrs. Barrett at Dorchester and by the way Mr. Barrett wrote you a letter before you left which he never received an answer from. He is very poor, poor man and wants to go to California, and if you can give him any encouragement he would go immediately. . . . He wants to know if there would be any use in applying for the Post Office in San Francisco—or if you could give him any mercantile employment—supposing you have anything yourself.

I hope you will have a care for him as he is an excellent man and has been a great friend to us.

Charlotte has taken up her abode with the Bowditchs who love her and make her perfectly happy. Jamie will be home to spend October with me. I don't know that we could be better placed than we are to be.

Dr. Twichell's houses were sold yesterday. Miss Carter's brought $2100. The Dr.'s $3500. The latter George bought for his Father. The former, Mr. Upton—machinist—for the Cheshire R. R. Miss Carter has bought the little office house and will live there.

Roxana wishes me to say with her good wishes that her bread got the premium at the cattle show.

I think of selling the pony which distracts George very much. I shall not let him go at a sacrifice and perhaps not at all, but as much of the 'live stock' as I can sell I intend to.

Ann Maginnis [one of the Wilsons' servants] does not seem very anxious for her pay, tho' I have informed her that she can have it anytime. I rather think she feels that it is better in my hands than in hers.

John Prentiss [publisher of the paper] thinks of sending you the *New Hampshire Sentinel*.

Jenny Lind is receiving golden opinions every where. She is a most glorious whole hearted woman and we all want to see her. . . .

I do not see but I shall be able to get along comfortably, if by the middle of winter you can send me some money it may be useful, as Lottie's and Jamie's bills come in.

I wrote Charlie March a complimentary note the other day telling him how much pleased you were with his book. I received a letter from Mr. Dixon giving account of the birth of another son.

I hope you will write us frequently as of course you will. Uncle Robert has been very kind and seems disposed to be very accommodating.

All is well. . . .

Your always loving daughter   M E Wilson

Annie introduced her father to the Fourgeauds, who, along with several other acquaintances in the East, became influential and wealthy in California. The Fourgeauds promoted California in the East and were thoroughly acceptable to the Wilsons on both coasts. Meantime, she planned to stay with another friend in New York—Mrs. Prosper Montgomery Wetmore, wife of a substantial dry-goods manufacturer and legislator.

Annie, who turned eighteen on September 23, loved exploring the New England countryside, especially with all the local young men—just as her father and brother loved hunting and fishing and Charlotte loved long walks. Only Lizzie seemed to have no interest in outdoor exercise.

✳ [ANNIE]   Keene Oct 28th 1850

My dear Father,

Your very kind remembrance of me, in the form of a birthday letter, is now in my Portfolio. It arrived in due time and was very cheering and delightful. I should have answered it immediately, but that I knew that there were already two letters awaiting you at San Francisco and I thought a little later date would be more acceptable than three of one week. . . .

For ourselves, I don't know what news to write you. We go on the same quiet way as of old. . . . I wish now that I were a Politician that I could entertain you with your favorite theme but all I know is that Mr. Perkins of Winchester is elected to your place in Congress if the towns lately added to this district are left out. And that he Mr. P. is going to contest with Mr. Morrison for his seat. It is supposed by the gentlemen here, that Mr. Perkins will have the seat.

Our European young gentlemen Frank Fiske and Mr. Bellows have returned, Frank looking very foreign and ferocious with a very unique moustache. Charles Adams and George Stale are also here so that excepting Horatio Peng our young beaux are all home. We had the other day a famous gipsy Picnic at Beach Stile—walked up, built a fire, roasted chickens and chestnuts, and walked back. The next day, a fine horseback ride, a new and beautiful one, to us. I presume *you* know it of old—up old Gilsum road, by the Wilder Orchard, and over a high ridge of hills turning off to the right came down back of the Upper glass Factory, getting an elegant view of Keene and the Monadnock at one glance. We were a party of nine making quite a formidable cavalcade as we rode in to the valley all abreast. . . .

We hope to get the affairs all settled and the house closed by Monday next. Roxana and Mary Ann [another servant] both go to Hartford, ready to come back whenever we shall want them. We had a letter last night from dear Charlotte who is well and happy. We shall soon be with her. Jamie too is doing nicely. He flourishes in a dressing gown made like yours which Lizzie made him and lined with red . . . [He looks at] least ten years older since it is finished. He is looking very elegant too in a complete suit of grey. He has won himself golden opinions from all the Boston young ladies who have spent the season here, by his gentlemanly bearing. I am glad to see him fond of ladies' society. I think the influence is good.

Our Fall is cold and bitter and sends shooting rheumatic pains through my shoulders. I long to flee from this cruel climate.

I hope you will see and know in San Francisco, Dr. and Mrs. Fourgeaud pronounced *Foor jo* (soft). You remember, perhaps, that I told you of them. We met in Washington. The Dr. is very rich, and has spent eight years in California, and now returns again. Mrs. Fourgeaud is a very sweet person and a great friend to me. Do write us if you have seen . . . any of our friends.

I am afraid dear Father that you will think I have spun out a great length, telling you nothing, but really our quiet life is so without incident that I fear to bore you. All our Keene friends are nicely desiring kind remember- ance to you always. The Sherwoods write me friendly and delightful letters often. Mrs. Wetmore has sent for me to spend December with her. She has a fine boy born in September and weighing at his birth, twelve pounds.

I send you a certain cure for cholera. It is much talked of, at present. If you do not need it yourself—which God grant—you may find it useful for some sufferer.

Kindest love from all your household and Uncle Robert. Hoping soon to hear of your safe arrival and good success. Believe me as ever (though 18)

Your fond child
Annie F. Wilson

Jamie, like his father, loved things military, especially the popular "mus- ter" in which companies of the local militias reenacted the glory days of the revolutionary war. He recounted his activities of the autumn in a letter to his father written months later, after he had heard of his father's arrival in California.

✳ [JAMIE]   Norwich Dec 23, 1850

Dear Father,
. . . It is only a few days to Christmas, and I wish very much, that you were going to be here to spend it with us.

. . . I remained at Norwich until about the first of Oct. when I went home to spend the vacation, which lasted the whole month, and I had a very nice time. While I was there they had a volunteer muster down on "Swanzey Plains." The companies were all uniform one, of which there were a good many, and it would have been a splendid one, if the weather had been more favorable, but it commenced to rain a little while after they went onto the field, which continued till night, and so it broke up the muster. However a little while after they had a "Cornwallis Muster" down at Troy, and Lizzie let George and I go down there to see it, . . . There were only two uniform companies and the rest were companies got up for the occasion. One was an old mans company, composed of the oldest men they could find in the place, and the others were made up of young men. The uniform companies represented the British, and the others the Americans. The British stationed themselves behind a little fort on a hill near by the town, where after firing a few times they fell back a little, and continued to retreat, little by little, until at last they reached another fort . . . where after firing all their powder away the British surrendered. After that they marched down into the village, where a gentleman made a speech, and then George and I took the Cars and came home. There were some of them dressed very queerly, for instance the Captain of the old men's company, old Capt. Wheeler, was dressed in small clothes, with white stockings, a long cue hanging down his back, with a Chapeau on, and an old powder horn, which reached almost around him. . . .

I had a pretty good time, at home with the gun, but I could not find much game, and as the house was going to be shut up this winter, and as you gave it to me in New York, I concluded to bring it with me, and so I have got it here now. I have been hunting two or three times, but I have not found any game, so I have come to the conclusion, that either there is not much around here, or else I do not hunt it right, which I think is much the most probably, for the market is full all the time, so the other day I cleaned the gun thoroughly and oiled it and put it up, and I guess I shall let it remain so for the rest of the winter.

I suppose that you have fine hunting, and fishing, in California, and I wish that in your next letter to me, you would tell me about it, and give me a description of San Francisco, and also tell me when you are coming home if you know yourself.

. . . I finished the third book of Ceasar on the 17 (of Dec.) which is all I am going to read at present,) and on the 18th I commenced Virgil. The first lesson, I took ten lines, the next fifteen, which is the lesson I take every day now, but I hope soon, to be able to take 20, and by the time you received this letter, to have got some half ways through the first book. . . . Hoping to hear from you soon and answering you that I will try to do as well as I can, in all respects while you are gone. I must now bid you farewell.

From your truly affectionate son   Jamie

Like his sisters, Jamie tells stories about what he is doing that might interest his father. Certainly, General Wilson would be interested in hunting, which he loved, and in the muster since he often participated in these events. In return Jamie wanted to hear about his father's adventures. Jamie's attitude toward writing letters to his father, the subjects he wrote about, and the tone of his letters help point up some of the distinguishing characteristics of his sisters' letters. While they felt obligated to post a letter in each mail, he seemed happy to write at length when he had some story he wanted to tell, but he hated to squeeze out a letter from duty. He told stories to entertain his father, but he never asked, "Wouldn't you like to be here to go with me to the muster?" By and large Jamie's letters are charming but far less intense than those of his sisters. Like Charlotte, Jamie did not cope with family finances, the cause of so much anguish, or many other family problems, which Annie and Lizzie imagined their father could solve if he only would. He had no message to deliver except the straightforward story that he wrote.

While Annie amused herself with picnics and Jamie attended musters, Lizzie organized the house for the winter, a task so arduous that she had to refuse "a kind invitation from Mr. and Mrs. Taintor of Hartford to go with them to New York and hear Jenny [Lind]" (Lizzie, 9-29-50). "I . . . put the silver and your trunk of papers in the bank as my property and Mr. Newall promised to deliver it to no person but me. I sold the old and useless things and they brought me about sixty dollars. George made me pay him thirty of it, but what with the sale of the wood etc I paid up Chardie's bills etc so far, and all the small bills before I left home—except Hagar and Whitcombs [a store] and a small one at Bridgemans [the grocer] and the meat bill. . ." (Lizzie, 12-1-50).

Underneath the domestic bustle and social flurry at the house at Emerald and Main lurked the wide-eyed fear that something would happen to James Wilson on his hazardous journey to California. "Mrs. Paige gave a splendid ball a week or two ago and invited us but we did not go as we felt so unhappy about you" (Lizzie, 12-1-50). By the time Lizzie and Annie had left Keene for Dorchester, the tension of waiting to hear of his safe arrival had become almost intolerable.

According to every newspaper report, they had reason to worry. Perils lurked everywhere along his route, but the worst were in Panama. The sixty miles across the tiny country were traversed partly by boat, though the last twenty miles of the journey included a five-day trek on mule back with no accommodations along the route. The primitive amenities of tiny Acapulco, at the end of the crossing, had been swamped by the onslaught of '49ers headed for California. No wonder Annie sent him a new cure for cholera, for besides the discomforts of blistering heat, torrential rain, mosquitoes, and fleas, Panama bred more than its share of tropical fevers—malaria, cholera, dysentery, yellow fever. According to one New York paper, Panama had become one of the "worst pest holes in the tropical worlds" (Oscar Lewis, *Sea Routes to the Gold Fields* [New York: Knopf, 1949], 192).

Understandably, Lizzie worried more than any of the other children about her father's well-being. Because she was the oldest and had traveled on the frontier, Lizzie understood better than Annie and certainly better than Charlotte or Jamie the trials and dangers of such a journey. She had spent more time with him in Washington the year she was sixteen, so she knew him better. She was enough older than her siblings that she wrote to him more as an equal. In fact, she was more like him—ambitious, charming, worldly—so she may have felt closer to him. No doubt she also realized that, heavy as her burden of responsibility was with her father so far away, chaos threatened if they lost their last parent. Economically, socially, and psychologically the children depended on James Wilson. The three daughters had no money, no way to support themselves and their brother, and no way to maintain their house. Their social position depended almost entirely on their father's political and business position. Finally, regardless of how far away he was, a father authenticated the family unit. Without him as the center, Lizzie would have found it nearly impossible to keep the family from shattering. The children would have been orphans. Their house in Keene repossessed to pay their father's debts, they would be farmed out to relatives and friends to become dependents in other families' households.

Friends cheered them through Thanksgiving and evoked the absent General Wilson. "We spent Thanksgiving at Mr. John Dorr's. He was surrounded by about sixty of his descendants. The first toast was 'absent friends.' He was courteous enough to drink 'Genl Wilson's health and prosperity'" (Lizzie, 12-1-50). Nor was he forgotten at the dinner table of the Eldredges, where Annie was visiting. "When I ate my Thanksgiving dinner with my very kind friends the Eldredges we drunk your health" (Annie, 1-4-51).

Gradually, tidings of their father's journey seeped back to the children. Lizzie and Annie were in Dorchester with the Barretts when they received the first letter from their father after his trip through Panama. Overwhelmed with relief, they freely confessed their terrible anxiety. Annie's concern for John Hatch's orphans and her discontent at living in other people's houses seem all a part of the same concern.

"Thank Heaven, my dear Father we have heard of your safe arrival at Acapulco and of your safety up to the 19th of October. I cannot describe to you the dreadful anxiety I have suffered on your account. I felt as if every pull on the door bell announced your loss. I have grown thin and pale watching and fearing and I hope never to have so much to fear again.

"I believe I have been with you in spirit every mile you have travelled and have aggravated every danger. Mr. and Mrs. Barrett have been very kind friends and have advised and counselled and soothed me very much" (Lizzie, 12-1-50).

✳ [ANNIE]   Dorchester December 9th 1850

My dear Father,
    . . . We are all 'in status quo' jogging on side by side, in the same old quiet way, while you are going through all manner of new and strange scenes.

We were very much delighted by the receipt of your letter from Acapalco, because our great anxiety for you was at Panama, and we were charmed to hear of your health and well being, after you left that place.

We are all well, and have been so ever since your departure. Lizzie has been very anxious for you and has not been at all like her self since you went until she got the letter from Acapalco, which raised her spirits somewhat, but still, every word that has a desponding accent in it, from you, almost kills her. In health she is very well and enjoys herself very much in her French which she is studying very faithfully. She is taking lessons in crayon drawings too, for which she seems to have a decided talent. She says she shall make her living by taking likenesses, when she is called upon. . . .

I hear no Keene news, but the death of John Hatch. His little orphans are alone in the world now. We are still, as you see, in Dorchester. The Barretts are very friendly and seem fond of us, but I am tired of boarding in other peoples houses, and quite long for our own house in Keene where I feel under no constraint. I wish next summer were here and we were all around our table at our home. Lizzie is going to Hartford about Christmas, when I hope to go and spend a month at New York, with Mrs. Wetmore. Mary Sherwood has gone to Havanna with John and their Mother to stay till the New Year. Jenny Wood is to be married to Mr. Tilton in the course of this month, and is going to Washington for a little while, then coming back to Keene, to spend an exciting winter. This I believe is all the gossip I can give you. . . . I wish I could write you a satisfactory letter 'on the State of the Union,' but I am not equal to it. . . .

I hear little of Washington, but have a faint hope of seeing it, before the Winter is through. . . .
fondly your daughter
Annie

Monday evening, Dec 9th 1850
We are rejoiced beyond expression dear *dear* Father to receive a letter from San Francisco. Lizzie spends this night in town and has only sent me word that the much hoped for letter has arrived. I have not yet seen it, but thank heaven that the news of yr safe arrival at the desired haven has reached us. God bless you my dear and only Parent. God bless you.   In haste, your
Annie

Thus, with grateful hearts the Wilson children celebrated Christmas and faced their first winter on their own. December 1850 and January 1851 were particularly cold and severe. After a fierce storm sleighing became all the rage during the Christmas season; then the snow ceased in Boston, but it remained bitterly cold. While James Wilson basked in the "mild and springlike" weather in California, in Boston Charlotte feared she would "lose [her] nose to Jack Frost."

Christmas arrived between storms. While Annie visited her friend Mrs. Wetmore in New York, Lizzie, Charlotte, and Jamie enjoyed Christmas in Hartford with the Goodridges. "I wish you had been with us this Christmas. We all had handsome Christmas presents. Jamie had numerous books from the young Goodridges and Lizzie and I had handsome embroidered handkerchiefs etc." (Charlotte, 1-4-51).

To young Jamie the early storm provided the opportunity for winter sports and adventures. "The snow fell here on the 15th about five inches deep which ended with rain, which has since frozen and the sleighs are flying merrily, and we have also excellent skating" (Jamie, 12-23-50). The next storm delayed his train on his return to Norwich after Christmas.

"I had quite a bad time getting here, from Hartford at the end of the holidays. . . . I suppose you know that in going from here to Hartford you have to change cars at Willimantic which is about 16 miles from Norwich. Well the snow on the track having delayed all the trains, we started from Hartford about forty minutes late, and as we had to wait about half an hour on the road for another train, we got into Willimantic over an hour late, and the train for Norwich had gone. There were several gentlemen there who were obliged to go to Norwich that night, for it was Saturday, and one of them plays the organ in one of the churches here, so they went to the agent of the H.W.R.R. *and I with them*, and told him that as we all had through tickets he ought to send us on (at the Company's expense I suppose they meant), but he was obstinate and would not, so after a good deal of talk, the conductor who was *a gentleman* stepped up and said that he would take the responsibility and send us through, so he went and hired a long narrow sleigh with the seats on each side, like an omnibus, and *without* a cover. It was about 7 1/2 oclock in the evening, when we started from Willimantic and about 10 when we got here" (Jamie, 1-22-51). On this snowy, dark ride Jamie caught a cold but otherwise escaped unharmed to regale his family with the story.

Not everyone escaped the effects of the weather so easily. In the fierce storm in December several ships were wrecked, and for a time the steamship *Atlantic* appeared to be lost with industrialist Abbot Lawrence's son aboard. Lawrence, who had made his fortune in the textile mills in Lawrenceville, Massachusetts, had become an international figure who interested the Wilsons perhaps because Lawrenceville was not too distant from Keene. All of the daughters wrote to their father about the missing *Atlantic*. Only weeks later did they learn that the ship had put in for repairs at Cork, and the young Lawrence was safe.

The uncertainty of the weather resonated in the lives of the Wilsons. During 1851, fortunes and misfortunes befell them at a dizzying rate. On the West Coast, General Wilson continually pursued confirmation of his appointment to the Land Commission; he suffered a painful accident; he became a hero, and he had an amazing stroke of good luck. In the East, Lizzie, Annie, Charlotte, and Jamie understood that he was only the titular head of the family. The sisters were often sick, they ran into serious financial problems, and a dear friend in Keene died. Of primary importance, romances blossomed for Annie and Lizzie.

Before New Years, Charlotte came down with the measles.

✳ [LIZZIE]   Hartford Jan 4th 1851

My dear Father,

   . . . she is quite comfortable and we are now taking care of her eyes which are not bad and which we intend shall not be. The most disagreeable feature of the whole is that she will probably have given them to me, and I am of an age when they go hard, but we have a good Dr. and Sophia [Goodridge] promises to take good care of me.

✳ [CHARLOTTE]

Lizzie wrote thus far and something prevented her finishing this letter the day she began it and since then she has been taken with the measles. Her symptoms are not bad at all and both Miss Sophia and herself think she will have them very lightly. Her eyes are rather weak so that she has to keep them covered but she does not suffer otherwise. I have recovered famously from my illness. But yet my sister does not wish me to go to school till a week is passed for fear of my eyes, which are not painful, however, except in a strong light. Then I shall study very hard, although I shall still be careful of my eyes. . . .

   Lizzie begs me to ask you to send her some money as she says she has some things to get when she returns to Keene. Your letters dear Father have been most satisfactory. We send them to each other, *always*, as you intimated in your last. We were all very sorry to know you had had the fever and ague. Away from home you must feel *very* lonely when you are sick. . . .

   Believe me my dear Father your loving daughter

                                             Charlotte J. Wilson

                                                         Jan 8th

   I have left this open to write you how Lizzie is. This her third day of measles and her most uncomfortable. She is pretty severely sick with them but has no dangerous symptoms. I am very well indeed but shall not return to Boston till Friday or Saturday when Lizzie will probably be better. I begin school Monday if possible. The weather is splendid and the sleighing fine. . . .

Believe me your loving
Chardie

Two weeks later Lizzie was recovering and considered accepting an invitation from Whig Senator Roger Baldwin. "I have recovered from the measles after a very severe attack which has affected my eyes and lungs somewhat tho' I hope care may cure both. I had excellent care and an excellent Physician. Measles at my age is attended by some very dangerous symptoms which I have escaped fortunately but I still feel a want of strength and energy that is unusual for me. . . . Mr. and Mrs. Baldwin whom we knew last winter have given me a very pressing invitation to go on to Washington with them. I am going for about ten days the last of the week if I am well and nothing happens. I have so much difficulty in getting through the day without any eyes, that I am growing less spirited and I hope for some help for my cough from the fine air of the south" (Lizzie, 1-25-51).

Wilson's new year began with a stroke of good fortune. By the time he had been in California for a month, he found gold at the Gold Bluff near Crescent City in northern California. There the tides uncovered treasure that prospectors sifted out of the sand. Wilson not only mined gold for himself; he soon organized an engineering project to supply water to others engaged in washing gold from the sand.

Despite the intensity of their correspondence it often happened that important news from General Wilson arrived in the press. At school in Connecticut, Jamie thought he read a report of his father's gold strike in a New York paper. "I saw a little while ago in one of the New York papers an account of a new and very rich gold mine, along the sea beach in California, which had been discovered by several gentlemen, one of whom was 'General *John* Wilson.' I did not know but what it might be you, the printer having made a mistake in the name. If it is you (as I hope it is) I wish that you would tell me in your next letter as I want to hear very much" (Jamie 2-24-51). But John Wilson proved to be John Wilson, partner of Colonel Collins—ironically, the man who resigned the appointment as collector that James Wilson expected.

James Wilson's strike followed very shortly, but the eurekas that must have echoed through Gold Bluff reverberated feebly in the East. Lizzie acknowledged without much enthusiasm that she was glad his mining business went well but that she had little confidence in the enterprise. A month later, when they received a sample of gold sand, Lizzie observed briefly,

"Your gold sand excites a great deal of interest here," then added, "don't you want your library? I met Gov. Hubbard in the cars the other day. He said he hoped you would cling to your profession as it was a certain fortune for you. I hope so, as California offices here are looked on rather as gambling affairs" (4-22-51). Lizzie and Annie continued to hope that their father would distinguish himself at the law. And what about his political appointment? "I see by the papers that L. Butler King is appointed Collector. What does it mean and what are you to have?" (Lizzie, 10-7-50). "I long to hear from you and know about the Collector business. I trust you will not be discouraged as your talents must command *something*" (Lizzie, 12-1-50).

Annie's ambitions followed the same line as Lizzie's. "I hear from diverse sources that 'Genl. Wilson is doing *great things* at the law,' which delights me beyond measure, and much more [than] to hear that he were doing *greater* things even at speculation" (Annie, 5-23-51). This was the beginning of a long tug of war between Lizzie and Annie in the East and Wilson in California. The two older daughters fancied their father in a respectable profession that produced a steady income and ensured the family a prosperous and respectable place in society in the East; meanwhile, their father—as distant in ambition as in place—often teetered on the brink of insolvency and disgrace while pursuing fortune and excitement in the West. While Wilson sifted gold-laced sand swept in by the tides, only his two younger children rejoiced with him. Perhaps that was because Wilson's gold strike did not immediately translate into cash for the family bills that Lizzie had to pay.

By the middle of the bitterly cold January of 1851, the money Wilson left for them was gone. The money Lizzie made in the fall from selling livestock and produce had been spent. Lizzie, who was in charge, wrote to ask for more money, and Annie, like a good sister, passionately supported her in her complicated and embarrassing predicament.

"The money you sent me was very acceptable as Mr. Webster had been rather dilatory. I immediately paid up Jamie's bills and sent Annie some which she wanted. However Mr. Webster sent some which I wrote for a fortnight before, just after yours came with a very kind note saying he wished to know how much his note was given for and how much he had paid, and that he wished me to consider him bound to furnish me with money while you were absent both now and after the note was paid. All of which was very pretty but does not make up for want of punctuality" (Lizzie, 1-25-51). It was just as well that Lizzie did not put too much confidence in Webster. By March, when the late snowstorm in Boston made travel in the streets treacherous, financial scandals had destroyed his credit in that city. "Mr. Webster is now in trouble . . . his connection with the

Boston and New York brokers [having been revealed], . . he wrote me with his last check, on the bank of Washington that he had no friends in Boston, and Mr. Goodridge had to endorse it to make it paid here [in Hartford]" (Lizzie, 3-16-51).

＊ [ANNIE]   New York February 7th 1851

My dear Father,
    . . . We had not heard from New England for some weeks till yesterday, when a letter from Uncle Robert came. . . . while M. E. was ill at Hartford, and before your remittance arrived, she got out of money, and sent to Uncle Robert, asking him if there was in his, or James Scott's hands any money from rents or other sources that she was entitled to, saying that our Father had mentioned that such would be the case. She wanted only ten or fifteen dollars *then*, . . . after a long time, comes this letter containing one hundred and odd dollars, and the information that far from any thing coming in to James Scott's hands, he had paid out *a thousand dollars* and that all the rents and money given R. W. [Uncle Robert] by you, had gone toward *'repairs* (?) taxes and interest paid to the bank.' But, remembering that a horse and colt were sold that belonged to M. E. [Lizzie] he had *borrowed* that amount and forwarded it with pleasure. All this distressed M. E. excessively, first that she had misunderstood you and sent for money where she had no right, and then that the business affairs should be in such a very uncertain and uncared for sort of a way. She accordingly wrote an entirely polite and respectful note back to Uncle Robert, *returning the money*, and saying to him that she regretted extremely having given him so much trouble, and thanking him for his kind attention to her wants, begged to return the money, as she fervently trusted that as long as [her father] lived she should not be driven to call on any other source. Uncle Robert said too, in his letter, that he had entrusted all his property to our Father's care, and he had never received any thing but promises, which he had found neither filled his stomach or clothed his back. (He never had broad cloth fine enough.) Now this seems heartless of me to write you I am afraid, but I am between two fires, and for myself alone I would not do it. But it wears terribly on Lizzie. She has grown older, and actually sick, since you left us, and really seems to droop under it all. This dreadful uncertainty she says, this fear lest your only home may be taken away from you over your head. She longs (as we all do) to go home to Keene and yet dreads to, lest some awful legal proceeding meets and crushes her. Now my dear, very dear Father this ought not to be so. It is not my place to advise or counsel you. You are older and wiser than I by far, but still you

will forgive me if I once remind you that it is a very great responsibility for so young a girl as Lizzie to be left with three younger ones to take care of, educate and look after, even if she has as much money as she can need, and nothing else to disturb her mind, but when in addition she has croaking friends round her, and creditors frowns to meet, and sheriffs mortifying notifications, and ten thousand other trials of this kind to bear, it is too much, too much and few can stand under it. *Girls* I mean. If we were boys it would be a different thing but for women who can do nothing but sit still and suffer alone and all within, it is a pretty severe trial. Father if it is in the course of human possibility you must come home this spring and attend to the house business. What it all is, I know not, only that the affairs are all at sixes and sevens. If you are to be many years away from us, leaving no head to the establishment is it not possible to get rid of all the immense amount of unnecessary property, and let us live quietly and undisturbed in our dear peaceful home. God grant that the day is near, when we own not a foot of land any where (but perhaps in California) but not in Peterboro, or in Keene or any where—no houses, no stock, nothing of the kind except our home and its garden and just its immediate surroundings. And now my dear darling we'll let this hateful disgusting subject go. I have never troubled you before, and I never shall again. I shall feel it my duty in this instance, and the duty is done. . . .

Write me an answer soon, and believe me in truest love your

                                        Annie

This dramatic letter, like the one describing Lizzie's anxiety over Wilson's trip west, is as much an expression of outrage at Lizzie's trials and humiliations as it is a plea for money. If it is Lizzie's responsibility to take care of the family, Annie commands from James Wilson the appreciation Lizzie deserves and the help she needs. Charlotte, who was not included in conferences on family finances, did not fill her letters with money worries. Instead, in the winter and spring of 1851, fifteen-year-old Charlotte wrote a series of fine letters in which we see a sensitive, observant, and intelligent young woman awakening to the social, political, and religious problems that plague her society.

Like all of the children, Charlotte pined for her father's return and worried about his well-being. Unfamiliar with the perils of earthquakes, hostile Indians, strange fevers, and ruffians that he faces, she worried about such everyday dangers and discomforts as taking snuff or eating poorly. Despite her overwhelming desire for his return, the romance of her father's adventures, with all the trappings of remote places, gold, and exotic savages, excited Charlotte's curiosity and fancy in a way it did not excite her sisters. Though at various times Charlotte expressed a wish to join him in California, more often she made the imaginary leap from her own experience to his. Instead of going to that mysterious coast, Charlotte concentrated on study and good conduct and taking care of her health. At sixteen, Lizzie circulated in the glittering social season in Washington, and at seventeen, Annie was an enthusiastic party-goer, but their young and deeply religious sister obeyed Dr. Bowditch's orders and went to bed early during the winter nights, took long walks, and observed what was happening around her.

A review of a book by atheist Harriet Martineau shocked Charlotte, who rejected Martineau's position out of hand. "I don't think she can be sane, do you? . . . I think she must be insane. . . . Altogether her reasoning is nothing but a succession of contradictions" (Charlotte, 5-5-51). Still, Charlotte supported many of Martineau's other reformist principles. In that chilly and turbulent spring in Boston during her last semester of formal schooling, Charlotte was ready to ponder new ideas. She developed a social conscience and explored the great political and social problem of slavery with her friend Mrs. Bowditch, who, with her husband, was an ardent and influential antislavery activist. Though the young girl and the matron never made the connection, they also struggled with the question of political rights for women (and Charlotte concluded that women had no business in politics) while they tentatively agreed that justice demanded that slaves have political rights. Despite her disclaimers Charlotte and Mrs. Bowditch, in the drawing room or in the kitchen, continued to discuss the question that haunted the nation.

* [CHARLOTTE]   Boston Feb 16th 1851

My very dear Father,

Since I have written you, so very little has transpired that my letter will have to consist of my private doings and thoughts. . . . I am very glad to learn you have such nice eatables in California, as it satisfied me upon one point concerning the place, that is, you won't starve. . . .

Boston people are now in an excited state about the slave taking law. Yesterday a runaway slave was taken into custody of the Marshall and some officers, when, much to their dismay, over two hundred negroes came to the place where he was kept and helped the slave to escape, while the officers of Justice were driven away. One of the negroes took the Marshall's sword of office, and wielding it *very* vigorously, drove *his honor* and his officers away. Dr. Bowditch and all the Free Soilers glory in it, but some of our quiet citizens smart from the indignity of having their laws broken by a 'pack of black dogs.' What do you think of it? Don't you like the spirit of the blacks? The beauty of the affair is that they wished to do no harm to any one, and did none, and after it was all over, the prime mover carried back the sword saying 'It was not his and he did not wish it.' Very amusing, I think, the idea of the Marshall fleeing before his own sword.

We have all feared, for this month almost, that the Steamer Atlantic was lost. The time for its arrival came, and passed, and still now it has hardly been hoped by many that she was safe. But, after leaving England she put into Cork, as *something* broke. . . . Mr. Lawrence's [industrialist Abbot Lawrence] son was on board. Oh if you had been there! I often thought how the friend's of the passengers must feel, and could imagine my own feelings if you had been there.

While I had to sit in my room with nothing to do, but to think, I longed so *very* much to see you. *Every* one is, and has been kind to me and I am *very* happy, though none of my family are with me, yet the thought of your coming back again makes me feel *too* happy. Oh dear Father if you could *only* hear the divine strains I am listening to. Mrs. Bowditch has been playing something that made me shudder, it was *so* exquisite. It touched 'The dark mysterious chord by which we're bound.'

I *don't* mean to be poetical but I felt it, and had to write it down here. I *do* love music *so* much. . . . I am going down to Mrs. Bowditch now. . . .

Good bye, dear Father, believe me ever your loving daughter

Charlotte Wilson

The mistrust of their own political insights that Charlotte expresses was so widespread among women that the intellectual activist Margaret Fuller addressed the issue directly. Fuller wrote to a woman friend about Harriet Beecher Stowe's *Uncle Tom's Cabin*: "Not read Mrs. Stowe's book! But you must. Her book is quite a sign of the times, and has otherwise an intrinsically considerable power. For myself, I rejoice in the success both as a woman and a human being. Oh, and is it possible that you think a woman has no business with questions like the question of slavery. Then she had better use a pen no more. She had better subside into slavery and concubinage herself, I think, as in the times of old, shut herself up with the penelopes in the 'woman's apartment,' and take no rank among thinkers and speakers" (Sandra Gilbert and Susan Gubar, *Madwoman in the Attic* [New Haven, Conn.: Yale University Press, 1979] 481). Charlotte was quite prepared to be shut up in the women's apartment, but even there she found herself drawn again and again to the questions that she had declared herself unfit to consider. Before the term was over, the Bowditches had moved out of town, and Charlotte had lost her friend and mentor as well as her boarding place.

Unbeknownst to Charlotte, Wilson had voted for the slave-taking law when he was a congressman. Still he, like most of the friends he left behind in the East, was not unsympathetic to the abolitionists' cause. He was an appreciative audience for his youngest daughter's remarkable letters during the winter and spring of 1851. They were, he noted on the one of March 23, "As usual Excellent. Dear Child how my heart is bound up in her. Oh! May God Bless her always. J. W." and of April 20, "A beautiful letter, very very beautiful. It is no common girl of 14 yrs of age who can write such a letter."

✳   [CHARLOTTE]   Boston March 23rd 1851

My very dear Father,

. . . I really envy you reconnoitering the coast of the Pacific, which always seems to me as far from here as the Moon. My idea of the world, being entirely devised from maps, is anything but clear. I should really expect to see the coast of the Pacific divided, into just such little projections, as one sees on a map.

. . . I am very happy, too. A quiet happiness it is, for 'I keep the even tenor of my way,' undisturbed by any excitement. . . . Dr. Bowditch does not let me go to any crowded assembly of an evening, that I may be well for school. That is the only way to keep such an excitable and inflamable person, as I am, cool. . . .

This morning I went to the Stone Chapel and heard Mr. Peabody preach a beautiful sermon upon the deaths of Coolidge Shaw, son of R. G. Shaw and Mrs. Mary Brooks, who was a Miss Chadwicke and married young Frank Brooks, grandson of Peter C. Brooks. She was about 21 and only married last May. A *very* lovely person indeed, both in mind and person. It was impossible not to feel great pity for poor Frank Brooks, and not to almost regret her death. But after Mr. Peabody had recalled to our minds her beautiful life and her trust in God, the church seemed almost filled with light. I could not doubt her happiness. Then he asked us all, if the summons of death should come to us as suddenly as it did to her, should we be prepared? And it startled me so much, to think how near I might be to death and still as frivolous and thoughtless as it is possible for any one to be. She died of congestion of the brain falling asleep quietly, and saying she felt perfectly well, at 9 in the evening, and never awaking till 10, the next day, in another world. It was *very* impressive.

The beautiful snowdrops are just in blossom here, much to my surprise, for it snowed from Monday till Thursday steadily, and left the ground with about 3 feet of snow on it in the streets, though it was only a foot deep else where. But it has gone even quicker than it came even. The only disadvantage we have suffered from it was the bad walking. That has been shocking, for when you thought yourself safely on dry land, the snow would give away and splash. You went into water up to your ankles. We have a worse time crossing, with our long dresses than gentlemen do.

I don't think you would immediately recognise your daughter Charlie, if you were to see me, with my little short hair. I wear it rolled back from my face. It is about 2 inches long now very nice and thick. I wish I could keep it as moist as yours is without water, but I cannot.

. . . The Free Soilers are now quiet. Charles Sumner the Free Soil senator was defeated by a small majority of Whigs, I *believe*. I presume you *know* by this time through the papers. I do not trouble myself much about Politics. . . .

Believe me your loving daughter   Charlotte J. Wilson

✳ [CHARLOTTE]   Boston April 20th 1851

My dear Father,

. . . I went to my new boarding place Thursday. I meant to have gone Tuesday, but when the day arrived, it rained very hard. . . . Wednesday, it rained and blew so furiously, that it was nearly impossible to go out without being blown down. Thursday afternoon I drove round to 44 Bedford st. with all my trunks. It rained from Monday till Thursday without cessation. The water came up into the houses near the wharfs sometimes above the basement. The poor wretches in Ann and Broad streets who lived in cellars had to leave them and were all crowded together in garrets. As soon as the water subsided they went back to their dark damp homes. Oh what a miserable life to pass! I should think that more than half the unhealthyness of a city would spring from the exposure of these poor beings to dampness and cold.

The wind blew a hurricane from Tuesday till Thursday morning. The shipwrecks are unnumbered as yet I believe. The light house, with two men in it, was destroyed. Just imagine the poor creature's agony all the time before it fell. The light was seen in it at 10 Tuesday night, but it was gone I believe at 12. The thought of their suffering haunts me. In a place such as they were in, alone with the waves dashing above and around them, every moment must have seemed a year. The English Steamer was nearly dashed on Minot's ledge in consequence of the absence of the light house. I have taken up so much room in describing the storm to you in order that you may appreciate the great excitement we were all in. . . .

The people with whom I board seem to be very goodnatured people. They are not very interesting however. I feel rather lonely there as yet. . . . My sister has given me permission to spend every Sunday with some one of my friends, as it will be disagreeable to pass the whole day with them. Miss Bixby is a very good person but she is not a person I should ever care particularly to know. She seems to be a very strict Unitarian which is much in her favor. I shall be in Boston but six more Sundays. Mrs. Bowditch wants me to come to their place one Sunday.

. . . Uncle Robert sent me a nice box of maple sugar a few days since. I wrote him a note of thanks by Lizzie. Mr. Nichols brought us a bottle of *gold sand*, last Wednesday. I have seen it and am the only one of our family who has. Lizzie went to Keene in such a hurry yesterday that I did not give it to her. It shall be sent to Keene by the very first opportunity. Every particle of gold was full of interest for me because I could imagine your pleasure when you discovered the shining metal. I rejoice in the brightness of your prospects and hope that your happiest expectations may be realized. I passed most of my evening at the Barretts reading your letters to the girls. I wish we could have letters from you *every* week. . . .

You have probably read in the Boston papers of the great slave case which has been exciting the minds of the Boston people. This is no other than the capture of a fugitive slave Thomas Sims. The Court house was in chains and guarded by a great number of policemen during the trial of Sims. He was taken back to the South. My commiserations were all engaged for the poor fellow. Though I have always thought a woman had better not meddle much with politics, yet I can't help feeling a great deal of interest in political questions. I do not agree exactly with free soilers in their tremendous ideas of reform and upon many other points, yet I feel that at some future time all these sufferings which they now experience will be looked upon as we look upon the persecutions of religious reformers. This idea occurred to me the other day while talking to Mrs. Bowditch. She expressed it just as I would have done so. It struck me as quite a coincidence that she should think of it just as I did. You are not Free Soil, are you? I don't know but that you think me very foolish to feel so much interest in matters so much above me, but it is involuntary with me. I cannot help it. . . .

Good bye dear Father. Believe me your loving daughter

Charlotte J. Wilson

During what turned out to be her last year of formal schooling, Charlotte's intellect and social conscience flourished at her lodgings under the influence of the Bowditches more than it did in the classroom. At school the measles forced her to limit her studies to French reading, writing, and grammar and English, which consisted mainly of memorizing a text called *Campbell's Rhetoric*. Her insights into the events around her she wrote to her father, Lizzie being more concerned about her health. "I intend . . . to have Charlotte come home before the hot weather to see if she cannot get thro' the summer without an illness" (Lizzie, 1-25-51).

Love and Money

W hen you thought yourself safely on dry land, the snow would give away and splash. You went into water up to your ankles"—the problem Charlotte experienced with the slush could serve as an epigram for the uncertainty of the sisters' fortunes. While James Wilson felt a burst of confidence and good cheer following his gold strike, the three women returned to Keene for the summer with their finances in disarray and the ownership of their house in dispute. Annie and Lizzie took steps to remedy that state of uncertainty. During these years, as Wilson focused his energies on making money, practicing law, and adventuring on the frontier, his daughters' most important endeavor was attracting suitable young men. For them spinsterhood was too fraught with economic and social uncertainty to be attractive. Choosing a husband was one of the few major decisions each would make, and on the success or failure of this undertaking hung their future physical and social welfare and that of their children, as well as the regard of their friends and family. Their assessments of the young men who courted them—the ones who were attractive and agreeable and might be pleasant to live with, the ones who could offer social position or wealth, the ones who were talented and might make a name for themselves—had long-ranging consequences. Thus, Lizzie's amusing accusation that Annie flirted with fools bears some fairly serious weight. Considering the consequences of bungling the enterprise, the women undertook this project with gallant lightheartedness, as we see in Lizzie's letters to Susan Colby.

The Wilson sisters pursued this business at official events such as the spring season at West Point and balls and receptions in Washington, as well as in the houses of family friends such as the Goodridges, the Wetmores, the Eldredges, the Taintors, the Dixwells, the Sherwoods. Although Lizzie provides some witty insights into flirtations and courtships for Susan Colby, the sisters don't often confide such things to their father. However, Annie, who was disappointed not to be part of Washington society as she had been the previous winter, sent bits of secondhand gossip from Washington society.

"The Sherwoods have just returned from their winters tropical sojourn [in Havana], charmed with every thing. They spend three days at the National, and describe Washington as pleasant, but not equal to last winter. There appear to be more married and elderly women, and fewer girls than last winter, and the whole thing entirely changed. Mrs. Wilcox Cabell is as pretty and silly as ever. Mrs. Ashley 'the lady mother' is very much the same state. Mrs. Hugh White and Mrs. J. C. Clark very much painted and very patronising. . . . Lady Bulwer they say entertains beautifully, and is universally a favorite. Mrs. Fillmore by way of giving ease to her receptions has Mrs. Spaulding of New York to help her receive, a woman at once fond of, and conversant with elegant society, as you undoubtedly remember. Mary S[herwood] went to one of the assemblies which she says was exceedingly brilliant. Miss Ellen . . . appears to have been the acknowledged belle. Miss Camilla Scott too is much admired. I have written this nonsense because I think when one is far away, these little nothings are particularly acceptable" (Annie, 1-27-51).

When the wealthy and proper Sherwoods invited Lizzie and Annie to visit them in Washington, Lizzie had not yet recovered completely from the measles, and Annie demurred: "we both feel the need of our dear Father there, to take care of us" (Annie, 1-10-51). The visit was therefore postponed until the Sherwoods' return to New York in late February when Annie would leave Mrs. Wetmore for a few weeks to stay with them. With eyes still weak, Lizzie remained in Hartford and left Annie to tell the news that Susan Colby had married James B. Colgate, a stockbroker, a philanthropist, "a very rich merchant, and I hear a very nice person" (Annie, 2-24-51).

What followed in April, after the announcement of this marriage, must have astonished General Wilson. On April 20, 1851, he received two letters in the same mail—one from Lizzie and one from Annie—telling him of some important plans of their own.

✳ [ANNIE]   New York March 10th 1851

My dear Father,

I am very happy to acknowledge the receipt of two most charming letters from you of dates 4th and 15th of January. . . . The cheerful and confident tone in which you write is very satisfactory to us, and makes us very happy. I don't know what to write you of ourselves. There is so little variety in our daily experience I fear to bore you by too frequent repetition. I shall go to see [Jamie] on my way to Keene . . . then home for several weeks of *undisturbed quiet*. I long for summer, for your return and a grande reunion under our own roof.

I have been several weeks with Mary Sherwood and have enjoyed [it] very much. . . . And now, comes a confidence between child and parent which it is your right to claim and my duty and pleasure to give. I have heard you say often, that you disapproved of an early marriage for women, and that remembrance makes me fear your displeasure when I tell you that I have conceived a strong attachment for, and have engaged myself to one of the young gentlemen of this family, the youngest, and the one you know least. His family you know, and know of, as he knows ours. In neither, is there aught to blush for. That he is fond of me I can hardly doubt, as he has nothing to gain by the connection.

His character I have studied and have had an opportunity of judging of, as I have seen him constantly for a long time in his home, and I think I am old enough now, and have a sufficient amount of common sense, to enable me to judge for myself in a case like this. Yet your presence would have been a great comfort to me, and it is now that I feel my dear Mother's loss more than ever before. In your absence, I have done what seemed to me right. I have given myself to the man I love, to one in whom I have entire confidence, who as my husband will love and care for me, securing for me the same position in which I was born, and have been nurtured, and faithfully and conscientiously perform this duty toward me.

If you would condemn, think my dear Father of your own youth, and of my pretty Mother's, and allow me to make my own choice. Your consent and blessing is all I ask now, to complete my happiness. My letter is full of self and selfish matters, but 'from the abundance of the heart the mouth speaketh.' Let me hear very soon from you, and believe me under all circumstances and in all situations I am as ever, fondly and affectionately your child   Annie F. Wilson

On March 16—a week after Annie sent this letter—Lizzie broke her news but in quite a different manner.

✳ [LIZZIE]   Hartford March 16th 1851

My dear Father,

The poor state of my eyes has made me for several weeks a poor correspondent, but I believe your other children have done their duty. I am now much better. . . .

I hear thro' Mr. Goodridge that you are doing a fine law business, and that one of his Captains says you can make $40,000 a year if you choose by your profession.

I am glad your mining business looks so well. Mining always seems so very uncertain that I never feel much hope, but brains are certain. Mine and yours I hope may prove available. I hope before the 1st of May you will send me 4 or 500. [dollars] that I may pay up some outstanding accounts. I begin housekeeping fresh. I am going to have James and Charlotte at home, as I cannot afford to pay their bills now without almost going barefooted and now Annie and I have no expenses. Mr. Webster's financial difficulties have cast a pall over the Wilson's prospects and Uncle Robert will allow me nothing and I have no resource but the little sum in the savings bank. Coleman and Stetson state their inability to get me that $300. and unless you send me some I don't know where I shall go.

Charlotte left me last Wednesday. Her health is somewhat improved. I shall not let her stay however after the hot weather commences.

The most important piece of intelligence I have to communicate is that I am engaged to Mr. John Sherwood, and that it is generally known. Of course I have no idea of being married until you come home, and not unless you are successful. I shall always consider my brother and sisters first. If you do not make money enough for them I shall go to work myself.

Mr. and Mrs. Taintor have been very kind. I have been spending a fortnight there.

Annie is in New York spending some time with the Sherwoods. She is going to Keene to stay with the Dorrs and Perrys a few weeks. I dare say you hear from her.

Hoping a kind Providence will ever protect you and that you will soon return . . . I am with much love your affectionate daughter

M. E. Wilson

The offhand manner in which Lizzie made her announcement suggests that it would not surprise her father, as Annie's engagement to the younger brother Robert would. Perhaps Wilson approved the match before he left, and Lizzie's intimate friends and family expected an official announcement. Still, Lizzie's marriage plans depended at least partly on Wilson's success. While propriety demanded that Wilson be present to give his daughter away, there was a more practical reason to wait until Wilson succeeded in California. Although the Sherwoods were a wealthy family, John himself had no independent income. The young couple would need money from both of their families to set up housekeeping. And there were the other Wilson children to consider.

Wilson raised no objection to Lizzie's engagement, but he strongly disapproved of Annie's. Lizzie, pleased with her own choice, heartily concurred with her father's opinion of Annie's decision. Just what was wrong with Robert Sherwood, Lizzie never said. The nearest explanation we have of his failings is Charlotte's observation some months later, "He is not amiable." In fact, the engagement was mentioned only a few times, but clearly Lizzie and Wilson set out to break up Annie's romance.

After wandering from friend to friend all winter, Annie returned home for the first time since Christmas, soon after announcing her engagement. She needed to contemplate in solitude the dramatic and surprise step she had taken. By April 22 Lizzie had joined her.

✳ [LIZZIE]   Keene Ap/l 22d 1851

My dear Father,

We are very happy to find ourselves once more in our pleasant home. I reached home Saturday night and found Annie and James safely established with Roxana, George, and Margaret, a very good girl who takes the place of Mary Ann who chose not to return. Uncle Robert is very kind and I am very confident we shall get along well. The season is very forward and with the exception of the dreadful storm which devastated the coast and blew down the lighthouse on Nichols ledge, we have had a delightful spring. . . .

Jamie has begun French with me and will begin his Latin and Greek the first of May. You are quite right about my disinclination to study languages. I have very little love of study and truly like those things which come easily, but I have overcome it in a measure and have very good and increasing knowledge of languages.

. . . Annie is to be housekeeper this summer. She has so much sense and firmness that she is particularly fitted for it and I let her give all the orders. I hope too it may divert her mind from the (as I think) unfortunate attachment she has formed, or *entanglement* rather for I don't think she loves him very much.

I am very happy in my engagement to the elder Mr. Sherwood. He treats me with every attention and kindness and is I believe a thoroughly honorable and excellent person. I hear from every source of his excellent character and good principles.

. . . believe me ever the faithful guardian of your best interests, your daughter   Lizzie

---

It must have been a jolly reunion for Annie, with Lizzie insisting that she understood her sister's feelings better than Annie did and that Annie didn't love Robert very much. Wilson wrote a diplomatic letter discouraging the attachment, but of course, it didn't arrive until June. Lizzie was less than diplomatic, and she and Annie had a huge row. By early May things came to a head. Annie's first letter explaining what happened to the engagement is lost. In June she treated the affair as youthful folly.

✳ [ANNIE]   Keene, N. H. June 8th 1851

My dear Father,

I hardly know how to thank you for a most kind, considerate and excellent letter from you by the last steamer. It related to a subject very near to me and allow me to say that if you had studied years to frame a letter that should cause me to reflect seriously on my conduct and to give up my absurdities you could never have surpassed that letter. Calm, just, cool, with no opposition or denunciations it was a master piece and would certainly have effected the desired end if that were not already effected. Long ere this reaches you, you will have received a letter in which I confess my fault and inform you of the termination of an affair which has done me no harm and has given me some useful experience. The circumstances of the case were these. I was in New York with my friend Miss S.[herwood] and happy and buoyant. Her brother was courted and flattered by other women around me and when I saw that he admired and liked me I was flattered by the attention. I saw him constantly, admired him extremely (as I do still) when he spoke to me of myself and his regard for me. I was just in this unsettled state of mind then, when I hardly knew how I did feel, when Lizzie heard of the state of the case. Her course then, though entirely conscientious was, to say the least, injudicious. I am easily persuaded, but hardly forced. She violently opposed me, without cause except personal dislike for Mr. S.[herwood]. . . . I looked upon myself as an injured young woman. I stood upon my rights—in short I was extremely absurd. I came home, away from opposition away from persecution. I thought seriously on the subject. I saw my error. I wrote to Mr. S. that our engagement (if it deserves the name) which was created and nursed by opposition having lost its natural [element] must languish and die, that I was convinced he already saw the absurdity of the whole affair, as I did, that we 'mistook the flicker for the flame,' and that I hoped we might neither of us be the worse for thus easily discovering our mistake. Where upon he wrote me a very gentlemanly letter acceding to my proposals and there is the end of the affair. I fear that I may have wearied you with this long recital but I like you to know the whole.

We are nicely ensconced here, and hope to get through a peaceful season in peace and quiet. May we not hope to see you in the Fall, just for a little while? John Sherwood is here today spending Sunday. He is very charming and loveable. Keene is almost a suburb of New York. . . .

All is well and comfortable. As ever fondly your child

Annie F. Wilson

One is tempted to doubt that any engagement could be entered into and broken off so simply, and this was not a simple situation. Whether Robert Sherwood agreed that he too had "mistaken the flicker for the flame," there was little he could do but acquiesce. The affair was widely known—even their friend Mrs. Fourgeaud knew about it in California—and any engagement publicly acknowledged and then broken is awkward. How, in fact, did Annie feel toward Lizzie for opposing her engagement? How did Mary Sherwood, Annie's friend, feel about her brother's engagement to Annie? How did she feel about Annie's breaking it off? How about Robert? He may have entered into the engagement hastily, but his pride must have been wounded when Annie shrugged it off so easily. What about John Sherwood, Lizzie's fiancé? The entanglement between the two families was far too complex for the affair to have dissolved without plenty of leftover hard feelings, but Wilson heard very little about them.

The end of this affair is not the end of romantic problems for Annie, though Lizzie hopes that Robert Sherwood will be Annie's last misstep. "I think now that she has given up almost the only mistake she has made, falling in love with Robert Sherwood. She is in a fair way to make one of these days a fine marriage" (Lizzie, 5-7-51). Certainly she would make a fine marriage if Lizzie had her way.

Lizzie's engagement was, of course, the subject of much discussion, but all engagements and weddings were a source of lively interest, if not approval. Across three thousand miles each of the three daughters sent the news of the engagement between forty-eight-year-old Hannah Newcomb and the ancient Gad Newell, a retired minister. All of Keene snickered at the story of Gad leaping over Aunt Lucretia's fence, and Wilson remained a part of that community via his daughters' letters.

"What *do* you think of Hannah Newcomb's conduct? Everybody thought that 'Gad Newall' was dead, years ago. It is said that he puts one hand on the pickets of Aunt Lucretia's fence and is over, with out opening the gate. He objects to having the wedding put off to July, ever, which Mr. Ingersoll says is not strange, as he has but a *few minutes* to live. Hannah says by way of excuse to Dr. Adams, 'Why Dr., you know my *Mother* is very old and will not live long, and I must have a home and some one to take care of me, and . . . then . . . (after great hesitation) *'I love Mr. Newall.'*

As a last and rather *un*important item!" (Annie, 5-23-51). Gad Newall said he was eighty-seven, but "most people here say he is as old as the Monadnock. . . . The only reason they say is that Hannah and Lucretia Dans are sworn foes. That old Mr. Newell is an orthodox pastor and has some property. Disgusting isn't it" (Lizzie, 5-24-51).

A week before the wedding Hannah was saved from this "disgusting" marriage. "Poor Hannah Newcomb's engagement is broken off by the intervention of friends. The poor old thing is wretched" (Annie, 6-23-51).

The local saga of Hannah Newcomb continued. In the summer her mother died; and Hannah was, as she predicted, left without a husband, however ancient, to provide for her. Hannah Newcomb died years later, poor and single, which, presumably, Lizzie found less disgusting than being the widow of Gad Newall with some property.

While Wilson's success at Gold Bluff glittered like Lizzie's promising engagement, his political appointment remained as unfulfilled as Hannah Newcomb's. The situation raised all of Lizzie's family pride, and she hastened to reassure him without mentioning the appointment directly. "You need never be afraid of our not being fond and proud enough of our Father, nor at our having any feeling but annoyance *that you are annoyed*. I do hope you will be amply repaid for all you have sacrificed for us, and if I may be allowed to hope or express a wish on the subject, I trust it will be *by your noble professional talents*, that you succeed. The Government can give you nothing that equals the offices you have held here, and I trust you will not need their help" (Lizzie, 5-7-51).

"Always remember we are very *proud* girls and feel we have a character to be supported as well as principles and love of you, to take care of us. I fear you give yourself more uneasiness than is necessary. We are too proud to be lightly treated, too proud of you to disgrace you, tho' all your advice is reasonable. Annie did not go to Washington tho' we both felt tempted to have a private interview with the President. But do not depend on this administration [Whig Millard Fillmore]. Depend on yourself dear Father. You can do much better than they can do for you" (Lizzie, 5-7-51).

Their reactions to their father's situation reflect the contradictory feelings of diffidence and self-confidence that informed these women's lives. Far from feeling impotent because their father's government appointment had not materialized, Annie considered going to Washington to intervene on his behalf with President Fillmore. On the other hand, she wailed that women were helpless in the face of financial problems, while Lizzie wrote dunning letters to the formidable Daniel Webster and tapped other resources, like Mr. Skinner. Even as Charlotte pondered the public matter of slavery, she depreciated her own opinions. The sisters' feelings of helplessness and strength ebbed and flowed as they viewed themselves primarily as women or primarily as members of their family or social class. As women they felt diffident and passive; as social, family beings they were proud and confident.

Gradually, the family trickled home for the summer. While Annie and Lizzie were in Keene coping with a series of family and personal problems during the spring, Charlotte and Jamie were still in school. Charlotte did not worry about her father's appointment; she missed the broken engagement and broken promises. When the weather in Boston turned hot and still, she fretted for home. "Boston is a very disagreeable and warm place, . . . The sun is scorching and there is no sea breeze to refresh one. And this is probably the weather you have had all winter. Well my dear Father I pity you. We have just had our first rubarb and asparagus. I remember your old fondness for new vegetables and wish you were to be here with us to enjoy them. . . . Jamie is at home and they are all as happy as they can be without you and *me*. I am going home now in about 4 weeks. I should love to jump over those weeks. However I shall be there sooner than you. Don't you sit sometimes and imagine your reaching home and seeing us all perfectly happy to get you back again?" (Charlotte, 5-5-51).

When he missed a connection on his trip home, fourteen-year-old Jamie had to spend the night en route and was pleased to find himself quite capable of coping. Along the way he encountered a hotel clerk, Mr. Moseley, who knew his father, and Mr. Ashmun, with whom the family had shared the boardinghouse in Washington the previous winter.

"I had quite a funny time getting here from Hartford, I will tell you about it. There was some accident happened on the New York road, so that they were very late into Hartford, and when we arrived at Springfield the Ashuelot train had gone, and I found that I could not get to Keene until the next morning. I was alone, and with eight pieces of baggage as I had some of my sisters so I went and asked the baggage-master if he would put it where it would be safe, and he said he would. (I had the checks all the way to Keene in my pocket.) I then went out of the Depot and I saw the Massasoit House. I remembered to have been there with you, once before, so I went in and inquired how much I should have to pay to stay all night and have my meals, and he said a dollar and a half, so I wrote my name on the book, and as soon as the gentleman, (whose name was Moseley) saw it he asked me if I was General Wilson's son. I told him I was, and he said he knew you very well, so he showed me my rooms, and I put my coat and carpet-bag in it, and then asked him if Mr. Ashmun was at home. He said he was, and as it was town-meeting day, he said I should most likely find him in the street, so I went out to walk but as I did not see him, I went and bought a cord to tie around the gun-case as it was a little cracked, then went to the Depot, and got the baggage-master to unlock the baggage room, fixed the case, and then went back to the Hotel, and read until supper time. After supper I read and walked around the house, until 1/4 of 9 when I went to bed. I got up about 1/4 past 6, had breakfast at 1/2 past 7, then I paid my bill, and went over to the Depot, and saw my baggage safely aboard the cars. I had just got in myself, and had got seated, when 'lo and behold' Mr. Ashmun came in. He said he was going to Greenfield. He inquired very kindly for you and the girls and then went off to another part of the car, and sat down and began to talk with some other gentleman. I had a very pleasant ride up the Ashuelot road, and at last arrived safely at Keene with all my things" (Jamie, 4-22-51).

* [LIZZIE]   May 7th 1851, Keene

My dearest Father,

. . . We are too happy always to get your merest note, imagine then the delight with which we receive and read the long and eloquent letters you send us. I wish I could give a "Quid pro quo" but Keene is so stupid and our lives so unvaried that I have scarcely anything to say, but blessed be such quiet, I say, unbroken by any sorry. The only events we care for are letters from you and the coming up of the peas.

I was very sorry the box had gone without "Alton Locke" the book you mistake in saying by Miss Brontë. Annie thought so when she wrote you. It is by a Mr. Kingsley a clergyman of the church of England but one who has nobly dashed off the blinders of prejudice and high-churchism and looks with the eye of a philanthropist and bold man on the struggles of the poor. It is a most powerful painful book. I was sorry I read it, but it may do me some good. However I fear I am rather radical by nature, with too little regard for "the law" and established usages, and need to be *conservatized* rather than liberalized. Therefore I consider that neither you nor I *need read Alton Locke*, for if you won't object to my paying myself a compliment at your expense, I think our minds are very much alike and sympathize quite enough with humanity—suffering humanity. . . .

We live very quietly, unmolested by any body. George attends to our outdoor interest and our place is looking beautifully. Our neighbors are *so* kind. If we had been queens we could not be treated with more kindness. I wish you would write Mr. Sumner Wheeler a letter. I think he ought to be canonized. He is the *best* man in Keene. Mr. Chamberlain too is so good. Uncle Robert is very kind and seems devoted to our interest, and we must bear with his infirmities of temper. I need not say we all treat him with respect. . . .

As for Jamie he is to begin in one month to recite to Mr. Torrence [former headmaster of Keene Academy], and in the meanwhile he studies French and is preparing the Latin Grammar. I do believe he will make a fine man and I know I have a powerful hold on him. He *never* disobeys me. He sometimes gets rather angry at his sister Annie whom he says "is a very severe disciplinarian and has not the care of him" but her clear logical mind in the long run has a fine influence upon him. I know where he is every moment. That influence must be very insidious *indeed* that gets at him without my knowledge, and if I have nothing else to do for him I sit down and hold him in my lap and tell him how important he is to us all and how much we love him. . . .

Annie is housekeeper now and shows a great deal of talent. Annie is very practical and needs only to soften and refine a little to make a very perfect character. She is not quite fond enough of reading and I hope you will advise her to cultivate those more elegant talents. She is very beautiful, very truthful, very capable and very thorough. . . .

Charlotte is elegant and accomplished and at the same time deep and thorough. She speaks French as well as if she had been in Paris, and she knows chronology better than most old professors. All we have to do is to keep her alive and well. When her nervous system is right she has a perfectly harmonious beautiful temper and disposition. I think she is in a fair way to have some health now.

. . . We are in a dreadful state here about a minister. I correspond with the Livermores. Mr. L. has waked up a great deal since he left here. His congregation are delighted with him but he finds Unitarianism rather below par there and he grows controversial. . . .

I have grown quite intimate with the family of Bishop [Carl] Chase, Bishop of New Hampshire. He was at the Goodridges with me and himself and wife and son are all great friends of ours. Sophia Goodridge who is the most rigid of all little church women insists upon it that he shall marry me and says she shall write the announcement "By the Right Reverend G. Chase, *Bishop of New Hampshire*, Miss Mary Elizabeth, daughter of Hon. James Wilson, etc." Whereupon I call her a little Tractarian, and formalist, but we can forgive so good a girl a far worse charge. . . .

Ever your affectionate
Mary Lizzie

Annie, having abandoned her ill-considered engagement and the illusion that her father would return in the summer, found tranquility at home following the restless winter. Only the nuisance of the patrons of her father's inn, The Emerald House, interfered with her peace. She cast a spell of incantatory language that seems to transform Wilson's letters into the man himself and conjure him into their midst like the tender fresh green of spring. Through the richness of her language and imagery Annie explored some of her most intimate and profound perceptions about him, the family and their home and garden. Wilson himself noted at the end that the letters were "Excellent" and "Beautiful" despite her indifference toward his triumph at Gold Bluff.

*   [ANNIE]   Keene May 7th 1851

My dear dear Father,

A charming pacquet of letters we have just received. How can I thank you for your thrice welcome, long, satisfactory letters to me. . . . We were *very* sorry not to have sent Miss Brontë's book. I will look out for a private opportunity and send you some books as soon as possible.

Seated around the back parlor fire place (for we have fires still) in a semi-circle, we take our turns in reading and enjoying your dear letters. And a general spring is made for the first sheet of your letter when I take up the second, my turn is through, having read them all and hasten to answer while Jamie sits opposite me deep in some one of the Epistles, confirming all you have said complimentary of him, by sundry expressions after each sentence like 'Oh'! *'Bless his heart'*! 'Yes indeed'! 'Well I *guess* I shall' etc etc etc.

We are so comfortable and happy here I wish you could look in upon us. Our place never was prettier. You know exactly how it looks now in its first budding tender beauty. The crab apple in leaf, the grass like velvet, that peculiar tender fresh green of Spring, the lilachs in bud and violets in blossom. This season is to me particularly charming, before the intense heat of summer has wilted or dried the grass or turned its color. Before another Spring you must be back again.

The affair of the golden bluff is very superb, but how is the climate? If it is not healthful don't go dear Father I beg. Think how very terrible it would be for you to be sick there.

I wish I had something to tell you new, but Keene is in status quo. Mr. Chamberlain says the State is turning around however. Think of the people's *not* reelecting Govr. Dinsmoor.

We are terribly bored by stupid divines. Last Sunday we had a man who preached on the new and interesting subject of 'peace.' The congregation went to sleep, and the poor minister was forced to contradict himself for the sake of argument.

. . . A letter in your box will set your mind at rest as to my absurd "affairs du coeur" (of the heart) as the french say. . . . I sent a letter to Mrs. Four-

geaud by your box. Thank her for her kind invitation. I should rather see her in New England than California.   As ever, fondly your
Annie

✳ [ANNIE]   May 23rd 1851

My dear Father,

The fragrance of a thousand flowers, 'mille fleurs' as the french call a favorite perfume, is coming into me at the window. Your old Robins (I suppose) sing from their nest in the grape vines and are this moment going through the very interesting ceremony of teaching the young ones to fly. Have they not been expeditious now before the summer is fairly here to have reared and forsaken their little family?

The apple trees, all over the place are laden with blossoms, and the lilachs perfume the house. As I write the breath of a little bed of "lilies of the valley" growing under the parlor windows floats in. Perhaps it wants to be sent to you. Did you ever hear of an instrument which is said to be used in the east, that is made outwardly like a piano, and instead of producing sounds, bring forth delicious combinations of fragrance! The perfection of the art is in producing an endless variety of perfumes without ever a '*discord*' or a false combination. This is a description of Melville's and seems like many of his things, slightly apocryphal. Nevertheless it is an original idea and the delicious combinations of nature this morning remind me of it. How far nature outstrips ere always!

I wish so much that you could see your place this very minute. I certainly *never* have seen it so perfect. Or, if I have, it never produced the same effect upon me. We have had a little row of fir trees put along on the edge of the north bank, that we hope may live, that shut off the Emerald nuisance entirely. How beautiful this must have been, before that lawn north of this house was touched. I don't remember it, but Lizzie described it to me the other day in glowing colors. . . .   I am as ever fondly your daughter
Annie F. Wilson

Could James Wilson have ignored her parable of the young robins forsaken by their parents?

In July Annie inspected their Eden minutely and declared: "Everything on the place looks extremely well. I was examining the little plum trees last night and I found one of the very small ones on the north bank, had *nine* immense plums nearly as large as an egg already. The two apple trees in the clothes yard, which you remember, are covered with apples and you know they are very nice. String beans and green peas we have daily from the garden and squashes in perfection. A little leg of roasting lamb with currant jelly and a little mint, new potatoes and the accompaniment of vegetables above mentioned makes a pretty nice dinner and one that reminds us of you.

"Every body is very kind to us, particularly Mr. Chamberlain and dear Mr. Sumner Wheeler, who talked to me over the garden fence last night and said 'I expect to see the General back here before long.' He was advising us that the fence which seperates (Is the tendency to misspell 'separate' genetic?) the yard and garden should be removed, and said that fences had no business in gentlemen's grounds. I love and admire this place exceedingly, but I still look to grandfather's place with longing eyes. It should be yours. It should be Jamie's. I wish I were a man—it should be mine. Now isn't that absurd, just as if I knew anything about it.

". . . Uncle Robert is very well and is much interested in the cultivation of roses and bees. He brought us some superb roses a day or two since, and [a] dish of elegant honey—white as snow, *almost!*" (Annie, 7-22-51).

But grounds belonged to men. It was more plausible for Annie to wish she were a man than to wish that she could own the property. Like Charlotte on the slavery question, Annie disclaimed not only any right to the property but the right to judge the question.

During a chilly June in Keene the daily routine at Main and Emerald streets settled into a not very contemplative domestic bustle, with troops of guests, including John Sherwood, adding to the distraction. Even Annie, noted in the family for her decisive character, found herself rattled by the confusion. "If my style is incoherent and apparantly careless you will pardon it my dear Father when you know what the surrounding circumstances are. Mrs. Thesta Dana and husband and child are here for a night, on their way to St. Albans. The two Misses Barrett also are in the house. The baby is crying, Charlotte playing, the clock striking an hour that tells me my letter must soon be in the postoffice . . ." (Annie, 7-9-51).

P. T. Barnum's traveling show and menagerie played in Keene in 1851. Barnum, who had sold the public on Jenny Lind's virtue as much as her voice, was himself morally suspect but always interesting. His traveling shows swept the country along with gossip about his quarrel with the incorruptible Swedish Nightingale. The scandals that whirled around Barnum diverted the Wilsons and their friends as much as the entertainment he organized. "Today there is a menagarie in town, belonging to the lover of 'filthy lucre,' Mr. Barnum. The people of Bridgport, whom I visited, think quite highly of him. They say he was as much annoyed by Jenny Lind as she was by him. The world, however, have heard but one side, and it is natural to sympathise with the weaker party. There is a good deal of kind feeling after all in the whole world" (Charlotte, 8-8-51). Jamie enjoyed the traveling caravan more than Barnum's menagerie. "There has been a Caravan and Museum here today, a thing got up by Barnum, and consequently a great humbug. I wish you could have been here, not to see that, but to see the Yankee pedlars. One man had soap to sell, which would remove (as he said) spots of grease and oil, tar, pitch, paint, rosin, wax, or varnish, and was also a good shaving and washing soap, a salve to remove warts, corns, or moles. Another man had knife sharpeners etc, and amongst them all it was a very funny set" (Jamie, 8-8-51).

He also planned to "go trouting with Nat Sears," son of a local businessman, but Lizzie, who censored every word he wrote to his father, added a postscript to his letter. "James has made but one mistake in this letter which is that he is going with *Nat Sears*, which by the way he will not do. He is very obedient and I have no fear that he will." Whether or not Jamie went fishing with or without the unsavory Nat Sears, Lizzie kept a close eye on his activities.

As Lizzie planned, Jamie studied Latin, Greek, and algebra with Mr. Torrence. Lizzie herself taught him French and drawing. Neither she nor Jamie had been altogether pleased with his schooling the previous winter. In an undated letter that probably was written during the winter, he complained to his father, "you know that Mr. Abbott has left us, and that a gentleman by the name of S. E. Brownell has taken his place. I do not like him nearly as well as I did Mr. Abbott, and I do not think he is as good a teacher by any manner of means. He has no rules at all, and the school is all disorder. In school we are whispering and talking all the time and out of school we do just what we please. He has no regular time to hear the lessons, but does it when it is the most convenient. I am sure I do not want to come here next winter and I hope you will not send me" (Jamie, ?). Since he and Lizzie had not been very well satisfied with Mr. Brownell during the past year, he changed to the University Grammar School in Providence, Rhode Island, run by Mr. Frieze and Mr. Lyons.

Lizzie was also concerned about the education of her two sisters. Though they no longer attended school, they launched a program of study with Lizzie as schoolmistress. Annie read *Conquest of Mexico* at Lizzie's behest; Charlotte practiced the piano and read *Bancroft's History of the United States*. "We all sit down after breakfast and read, and ask Lizzie questions about what we know nothing of, and are surprised to see how much she knows that we do not. She has picked up a great deal of knowledge" (Charlotte, 10-5-51). Though they read these histories of the Americas, they ignored American fiction, like the recently published masterpieces Herman Melville's *Moby Dick* (though Annie mentions Melville) and Nathaniel Hawthorne's *The Scarlet Letter*, favoring instead British novelists.

They took lessons in French with the same woman who taught Charlotte piano, Madamoiselle de Sandraus, a Frenchwoman who was visiting her mother in Keene. Charlotte observed, "They are very amusing people indeed, except that they talk a little too much about the great people they know. What a very common fault this is, by the way, and what an *exceedingly* disagreeable one" (Charlotte, 7-9-51).

Keene was not always the secluded refuge that Lizzie, Annie, and Charlotte depicted. The railroad, which provided the children with easy access to Boston, Providence, New York, and Washington snaked along the Ashuelot River at the foot of their property. During the building of an engine house in the summer of 1851, the Ashuelot Railroad created havoc on their property and destroyed much of their crop of hay.

"I think you would hardly know our field if you should see it, it is so cut up. The Ashuelot Company have built an engine-house just south of the Cheshire one and there is a broad expanse of sand directly in the middle of the lot. The patch between the railroad and the river and the yard [is] all we had to get hay off of this summer as a good deal of the ground is taken up with corn and potatoes. All that south of Emerald Street is, while that north of it was used for a pasture for the cows, but now they have eaten it so close, that Uncle Robert has had to have them turned into the lot between the railroad and river" (Jamie, 8-8-51).

Financial woes further blighted their contentment. Uncle Robert continued to be unpredictable.

". . . We got your last remittance and get along very safely and agreeably paying as we go. If it were not that I am perpetually requested to pay old debts I should have no trouble. But there are several men who bring in little accounts and keep me embarrassed all the time. . . . If it is not too soon to ask and it will not be when this letter reaches you, shall you not be able to send me home enough to pay Roxana? I pay her $50 and $100 whenever I can to appease her, but so long as we are in her debt we are the servant of servants. Her note is reduced to $350 now I believe. And it seems to me that some portion of the rents might come to us. Uncle Robert lives very extravagantly and gives us nothing, while the Brink Store and the Emerald and the Stable and the houses all pay well. I hope you will ascertain as soon as some of the outward debts are paid how you stand and not be so implicit in your reliance on that bad man who is no friend to you. Let us be free of him and quit him forever.

"I was sorry you sent to him for your books. We could have sent them just as well, and he does domineer over our household arrangements so unpleasantly. . . ." (Lizzie, 6-9-51).

Sending things like books, pictures, and money to and from California provided the women with a tangible link in the bridge their letters constructed to their father. Sending his law books would have given them a little role in their father's career. The people they met who were part of his life and work in California further linked them to the place from which they felt very remote. John Sherwood was engaged in a lawsuit with Captain Joseph Folsom, a New Hampshire man who went to California with the army and stayed on to become one of the wealthiest and most influential men in San Francisco. Folsom, a shadowy presence in these letters, probably played a significant role in Wilson's career. He took the opposite side in the important and lengthy Limantour case with which Wilson struggled for many years.

Place and time are no more inextricably intertwined in Einsteinian physics than they are in letter writing. From the beginning Wilson's three daughters perceived California as a strange and threatening place. They had little idea even of the weather in San Francisco. As Charlotte observed, California seemed as far away as the moon. Not only had it lured their father away from them, he and other sojourners raved about its attractions until it sounded like a land of enchantment that might prevent him from ever returning home. Furthermore, this enchanted place was filled with danger from hostile Indians, inhospitable terrain, and lawless ruffians. Lizzie, Annie, and Charlotte perceived the full implication of the distance between themselves and their father during the summer of 1851, when the family experienced a multitude of major events on both coasts. First there was bad news from California. Their communication with him broke down as it did on so many important occasions, and they learned about it the same way they had learned about his original plan to go to California—by reading the newspaper.

* [CHARLOTTE]   Bridgeport June 22nd 51

My very dear Father,

Day before yesterday I read in the paper that 'Gen. James Wilson though severely burned, is pronounced by his physician entirely out of danger.' It was the first intimation I had received of the fire even. Oh my dear Father how can I express to you how much I longed to be with you! And when I think that a month since I was just as happy as I could be, about going home, and you were suffering intensely from that burn, it makes me feel more sadly than ever. I suppose the girls have letters in Keene from you, or your friends, but as I am away from home I have heard nothing from there. Mr. Greene brought me a letter from there Friday, and after I had read it, supposing it related to your injury, he said 'Your Father however is entirely out of danger.' It startled me very much. May God preserve you from further suffering.

Well dearest Father every thing is for the best. Perhaps this will bring you home sooner. When you come you know I shall keep house for you. I do not mean that you will not have the girls for a good while yet. Annie I am sure you will, but of course they will get married sometime and as I am the youngest I shall be yours entirely. I mean to learn to keep house nicely that I may at some far distant time preside with grace over yours. Oh Father we will be very gay and happy won't we?

I am staying at a delightful Country seat belonging to Mr. Greene a brother in law of Lizzie Eldredge. Two young ladies from New York, Minnie Choate and Lizzie Eldredge are staying here too. We have fine times together. We drive every afternoon in their barouch. In the morning Lizzie and I go out in the yard, and sit in a willow tree near the house. We take books with us, and the wind blowing through the large boughs refreshes us very much. Then Mr. and Mrs. Greene are delightful themselves. They are kind and polite to all of us. I shall never know how to repay so much kindness. Yesterday we drove down to the beach. When I looked at the sea I thought how far you were from us and I longed so much to be wafted to you in a moment. I love the sea. I love it more than trees or grass or hills. I am perfectly happy when I hear the waves breaking on the shore. It always fills me with a longing to gain something which I cannot express or understand. I wondered yesterday if I wanted to be on the ocean or what it was which I so earnestly desire, but I decided, that it could be no earthly pleasure but rather a longing for infinitude, for the 'far off unattained and dim.' Oh, my dear Father, when I hear the birds sing, when I see the ceaseless waves, when I am happy, it seems to me as if God were almost within reach. Do not think me romantic, Father, for I am sure it is a deeper feeling than romance which I experience. A second life, apart from the real one, makes me happy.

Today is Sunday and we have all been to church in Bridgeport. The Unitarian church is poorly filled here as most every where in Conn. What do you do on Sundays? . . . Our church is in a miserable state in Keene. Every body of people needs a head, but we have none, unless one can call a multitude of Prentisses, Hales etc *head*.

. . . I hope a letter arrived for you at the time you were in so much pain as you must have been. A letter from home is the next to being there. Who took care of you, and did you not want us very much? . . . To think you have been so ill shocks. I can't believe it. Annie and I have talked lately about the few accidents which had ever befallen us. Annie hushs me and says I must not boast of it. I do not, but am truly thankful they have been so few. May you be spared however particularly. Dear good Father I hope you will not suffer any more from burns or any thing of the kind. If my wishes can help you, you are safe.

. . . Believe me your own loving daughter,   Charlotte J. Wilson

✳ [LIZZIE]   June 23rd 1851

I shall not attempt to discover to you my dearest Father, the immense agony and sympathy we have felt for the last few days. While you are probably well and happy, we are mourning over the events of nearly six weeks ago. But thanks be to God, you are alive, you are in the hands of kind friends and you have the delightful satisfaction that you were inspired in the noblest of causes, and that the whole United States are talking of your heroism and self forgetfulness. More fortunate a moment was that we were led to dear Mrs. Fourgeaud's sick room in Washington? Is not she a noble woman?

Almost at the same moment I received the intelligence of the fire I heard that you were appointed Land Commissioner. I am thoroughly happy as a certain salary will not be an uncomfortable thing and Charlie March advises me that one can make much money out of it.

. . . How *could you remember* not to *breathe* when you were laying there in that fire! That piece of presence of mind was wonderful. I talk of it so much to James that I suspect he imagines you are holding your breath, as a matter of principle, yet.

Mr. Sherwood has just been over to see me. He has also just returned from the West Indies where he has been on a singular law case. He says perhaps you will be on the opposite side. It is a case wherein a Capt Folsom is concerned. The property of a certain ship master which lies in San Francisco is the matter in question. If you are the opposing counsel you must not abuse your antagonist as you know I am going to marry him.

Do write us what effect this appointment will have upon your absence. When will you come home.

Now do allow us to request that if there is another fire you will *not* go into it. Remember you have *served* your day and generation in that line. That you are older now than you were. That you cannot recover from injuries so readily. That you have *four children* each one of whom suffers any pain you suffer. Do be careful dear Father.

We are all well and in good condition. Mr. Webster has just sent me $100.

Hoping to hear soon I am ever affectionately your daughter,

                                                        Lizzie

✳ [ANNIE]   Keene June 23d 1851

My poor dear Father,

   God only knows the awful agony which we have endured the last three days, since the arrival of the Crescent City, with the news of the terrible fire. For the Crescent City, you must know arrived with the papers long before the 'Cherokee' with the mails. And all that could be learned was that 'Among those seriously injured, Genl. James Wilson of New Hampshire' thus leaving us no doubt of the identity, and in an awful state of suspense. We could not know if you were alive even. God grant such another time of suffering may never be passed. By this time you are well I pray most earnestly, and you will receive the news of your appointment (which Mr. Webster sends word to Lizzie will lead to fortune), before this letter reaches you.

   How can we thank Mrs. Fourgeaud for her angelic kindness. I shall endeavor to do it but I can never express to her the deep, deep gratitude, which fills my heart. My God bless her, and hers. . . .

   All your friends came down to see us as soon as the news reached us, and vied with each other in their efforts to mitigate our distress. Thank God the worst is over and we see in your own hand writing that you are out of danger. Believe me dear dear Father, our sympathy with you is very great and although it comes too late, and our letters full of hope and joy will reach you first at the time of your sufferings. Still you will not doubt the genuiness of it. Perhaps it is best that the cheerful letters should reach you first and the sympathizing ones come when you are better able to bear it.

   We never realized before, how far you were from us. More than a month now since your accident. It is truly frightful.   As ever, your daughter
                                                                  Annie

   Perhaps no other event provoked the Wilsons to examine the problem of communicating by letters more than their father's injury while saving others from a burning building.

   This incident reminded them of how acutely time and distance limited their control of their communication. The daughters felt the inadequacy of their response to their father's danger and the irony of the juxtaposition of their cheerful letters to his sad condition. While he suffered and healed in due time, the information *about* his suffering had to travel the distance he had imposed between him and them. During the time he suffered, they were happy. By the time they learned of his injury, he no longer needed their sympathy any more than he needed the salve or bandage they had not been there to apply. They were overwhelmed with gratitude for Mrs. Fourgeaud's help but felt guilty for not having nursed him themselves. Since it was too late to sympathize with him, their sympathy could as well be applied to their shock at receiving Mr. Greene's consolations before they had heard about their father's injury and their agony of waiting three days to know whether he was well. Annie's cry, "God grant such another time of suffering may never be passed" and "It is truly frightful" can apply equally to her father's suffering and to that of his daughters on his behalf.

From July 5 until October 19 they heard not a word from Wilson himself. During the summer after the fire in California, Wilson, quite recovered from his burns, went to the Gold Bluff in northern California, worked his claim, and set up the water system for washing gold. He did not read these letters commiserating with his injuries until he returned to San Francisco in September.

During those long months of silence the fortunes of the divided family began to change. Lizzie's engagement and Wilson's gold strike seemed to promise a new family structure and renewed prosperity. Although neither of these changes, not even the prospect of being rich, was greeted with unmitigated enthusiasm by every member of the family, they held out hope of a more stable and secure future.

Though Wilson did not write to his children, in July he sent them a substantial amount of gold. The physical presence of the gold and his enthusiasm finally aroused some confidence in Charlotte and Lizzie. Curiously, Annie did not mention his recent successes at all.

Charlotte regarded the gold, with qualified enthusiasm, as an exotic curiosity. When she stopped by to pick up a sample sent to Wilson's business associate, Mr. Francis Skinner, in Boston, she found it less interesting than Mr. and Mrs. Skinner themselves and Jamie's fishing. "Saturday I went to see Mr. Skinner about the gold. Saw his wife, he not being at home. She was very polite, but knew nothing of the gold. Sunday evening Mr. Skinner called on me at the Elderidges. Was very pleasant indeed. What a sensible person he is. I think he must be a very shrewd man. He thought he should go to Keene with the gold. I told him he would find fine trout fishing, which I suppose Jamie has described to you. How strange it seems to me that any one should enjoy fishing or any thing of that kind as boys do" (Charlotte, 6-22-51). Later, when she thought about the gold, she worried about its effect on her spiritual life. "I thought and prayed inwardly, that if we were prosperous, (as we shall be probably), we might never forget for a moment that there is yet another life, to obtain happiness in which is more desirable than here" (Charlotte, 7-24-51).

The gold finally inspired doubting Lizzie with hope that their money problems were over. Lizzie, who had been scrounging for money for a long time, saw nothing but good in the prospect of being rich. She analyzed the whole situation of her engagement and its effect on both the Sherwoods and the Wilsons with as keen an eye as any CEO could analyze the ramifications of a company merger. Long before this the clever and perceptive Lizzie had observed the Sherwoods very carefully—their financial situation, their attitude toward her father and her marriage to their son. With these observations in mind she struggled to reconcile her own desire to marry, the needs of her own family, her ambitions for them, and the Sherwoods' ambitions for their son. In fact, Lizzie saw her marriage as an entrée for Annie and Charlotte into a secure position in society—something General James Wilson had failed to provide. From this secure position her two sisters could more reasonably expect to find proper husbands—another responsibility shirked by James Wilson. Thus, she figured as exactly as she could how this marriage would affect the Wilsons, and she concluded that it would be for the better, for herself and for her siblings.

After their father's departure, the children created a new family structure, which Lizzie's engagement compelled them to rethink. The incorporation of John Sherwood would provide the much needed male protector for Annie and Charlotte. Fortunately, he was not an interfering man, and they could continue to run their household pretty much as they saw fit. Lizzie could become a figurehead mother while Annie took on the management of the family. Lizzie had already begun to groom her for that position by making her responsible for the house during the summer. Aware that her broken engagement freed her for the job, Annie acknowledged her willingness to step into her sister's shoes. "Long before this reaches you, you will have heard of my determination not to leave my home precipitately. I shall stay and perform my duty as well as my weak human nature permits, and if Lizzie chooses to marry, it will be my greatest pleasure to make Charlie and Jamie as happy as I can, and the home which can never be *perfect*, until yr. return, our dear and much loved Father" (Annie, 7-22-51).

These reassurances did not propel Lizzie into marriage. Lizzie would not be content with crumbs of stability and propriety. Just as her father sought his fortune in California, so Lizzie would seek her fortune in New York. She planned to launch herself on a wildly ambitious career as a socialite in New York, a scheme that demanded a great deal of money. Her plan required a proper establishment—house, carriage, servants, and clothes. She figured she could count on some money from her father's newfound wealth, but from Uncle Robert's reports she gauged that there would be little forthcoming from the property in New Hampshire. She also had problems with the Sherwoods that needed resolution before the time would be ripe to launch her scheme. They obviously would have to contribute handsomely for her career to succeed. Advantageous as her marriage might be, at the end of July Lizzie thought that on balance it would be better to wait.

✱ [LIZZIE] Keene July 24th 1851

My dear Father,

I was made very happy by your last letter, narrating the good news from the Gold Bluff, and your now entire recovery (How fortunate it is that you have such a constitution.) Now you have apparently two roads to a fortune, the Land agency, and the Gold Bluff. Do make a splendid fortune if it is possible. Every year I live I see how important money is to happiness. I no longer believe the twattle of poverty and happiness—poverty pulls down the best and noblest while wealth makes them comfortable. Look at Abbot Lawrence, with his ignorance and pretension, and by his wealth, a great man, the companion of princes and filling all Europe with his magnificence. I want to see you a very rich man for then I think you will have an opportunity to fulfil every wish of your heart your generosity, your love of travel, and your love of your children.

You speak of a very important topic, my marriage. I dislike to think that it must take place before your return, but I suppose it must, if you are not coming for so long. But not this winter. I do not feel that I can leave the children this winter. My idea was that I had better be married this fall and take the girls to New York with me, but I find we cannot afford to take such a house as I should want, at present. Mr. Sherwood's fortunes are in this wise. He has an excellent business and a good income resulting from it. His Father has a great deal of property but has speculated and involved himself somewhat, so he does not feel like giving his son much. The family were disappointed because John, who is the idol, and who has been very carefully educated and sent to Europe etc. did not marry an heiress whom they had picked out for him as I have recently found out, and disposed to dislike me for my poverty. Understand this I have found out by slight *indicia* not from any *statement*. Now since your appointment I find they admire me *more* than they did before. John has no part and parcel in this. His attachment to me is sure and he only regrets he has not now to offer me [a suitable home]. But I think he has much. Fine character, excellent talents for business, and great goodness of heart. Now I am disposed to put off my marriage until you can give me something—that the Sherwoods may not feel so very much that their son has made a bad bargain, nor we that we are living on an uncertainty. John is as much interested for the girls as we are. If I could live in New York, winters, and have them with me, it would be much better for them as Keene is the most dismal and forbidding place now, winter or summer. Summers we can get along but I don't know how we are to drag thro' the winter. I shall not be neglectful of the girls and Jamie I can assure you, even if I am married and I wish I could be, more for their sakes than my own, for then they would have a protector in John, always.

But we are to stay here this winter. George is to be married and to a very decent person who is a good cook. With Uncle Robert's approbation I have hired them for the winter. Roxana is getting past heavy work but she is to stay and sew for me and do what she likes for her board. Jamie I think will go to Providence. He is exposed to so bad an influence here thro' the continguity of the Emerald House and the awful awful set of boys here that I dare not expose his as yet easy virtue. He is an excellent and obedient boy, but he needs the care of a vigilant man on his studies and I am certain *no* place can be as bad as Keene in point of morals. The school here is very poor.

Now I might be married, and go to New York and board this winter at the New York Hotel and have a nice time, but here would be the poor girls up in New Hampshire having a lonely and sad winter. So I am determined that I will not be married until I can have a house and a right to take my sisters to it. We could come back and live here summers and they could spend their winters with me. Now is it not best, as they need me so much, that I should wait and see what happens? If you continue to . . . have $60,000 a year I think you can perhaps afford to give me $15,000 or so when I leave you.

And my dear Father, instead of being a beggar upon you, how much I have hoped that I could bring in a fortune *to* you, but such alas is not my fate. I have been disappointed ever since I can remember, in every thing I ever wished for very much, except your affection. That I believe will always be mine. The children too, are as dear to me as to you and I shall always regard them as sacred charges in any contingency.

Uncle Robert has had an offer for the Emerald House, $12,000. But he will not sell it. He says he wants $16,000. But when I reflect how easy that sum would make us, when I remember how we suffered for $1000 last summer it seems to me he might sell it. Mr. Holbrook of Surry made the offer and can pay $10,000 right now. I hope Uncle Robert will be paid soon for he is growing horribly avaricious and I think means to make as much out of us as he can. He sells our vinegar our manure, our hay, and takes the money for it. So if we have any right here let us have an exclusive one.

Before I get an answer to this letter it will be the 6th of October. By that time I shall want to know your opinion on all these points and I hope you will be able to send me some money to pay Roxana. She is very troublesome and every month I have to pay her some on her note which keeps me straightened all the time. Don't however write her or let her know that I say so, as my object is *peace* above all things.

I feel a great deal concerned when I hear you are at the Bluff. It seems to be a rather dangerous place. You have heard of poor Sarah's death. We all feel it very much. The family seem calm as they found much to comfort them in her death. James is slightly ill today with a headache and little biliousness. He sends his love but cannot write. He is subject to such attacks, which I treat with Eliz. Pro. He thought his letter was elegant, from you.

Remember us all to Mrs. Fourgeaud and tell her how much we love her and how glad we are to hear of the dear daughter.

Ever affectionately your daughter   Lizzie

I am very sorry about one thing. I did up a package for you of books and a beautiful daguerreotype of Chardie (who has got back all her lost beauty) and gave it to a man who was going to California. He came back the other day and said he was not going. So you will get a letter describing them but no picture. Then your box of shirts and books. I don't know when they went or how. I hope you may get them.

In the course of the twelve years during which Lizzie, Annie, and Charlotte wrote to their father, they told him many stories—love stories, stories of journeys, revealing anecdotes, entertaining gossip, accounts of public events, and dozens of others. From the comments he wrote on their letters, we can surmise that he appreciated a well-told story and that the sisters did their best to please him. Since they were enthusiastic readers of contemporary fiction, it is not surprising that they, like many letter writers, borrowed some of the devices, language, and details of novelists such as Dickens, Thackeray, Stowe, and Kingsley. The similarities between their private stories and public literature is especially striking in three narratives of the deaths of women: Lizzie's account of Mary Wilson's death and Annie's and Charlotte's descriptions of the death of their friend Sarah Adams, daughter of the Wilsons' physician, during this summer of 1851.

* [ANNIE]   Keene July 22nd 1851

My dear Father,

   . . . Our hearts are all bowed down in sympathy and sorrow at the most sudden death of dear Sarah Adams. She has been all summer in New York with Martha, until about a fortnight ago, when she went to New Haven to stay with her friend Miss Blake. Last Monday, Miss B. wrote to

Mrs. Adams that Sarah was ill, and remembering Daniel's sad death away from home Mrs. A. went on directly, but totally unprepared to find Sarah in the state she was, delirious with fever on the brain. She telegraphed the Dr. who went on directly. Charles too and Eliza even sent for, and Sue and Mary claimed all our attention here to keep them calm till Friday when their father wrote them that Sarah was *better* and our hearts were all gladdened in consequence of which the shock of the next news, was increased. Saturday they all arrived in town, with all that remained of the sweetest and loveliest one among us. Poor Martha never heard a word of her sickness, and a dispatch announcing the death, was the first thing she received. It has nearly killed her. John too poor fellow was at College, and equally unprepared for the blow.

Sarah knew all her family and bade them goodbye saying to her friend Miss Blake as she took off a ring from her finger, 'Hetty, when I am in Heaven, you will wear this.' The Dr. was deceived as to her condition, by a revival that took place just before her death, when he wrote the children. She sang the hymn beginning 'One more night on earth, and *One more soul will be in heaven*,' and then died, calmly and peacefully in perfect consciousness and happiness.

I cannot tell you what a gloom this throws over our whole village. This afternoon Tuesday, we are going to her funeral which has been postponed thus long that Martha might arrive. Sarah is in a metallic coffin hermetically sealed which enables them to keep her. She died on Friday night, July 18th. . . .

. . . Give a great deal of love to the dear Fourgeauds and believe me as ever fondly yr child   Annie F. Wilson

✳ [CHARLOTTE]   Keene July 24th 1851

My dearest Father,

. . . The same day we had your charming letters, Sarah Adams was buried. Of course, my dear Father, you can imagine how very deeply the whole family are afflicted. All of us feel her loss very much. But in her 'Father's house are many mansions' and we can not doubt that she is with Him. As soon as we heard of her illness we all thought she would die, for she was *too* beautiful and good to live. Dr. Ingersoll officiated at her funeral and rendered the whole services very touching. They sang a hymn which she sang every Sabbath evening. That melted us all more than anything else. Music seems to me the medium through which we approach Heaven. The shock was very great at first, but as everything connected with her life and death was perfect, it has left on my mind the most melodious effect.

Her death was like the dying away of a beautiful strain of music, whose harmony although silent to the ear yet lives in the soul. . . .

Believe me your truly loving daughter,   Charlotte J. Wilson

Annie and Charlotte used many of the rhetorical devices and details to describe Sarah Adams's death that Lizzie used to describe her mother's death. It is interesting to see that their descriptions included many of the same details—perfect consciousness, lack of pain, resignation, music, peace, and promises of a better life hereafter—that appear in such famous death scenes as the death of Nell in Dickens's *Old Curiosity Shop* (1841) and the death of Eva in Stowe's *Uncle Tom's Cabin* (1852). Literary models, no doubt, were helpful in providing a form in which to describe such an emotional event. Lizzie acknowledged as much when she suggested that the details originated in the family's retelling of the story. "The family seem calm as they found much to comfort them in her death." Whoever provided the details, Sarah, like Nell and Eva, was canonized in the fashion of the nineteenth century.

Interestingly, the Wilsons described other deaths close to home without using these literary models. "You will be shocked and distressed to hear of our cousin Jane Wilson's death, Jane of Peterboro. She died during our absence. Jamie went down to her funeral with Uncle Robert. Chardie was not well, and Uncle R. would not allow her to go, on account of her headache, the day being very hot, and the brain fever has been so prevalent. Poor Jane, died of a typhoid fever, it seems, after an illness of two or three days only. We are very much distressed to hear of it. I am going to write to them today" (Annie, 8-23-51). Why no one created an interesting narrative for poor Jane we cannot guess, unless typhoid fever, a plague that they had seen a lot of, was too commonplace to command such excitement.

As faithful Unitarians, the Wilsons, like the women whose deaths they described, turned to the church for consolation in their grief at the loss of their friend and their cousin. While they were moved by Dr. Ingersoll's conduct of Sarah's funeral (he was a well-known preacher who had retired to Keene), he was not the pastor of their own Unitarian Church, to which they were devoted. With the Reverend Mr. Livermore's position still vacant, their church had little solace to offer. Livermore had exerted a strong influence on the Keene church with the "sustained high thinking and literary charm" of his preaching, and his move to Cincinnati was a blow. For Charlotte, whom Livermore referred to as "the first lamb of his flock," his departure was particularly painful (Charlotte, 8-23-51).

Finally, in June 1851, the church called Mr. White, who soon became a good friend of the family. When he delivered his first sermon on October 5,

Lizzie announced with satisfaction, "there is a feeling of respectability in going to hear our own minister" (Charlotte, 10-5-51). To celebrate the installation of the new minister and his "fascinating" wife, "the ladies of our Society had a levee at the Town Hall, to which all the Society came. Every one had an opportunity to see Mr. and Mrs. White. All the ministers in town were present. Mr. Barstow asked grace before we partook of the numerous good things spread before us. It was quite delightful to have any of that society *deign* to be present and quite as pleasant for them. . . . The evening passed off well without *dancing*, which *we*, the younger portion of the assembly, thought agreeable" (Charlotte, 10-5-51). While they joined the general rejoicing at the arrival of the new minister, they remained friends of the Livermores. At his daughters' request James Wilson began a correspondence with him, and Lizzie once visited him and his wife in their new parish.

Nothing, of course, in either Keene or California was as exciting as Lizzie's engagement to John Sherwood. To the delight of the sisters he visited Keene often in the summer of 1851. In August his mother, his brother Robert, and his sister Mary came with him on a trip through the White Mountains of New Hampshire to Mount Washington, tallest mountain in northeastern United States and destination of many summer visitors. The Wilsons had apparently never considered making the trip until the Sherwoods suggested that Lizzie and Annie go with them. The very idea amazed Annie.

* [ANNIE] Crawford House, Whit. Mts. August 9th 1851

My dear Father,
    Doesn't this astonish you? a letter from me in the Whit. Mts.! We started off most unexpectedly with the Sherwoods, and Mrs. Dorr for a matron, on Tuesday last, the 5th of the month and here we are today, at this beautiful new house just built near the White Mountain notch, and kept by a man named Gibb.
    You will get letters from Charlie and Jamie who will tell you of their well being. I felt quite distressed to leave them, but Mary S. had come on, on purpose, and was very much disappointed by my decision to stay at home. Lizzie urged, and Roxana promised to take special care, and so here I am.
    The first day after leaving Keene at eleven o'clock we arrived at the Lafayette house at the Franconia notch, and what a superb place it is! We saw there the old man's profile, the Mountains about, Echo Lake and the notch in which we were, and the next day went to the Flume which is another most magnificent place, passing on the road the basin and enjoy-

ing very much the superb views. At the flume is a charming hotel where one gets all the luxuries of a city. We spent a night and part of a day there and then came on the Fabians house five miles from this point. Our party of six fills an extra [wagon] all along and we travel most comfortably all the time. We went to the Willey House. . . . This is an elegant house and the place, which is near the old Crawford House, is truly superb.

Today being a bad one we have been unable to go up Mt. Washington. We drove up Mt. Willard and saw from thence the range and the Willey House standing in the notch. . . . The trip is most charming as you know, and I am charmed to have taken it for I am always ashamed to confess how little I know of our own Country. . . .

We are getting along very nicely in every respect, but we want you, very much. Mr. Sherwood is everything that is delightful, a true, safe, and sensible friend and adviser, as well as a most cultivated and refined man. His attentions to us are unremitting, and for numberless kindnesses, we are indebted to him. . . .

When we have stopped at night I have been too tired to sit up a moment. This traveling in lumber wagons is pretty tiresome in these days of rails.

. . . Mary Sherwood is in ecstacies over New Hampshire scenery as are we all.   as ever fondly and respectfully yr. child
                                                                                Annie F. Wilson

While the trip confirmed everyone's good opinion of John, Charlotte, who stayed behind in Keene to take care of the house and Jamie, knew that Annie's broken engagement to Robert would cast a shadow over the party. She observed more critically than usual the relationships among the travelers. "We had a letter today from Franconia where the girls were. They wrote in excellent health and spirits. Mr. John Sherwood is a lovely person, I think, and we are all very fond of him. I think Lizzie and he will be very happy together. Their literary tastes are the same. Annie and Robert although they are both of the party will have very little to do with one another probably. I am glad he is not to be a brother of mine as he was never a favorite" (Charlotte, 8-8-51).

Lizzie, unlike her sister and Mary Sherwood, was not overwhelmed by the scenery, but she could still admire a fine hotel. More important, this trip to the White Mountains confirmed Lizzie in the wisdom of her engagement even though she recognized that John Sherwood probably would never make a great name for himself. Though Lizzie loved and admired her father, whom she described as "impulsive and lavish, imprudent and always in hot water . . . a man of genius" (*Epistle*, 5–6), she loved her fiancé for many qualities her father lacked.

*   [LIZZIE]   Gibb's, White Mountains, Aug 18th 1851

My dear Father,

We accepted an invitation of Mr. Sherwood to accompany him and his sister to the White Mountains. So here we are. The Mountains are the same I dare say as when you last saw them but there is an elegant Hotel here now kept by a man named Gibb. . . .

I believe I wrote you that George and his wife are coming to live with me this winter. I feel it best for us to stay at home. Charlotte and I are certainly to be there pretty constantly. Annie will go to Hartford and Boston possibly during the winter. I wish it were possible for me to be married this fall, but I do not see any very present prospect of it. It is rather sad that I must be married without your presence.

I must say to you how happy I am in my engagement. How every day I see more and more reason to congratulate myself on my choice. Mr. Sherwood is a very sterling character. He has all those virtues so useful in every day life, judgement, truth, kindness and firmness. And altho' he has not so much demonstrative talent and may never make a figure in the world he is highly cultivated, very much respected.

I am going with Mr. and Mrs. Sherwood to Delhi where Mr. Sherwood's country seat is, to visit my new relatives. It is rather a nervous undertaking but as Mrs. Sherwood has pressed me to come, and Mr. Sherwood thinks it my duty I shall go for a few days.

The whole party wish to be remembered to you. God bless you dear Father.   Ever with much love yours
                                                           Lizzie

Lizzie went from the White Mountains to visit the Sherwoods at their summer estate in Delhi, New York, a visit that made even the polished Lizzie nervous. While she was away, jewelry the sisters had ordered for themselves and their friends—Mary Chamberlain, daughter of Levi, and the daughters of Dr. Adams—arrived. "Our beautiful gold ornaments have come home from the jewellers since I wrote you. They are extremely handsome, just what we have wanted, for so long. Nothing is so fashionable as ornaments of plain gold, and when we have seen them on other girls, we have always spoken of them, and wanted some. Charlie and I, each have bracelets of wrought gold, and Lizzie preferred hers made into a pin, which is very superb. Jamie preferred to keep his gold, until he is old enough for a watch guard or whatever he may need bye and bye. The rings are extremely handsome, and satisfactory. I have not yet seen the young recipients" (Annie, 8-23-51).

"Yesterday my bracelet and rings arrived. Although you sent the gold some time since, it has not been convenient for us to have them made till quite lately. When it came it seemed to bring you nearer to us. We knew you thought of us and loved us just the same as if we were with you, and *of course* we do you too, but it was very pleasant to have some tangible token of your remembrance. The kindness which characterized your little gifts to my friends is fully appreciated by them and by myself. Annie, I suppose has written you about our choice of articles to be manufactured from the gold. When the bracelets came I decided in my own mind what one I wanted and so did Annie. We discovered that we had selected different ones, and were both satisfied with our choices. The rings were sent to Mary Chamberlain and to the Adams with a little note which was certainly 'affectionate' enough if not 'sweet.' They admire them and Sue meant to write you a note of thanks. . . . Your beautiful presents arrived a week before my birthday. I am sixteen a week from today. Sixteen was at one time the very height of my ambition. I am very glad to be so old for I am tall enough to be as old as Annie. Not quite as tall as she is now though. My hair grows finely. It is just below my eyes now, but as it curls up a little at the ends, it just hangs *into* my eyes. . . . I forgot to say that Annie selected our ornaments, or chose the styles for them, and that her taste ought to be *highly* commended. They are beautiful. . . . Mary Chamberlain wishes to express her grateful acknowledgment to General Wilson for the valuable present of a gold ring, which she has received from him by Charlotte. She hopes to keep this token no less on account of its value than as a mark of her gratitude and respect for the giver." (Charlotte, 8-23-51).

✳ [CHARLOTTE]   August 31st 1851

My very dear Father,

I cannot let this, my birthday, pass without writing to you. Today I am sixteen. A birthday comes but once in a year and is always to me a day of thoughts which do not occur at other times. It recalls to one's mind the number of years they have lived, the number they may live, and a thousand comparisons between the Past and the shadowy Future are made which cause one to feel the great uncertainty of life and every thing relating to it.

The thought of your exposure to Indians, to fires and a thousand dangers which we do not have cause to dread makes us extremely anxious. But I often think how wicked it is for us to fear so much more for you there than here. The same God watches over you every where. People die here as well as in California. . . .

How much we would love to have you with us it would be impossible to tell. I can almost imagine you here when I go down stairs and look at the table with my presents on it. Your beautiful bracelet is there and I can almost imagine that I hear your dear kind voice saying "This is for you my dear child." You really seem before me. I wish you were here with all my heart.

Lizzie gave me a beautiful collar, Annie a pair of very pretty cuff pins, you the *splendid* bracelet and ring, and Uncle Robert brought me up the most magnificent basket of flowers. Roses of every kind which blossom now, marigolds, asters, geraniums and the most immense quantity. Six vases of them. I wish very much I could send you some. I will send a four leaved clover. May it bring you good luck dear Father.

Ottie made me a cake, and she wishes me to tell you, that she wants to send you some very much indeed. Dear little Jamie looked quite disappointed that he had nothing to give. I only want him to continue to be a good boy. While the girls were at the White Mts. James was very kind and devoted to me. We were rather lonely, but they came after 10 days' journey. Dear Lizzie is visiting the Sherwoods, who are very fond of her, I believe. They can never love her as well as we do. But we must and ought to relinquish her. It is a funny day. The sun shines a little while and then it showers, but the sun predominates. I look at it as a favorable sign that my next year, although there may be little clouds, yet sunshine will constitute the principle feature. "Sorrow is of our own seeking" generally, but I am determined to have the sunshine. Sometimes the clouds into which our "spirits enter merely refresh them with a little shower." I hope it may be so.

Good bye my dearest Father. Accept the love of your *little* daughter on her *sixteenth* birthday. Your loving,   [Charlotte]

✳ [LIZZIE]   Delhi, Del. Co., Aug 24th 1851

My dear Father,

You will be somewhat prepared for a letter from Delhi, as I have written you that I was coming here, sometime since. Mr. and Mrs. Sherwood and I left Keene last Tuesday and reached New York Tuesday night, and spent two days there very delightfully and on Wednesday we reached Delhi. Mr. and Mrs. Sherwood have received me very kindly and I have felt as I could wish, toward the family of which I am to become a member. Mr. Sherwood built this place nearly fifty years ago. It was commenced in 1802, and finished 1804. Mr. Sherwood cut down the primeval forest and rooted out all the stumps from around his place. It is a very beautiful old stylish house with any quantity of rooms and carved work and niches and a variety of ornaments and situated very charmingly just above the Delaware river. The village is a mile off and we approach it by the most excellent and picturesque of roads. Mr. Gould [Herman Gould from New York] whom you remember in Congress has a place here, a very handsome one too, but the poor man is a . . . paralytic now. He has a fine set of boys, a handsome fortune and a lovely attentive wife, so his case is not so very unpalliated. . . . We drive and walk and read and do whatever our fancy suggests. Mr. Sherwood owns hundreds of acres here and plenty of horses and carriages, so we can drive some length without going off our own ground. . . .

Mr. Page and Mr. Whitcomb [legislators] have both written me about you since you went away, very good intelligence. I long to hear about your reception of your office, how it pleases you etc. I hope if you feel able you will send me a little more money as I find it very tight squeezing to get along with the little I have, and the constant demand of old debts. Mr. Webster has done sending any tho' he owes $360 yet, but I suppose he thinks he has done his part in giving you an office. The country is quite excited about the Cuban invasion, and the murder of fifty Americans, as they call it. It seems quite desirable that that rich little island should belong to us tho' I hope it never will. The revenues are immense. . . . Still it would only be a slave state . . . we better let it alone. . . .

Believe me always your affectionate   M. E. W.

All the Sherwoods desire to be remembered to you.

As the summer passed, even the elemental excitement of love and death could not redeem life in Keene. Jamie observed that while he enjoyed himself in Keene, "I believe the girls find it rather dull, though I do not wonder at them, for they cannot hunt and fish as I can, and it seems to me, that is all there is to do here" (Jamie, 8-24-51). And despite the trip to the White Mountains and Connecticut, the stream of visitors, the arrival of the gold and Lizzie's engagement, they do find the town dull. "New Hampshire is not like California or Cuba, changing every day, so as to make letters from it replete with exciting news. In fact it is exceedingly *slow* and consequently every letter written in this town is like every other one" (Charlotte, 9-8-51). In early September, when a heatwave struck, Annie felt that "we, in Keene, are literally standing still. The heat is intense beyond anything we have experienced this year. In fact our summer has been so cold that there was great fear lest the crop should not ripen, but we have heat enough now, to roast the corn."

His daughters wrote him local news of friends and neighbors and news of the world, which would cast doubt on their complaints of boredom. The war in Cuba elicited an astonishing amount of hostility from Annie, who read "the accounts of a Spanish war with savage delight" (Annie, 9-8-51). The Wilsons were shocked at the death of Levi Woodbury, a leading New Hampshire politician who had been touted as a potential Democratic nominee for president of the United States. Several of the Wilsons' friends speculated that Sam Houston would be nominated instead, but they were wrong. Franklin Pierce, another New Hampshire Democrat and no friend of Whig James Wilson, won the nomination and the election.

As they ever do, friends and relatives got sick, died, married, retired, moved away, or simply did eccentric or kind things. Frank, the young son of their neighbor Sumner Wheeler, became very ill but managed to survive. George Balch, the gardener, married and brought his wife to work for the Wilsons. Her job would be to work with Roxana, who was getting old and spent part of her time in Hartford. Their friend Judge Haskell sported a more flowing wig than he formerly had; Uncle Robert grew flowers and brought them roses every few days.

Charlotte did not imagine that this kind of village life would ever content her father permanently. As an alternative she proposed Europe, not yet aware that her father has already found his Shangri-La in the West. "I don't think Keene would satisfy one all the time without some change, but if you return wealthy we shall be able to stay all together, I should think in some part of the globe. How pleasant it would be to go to Europe at some future time! . . . Keene is different to us however. Without either you or Mother it seems lonely" (Charlotte, 8-23-51).

Despite the limitations of Keene, she gives him a peek into their pleasant and comfortable family life, in which he could star if he gave up the great world outside. "I wish you could look in upon us when Mr. Sherwood is here, and at all times, but we love him so much that we are always happier when he is here. When we are all seated in the parlor, Mr. Sherwood and Lizzie conversing in an undertone and looking *very* happy, Annie working at the centre table, Jamie reading, and I wandering around, sometimes playing and sometimes interrupting Mr. Sherwood with a commonplace question. We often look at one another and think this would be *perfect* happiness if 'Father were only here.' We had corn and beans, or suckatash (oh what a word to spell!) for dinner today and yesterday, and we said we wished you were here to enjoy it with us." (Charlotte, 9-8-51).

"Annie is a notable housekeeper. She has so much energy, that all goes smoothly. My admiration for Annie is only equalled by that which I feel for Lizzie. They are the best two girls I ever knew" (Charlotte, 9-8-51). "Lizzie [is] the most gifted and amiable of us. . . . [Jamie] has improved very much in writing I think. . . . He has lately realized the necessity of studying *hard* while at school in order to go to College. Till quite lately he has not applied himself to his studies with the assiduity which he now does. We have talked with him a great deal this summer about his examination at College and he will, I think, study very devotedly. His letter is beautiful" (Charlotte, 9-24-51).

How could their father resist the pleasures of family life? How could he ignore such loving and admirable children? But he did. Lack of mail from their father distressed them more than the tedium of the long summer in Keene. Then at last a letter arrived from him and brought "joy to their hearts" (Annie, 10-24-51). "We always feel so happy at receiving your letters. We all sit down together and taking our own letters read them, then we read each other's. It seems as if we had been with you a little while in the day. The rest of the day we talk about you more than ever and say more than once, Oh if Father were only here!" (Charlotte, 11-8-51). The letters that broke his silence were dated September 15, and he was not pleased with his children.

He reprimanded them for not acknowledging promptly the gold he had sent from California and for failing to thank Mrs. Fourgeaud adequately for her kindnesses to him when he burned in the fire. Perhaps their letters were delayed, for they certainly intended to do so and finally did.

He also expressed his surprise that Lizzie imagined that he would afford $15,000 for a marriage settlement for her. Perhaps she had written "15" when she meant to write "5," or perhaps she didn't want to appear grasping. Proud Lizzie, who suffered acutely from the Sherwoods' contempt for her poverty, may well have imagined that her father would give her a handsome settlement since he often wrote of his success and sent them gold to have jewelry made. His account books of this period show him sometimes writing checks for several thousand dollars in one day, which would corroborate his success. Still, he found Lizzie's request outrageous.

For all of these failings they sent apologies and explanations and excuses, but they had other things on their minds. Events in Keene had overtaken these matters long since.

"A Splendid Wedding"

During the summer in which they heard not a word from James Wilson, a silent battle of wills had taken place between Lizzie and the Sherwoods. Eager as she was to be married, Lizzie would not set a date until she could move to a house, appropriately furnished as a backdrop for her debut into New York society, to which she could take her sisters and brother. Her father had not yet responded to her request for $15,000 as a marriage settlement, and John Sherwood, though a promising young lawyer, could not afford such an establishment. John's wealthy parents showed no inclination to subsidize their son's marriage to Lizzie. Lizzie refused John's suggestion that they could be married and live at a hotel. All through the summer—the trip to the White Mountains and the visit to Delhi—she was adamant. Though she dreaded spending the winter in Keene, she would not marry without a proper establishment.

Near the end of September, after Lizzie's visit to Delhi and weeks before she heard from her father, the Sherwoods relented and provided the young couple with the money to rent a suitable house. With whatever money her father gave her Lizzie would furnish the house, but with or without support from him, Lizzie decided to be married. Wilson's scolding letters, arriving in the middle of plans for Lizzie's wedding, seemed fairly irrelevant. The narrative of Lizzie's marriage, which totally absorbed the family, was reaching its climax, and Wilson was a minor character in that story.

On Annie's birthday Lizzie wrote the news to her father and explained the arrangements she had made for the rest of the children until she returned from her honeymoon.

✳ [LIZZIE]   Keene Sept 23d 1851
                                                Annie, 19, today
My dear Father,
    . . . The most important subject in my mind now is my approaching marriage. Mr. Sherwood wishes me to marry him in November. I have consented. We are then going to the West Indies for a few months as Mr. S.

has business there and thence to housekeeping in New York. I do not know what I am to do for a wedding trousseau as my finances are in a desperately low condition. We have rec'd no money from California for three months. Mr. Webster has nearly paid up. We have been forced to take nearly all our money from the savings bank. We are literally without a cent. I hope to receive some money from James G. Wilson but as he has failed so often I don't know as I have any reason to hope. I write you this because it is positively necessary that you should know how we suffer for want of money and make some arrangements for us. Uncle Robert is not approachable on this subject, as he has to borrow money to pay Charles Perkins' debts who has failed. [Perkins was a carriage manufacturer].

I hope 'ere I am married to receive some money from you to make some provision for my house. Mr. Sherwood has taken a nice house. His father has behaved very generously to him and I feel that we too should do something. It is an occasion which will not happen again soon and I think deserving of some exertion.

The girls will stay here and Aunt Sylvia Richardson is to be invited to stay with them. George and his wife will remain as their domestics and I trust they will be happy and well cared for.

Mr. Sherwood is all we could wish, kind and attentive and very high minded and honorable. He is truly an honor to us and the family have behaved very kindly to me.

We go on tranquilly enough except our want of money. George has married a good woman who cooks etc. Roxana is sewing for me. We hate to think of you in that barbarous land and pray every day for your return. James is in Providence at school. He is well placed there and doing well. I am going down to see to his winter arrangements as soon as I can conveniently.

Charlotte and Annie are fagging away at history, Chardie at music and making great progress. . . . I long to hear how you like your appointment. We enjoy your letters intensely but I don't enjoy being married without your presence.

Give my love to Dr. and Mrs. Fourgeaud and believe me always and ever your loving daughter   Lizzie

Plans for the wedding went forward apace, and the three sisters unfolded it in all of its details for their father. Understandably, the whole family suffered misgivings about Lizzie's marriage. Despite Lizzie's plans for their care, regardless of Annie's competence, they were losing a second mother. With generosity of spirit they tried to muffle their dismay, but it frequently burst out. As they prepared the house and the trousseau for Lizzie's marriage, they also fortified themselves to live without her constant attention.

For that attention Annie wanted to compensate her sister with a handsome wedding present from the family. So she wrote without mentioning that it was her birthday except for underlining the dateline.

* [ANNIE]   Home *September 23d* 1851

My dear Father,

The California mail arrived in New York on Saturday last, September 20th and to our great disappointment brought no letters from you. We are indebted to Mr. Whitcomb and Mr. Paige for letters informing us of your absence from San Francisco and the more cheering news of your daily anticipated return.

Our number is reduced to three again by Jamie's absence at Providence at school, and just now in the midst of the equinoctial storm and with the prospect of Lizzie's speedy marriage we are quite as the French express it 'desolee.'

I rejoice too in L.'s marriage *for her*, for Mr. Sherwood is all in all to her, and is a most charming, excellent, and loveable person, and I think will make Lizzie's life happy. It is a great disappointment to us all to *her* particularly, that you can not be here. It is very sad for her to be married without either parent. Still, it seems necessary. I feel very anxious, as I know you do my dear papa that the gifts from L.'s family to herself should be handsome and servicable. She expresses a wish for silver, and I find that in Boston a very handsome service of course I mean a simple tea and breakfast service of silver can be obtained for from an hundred to a hundred and fifty dollars. These things now a days are necessaries, you know, and *it*, as a combined present from our dear one's father, sisters, and brother will be a beautiful and acceptable, although an inadequate expression of gratitude to her, for all she has done for us. My idea is to have the large and elegant pieces of silver marked "Lizzie Wilson from her Father," and one small piece marked from each of her sisters and one from her brother.

Will you write me what is your idea on the subject as soon as possible, as they propose November as the time for their wedding. I shall urge its postponement until late, that we may receive your answer.

Keene is standing still. Next week our new Minister, Mr. White, is to be installed, and in the evening we are to have a town, or rather, society, levee, at the town hall. . . .

. . . Charlie is growing lovelier daily. Every one who sees her is struck by her beautiful face, graceful pretty figure, and elegant manners. She dances beautifully, plays finely, and promises to be a splendid woman. Lizzie is what she always has been, and that is saying enough. Jamie is a splendid boy, charming and fascinating every body he sees, and I am, my very dear Father, most fondly and devotedly *your child* Annie F. W. and isn't that enough?

Annie's letter was delayed and did not reach Wilson until November 5. He answered it November 13, a day after Lizzie was married, but plans went forward.

✳ [CHARLOTTE]   Keene Sept 24th 1851

My dear Father,

    ...We are feeling very sad now at the prospect of losing Lizzie. Mr. Sherwood and she wish to be married in November or December. We (Annie and I) shall be well taken care of I know but we *must* miss Lizzie dreadfully. As yet we can not realize that she will not always be right here to advise us when we desire or need advice and to sympathise with us in all our little troubles. I cannot imagine our house being agreeable without Lizzie the most gifted and amiable of us. We shall exert ourselves to help one another but we can never again find a person like Lizzie. It is *very* selfish I know, but we do love her so much that we can but feel her absence.

    I take a walk of two miles, *almost* always, and *often* more, after breakfast. I either walk after dinner or tea a mile or two miles more. My health is improving under this treatment. I eat no meat but lately I have had an immense appetite. I wish you were here to walk with me dear Father. . . . Neither of the girls will walk, but they too are well.

    Today is the annual cattle show day. We have been up to the Town hall an hour or two this morning. Lizzie sent a beautiful piece of painting she has done lately. . . . There are many very pretty pieces of fancy work. . . . Mr. Chamberlain being on the "tasting committee" allowed us all a piece of pie. . . .As the mail closes . . . I must not keep George waiting. Believe me dearest Father your truly loving daughter   Charlotte

To soften the psychological and social stigma of performing this important rite of passage without the legitimizing presence of a parent, they hung the house with pictures of their father and mother. "We have a pretty new . . . carpet on the parlors, and with a nice picture of 'our eldest' and a lately finished 'Wheeler' picture of our beautiful Mother, an inimitable crayon of our very dear Father. The rooms look quite bright and cheerful" (Annie, 11-9-51).

✳ [LIZZIE]   Keene Oct 8th 1851

My dear Father,

. . . We have installed Mr. Wm. A. White, son of Judge White of Salem as our minister and we are quite fortunate I think. He married Meggy Harding and she is lovely and of good report. By the way Annie congratulated Mr. Ashmun on his daughter Lizzie's engagement to a son of Gov. Morton [Florida Whig Jeremiah Morton]. "O! don't! Annie" said he. "Lizzie is engaged to a free soiler—don't congratulate me." I am sitting to Mr. Harding for my picture. Mr. Sherwood asked me to and he has got a good likeness and pretty picture. We have also an excellent picture of Mother by Mr. Wheeler which he has just finished. The face was painted in 1840. It is very like her and a great blessing.

The twelfth of November is fixed for my wedding day and I hope you will be here in spirit. I think of your daughter who so much needs on this occasion your sympathy and aid. We are to be married at half past eleven in church, and come home to receive our guests, from twelve to two, and at three leave for New York. We go then on the eighth of Dec. to the West Indies for two months, as Mr. Sherwood has business there. We are to be married by Bishop Chase in the Episcopal form as Mr. Sherwood prefers. I need not say that I am full of anxious and solemn thoughts. I wish you were here to be as you have always been my dearest and kindest friend. But I feel I could not have done better nor secured a more valuable and excellent husband. The leaving the children is all that is unpleasant and that will be adjusted right I hope. They will stay here until I have a home to offer them, which I hope will happen soon.

Uncle Robert is taking measures to send your library by the ship Versailles which leaves Boston next week. I shall put in some of the modern books for your reading. . . .

We are enjoying a true fall, beautiful autumnal weather which gives us fine opportunities for walking.

I was obliged to borrow $200 of Mr. Skinner last week as it is now nearly four months since we received a remittance. Please remember it and pay him. He very kindly asked us to draw upon him when we needed. But we shall try not to do so again. Hoping this may reach you safely and that you will not fail to write to me as often after my marriage as before, I remain as always your most affectionate daughter

                                                              Lizzie

Enclose for the present your letters to me to Annie as she will know my direction.

✳ [ANNIE]   Home Oct. 8th 1851, Wednesday

My dear Father,

   . . . We are here, all but Jamie and quite sad at the idea of Lizzie's approaching departure. Their wedding day is fixed for the twelfth of November, the same month of your and Mother's wedding. I am sorry that they won't wait until we can hear from you, for I should like Lizzie to have some money, and some presents from her own family, but John is going to the West Indies on the 8th of Dec. and he wishes her to accompany him. Jamie is in Providence and very happy as you will hear from himself. Chardie and I shall stay here, I suppose the greater part of the winter. There is protection in these walls for us.

   . . . Our Autumn is superb. A glorious indian summer is repaying us for the wretchedly cold six weeks we have been shivering through. Isn't this a climate to "try men's souls" as Charlie March used to say, and women's lungs I shall add.

You will hear with regret of Mr. Webster's declining health. Mr. Harding says he doubts if he ever goes back to Washington. Isn't that sad?

Somebody was saying the other day that you would come to the United States Senate yet from San Francisco. Won't that be splendid? Don't do it dear Father until you are a sort of Croesus though.

There was a sort of crazy, coarse, illiterate western New Yorker here the other day who stalked into the parlor and sat down, looking as if he would cut our throats with pleasure, who informed us that his name was Davis, and that he met you in 1840. He inquired all about you, and California and upon Lizzie's telling him that you had an office now, the duties of which would occupy you chiefly, for sometime, he rose and said, "then my hope is gone, my object frustrated." We ventured to ask what his object was, and he said to go into partnership with *you*. We were very much amused. I think I see you with *him* as a *partner* in your office. Do you remember him?

. . . truly and fondly your child   Annie F. Wilson

✳ [ANNIE]   Home Oct. 24th 1851

My dear Father,

   . . . The three hundred dollars was a perfect Godsend to Lizzie in the purchase of her wedding 'trousseau' "as we say in Paris."

. . . Lizzie will be married on Wednesday the twelfth of November. Aunt Sylvia is here and will spend the winter with Charlotte and I, which delights us extremely. We two young girls could never stay here alone, and Lizzie

AN ECCENTRIC AND CURIOUS THING

says she never could have left us alone. Jamie is coming home to his sister's wedding and we shall then have quite a reunion only. . . . Oh dear father what a vacancy your absence, and our Mother's, will make. Mr. Sherwood wishes to be married by the Episcopal form and Uncle Robert will give Lizzie away. Our Fall is cold and harsh promising a blustering raw winter, but by means of numerous soap stone stoves and open fires we hope to keep animate.

Enclosed you will find David Tillson's bill. He came up here and was very importunate and blustering, but I quieted him by telling him that I would write you immediately, . . . treating him civilly. . . .

Keene is verily getting to be a summer retreat alone. This winter the Hales shut up their house and are going to Boston to board. The Prentisses think of doing the same, the Perrys, and the Ingersolls. The latter are going to Charleston, S. C. on account of Allan's health. We have a lonely prospect, but Lizzie says next winter we shall spend in *her* house. She has gone to Boston to make the necessary purchases and it may be that she will not find a moment to write, by this mail. She is *very* hurried, and if you receive no letter you will attribute it to that. . . . We hear excellent accounts of Jamie. . . . Aunt Sylvia sends much love. For great haste, hoping soon to hear from you, your child   Annie F. W.

✳ [CHARLOTTE]   Keene Oct 24th 1851

My dear Father,
    . . . We were inexpressibly delighted to see another letter in your dear hand. Our anxiety for you has been great since you have been from San Francisco. When you leave there (which I always look upon as a savage place) it seems as if you were abandoning civilized society and going among perfect barbarians. . . .

We are all very busy, preparing for Lizzie's wedding, which is a fortnight from next Wednesday. There is a great deal to be done in the way of sewing. Her wardrobe will not be very magnificant, as she is unable to get one, and because every one advises her not to get a great quantity of things, which she cannot wear out till they are old fashioned. The minutiae of her wedding will not be as interesting to you as to "us girls."

You have probably heard the "order of the day." That she will be married in Church, at twelve in the morning, and receive her friends here afterwards. We shall probably have our house full of people. It seems as if you *must* be here. I can imagine your strong desire to come. We really miss you *more* and *more* every day. Aunt Sylvia arrived yesterday. She looks older and thinner than she used to. Otherwise she is unchanged as cheerful and good as ever.

Lizzie left us Tuesday for Boston and New York. Annie and I went to the Depot, and as we returned without our dear sister it burst upon us how we should miss her. I don't think I have realized till lately, and I don't expect to till she is fairly gone. That our darling Jamie will come home to her wedding is an agreeable thought. . . .

Keene is so very quiet that we live the most secluded lives. We withdraw into ourselves, as it were, for amusement. I have been devoting time and attention to Bancroft's United States, and had reached the middle of the second book when my duty to Lizzie called me away from it. I have become much interested in it. . . . The girls sew and prepare work for the rest of us.

Every one in Keene seems about as usual. . . . The Adamses behave beautifully about Sarah's death. They try hard to keep cheerful. Mrs. Dow is well, so is Miss Frost. Mrs. Dow is really having a new fence. She is also having said fence painted black. It presents a very melancholy appearance.

Lizzie is going to join the Church. Do you think I am old enough to do so? It was always my desire and intention to become a member when I felt myself capable to decide upon my own religious belief. I have read some Unitarian tracts and books. I shall study them thoroughly. I don't wish to become a member of the Church of Christ without first considering what I am doing. It may be partly from a feeling of conservatism and partly from a desire not to shock the members of the Church, that I should wait till I was older. I don't wish them to feel that they have with them, to partake of the Lord's supper, a *very* young flighty girl who does not know her own mind at all. But I should like the incentive to be good, and the almost *tangible* presence of a promise to God and man to do as well as one can.

. . . With much love to you from all, including Aunt Sylvia, believe me most truly your affectionate daughter   Charlotte J. Wilson.

Jamie was too young, too far away, and too wrapped up in his own affairs to think much about what was going on in Keene during his absence. After Jamie left for school, he reported on his own work and pleaded for stories of his father's hunting adventures—even the killing of Indians. With his sister's wedding less than a month away, he was far more concerned about the crises in the money market and the numerous business failings than he was about events back home that would change his life.

✳ [JAMIE]   Providence R. I. Oct. 24th

My Dear Father,

. . . I do not think that I ever knew, what *real hard study* was before, but now I not only know what it is but also have to practice it . . . there has not been a night this week, but that I have commenced to study at half past six or seven, and continued until after eleven. In Latin I am reading "Cicero." . . . In Greek . . . I have very long lessons, still I like it very much. I am also studying Arithmetic. . . .

I find Providence a very handsome and pleasant city, and I am very happy, although I know hardly any one here. Still I have not felt one pang of that disagreeable malady called homesickness, since I left Keene.

I suppose you have heard of the great pressure in the money market here (as the mouse said when a keg of specie rolled over him.) Every one is failing and change is so scarce that if you give a bill in pay for any article, the storekeeper will be almost sure to ask you if you have nothing smaller. I do not know the exact cause of it, but I think that a great deal of the silver and gold has been shipped off in pay for foreign goods.

We received a letter from you a short time ago, telling us about your tour into the wild regions of California. I was very glad to hear that you had met with no injury. I wish you would write me all about it . . . and also tell me how many Bear, Deer, Elk, and *Indians* you killed, whether your rifle that shoots twenty-four balls in a minute is a good one or not. . . .

From your most affectionate
Jamie

I am almost ashamed to send you this dreadful looking letter . . .   J. H. Wilson

A week before the wedding Annie and Charlotte tried to explain why they had not thanked him properly for the gold, but the whole matter seemed too minor to distract them from the important events happening at home, as Annie explains bluntly.

✳ [ANNIE]   Keene Nov. 9th 1851

My dear Father,

. . . Our gold, you will have ere this received many thanks for. None of us were able to go to Boston very soon after it arrived. . . . As soon as possible, *I* went to Boston, and got the gold (which was really superbly rich), and had it worked. Our ornaments are very beautiful, and much admired. . . .

My mind is so full of our dear Lizzie's marriage that I can hardly think of any thing else. For the last two weeks we have been so busy that we are now almost tired out, and thankful to say that we can see through. Next Wednesday is the day. She will be married at eleven in church, Mary Sherwood and I being her bridemaids. After that, she is coming home to receive her friends here, and as handsome a table as our means will allow, will be spread. Three hundred dollars received in yr last letter, was more than acceptable to us. It enabled me to buy for Lizzie some pieces of silver which she particularly desired, "from her Father." Also to defray the necessary expenses of her wedding. I shall pay George and Roxana from the next remittance.

Aunt Sylvia you will be glad to know will spend the winter with us. Every body is very kind to us, and I do not doubt that we shall get along nicely. I shall try to perform my duty to Chardie and Jamie, but doubt my capability.

. . . In Mr. and Mrs. White we have a second Mr. and Mrs. Livermore.

You will be gratified to know that Lizzie became a communicant in the Unitarian church last Sunday. I thank all the people who have persecuted me for my Unitarianism in Washington and New York. By that means I was led to look into its beauties more deeply and so enjoy more its goods, "the greatest of which, is charity."

Mr. and Mrs. Barstow were much gratified by yr mention of their Son. They have not heard from him for a long time. All yr many Keene friends always desire to be remembered. God Bless you dear Father. Ever, as now, fondly yr   Annie

✳ [CHARLOTTE]   Keene Nov. 8th 1851

My very dear Father,

Last Tuesday we received a splendid lot of letters from you. . . . We all sit down together and taking our own letters read them, then we read each other's. It seems as if we had been with you a little while in the day. The rest of the day we talk about you more than ever and say more than once, Oh if Father were only here! But this exclamation is repeated oftener than ever now. It seems very sad that our dear Lizzie should be married without you to give her away. Uncle Robert is to do that, but when he does so, we shall all remember that dear Father of ours, who has the first right to bestow such a girl on another.

Lizzie means to be married at 1/4 past eleven. Bishop Chase will perform the ceremony as I suppose the girls have written you. With Aunt Sylvia for our officiating clergyman we have performed the ceremony once. *Annie* is the *bridegroom*, *Lizzie* the *bride*, and *I* give her away. I was so overcome by the thought of my responsibility that I *said*, "I do," when asked who "gave this woman etc." I ought to have bowed. Annie, as Lizzie's husband, did her part very well. Today is Saturday. Next Wednesday she is to be *married*. We *cannot* realize our great loss yet. Annie and I tremble to think of it. But, despite our own sorrow at losing her, we do *not* forget our dear Father. You must feel more deeply than we, if possible, the loss of one so dear to us. Annie and I have both resolved in our inmost hearts to do our *best* to make home as agreeable as ever. Not that we flatter ourselves that it will be as much so as it has been heretofore. Annie and I will "cleave unto each other."

Darling Jamie comes Tuesday. Mr. John Sherwood comes Tuesday morning. The rest of the party Mr. and Mrs. Sherwood, Robert, Mary, their cousin Miss Bostwick and Mr. J. Sherwood's friend Mr. Murray come Tuesday night. We are not to have them all here. Mr. J. and R. Sherwood and Mr. Murray go to the Cheshire House. . . .

You ask where my note to Mrs. Fourgeaud is. When I wrote your letter, in which I said, I sent her note, I *think* it was carried immediately to the Post Office. I know that I meant to write the very first time after we received your letters about the fire. . . . I will try to express my *heartfelt* gratitude to her in some more substantial form. Do forgive me dear Father for doing what I ought not to have done, or rather for "leaving undone what I ought to have done."

. . . you speak of our not mentioning the gold. . . . I thought it better remain in Mr. Skinner's safe till some of us went down to Boston and could have time to see about the ornaments to be made. Was it not better than to take such a valuable parcel to Bridgeport then to Keene and then back again to Boston? I ought to have written you that it was safe . . . but I thought it would be better to wait till we had it in our possession. Need I tell you now dear Father again how *perfectly* beautiful it is? Our ornaments are very much admired. . . . [Susan Adams] admires her ring. Mine, on my *3rd* finger, reminds me constantly of you. . . .

. . . We are all well but very *very* busy. Good bye dear Father. A great deal of love from every body and a thousand kisses from your truly loving *little*
Chardie

I am *delighted* that you are leaving off snuff.

Wilson received Chardie's letters of October 24 and November 8 on December 17 and answered them on December 27. Along with that information, he appended to this letter a notation: "Sent with the ansr a Draft for $50. to Chardie. Charming as usual."

Lizzie, too, answered her father's critical letters with excuses for asking him for far more money than he would consider giving her.

✳ [LIZZIE]   Nov 9th 1851

My dearest Father,

I have received your kind letter of the last of September. I am sorry any carelessness in figuring should have led you to think I ask for so unconscionable a sum as *$15,000*. *$5000* was my *intention* and I thought from all I heard of your prospects, *that* would not be unreasonable. John has been so kind and so anxious to do every thing for me that I was anxious to do something too. But of course I am content with a moderate establishment. I only wanted to feel that those things usually furnished by the lady should not be wanting for me. Old Mr. Sherwood has been very generous to us and John is the most generous and unselfish of [men]. So I cannot be more happy unless you will come home and make me so. . . . I hope you will write to me just as often as if I were still under your roof.

. . . I have also been provoked that we should have forgotten to thank you for the elegant gold ornaments which have delighted us so much. Jamie's 'dust' is in the safe waiting his pleasure when a man. I have loaned him my watch as he needs one, and Mr. Sherwood has given me a very elegant one. I have had many beautiful presents from many people, Silver and other valuables. We are going to receive our friends in the morning from 12 to 2. I leave in the cars at 1/2 3. Uncle Robert is to give me away. . . .

I rather think I should be happy to see you at my house in New York when you arrive there, and will give you a good dinner and a 'nice little bed.' . . . I have not invited our Peterboro friends as it was a morning wedding, and they all in black for poor Jane. . . . I shall receive any letters directed Mrs. Sherwood, Care of John Sherwood Esq. 142 Broadway and you will write to me just the same won't you? Dear Jamie comes up to the wedding in great state. Give my love to dear Mrs. Fourgeaud and believe me ever with great love your daughter   Lizzie

Frank Fiske thinks a little of going to California. He suggests the possibility of being secretary to the Land Commission. Will you be kind enough to write him if he could get such a thing? Or if there should be any opening. He is a fine manly fellow and I should like to have him near you.

Wilson himself was touched that he not only missed Lizzie's wedding but missed participating even vicariously since he did not learn that it was happening until it was over. On this occasion, at least, he seemed to have pondered the strain that time and distance placed on his relationship with his family for he returned to it to note: "Lizzie's Letter Nov 9th 1851; Recd Decr 17 1851; Ansd Decr 27 1851. This is her last Letter to her father before her marriage."

Though a remnant of her mother's Puritanism prompted her to protest that she was not anxious "make a display," Lizzie listed with satisfaction the wedding presents she received and turned her attention to establishing herself in New York immediately after her wedding. She remarked particularly on the attention she received from the Sherwoods' relation Samuel B. Ruggles, whose friendship and influence Lizzie and her sisters valued for years. In fact Ruggles, a noted jurist and civic leader known especially for his promotion of the value of open spaces in New York City, cut a pattern of behavior Lizzie probably preferred to that of her adventurous father. While Wilson followed his California dream, the urbane Ruggles invested in the founding of Gramercy Park and Union Square and represented his country in international monetary congresses.

For her entrée into society Lizzie relied on the Sherwood family. If they introduced their new daughter-in-law with some fanfare, then she would be launched on her career as a socialite.

* [LIZZIE]   New York, Nov 24th 1851

My dear Father,

This mail finds me comfortably married, and living in New York or staying for the present with Mr. and Mrs. Sherwood. I learned by accident today that the Georgia sails two days earlier so I fear the children's letters are not yet sent. I have letters from them nearly every day and they are well and comparatively happy. The wedding was a most satisfactory festival except for your absence. Mr. and Mrs. Sherwood and daughter came and staid with us. I had some Boston waiters to arrange the collation, and we were married at 1/4 past 11. in the morning by Bishop Chase. Uncle Robert gave me away. The church was crowded. The organ was playing and there was a beautiful wreath of white flowers on the pulpit placed there by dear Chardie. It was a very impressive ceremony. We both took most solemn vows upon ourselves and I hope by the grace of God I may keep them. Annie and Mr. Robert Sherwood went in first, Mr. Murray, a friend of John's and Miss Sherwood next and then Uncle Robert and myself, with John the other side of me. There was a light snow on the ground and the day was dazzling in brightness. We got home and got composed, when at twelve our friends arrived to congratulate us. Mr. Chamberlain sent me a beautiful portfolio with a note saying it was from my "friend and admirer" Levi Chamberlain. He told me with his funniest look that I better not tell Mr. Sherwood anything about *that note*!

Mr. and Mrs. Sherwood brought me two dozen silver forks and a set of dinner and dessert knives, Miss Sherwood a splendid fish knife and fork, Robert Sherwood a silver basket. Mrs. Little and William Parker sent me silver card baskets. Mr. John Dorr of Boston sent me a very handsome and heavy pudding knife of silver. The Barretts all sent me something. Two heavy silver napkin rings from Mr. and Mrs. Barrett. James Elliot sent me a silver napkin ring. Frank Fiske a beautiful little silver pepper box, John Prentiss a beautiful fan. I had a table covered with beautiful and valuable gifts. Annie invested $160 in a silver tea set of which the principal piece was marked "M. E. W. from her Father." No one forgot me but the Dixons. Charlie March wrote me a beautiful note full of good wishes. Mr. Trumbull came to the wedding in great style and *staid with Mrs. Dorr*!! He was observed whispering soft nothings in the widows ear several times. James Wilson came up from Providence in a new white overcoat looking like a rosy young bear. He was so large and full of life he was quite splendid. He kept close to me every moment and quite amused me by getting between John and myself while we were receiving. At 1/2 3. the newly married started for Springfield and came gradually down to Albany and to New York. . . . We were met by a deputation of the [Sherwood] family which amounts to about fifty in all its branches. Mrs. Sherwood had a family party the evening we arrived for us and Mr. Samuel B. Ruggles the most distinguished man in the family brought me an elegant bouquet. He is very delightful. You know him probably by reputation. He is fortunately a great friend of John's. Since then I have been feted and caressed to my hearts content. Two handsome dinner parties have been given us by John's cousins, and we are engaged for several parties for the evening. Mrs. Sherwood gives a morning reception for me on Wednesday, and I have nothing to complain of in the way I am to be socially presented in N. Y. a fact which it is very agreeable to have adjusted comfortably. Now don't imagine I am anxious to make a display. No such thing. But I am anxious to have an agreeable place in society here and that I have found.

As for *my husband* (don't it look funny?) he is the sweetest tempered and most thoughtful of men. I shall be a very bad woman if I am not happy with such a character. I find him most extensively respected and wholly excellent. I have never seen a trait of meanness in him yet. He may not always be as charming to me as he is now but I am sure I shall always respect him and have the fullest confidence in him.

. . . My dearest Father, I trust I have written enough to show you that I am very happy and well placed, that my lot seems to be a very fortunate one. My husband loves me and all my family here seem to approve his choice. If now I can hear that you are doing well and that you are prospered in every way, what more can I ask of Providence.

Annie has shown an immense amount of energy and unselfishness in helping me off. I hope you will write her fully and gratefully for her conduct deserves it.

I enclose you my card of invitation, Mrs. Sherwood's reception card, and my own visiting card, that you may be "up" to our arrangements. Also a card for Mr. and Mrs. Fourgeaud. . . .

You will write me by every steamer won't you. John's address is 142 Broadway.

I wish we could strike across from the West Indies and see you a little while. When the Panama R.R. is done I think we *can* make you a little call.

Although I am no longer "head captain" of your forces you must re-member past services and give me a good pension of letters.

Ever with truest love and respect

Your daughter   Lizzie

Accounts and recounts of so momentous an event as Lizzie's wedding quickly passed into the annals of family mythology. As Annie perceived, they don't simply want their father to know Lizzie was married; they want to re-create the event for him. Since each of them viewed the event from her own angle, each had to perform this act herself. The story, first written by Lizzie, was codified and entered in the family archives in accounts by Annie and Charlotte, vivid and enthusiastic descriptions tinged only slightly with the melancholy they felt at being deprived of Lizzie's good company and care. Young Jamie, to whom Lizzie was nearly a mother, mourned without apology, finding no joy in the wedding itself. "It was a very sad occasion to us, and I could hardly believe, that she was going away to leave us forever. She was married in the Episcopal form, by Bishop Chase, of N. H. I think I never saw her look more beautifully and she was much more composed than Mr. Sherwood. Her presents were *elegant*, but I suppose the girls will tell you about them" (Jamie, 11-25-51).

Charlotte, more composed and very observant, noted every social nuance and every quavery voice. She alone appreciated the tact with which an old friend smoothed over the awkwardness of a young woman being married without her father by genially invoking his name.

✻ [CHARLOTTE]   Keene Nov 25th 1851

My dear Father,

. . . Today the 25th of Nov, is a cloudy muggy looking day. Yesterday
Annie went to New York. Lizzie wrote her she wanted her to come Monday
and stay till Saturday, as Mrs. Sherwood is to give *young* Mrs. J. Sherwood
a reception. Wednesday, tomorrow is the day fixed upon. Annie has needed
a little change I think and Auntey and I are glad she has gone. She hated
to leave us here a week alone and over Thanksgiving too, but we made her
go. Of course Mrs. John Sherwood wants her bridesmaids at her reception. Day after tomorrow is Thanksgiving day. Auntey and I are going to
Mrs. Dow's to dine. Our Minister and his wife will be there too. We shall
doubtless have quite a nice time. Oh dear Father how happy we should be
if you were here. I will think of you as I always do on every occasion of
joy or Sorrow. We certainly ought to be thankful for having had our lives
spared to us for the last year. How happily every thing has happened for
us! God shields us always.

Our dear Lizzie was married the 12th of this month. In the letters which
we received a week ago today from you, you did not mention the 12th,
from which we inferred of course that you had not heard when you wrote.
But we hope you heard before the day. We all thought of you a great deal.
Mr. and Mrs. Sherwood were very warm and pleasant in their manner to
us all. They came with Mary and her cousin Miss Bostwick to stay at our
house. The evening before the wedding we all sat in the parlor. The Barretts
came down from the Dows' to see us and old Mr. Trumbull also called. He
was so affable and genial that his presence alone would have thawed all stiff-
ness out of our circle. But it was a very pleasant group and but one thing
wanting to make it perfect—your dear presence. We all spoke of you. Mr
Trumbull repeatedly shook my hand during the evening and said 'I miss
the General.' 'If he were only here to meet us with his cordial welcome, it
would be delightful.'

The Bishop did not arrive till 1/2 past ten the morning of the wedding.
Lizzie and John felt much excited about it. At 1/4 past eleven Wednesday
12th of Nov. Mrs. Sherwood and her husband, Miss Bostwick, Aunt Sylvia
and I went to the Church. The moment the Bishop entered, the organ
struck up. In a few minutes Annie and Mr. R. Sherwood, Mary Sherwood
and Mr. Murray, Lizzie and Uncle Robert and Mr. Sherwood entered the
Church. Lizzie dressed in white watered silk, with a long white veil float-
ing from her head all around her, looked like an angel, but just as white as
marble. We all feared she would faint, but she responded in a clear audible
voice. Mr. Sherwood's 'I will' was emphatic but his voice trembled very
much the rest of the time. We returned home and in about 1/2 an hour all

the Keene people and the gentlemen from New York came to our house. At 1 o'clock the back parlor was thrown open and we entered to partake of a splendid entertainment prepared by Smith of Boston. He sent up waiters with every thing that one could desire to eat and drink. Uncle Robert seemed to feel quite proud that every thing was so well done. It was a *very splendid* wedding. Mrs. Sherwood said she never saw such a handsome entertainment in New York.

The front parlors were devoted to receiving people. Lizzie and Mr. Sherwood Mary S. Annie, Robert Sherwood and Mr. Murray stood directly before the first door, the south door of the parlors. The north door was open and people walked through into the Office where there was a bright fire in the stove and Lizzie's presents on a table. Every one seemed happy and pleasant. The rooms were crowded so that it was not stiff, and yet were not too full. . . .

At 1/2 past three Lizzie left for Springfield. The next morning the Sherwoods returned to New York. Then we felt the reaction from all the excitement. Dear Jamie tho' I have not spoken of him was here and stayed till Friday at 9 o'clock. He came Tuesday afternoon. Dear little fellow, he was very well and happy. Looks well and strong. Is spreading out into a manly handsome fine looking boy. His face and manner is just like you. The resemblance is striking and increases every year. Says he is studying very hard. Has high marks, and feels ambitions to excel others and himself.

Since Lizzie left us we have fallen into our old quiet habits of life. Annie reads, and sews, and keeps house *finely*. Aunt Sylvia reads and sits quietly by the fire in the back parlor. I am active in my way. I walk a good deal, practise an hour or 2, sew when agreeable, read History and write a great deal. . . .

My little friend Lizzie Eldredge wants me to visit her this winter. . . . We are so lonely alone here when one is gone, and I shall only stay a fortnight or so with her. . . .
Believe me dearest Father your loving and devoted daughter

Charlotte J. Wilson

A week later, when Annie returned to Keene, she delivered her description of Lizzie's marriage. Though she knew he had already read other accounts of the wedding, Annie, always sensitive to the power of language, insisted on rendering her own version of the story.

✳ [ANNIE]   Keene Dec. 7th 1851

My dear Father,

On the 24th day of November I went on, to New York, as one of my sister's bridesmaids, to be present at the wedding reception, given by *Mrs. Sherwood*, to *Mrs. John Sherwood*. My first question on my arrival, was if a letter which I had for you, might be sent to the post office, and was informed, then and there, that the mail which should have left N. Y. on the twenty sixth for some reason or other, was then, the twenty fourth, gone. . . . I fear that no letters can have reached you from us, till this mail since the tenth of Nov. two days before the wedding.

First and foremost, the wedding, an account of which you have already had undoubtedly, but not mine and I must be allowed to give it.

Our bride was superb, in white watered silk with a veil falling from her head all about her to her feet. John, Robert Sherwood and Mr. Murray of New York Miss Mary and I as bridesmaids in pink, behold the bridal party. Lizzie entered the church on Uncle Robert's arm, first Robert and I, then Mr. Murray and Mary, a minute after. Lizzie and Uncle R. following. Bishop Chase rose and commenced the moving service of the English church which has hench forth a deeper meaning than ever before for me. After the service which was finished by twelve o'clock, the invited guests began to come. The parlors were trimmed with evergreens, the office open and in it a large table covered with all Lizzie's superb presents which were too numerous to mention. One among them, however, as the editors say, attracted our attention particularly, a beautiful classic shaped tea pot of silver, on which was very elegantly engraved "M. E. W. from her Father" and standing each side thereof a cream pitcher and sugar bowl from her two sisters and a pair of silver salt cellars from Jamie.

We had a man from Boston who got up a very elegant entertainment the doors being thrown open at one, General Wilson's taste in wine often praised and his health most heartily drunk. At three, the bride and groom left us and went to Springfield, the family remaining till the next morning, charmed with New Hampshire with its snow mantle on, charmed with everything and charming all.

After a fortnight of quiet loneliness, they sent for me to come on. . . . Spent a week found Lizzie perfectly happy and looking superbly, receiving every attention and the center of attraction as she deserved to be. Tomorrow, Monday the 8th they, John and L. sail for the West Indies. And now that subject is done up, not brown, I hope.

In yr last, you ask about a draft on B. R. Curtis of Boston from Argenti and co. for two hundred dollars. I remember its arriving, and being cashed. . . . We have not received any thing by the last two Steamers. The six hundred, three in two successive Steamers was the last. I hope we shall get some by the next as the expenses of L.'s wedding were necessarily great and took off our money fast, as it was the last thing we could do for her. I was particularly anxious to do it well. And now let me ask you dear Father to send us small sums, *often* as after Jan. 1st I don't intend to have a *bill anywhere* and to pay on the spot. I must have ready money. Jamie's expenses too draw on me largely, and it is no joke to buy wood, potatoes stores, carpet etc etc. In fact to keep house.

. . . Give much love to Dr. and Mrs. Fourgeaud and to all our acquaintances in Cal. and believe me as ever   Devotedly yr. daughter
                                                                        Annie F. W.

Since Annie, Charlotte, and Aunt Sylvia would live in Keene, it was wise that Lizzie had prepared the house for the winter season, for a deep chill gripped Mount Monadnock and froze the Ashuelot. The chill, however, was inside the house as much as outside. Only two years before they had lost their mother. Only fourteen months since, their father had left them, and now Lizzie was gone too. Good Aunt Sylvia, their mother's sister, failed to fill the shoes of their precious Lizzie, and Charlotte confessed that she and strong-willed Annie did not always get along. "Without our very dear Sister we feel quite desolate now but we are endeavoring to do for each other more. In the abstract Annie and I are very fond of and very willing to help each other, but we jar against each other sometimes.

"Today I made up my mind to make the day pleasant to Annie and not do any disagreeable things. But I have been *crosser* and more petulant than usual. You *never* see this in me dearest Father but the girls will, together with myself, own that my temper is obstinate and easily given up to.

". . . when I remember [Lizzie's] caressing hand which averted from us all possible pain and trouble, and that dear presence which made us all so happy, I cannot feel but that our separation is sad and hard to bear" (Charlotte, 12-8-51).

Self-confident and loving, Lizzie was the long-standing mother surrogate in the family. When Annie, only two years older than Charlotte, assumed the helm she did not automatically assume Lizzie's authority or experience. Nor did she have Lizzie's ability to put the eternal creditors out of her mind. "The few things necessary to make the house comfortable for that affair—new carpets for the parlors in place of *straw* which were rather cool for Nov. Stoves, and a little painting, with her wardrobe and bride's outfit, her entertainment etc etc, with a claim from Roxana at the precise moment and it seemed to me more *old* bills than ever before, with all this I say, six hundred dollars seemed not to go as far as it ought" (Annie, 12-21-

51). They had not received any money on the last two steamers, and Annie was indeed learning "it is no joke to buy wood, potatoes stores, carpets etc etc. In fact to keep house."

Of course, the stoves and carpets chalked up to display for Lizzie's wedding actually prepared the house for Charlotte, Annie, and Aunt Sylvia to live in during the bitter winter. "Aunt Sylvia, Chardie and I have led most entirely quiet and peaceful lives during the winter, which in its unyielding severity is almost new to us, so long is it since we have before felt it. On Wednesday the 17th we had the thermometer at thirty *30* degrees *below* zero" (Annie, 12-21-51).

In contrast, on New Year's Eve Lizzie basked in the tropics on Santa Cruz. There she was gratified by the company she and her new husband kept. She again mentioned Captain Joseph Folsom, who would soon be involved in the massive Limantour case with General Wilson.

Lizzie, who hated the American South most passionately, had the unique opportunity to observe firsthand a society with freed slaves, a tale she told along with several other traveler's observations.

✳ [LIZZIE]   Santa Cruz Dec 30th 1851

My dearest Father,

John has just come in and told me of an opportunity of writing you or rather of sending a letter to Nassau. We left New York Dec 8th by steamer Merlin for St. Thomas. I was very seasick all the way and thought often of you and wondered if you suffered as much in the gulf stream as I did. At last I grew so weak that my husband made up a bed of shawls and cloaks on deck as I could not sit up even during the day. I cannot sufficiently praise all his goodness and patience. It was much tried and bore it well. We remained but two days at St. Thomas and thence came here, where we found a most agreeable home in the house of the episcopal minister. . . .

Although the thermometer stands at 80. most of the time yet the heat does not oppress me, for there is generally a cool breeze. Mr. Hanley was one fellow passenger in the Merlin and *insisted* on our coming to stay with him. He has a well filled cellar. Good maderia, and excellent claret, port, Porter and genuine *Santa Cruz*. John is of course my authority in these matters. I drink a glass of Porter for lunch, for I find unless I do I feel very weak and miserable during the day.

But I am enjoying for the first time the splendid luxuriance of the tropics. The flowers, the fruits the charms of this lovely island are indescribable. You have seen what it is, so I need not describe.

We are treated with much respect and attention here. I find John is respected here as every where he is known. We are invited to a beautiful dinner party on Christmas day, and we found the lady of the house Mrs. Abbot had been the widow of Capt Blakely of the *Frolic*, so celebrated for its victory over the *Wasp*. As I went in they all exclaimed how much I was like Miss Blakely the deceased daughter of this lady and Capt Blakely and there was a picture of her on the wall taken at sixteen, the precise image of Chardie! Was it not a singular coincidence. We are already engaged to several parties and to a New Year's dinner, so you see we are getting acquainted here.

John would give his eye teeth to know what your letter relative to Capt Folsom is to say. We shall be obliged to stay here until the 1st February when we leave for Havana and hope to be home by the first of March. That is a month longer than we meant to be gone but John says he must wait. If I could only hear good news of all my people I should be content, but I really feel guilty sometimes at being away from the girls, and Jamie. However that I suppose is not right. I must leave you all in the hands of Providence and trust that *he* will keep you all in his tender care.

The negroes here seem better off and more respectable than I have ever seen them but they say they are much the worse for emancipation. The late Gov. Van Shotten gave them their freedom one day because he was frightened and the Danish government cannot get them back of course. The inhabitants here all execrate his memory as well they may, for it has impoverished many of them.

The people all look very pale and poorly and seem very languid, but they all say it is very healthy and very enlivening and most admit they haven't all the energy in the world. We live delightfully here. The cooking is very nice and the fruits and vegetables delicious. The fruits I have not learned to like yet all of them, but the pines [pineapples] and oranges are delicious.

We dine out frequently in the country and the views of the ocean and the hills on the island and the curious vegetation are all very agreeable to me. Every thing is new. I suppose palms hardly grow in California.

I went to see a baptism in the Church on Monday. I should have said that Mr. Hanley is a bachelor and keeps several servants, and that another gentleman lives here, Mr. Linling, an English creole. The servants all live in a yard attached to the house. So as one of the little *niggers* was to be baptized whom I had seen in the yard I went on to see the whole thing. There were sixteen black babies all screaming at once! But Mr. Hanley did not seem discomposed at all, and gave them all their romantic names— "Albertine Louisa" "Ernestine" "Rosalie" etc etc without winking.

The names of the estates here are remarkable "Diamond and Ruby" "The Pearl" "Anna's Hope" "Work and Rest," "Prosperity, Bethlehem

Castle Copeley, etc, etc. They make about 60,000 hogsheads of sugar yearly on the island.

The gigantic windmills remind you of Don Quixote. They are however now introducing steam engines to work the sugar cane. Hoping you are enjoying excellent health and good fortune and that I may soon hear from you I am as ever your loving daughter   Lizzie Sherwood

John wishes me to add his best respects and good wishes.

The next month Lizzie got pregnant, which must have made the sea voyage home in March worse, if possible, than the one south. Aunt Sylvia returned to her home in Waterbury. Though their circumstances had altered dramatically, Annie, Charlotte, and Lizzie were reunited.

PART TWO

"Being United, We Three Girls"

(1 8 5 3 - 1 8 5 5)

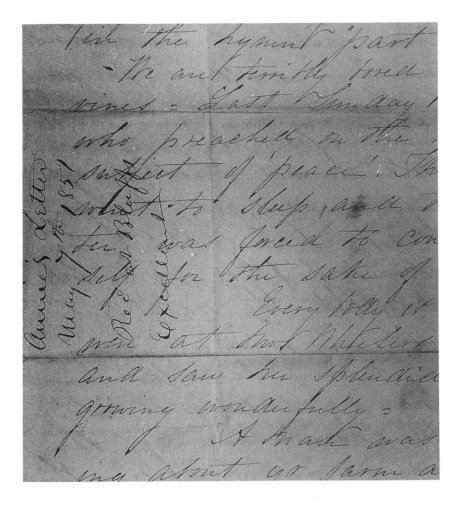

Having a Roof of Their Own

For the next several years, James Wilson's children continued to expect his return with undiminished fervor but at the same time entered a three-year period of relative domestic tranquillity. The four children settled into a new family routine and developed markedly tender and loving ways of nurturing each other's needs and supporting each other's situations. Annie and Charlotte adopted Lizzie and John Sherwood's home at 6 West 11th Street in New York City as their winter home; Jamie visited there too during vacations from his school in Providence, Rhode Island. In the summers the house at Main and Emerald streets in Keene remained the home of their hearts and sometimes their tempers as questions concerning its financial disposition continued to plague them.

For the next three cycles of seasons, Lizzie, Annie, and Charlotte reigned (each in her own way) over a society of women. Lizzie came home from her honeymoon pregnant and soon gave birth to a son, dedicating her days and her heart to her child's care. At the same time, she began to develop a skill at wordsmithing, which her mother had undertaken to quench years earlier. Balancing the duties of motherhood proved to be much easier because Annie and Charlotte, for whom she still felt a motherly responsibility, eagerly accepted their roles as nursemaids for their nephew. All the while, Lizzie remained attentive to her sisters' social lives and graces lest they become domestic ugly ducklings. Young Jamie, of course, continued to be the focus of true republican child-rearing zeal, barely escaping his sisters' scrutiny at any turn. On the surface at the very least, the Wilson sisters fashioned a tranquil domestic life for themselves. They traveled to visit old friends. They attended weddings and funerals. They found encouragement and new ideas from their conscientious Unitarian practice. They comforted each other in illness and commiserated over tardy recoveries. They devoted themselves to children. They read the latest books from England and enjoyed employing versions of Dickens's and Thackeray's plots to describe and validate their own conventional response to their unconventional family situation. Puzzled by the radical stirrings of Margaret

Fuller and "that Jane Eyre woman," they made no room in their family narrative for new voices like those from Walden Pond. Instead, we read of days of domestic felicity, of tranquil and purposeful cultivation of a new family order patterned after the accepted domestic ideology of their day.

Not again would they endure the desolate winter in Keene nor the uncertainty of drifting from the house of one friend to another with no place to go to be together. Furthermore, life with Lizzie in New York in the winter included the promise and excitement of the social "season." The winter of 1853 could not have been more different for the three sisters than the winters of 1851 and 1852.

Charlotte's letter of January 19, 1853, and the contented order it depicts must have pleased its recipient for he added, after the usual annotation describing its receipt and answer, "*Very Excellent.*"

✱ [CHARLOTTE]   New York Jan 19th 1853

My dearest Father,

We received last week letters from you, dated Dec. 15th. I was glad your law case was postponed. Otherwise I am afraid I should not have had any letter from you. You speak of the happiness we must feel on account of being united, we three girls. We are very happy indeed. Lizzie is improving in health. She is very much charmed with her *superb boy*. He is one of the finest children I ever saw. He is about 2 inches taller and larger every way than when I wrote you a fortnight since. He grows out of his clothes just as his Uncle Jamie always did. He is a very sociable little boy too, and amuses us much by his endeavors to talk. I try to make all the sounds I can to amuse him, but can never make the peculiar whistling one you do.

We have not heard from Jamie since he went back to Providence. He is a brilliant talented boy. While he was here we took him to the Theatre a good deal. He is fond of it, and we wished him to enjoy his vacation. He had a thorough appreciation of the beauty or wit of the plays. He is rather silent with gentlemen and ladies older than himself and listens very attentively to conversation. He says he wishes he were not so very large of his age—people expect him to know more than he does he says—but I am glad he has that feeling, although disagreeable to him. It will prevent his being loquacious and self sufficient, as young men are inclined to be now a days. Were they formerly just as much so?

I waste my time here very much. I practise very little. I read History a little. I walk a great deal and I love the baby a very great deal. I did not hold him well at all when I came here first. Pins about my dress used to prick him and he was generally uneasy with me. But now I can hold him a little better. Annie takes a good deal of care of him. She can do every thing. I wish I could be one half as practical a person as she is. You don't know my darling Father what a useless little girl you have in me. Annie manages all Jamie's and my affairs very well. She is an *exceedingly* reliable person.

I think more and more of you every day. A year from next March is the longest time we can wait to see you. It is some comfort to look forward 13 months and think you may be visible to us then. But we have waited so long. It seems so wrong, my dearest Father, that you should be working so hard for us, and all alone in a new country. You have had many disappointments in your life haven't you? I always pray that we may always be able to compensate with our love for your trials. We remember you every hour. The baby even is told about his dear Grandpapa. It makes us feel quite old to be Grandfather and Aunt does it not?

In the way of amusements we find no lack of them. Very quiet domestic ones. Lizzie had some fine tableaux week before last. Jamie and I were in one together and *we* think it was a fine one. The scene was from the "Song of the Bell." A young boy is just starting forth to explore the world. His parents and little playmate are partly clinging to him. Jamie's position was very fine. He expressed in his face sorrow at leaving us but at the same time one foot was forward and showed impatience to be gone. Annie was very handsome in them, as was Lizzie. Small family parties too have been frequent. Broadway is in itself enough to make a place delightful. Nothing makes you feel "smaller" than to live in a large city, I think.

We heard from Ottie yesterday. Poor old woman she is so homesick away from us. She has a very warm heart. *Aunt Sylvia is in Waterbury now I suppose with Porter.* She wrote us she should come to New York the last of this month. We hear from Keene often. There is fine sleighing there now. It is cold here at last, but the winter is a mild one compared to the last one.

We all talk a good deal about Lizzie's coming up to see us next Summer with the baby. He fills the house with his dear presence. We all consider him a wonder.

Susan Colby, or Mrs. Colgate, we see often. She is very comfortably situated in the upper part of the city. She invited us to her house, to a small party, last week. Is just as amiable and hospitable as ever. Insists upon our coming to stay with her. Her Father has been here several times lately. Lizzie saw him, and admired him exceedingly. Robert Colby had been here too. They are all warm friends of your's, as ever.

Be very cautious about your troublesome rheumatism, dearest Father. We are all well and comfortable. May God continue to bless and keep you. Most lovingly your daughter   Charlie

Don't take much snuff dear Father. It may hurt your voice, you know, and then you can't argue cases, or, (still more important), you can't talk so much to us when you come home!

United under Lizzie's roof in New York and at home in Keene, the sisters devoted hours of each day and pages of the correspondence to descriptions of the care and nurture of Wilson's son and heir, Jamie, and Lizzie's first son, Wilson, who all the three sisters declared and neighbors reiterated "looks precisely like General Wilson" (Annie, 2-4-53). The reader can easily speculate that the energy the sisters brought to preparing their brother and son/nephew for manhood not only flattered James Wilson but provided a constant reminder of his abandonment of his parental duty.

Many temptations and distractions attended the sixteen-year-old Jamie in 1853, as his sisters undertook to ensure his preparation for Harvard. "A brilliant and talented boy," according to his sister Charlotte, Jamie succeeded from being like his father, a "boy-man," socially precocious on the one hand and susceptible to all of the foibles of boyhood on the other.

In the same month (January 1853) Annie captured the conflicting currents Jamie was navigating when she wrote: "Jamie is very splendid, I think. He is evidently growing older since he appears in a black frock coat and does not like being directed but rather requested. Secretly I am glad to see him get a little obstinacy for I have always feared that he was too yielding. However don't tell him that" (Annie, 1-4-53). Established for the winter with his old teacher, Mr. Hall, in Providence, Rhode Island, it is hard to know whether the overbearing attention and scrutiny of his sisters, his smoking, lack of exercise, or his surge toward manhood produced the frequently mentioned headaches. At any rate, Annie was concerned enough to travel to Providence in March; when she returned, she reported to her father:

"I think you are needlessly alarmed about him. As far as I can judge he seems a very good boy, and all his friends at Providence seem to think so too. He was not very well when I was there, and said he had suffered from severe headaches for some time, produced I think by want of exercise, which we, full people, all need. This accounted for his not writing to any of us, as it was as much as he could do to get his lessons. I do not believe he has contracted bad habits, or that he has bad companions. He likes play better than study and so do we all. Mr. Frieze said about his entering College, that he could get in, but he would have to work hard after he was in, where if he waited another year, his first year at College would be easy. Now this is I think false reasoning. I don't think anything could be so injurious to him as to enter Cambridge College and have nothing to do the first year. He had better to work hard then. It will keep him out of mischief" (Annie, 3-17-53).

For his part, Jamie wrote to his father occasionally during this year, each time apologizing for his infrequent letters, assuring his father of his earnest application to his studies, and detailing his boyishly routine attempts at reformation of character. Once or twice he varied the formulaic and doggedly dutiful letters with details from the heart. In March, for instance, just before Annie's visit, Jamie wrote: "How are you getting along. Oh what wouldn't I give to see and kiss you. I wish you could be in business in some of the Atlantic States, where we could be together all the time. It would seem so much like our old home, before Mother died. I wish I had never been away from home. I should have been so much better a boy. I try to be good, but I have a great many faults, which I should not have contracted, if I had always lived at home" (Jamie, 3-3-53).

Lizzie reassured her father that Jamie did not "have any proclivity to evil" and continued, ". . . I think he will probably be more cautious than if he were under constant watchfulness" (Lizzie, 3-21-53). Annie echoed this sentiment, adding, "Jamie requires you more and more daily. He is growing away from me and although he is a good boy in the main, he needs you vastly. I am afraid to have him grow up with the idea that he has no one to keep any watch over him" (Annie, 7-3-53). And the watchfulness Lizzie and her sisters particularly wished for from Wilson is clearly reflected in a letter from Jamie to his father, a letter that provides one of the lighter moments in the correspondence while underscoring the complex problems of unnamed vices the sisters faced: "I received a letter from you a short time ago in which you mentioned a 'certain secret habit of youth,' which always proves fatal to both mind and body. I know perfectly what you mean, and in fact I know a great many boys, who are addicted to it, but I can truly say that I am entirely free from it, and I pray to heaven that I always may be" (Jamie, 1-2-53). For three women who speak freely of their own illnesses and remarkably freely about their pregnancies and childbirths, their treatment of Jamie's need for sex education and concern for his potential addiction to masturbation reminds us of what a gap Wilson's absence created.

Constant apprehension for Jamie's well-being and fears over his being on the precipice of dissipation continued unabated. In one letter after another his sisters lamented Jamie's overactivity and inactivity, studiousness or playfulness, good judgment or lack of judgment, choice of friends or confinement. In an amusing if not somewhat indicative foreshadowing of the stereotyping that would sweep the public arena in the 1860s, Charlotte confided details of a visit from a friend of Jamie's: "There has been a very disagreeable boy in town, a student from Yale, who stayed with Jamie a few days. He was a Southerner, and perhaps his faults are partly expiated by that unfortunate circumstance. He was, or seemed, such a deceitful, impure, double-handed person that we hated to have Jamie with him. Jamie was rather pleased with his conversation—which I believe all the boys like—and after seeing him one day asked him to spend Centennial here. Jamie's misfortune is to be too open, too trustful himself. It is a loveable weakness however, and not a fault. I am delighted to say that Jamie disliked the young man as much as we did" (Charlotte, 6-17-53). As for Jamie, who not surprisingly omitted mention of the "deceitful" Southerner, his accounts of the summer bristle with the more private details of trout fishing ("we got two hundred and seven trout" in a few days) and pretty girls ("the first objects of interest") and occasional mention of studying Homer, Livy, and Ovid.

By the middle of September, Annie had resettled Jamie in Boston with Mr. Thomas Bradford, a teacher whose reputation for preparing boys for Harvard seemed more appropriate than the situation in Providence. "Boston has a great many temptations," Annie wrote, but as if to finally give Jamie some credit for diligence, she justified her choice by concluding: "But then the boy must learn to shun temptation. He must begin to fight with it. No schools are as good as Boston schools to fit a boy for Harvard. Exeter is considered by some a fine place to fit boys for Harvard, but I believe it is a very bad place" (Annie, 9-15-53).

By their repeated anxiety over Jamie's hazardous position, constant temptation to dissipation, efforts at resistance, and inevitable backsliding, the sisters fulfilled their duties to their father and their brother. In the end though, for all of their worrying, the young man, who, they noted, had grown from pantaloons to a frock coat of his own choosing, might, like his father, try to evade all efforts at feminine nurture and control. Of course, he never really did, and Annie predicted that when she wrote: "He has inherited your faculty for making friends all over the world which may do him good and great haven. He is easily influenced for good or evil, I fear, but he has a high sense of honor and a kind heart" (Annie, 9-2-53). Like father, like son, Jamie confided to his father an insight that might not have pleased his sisters: "Everybody here and even in town seems to know you. There is a Mr. Shannon here and a Mr. March, who both say that they have known you for a great many years. There is a gentleman lives out at Wellington Hill, by the name of Sam. O. Mead who is very rich, and has a superb place out there, who claims a long acquaintance with you. I am very intimate with one of his sons, and I go out there very often to spend Sunday. Two or three weeks ago, while I was out there, I was introduced to a Mr. Bates, son of the President of Middlebury College [Joshua Bates], who says that you were a very fine fellow, but rather wild.!!" (Jamie, 11-30-53).

Equally gifted in the art of attracting people to him, Lizzie's young son, who as a baby bore not only his grandfather's name but also his visage, occupied much of his mother's and aunts' time during 1853. All of the correspondents wrote enthusiastically to James Wilson about each entertaining change in the baby's behavior. From accounts of the two inches the "superb boy" had grown in a fortnight to his battle with new teeth, his growing mind, and his first attempts at words to speculation on his fitness to be president of the United States, the sisters affirmed in unison that young Wilson had begun his life well. As Charlotte commented: "He is not one of those angelic looking children who always startle you with their beauty, but he is a great strong boy. Screams like a boy and laughs like one too" (Charlotte, 2-20-53). And of first importance, of course, as Annie recounts, "Martha Adams exclaimed the other day, 'Why! he's a perfect beauty Why! he looks precisely like Gen. Wilson!'" (Annie, 2-4-53). The sisters also reminded their father often (and, we suspect, reminded themselves) that health is a gift bestowed and not assumed, and over and over again they lapsed into a conventional literary sentimentalizing of life's fragility. With an unsettling prescience, they seemed to know that Wil might not live to manhood.

Charlotte's letter of early April, which began with a comment about time's rapid flight, continued: "The dear baby is not very well. He has two little teeth just through and his gums are troubling him very much. The Doctor said nothing was the matter with him but his teeth. He [the baby] is so charming and bright that every one feels fond of him. I don't know how we can help it, but I am afraid we are too fond of him. I congratulate myself every day upon his having a turned up nose. It seems cruel to speak slightingly of that little feature, which I don't mean to do, only it is not quite Grecian. If he were entirely perfect I should be afraid we could not keep him. I don't know whether I would rather have him become a little angel now, before he has 'soiled the robe which God has lent him,' or live. When he is asleep sometimes, and looks as white and as pure as anything can look, it seems as if we ought to let him go now, without a sigh" (Charlotte, 4-4-53).

Their sentimentalizing aside, the young Sherwood, like his Uncle Jamie, received the ritual attentions of a prince. As the family gathered in Keene for the summer, Annie and Uncle Robert made alterations in the homestead to afford comfort to the youngest member of the family. His mother wrote: "Well, I and my 'young barbarian' are at Keene enjoying all the comforts of our home. Uncle Robert and Annie, who would tunnel the Alps with their joint resources in one day, knocked a hole thro' the office wall, thus affording a door into the upper kitchen, fitted up the office for a nursery and removed one bookcase with great care, so you can have it all intact when you return. The hot and cold water which Master Wil requires in large quantities is thus easily transmitted and he and his nurse laugh, eat and grow fat in there together. Mrs. Wheeler immediately sent him up a wicker work wagon which her boy had outgrown and he rides around immensely flattered and admired" (Lizzie, 6-15-53).

Annie, who had a keen eye for symbolism, took great pains to advise her father that though his office has been altered to become a nursery, Wilson might reclaim it at any time and find his belongings undisturbed. While the choice of Wilson's office for the nursery might have seemed logical, the displacement of their father's office required detailed and lengthy explanation.

✳   [ANNIE]   Keene June 17, 1853

My dear father,

. . . Our splendid baby and his dear Mother are with us at last. Have they told you what a fine nursery I have made of the Office? Took the empty book case out, simply moving it without scratch or injury, cut a door through behind it to the upper kitchen so that it is now the most convenient room in the house, and whenever you want it back again for an office nothing is easier than to move back the book case and shut the door up again. I put a straw carpet on the floor, put some curtains to the window and hung your 'Marchand' picture over the fireplace so that you could superintend the education of your grandson, and now you know exactly how it all looks. The baby and his Nurse sleep here and there never was better Nursery. I have your desk in the little room over the Piazza known as Jamie's room which he has outgrown, so that bed is in the 'nursery,' and the little room makes an elegant place to write letters in. The doors and drawers containing some of your papers are locked and undisturbed. I forgot to say that the lower part of the bookcase which had some old books and papers in it was undisturbed also. So you see I didn't do any harm and I don't know how we should have got along without the new room as we could not give to James Wilson and Nurse the only spare chamber in the house. Sometime you must make some chambers out of the 'back chamber.'

Lest you may not know exactly how it is, I will tell you that the baby's bed stands in the north west corner of the room the new door being at the foot of the bed, where you must imagine Roxana to be standing *most of the time.* Uncle Robert knocked the hole through the *12* inch wall himself. It is funny to see his intense interest in the little boy. He says he is going to put a notice over the door to the effect that the former patrons of Hon. James

Wilson are informed, that his late office is occupied by Wilson Sherwood, Esq. who will attend to any business in his *Grandfather's 'line.'*

Jamie has gone to Peterboro. George Wilson was up here and invited him so urgently that I thought he had better go. Mr. Torrance I am sorry to say finds it impossible to give Jamie time enough for his lessons. I regret this very much but I still think he had better stay at home till the Autumn, as he is in much [better] health. I want to look after him. He has left off cigars which I think is one great cause of his improved health. I think my influence is worth something to him. He says he won't write to you that he has left off smoking *now*, as it is only four weeks and you won't believe in it. I frightened him so much about his health that I think he is fairly cured. Still I don't want to send him right away, and when he comes home from Peterboro he is going to study certain hours of the day, whether he can get any body to hear him or not. The habit is worth a good deal.

My finances are rather low. I have done as well as I could to make the $150.00 received in May last, but $25.00 to Wheeler for Mother's picture, $13.50 pen rent, $18.00 piano rent for the summer, $13.00 for Jamie's coat, $14.00 for some wine for summer visitors, and about $40.00 paid for 'wood, eggs, plates, papering the side of the office and innumerable other items in my acct. book make up no less a sum than $100.00 already gone. I shall do very well if I get some more in July. Do you think me insatiable?

I shall lose the mail if I write you another word so Good bye.

God bless and keep you prays your ever fond child

Annie F. Wilson

Old Mr. Trumbull lies on his tranquil death bed from paralysis.

Somewhere below the surface of all of the reminders to James Wilson that the family heritage had been nobly transmitted to young Wilson Sherwood, it is easy to guess that Wil's mother and aunts alike might have wished their absent father to be as profligate in his attention to them as they have been to his son and grandson. Charlotte opined: "Let it be whispered *sub rosa* that his Mother may be wanting in discipline toward him. She believes that mothers were made to ameliorate the condition of their little boys." And Annie rejoined: "I believe I have got to do the managing of Lizzie's children for they will get none elsewhere, Lizzie being determined that they should be happy and love her at any sacrifice and not seeing that the surest way to secure both is to teach them obedience" (Annie, 12-4-53). Nonetheless, it was more often young Wil's "sovereign will" and "Herculean lungs" that ruled. Lizzie, Annie, and Charlotte each remarked that by the end of the year young Wil Sherwood might not be able to walk but had mastered speech and continued to polish the art of attracting people with his exhortation "Take care."

While the sisters took care of each other and their brother and Lizzie's husband and son, reporting with relish their successes and not infrequently lamenting their lack of control, the undercurrent of understanding existed that they were only caretakers or stewards of their father's unattended offices. More and more often in this year of birth and change, the mature awareness of their father's three-year-long absence caused the twenty-seven-year-old Lizzie, the twenty-one-year-old Annie, and the eighteen-year-old Charlotte to ask repeatedly and urgently: "When will you come home?" By the end of the year that question had very nearly become "Will you come home?" Will you, they asked, come home to watch over Jamie, see the baby, take care of us? By the end of the year we sense too that each of the sisters had at some level begun to explore the question "What if you don't come home?"

The sisters asked the question in many ways, putting the question to Wilson in many forms, trying to forestall the answer "I'm not coming home." One form of the question continued to be the repeated reminder to Wilson of the details of their setting, the content of their daily life. By their intense evocation of setting, they tried to draw Wilson into their circle, remind him of what he was missing, involve him in small decisions. Sometimes the reminders were as simple as the sharing of literary tastes. What did he think, Charlotte asked, of *Uncle Tom's Cabin*? Had he read the year's current books—Elizabeth Gaskell's account of "the small peculiarities and absurdities of narrow-minded people" in *Cranford*, or the new book by "that Jane Eyre woman," or Thackeray's lecture on the English poets, or Rufus Choate's eulogy for Webster, or Joe's touching death in Dickens's *Bleak House*? On another occasion, in a letter written while recovering from painful dental work, Charlotte drew Wilson into an engaging invitation to discuss DeQuincey's writing: "I think pain makes people more brilliant sometimes. Did you ever read any of DeQuincey's writings? He was an opium eater, and under the effect of opium writes most brilliantly. He hurls out anathemas against the habit of eating opium, while he is most intoxicated with it. He wrote one very original article, on Ford Rosse's telescope, in which, he tries to conjecture how old our Mother Earth is. He says it will be impossible to decide whether she is young or old, for even if we discover that she is 4 or 5 million years old, we can not tell whether she is considered a young flowering girl, or stately matron, by her associates, the sun, and all the heavenly bodies. I think that is very funny, don't you?" (Charlotte, 11-1-53).

All three sisters, but Annie in particular, drew their absent father into their waiting present by evocative observations of the natural world. At the opening of a midsummer's letter, Annie pulled her father directly into the present with her most intense poetic references to the past, the present, and the future. Here, while at the window writing to her father, she sweeps him right through the garden with her: "I am very much as of old. Most twenty years old, and very practical and unpoetic. I have spent my morning in walking around the yard and garden, cutting off a dead branch here, and watering a living plant there. The place looks exquisitely. I see the Peas, Beans, Corn, Onions, Beets, etc. etc., from my window all looking well thanks to James Wright's excellent care, tho' they all pine a little for rain. We are really suffering for a little moisturing. As I speak the little drops, precursor of a good shower are wetting my window" (Annie, 6-17-53). Or again, Annie pulls her father into the familiar setting of Keene, when she observes at the end of an exhausting day of housekeeping: "It is the finest night on which the moon ever shone and West Mountain and the meadow never looked more picturesque" (Annie, 7-18-53). Charlotte, always inclined to contrast her father's setting with theirs, wrote ardently of the New York scene: "I have wished all day you were here with us. It is the very most perfect May day you can imagine. And doubtless brighter than in a more uniform climate, for we can remember days when broadcloth and furs were in requisition—without any effort of memory too. Now in this desert of brick there are beautiful oases of green grass, willows and budding trees" (Charlotte, 5-1-53). And later, having arrived in Keene for the summer, Charlotte put yet another double-spin on the wish-you-were-here theme, writing at the beginning of the letter: "I wish you were here today. What day couldn't I say that? It has been so hot that we were almost too warm, being supremely uncomfortable, though high-spirited. But today it has attained the *juste milieu*. The sun is bright, but one of our fresh invigorating mountain breezes is playing rather rudely with our curtains" (Charlotte, 6-17-53). And she concludes (using prepositional phrases to their full advantage): "I wish you were here, instead of in your wretchedly high room, in a wooden house, in San Francisco. Can't you get the first floor? Do dearest Father. What would you do if the house should take fire? Is it surrounded by wooden houses? Do have a ladder put where you could reach it in case of need. God I know will keep you in his care" (Charlotte, 6-17-53).

Lizzie, though understandably distracted from her natural surroundings, was always more inclined to try to lure her father home by commenting on the social milieu. Speaking with her father as if he were a co-conspirator, Lizzie provided arch and acute comments on the changing life in Keene: "The house is in excellent order and appearance. It never looked more beautiful, but all that made Keene a pleasant residence is gone. It has become a mere abiding place of Elliot's and Faulkner's and the charm and sociality has passed away forever" (Lizzie, 8-3-53). Later in the fall she observed: "Your remarks about Keene people are very fine, but far from despising us or you, I suspect they envy us much more. We have had talent and determination. We have known the best people of our day and we have made ourselves a position in the land. They cannot forgive us for it, and I wouldn't if I were they. Mr. and Mrs. Edward, the Dinsmoors and etc. tho' selfish people, are very much above this meanness, and like us better for being *somebodies*, but the vulgar faction and a few like Mrs. Dorr, Mrs. Ingersoll etc., feel personally injured. But never mind them. We are quite capable of taking care of ourselves" (Lizzie 10-31-53). Annie, too, lamented changes in Keene, writing: "Keene is stationery. A house is going up on the south lot of the garden. I don't know the owner of it. It will hurt our place. The town is being filled up with a low class of people and you might walk the length of the street without seeing a familiar face" (Annie, 9-15-53).

In 1853, whether the girls wished for their father's watchfulness over Jamie or his attentive pleasure in Lizzie's son; whether they tried to lure him into their company by shared reading, shared gossip, and shared headaches, no one subject dominated the letters with more force than the question of how Wilson intended to protect his children by securing the house in Keene—unencumbered by debt. In this year it became painfully and indelibly clear to Lizzie and Annie that Wilson's continued absence seriously threatened their financial security and perhaps even the harmony they had worked so hard to establish. By the end of the year the tone of the letters had become more desperate. "Take care," young Wil's new phrase, had an ominous ring for his aunts. "Taking care" meant protecting "home"; "taking care" meant protecting the family and the family patrimony. How, the women asked, did Wilson mean to protect them—summer, fall, winter, and spring? Unaware that their father was dazzled by his adventurous life in California, their queries were rooted in how his success might ensure their security. Their daily concerns, it appeared, could not be more different from his. Their life could not be more different from their father's. At first the letter writers approached the question abstractly or obliquely. Charlotte, for instance, speaking in her characteristically reflective, tenderly quizzical voice wrote: "How quiet our life must seem to you. I think I should like an object to work for. I mean I should like an exciting employment, with the prospect constantly before me of reaching some goal. Will you be satisfied with a quiet life of leisure when you have become comfortably well off? California seems to create a ceaseless desire for motion and 'go-a-head-ness' in peoples' minds. Every new country accelerates the ideas of people doesn't it? What would become of us if a new California should be discovered?" (Charlotte, 4-4-53). Although Charlotte's question sounds naive, in the light of daily newspaper reports of worldwide mining prospects, her father's enthusiasm for California's challenges might have seemed a foretaste of adventures to come. In the early months of 1853 the *Keene Sentinel* was reporting expeditions to the North Pole; news of Australian gold mines, richer perhaps than California's; and gold sightings in India. The Keene paper, like all of the East Coast papers, was filled with news of numerous vessels leaving for California (thirty-four from Boston alone in January), and bimonthly gold dust arrivals from California ($3,700,000 in March). Along with the report that James Wilson, Jr., had presided at the monthly meeting of the New England Society of San Francisco, the *Keene Sentinel* also reported in the early winter of 1853 that a severe winter and the lack of provisions had forced seven hundred miners to subsist on acorns. Later in the same winter the local paper devoted considerable ink to a criticism of the "God of Success," quoting their beloved ex-minister, the Reverend Abiel Abbot Livermore, as declaring: "There is no success in life worth the name" (*Keene Sentinel*, 2-11-53).

And of course we might expect the children to inquire about their father's "success," dependent as they were on its fruits to provide them with security. In a familiar vein Charlotte wrote: "Even if you are not so successful as you hope now still with your wealth of internal resources you need never, it seems to me, be poor. A little more selfishness and hardness of character which seems an element of success in this country and perhaps everywhere would have made you rich years ago" (Charlotte, 10-31-53).

Niceties, abstractions, gentle cajoling aside, by midsummer Lizzie and Annie's entreaties to Wilson took on darker and darker tones. The "dark cloud of despondency" that Lizzie mentioned earlier continued to cast its shadow on her days, and she wrote that she was struggling to understand "how intimately soul and body are confined and how the enfeebled nerves carry dire messages to the brain" (Lizzie, 6-16-53). September brought a message from Lizzie that set the stage for a series of tortured letters from Annie, the daughter now most intimately concerned with the children's finances. Typically, the letter began by recapitulating family news, but at its heart the message was urgent. In one of the correspondence's most compelling narrative moments, Lizzie detailed the children's circumstances in a letter that she adjured her father to DESTROY.

* [LIZZIE]   Keene Sept 2d 1853

My dear Father,
    You see we are still here. William Sherwood, an elder brother of John has come to Delhi from the West where he lived,—to die, as they fear. He

seems in quick consumption and therefore we didn't go as we intended, the middle of August. He has been a very dissipate man and has ruined his constitution. He is not married, and perhaps the best thing for him is to die. Still he is a very gifted pleasant person and they all feel very sadly about him.

The girls seem quite delighted to have their nephew with them still longer. They have been very kind indeed to us, taking care of him and me and I am much better. The perfect rest and good air, and Time, have all helped me. The baby has never been any other than very well. He is a great handsome creature nearly a year old. He has been made acquainted with his Grandpa's picture and will love you as well as you desire. He is very smart and engaging and shows a lively aptitude for learning to talk, so I suspect he has a distant relationship to you and the old Scotch Irish ancestry.

I know our letters since June have relieved your mind about Jamie very much. He has been behaving splendidly all summer. I think his languor and silence last spring was owing to his health which was in one of those depressed conditions incident on rapid growth. He has waked up astonishingly and we make so much "fuss" over him that he would be apt to. I do not believe he is a bad or dissipated boy *at all*. He will have breaks and scrapes I presume, but I feel very much encouraged about him. His ambition seems thoroughly aroused now to be a good scholar. It will be many years probably before he talks or thinks much like Mr. Webster, or even reads his speeches with much interest, judging from myself and I think my mind was a precocious one compared with children generally. I did not enjoy Mr. Webster until I was twenty. It requires matured taste to enjoy that Doric simplicity and grandeur, and if *Jimmie* will only learn Greek and Latin and mathematics now it is all we can ask. He will no doubt be a man of whom we shall all be proud, but first we have got to endure much anxiety and many youthful excrescences. He is neither a loafer nor a drunkard nor a licentious boy, *as we believe*. John has observed him closely and he says that he is a very uncommon boy. We have given him a little holiday and he has gone to Delhi to see Mrs. Gould's boys, John's nephews.

We are hoping now to get Jamie in one of the excellent Boston schools. Mr. Sullivan is looking out for him, and if we can get him an excellent *responsible* boarding place we shall then be easy. We are using all our friends as *scouts* to pursue such an one.

If care and attention and entreaty, if emulation and three ambitious sisters, can do anything James is well off. You know you had no such guardians in your youth, so it was not surprizing you should have lost some precious years, but I think you "caught up with them" after hand.

Annie says you speak of selling the house. If you do (if you can get a good price for it) it would be a good thing no doubt, but before you do it I want you to consider that it is best for these children to have a home of their own, and unless at the time you sell, you can invest a fund for them so they will be sure of a resting spot, I think you ought not to sell the house. If you could pay your debts and sell *all your other property* here and elsewhere and keep this place unencumbered I should be glad. Not that I can wish you to live here, or expect you to do so, but it is all important that the three children have a roof of their own. My house and heart is always open to them, but old Mrs. Sherwood is a very hateful person and would like to make us all uncomfortable if she could, but while we have this excellent and respectable retreat, whither every body is glad to come in summer and where she knows I will come with the baby in preference to going to her country house, if she tries any of her amiable tempers upon me, why it gives us an incomparable advantage, don't you see? Now John is a most excellent man, generous and faithful and devoted to me, but still he is influenced by his *Mother*, and thinks of her as every son does, and ought to, perfection (I am sure if I am come so, ugly and bad I hope my son will love me.) and I have been afraid that if the girls were not perfectly independent they might sometimes be very much inconvenienced. But I merely throw out these thoughts for your better consideration. If *you could* get $10,000 for the place and thus *pay up* and have something left, why I should be perfectly happy, provided you secured the children from want first and foremost. Consider if you and I should die, how hopeless their position. *Destroy this letter* I beg of you because I do not wish its contents to meet any eye but yours, and never mention any thing I say about my husband's family because I wish always to live on good terms with them. Mary Murray is an excellent woman and loves Annie devotedly. Her Mother I suppose is jealous of that fact. She dislikes me because I have not any money, and because I always *succeed* in society in spite of her, so it is well to be perfectly independent of such a person. $10,000 is a good sum, better perhaps than you can get. Mr. Franklin Adams is about moving away and wishes to sell. Governor Dinsmoor is also going to France for four years, and will sell or let his place. None of them compare with ours, however. It is in perfect repair and very beautiful. Its propinquity to the Emerald hurts it somewhat, but it is a very nice place.

The Emerald and the old store are all going to rack and ruin. The Emerald looks a hundred years old, and I wish it were burnt. As soon as any money can be advanced I hope you will pay off the mortgages and advertize it for sale, as I don't doubt you would be glad to do. . . . Ever affectionately yours dear Father,
Lizzie

For all of the intensity and drama of Lizzie's language, Annie's steady despair and careful re-creation of the daily snipes from neighbors must have quickened if not activated her father's sense of duty. In July, Annie, whom Charlotte had described as having a "womanly trusting character," still sounded as if she were leading a discussion rather than an assault, when she wrote: "There is no position in the world so distressing as that of a lone girl. I am as able to take care of myself as most young women of my age and position, I suppose, but there certainly are times when it seems too much for Charlotte and I to live and wander about alone. Jamie is no help in this respect yet, and Lizzie is all absorbed in her husband and child. Oh! my dear Father we want you terribly. I am always distressed to hear of your interests in any mines. If you could only pay all your debts and come home, and not invest money or encourage any interest in California, I should so thank God. It is not possible that you should live there. Every thing opposes it. And it seems absolutely wrong that one should be forced to spend the latter years of his life away from his home, his children, his all. I don't know but you will think it utter folly, but I must say what runs in my head so constantly. Do send home your money. Pay off these enchaining debts that trouble you, and don't invest anything more in California mines or anything else" (Annie, 7-3-53).

By August, Annie's worries had compounded, and she was forced to write a lonely and anxious letter in which she lamented a woman's vulnerability. This questioning of the disadvantages of her gender became a more and more frequent subtext, along with the related issue of the advantages to be attained or lost by changes in class structure.

* [ANNIE]   Keene August 3d 1853

My dear Father,

Your short letter to us from San Francisco, written just before yr departure for Monterey, of date June 25th and mailed July 1st arrived about the 26th July. We were glad to hear of yr continued good health and the cheering prospects from the "land cases." You must be sure to let us know how the Monterey testimony turned out. We always rejoice over any *legal* news.

We are quite well. Jamie studies well, and recites to Lucius Hall. We are making every exertion to establish him well for the winter. We are particularly anxious that he should go to Boston, but I don't know that we shall succeed in finding a home for him that will satisfy us. We have written to Mrs. Bowditch and a good many of our kind friends are on the look out for him. He is a good boy in the main but a little jealous of my control, which I told him I should tell you, so it may be as well for you to suggest to him that it is a cowardly and unmanly thing to trouble and perplex his sister. I told him I should write you, one day when I told him he must not be out at night, and he answered, "I shall go where I choose." Nota bene, he *did not* go out nights afterwards. Obeys me very well generally but I told him I should tell you, so I must.

Charlotte is very well and takes the world easily. Lizzie is only pretty well. Wilson Sherwood is splendid, but has learned to say "Take care," which we consider ominous that he means to be a dangerous antagonist. He is a remarkably beautiful child, (other people say) and very funny and bright in his ways, as is envinced by his shaking his head in imitation when we say "No, No" to him.

I have been obliged to borrow fifty dollars of Mr. Newell, as the $450 received in May has given out. I had with it to pay Mr. Wheeler, church tax etc. which I have already written you, beside finding the wood shed empty (owing to Uncle Robert's neglect) and having to fill it *at this expensive season*. I shall hope to receive some funds by the next mail.

Uncle R. informed me the other day that "our creditors have got a judgement against us" which I did not understand at all until he added, "if something don't turn up money soon we must lose everything." I was sick and nervous and out of money when he told me and the prospect of being turned out of house and home, of losing even this roof which covers us kept me awake a good many nights. It is the harder to bear being a woman and unable to *do* anything. Men say women don't know trouble, because they don't have to *do* anything. I can tell them it is a hundred times harder to sit and wait and watch and expect a blow without any power to avert it, or run from it than it is to struggle with and take it. This constant anxiety and tension wears me out. If I could feel sure of my home it would be a relief. I find my nerves so shattered that I start at every step. The opening of the gate sends my heart into my mouth. Now this may seem ridiculous Father but consider my position. Uncle Robert comes to me with every disagreeable thing. Roxana too, keeps my ears tried, and I can only receive it all with out a single person to turn to. Lizzie is too sick. I don't dare tell her a thing. Charlotte I never tell anything nor Jamie. It would only make them unhappy and do no good, and I am so full sometimes it seems to me I shall burst. I can't walk up street that I don't read in every face coldness and cruel expression. The Elliots are a constant torment to me, and yet with this weight at my heart I have to be as cheerful as possible. Charlotte even is asking me this minute if she mayn't have a party.

I am ashamed to distress you, dear Father, but I thought there was nobody else in the world I could speak to and I *could not* keep it all in any longer. If we were near you or you could get to us, if there were any place where we could escape this constant reminding of our troubles I could get over it, but here there seems nothing but suffering forever.

Uncle Robert sold the pony in the Spring but I believe he is not paid for and we have had to hire a horse when we have needed all summer.

The place, and everything about it looks beautifully, much too beautifully to fall a sacrifice to the Elliot clique. Nothing ever will be done till you come to do it. Uncle R. either can't or won't do anything. He is at times very generous and kind to us and then comes the next day and paints me a picture that haunts me night and day for a month.

We shall send you a daguerreotype of the baby as soon as we can get an opportunity.

Let us hear from you as soon as possible dear Father. Take good care of yrself, and believe me as ever devotedly and fondly yr daughter

Annie F. Wilson

Two months later, wearied perhaps by a busy season of housekeeping in Keene and settling Jamie in Boston and certainly exhausted by her financial responsibilities, Annie sent her father another tortured letter. Written in short sentences, with energy fueled by urgent parallel constructions, its contents might be expected to haunt the correspondence for months. It is a small wonder that Wilson did not destroy this letter.

✳ [ANNIE]   Keene Oct. 18th 1853

My dear Father,

Your letters of dates Septr 15th and thereabouts came duly to hand, and we were glad to know of yr continued health and plenty of business. Your letters found us well, and again scattered to the four winds, Lizzie and little "Wil." gone to their home, and Jamie at his school in Boston, Charlie and I alone in our own home. We are making preparation to leave by the sixth or seventh of November, and are nearly ready. I believe I have already written you that we go to Boston first. I shall stay, solely for Jamie's sake, about a fortnight; a few days with Mary and Lois White, at Cambridge; a few days with the Barretts, at Dorchester; and a few, with Mary Jennison, who will accompany me to New York. Charlie will go with me till I leave Boston, when she is to go to her friends the Eldredge's for a visit. She will join me in N.Y. later.

Thanks to the unusual amt. of money in my pocket, I shall be able to meet my expenses, I hope. Though the Summer has been an expensive one, I have paid off some long standing demands. I leave our home with unusual concern and regret, since a conversation with Uncle Robert yesterday, has led me to fear that we never shall have the privilege again to it. I almost feel inclined to cling to it now, through any thing, Winter, and cold. I would, but for the needless expense of keeping it open.

Uncle Robert says the property is mortgaged for nine thousand dollars, which staggered me, and that it takes all he can get to pay the interest, notwithstanding which the creditors threaten every day to foreclose. Dear Father can't you do something about this? Can you not save this home to us in some way? Can not something be sold to clear off this mortgage? It is easy to say go out of yr house peacefully, and give up yr home, and the roof under which you were born, but where shall we go? Children with neither Father or Mother to go to. Girls unprotected and alone, and a young boy of fifteen. Oh Father it is awful. It is not as if we were boys, and could earn our living. It is not respectable for girls of our age and appearance and position to wander about alone. John and Lizzie will and do, do everything for us in their power, but John is a poor hardworking lawyer, and Lizzie, with always a baby in her arms, (as she will always have,) has neither time, or health, to devote to the care of us. I will do almost any thing that I *can* do. I will stay with the children, and by them, while I live, if it is best, but Father we *must* have a roof to cover us, since we have no other protection near us. Don't let us be deprived of the respectability of our Father's *roof*. It almost kills me to write this, and I would not, if it were not that I *know* there is danger overhanging us. I see even through my wilful blindness to slights and insults, how, even Mr. Chamberlain avoids one, or passes me with a curt nod. It has been increasing for a year, and there is no disguising the matter. People are out of patience, and seem to *grudge* us the bread in our mouths. People hear that you are in receipt of large sums. They don't stop to consider expenses, distance, the vagueness of humor, or anything. They want money, and Father, whether it is true or not, is it not better to make a great sacrifice, than to have us thus uncertain and helpless. I don't mean to dictate, I don't mean to put my judgement beside of yrs, ever. I only think that at a great distance from us, you can not realize the distressing position in which we are. It would be better to sacrifice every thing else you own, or have an interest in, than to deprive us of this our home, except we have another.

I beg you will not treat this as a piece of disrespect, or impertinence. Neither regard it as the result of a woman's timid nervousness. I am not timid, I am not nervous. I *know* we have reason to be anxious and I can not be silent.

Jamie likes his school and stands well in it. He disturbed me by going into Boston to spend one or two evenings last week, as his, and our, devoted friend Mr. Jennison, immediately informed me. I wrote him that I should write you, and so I must. I enclose his answer. Mr. Woodward is the man at whose house he boards. He—Jamie—learned to play billiards at Providence at the "gymnasium," where he used to go with Mr. Frieze and I am sorry to say, plays a remarkably good game. I felt it my duty to tell you this, but I think it will not be wise to be very severe with him. He must meet the world some time, and I really think he means to be a good boy. I don't think it's well for him to have much money, tho' he should never feel the mortification of being unable to pay his bills, so I am careful to send the exact amt. of his bills to *him* and allow him to pay them.

And now dear Father I have got through a hard duty which has weighed upon my mind for some time. I have written you a disagreeable offensive letter which (as you used to say to me when I was to be punished) has been *really* a thousand times harder for me to write, than for you to read. I wish it were not my fate always to say, and write, the disagreeable things.

Let us hear from you always regularly. Wilson Sherwood has learned to point his little finger to yr picture when we say "where's Grandpapa?" and make up his mouth to kiss it.

God bless you, dear Father, and good bye. Believe that I am always fondly yr child   Annie F. Wilson

Meanwhile, Jamie grew in grace and dissipation; James Wilson Sherwood pleased his family with the enjoinder "take care"; Lizzie struggled back to health; Annie bore the family burdens and fell in love; Charlotte observed quietly and heaped blandishments upon her father. And what if he did not return in the spring of 1854, as he had hinted he might do? Should the women find ways to support themselves? "I never could understand why women should wish to be either M.D.'s or D.D.'s or L.L.B.'s," Charlotte wrote. "If they want to study a tiresome profession I should think we would be rejoiced to let them" (Charlotte, 2-17-53). According to Charlotte it was a pity Lizzie "could not be in the Senate or somewhere where her eloquence would be more widely enjoyed" (Charlotte, 3-13-53). Annie, too, explored the subject, asking: "Isn't it a pity that I wasn't a boy? To earn my own living?" (Annie, 7-3-53). Returning to the subject later, she wrote that when John Sherwood came home at night, he often said, "Annie, I've got a very interesting question for your legal opinion tonight." And to this Annie commented: "If I had been a man, I would have dug at the law" (Annie, 11-2-53).

At the year's end the children's questions remained unanswered, and their domestic rituals become more complex. Instead of going to the Senate, Lizzie gave birth to another son, named Samuel Sherwood, Jr., to honor his paternal grandfather. Tantalizing news began to trickle out about a romance for Annie, whose future had been a concern to Lizzie for some time. The romance had a character of intrigue and remains the Wilson narrative's most complicated and mysterious love story. Lizzie offered her reservations early (not to be mentioned to anyone else, of course). With an ever clear eye to advantageous marriage, Lizzie noted that other members of Annie's beau's family have married well, for James Watson Webb, a Whig journalist and diplomat she mentions, would have been well known to Wilson. So she observed:

"Annie shows symptoms of getting married. One Mr. Clarence Cram has showed the firmest intentions of having her for three years. She has never favored him till lately. He is a young man of extraordinary talents, good looks, and a very rich old Father. So far very good, but he is only 23, has no business (as yet) or profession. So far rather good. I don't want her and she don't intend to marry him in any uncertainty, so the 'grand finale' is not yet arranged. I think she likes him, and if the old gentlemen will 'fork over' it will do. Old Cram is worth a million it is said, and has four children. He is old and gets drunk so I don't consider him very safe, as he has two ambitious daughters, one of whom married Col. [James Watson] Webb of the Courier and Enquirer, and they try and get an influence over him, and his money. However young Cram is as yet a favorite, is very gifted has honorable feeling and loves Annie to distraction. She is smart and shrewd as all her ancestors could desire and altogether I don't know but we may consider it a good thing. However it is not settled yet and you must not say one word about it to anyone. I think Annie will break it to you. Annie is a 'stunning' beauty as Jamie says and has many admirers, none of them quite up to what she deserves and desires. She says no sensible man ever did admire her but Mr. Cram, and I must say she has as you say 'escaped some great mercies'" (Lizzie, 9-16-53).

Annie never mentioned Clarence Cram to her father in 1853. In fact in September, while repeating an entreaty for his return, she commented: "Will you come home in the spring? I have said so, so often, that I should be dreadfully sorry to have you contradict it all, if for no other reason. I do want to see you dear father, 'awfully'. It will be a charming sensation to go about under your strong arm feeling sure that there is one person in the world to take care of me, personally. I have learned to take care of other people a little, and now I want the fun of being taken care of" (Annie, 9-2-53). "Times," as she often commented this year, "are hard and money is tight."

Lizzie, Annie, and Charlotte would continue to perfect the art of taking care of each other more than a little before experiencing "the fun of being taken care of." Letters from Annie and Charlotte at the year's end express both their contentment and their expectation of "the speedy eligibility" of their father's return. Letter, gifts, and family friends arrived at Wilson's behest, but Wilson himself stayed firmly rooted in California, while his daughters waited.

✳ [CHARLOTTE]   New York Dec. 16th 1853

My dearest Father,

I did not write by the last mail—this of course you know—and I only mention it to try to excuse myself on the slippery ground of not knowing the day of the month. But I am as sensible as you of the absurdity of this excuse. It is my duty to know the day on which I am to write to you. Will you try to forgive me once more?

We received today your very splendid presents by Mrs. Berry. They are very handsome indeed, and we are very much delighted with them. I was not at home and Annie was the only person visible when Mr. Berry called.

Lizzie has a superb boy. Born last week Thursday, Dec. 8th 1853. He is very dark and rather red as yet, but he has jet black hair and promises to resemble his dear Mother. He weighed 12 pounds when he was born.

Lizzie is very well and comfortable. She says the baby looks like you. I asked her what I should say to you from her, and she said "Tell him I have a son." That of course will satisfy all your expectations. He is to be named 'Samuel,' for old Mr. Sherwood. The oldest one—Wil—is a splendid fellow. He is very bright and precocious. His ankles are rather weak and we don't dare to let him bear his whole weight on them, but he walks somewhat. He is nervous and excitable, but healthy and good natured. I only wish you could see both the darlings. Lizzie is so proud of having two *sons*. We are all entirely satisfied. Jamie is delighted.

James Wilson *Jr.* is well and happy. He came to see me often when I was in Boston. Mr. Bradford, his teacher, reported most favorably of his conduct and progress at school. He is studying conscientiously Mr. B. says. His only fault, when he came to school, was superficiality, but his teacher told me how he had improved, how much more thorough he was now. Mr. Bradford is a very fine teacher. He eradicates faults, and does not try to cover them up, as so many teachers do.

. . . I wrote you, I believe, about the death of young Mrs. Eldredge, Lizzie's sister in law. In consequence of that event we were very quiet indeed, but I enjoyed Lizzie's company very much. I saw a good deal of the Hales in Boston—Nat/l. Hale's family. I suppose you know him.

Young James Eldredge returned from California while I was in Boston. He had seen you in San Francisco he said.

Boston seemed so small after New York. How does San Francisco compare with New York in point of size? Is it as large? New York has changed since last winter. It is larger and more dirty and noisy. Everything is moving up town. There is not room enough 'down town.' What an idea of noise and confusion those two words give one! I remember when we stayed at the Astor House, Canal Street seemed to me very far up town.

We heard a report yesterday, a very authentic one, that Clement March was married to Adelaide Smith. Is not that a singular termination of such a belle's existence? Clement is becoming very rich. But Addie never liked him at all, Annie says. How can people marry disagreeable people because they are rich. What good does money do one if one is to live always with a person whom one cares nothing about. It is rather uncharitable to suppose any one marries for money alone.

. . . Captain Folsom the rich gentleman has just gone to California. Is his health improved? I saw him last Spring and thought him a very agreeable man. He was just going to Europe for his health. I suppose you see people by almost every Steamer that you knew here or that know us. Is it not so?

We are all well and Annie will write tomorrow or the next day.

Remain assured that you are always remembered in the prayers of your daughter   Charlie

✳ [ANNIE]   New York Sunday Dec. 18th 1853

My dear Father,

Your agreeable letters and my beautiful Christmas presents are all re-ceived safely at last altho' the Steamers are somewhat behind hand and poor Mrs. Berry had a hard passage, but she is now here all safe. The regular mail beat the Nicaragua line this time. We rejoice to hear of your good health and fine prospects but Mrs. Berry distresses me very much by suggesting that you may not come home for two years. I don't think we could stand that possibly.

You will rejoice to hear of the birth of your second grandson who ar-rived on the 9th of December. Lizzie is very comfortable and has been sitting up today looking from one boy to the other. She has been uncom-monly well since her confinement. The baby, No. 2 and named "Samuel Sherwood Jr" by the way, weighed twelve pounds when he was born and is in every respect a fine, perfect, healthy boy. Lizzie is enchanted, and says if she has ten, she hopes they'll all be boys. The name of Samuel we think is dreadful but Lizzie is very fond of the old gentleman, and since we had the privilege of naming the first one for our own dear Father, she feels it a duty to gratify the good old Grandpapa by naming the second for him.

Mrs. Berry was amazed to hear of the birth of "our second." She did not expect it so soon. Nor did we, but we are very thankful that it is all over so soon and so well.

As for the rest of us, we are quite well, and content, except that there is so little prospect of your speedy return. Jamie will spend next week with us. I hope he will write you by this mail. Charlotte is already here, as she herself has told you. She is a great beauty, and never looked better than she does this winter. She is in perfect health, and takes great care of herself.

I have not told you how much we admired our beautiful card cases. It is rather a funny circumstance that in all my visiting I never have had a decent card case. I have always borrowed Lizzie's, and always thought I would get one, so you could not have sent me a more useful or acceptable present. If you find it convenient I hope you will send Lizzie a little money. She has so many little things to get for her babies and herself which don't come under the kind of necessities exactly, but which she would like to get if she had her own money, and altho' John would give her whatever she asked for, she knows that his expenses are very great and that he has to work pretty hard to save anything. So when ever you feel inclined to send her any thing, when you can, send her a little money, fifty dollars or so, and it will be a great pleasure to her and the means of procuring a good many little gratifications for her which she desires and wants. Both she and dear John are most devoted in their kind attentions to us *all* and I am always glad to give them what little help I can.

I don't hear from Keene at all. Charlotte heard from Susan Adams that Mrs. Willard has a living child at last, a daughter. Charlotte met Aunt Elizabeth in the Street a few days since and spoke to her. She is well and is living in Brooklyn this winter. Mr. Hunter has broken his leg or ankle or something. Aunt Sarah is at West Port. We heard the other day that Addie Smith was married to *one* of the Marches, which, I could not learn, and as I can hear nothing more about it I am inclined to doubt its authenticity.

There has been a good deal of disturbance in the city of late in consequence of the street preaching of the Methodists who abuse the Catholics. It threatens to end in a regular controversy of Protestants against Catholics. I have been personally very much incensed lately at the persecution of a young Unitarian who was nominated for Professor in Columbia college here—Professor of Geology, I think—who was objected to on the ground that he was a Unitarian. Isn't that enlightenment for the nineteenth century, and in the great city of N.Y. I told Mr. Ruggles I would not build any more colleges for boys. I would build one for their Sires if I were he.

God bless you always prays yr loving child   Annie F. Wilson

When you have time I wish you would write to Uncle Farnsworth.

·

"*Real* Ladies Society"

·

With less assurance of their father's speedy return and stronger and stronger indications that they not only took care of each other satisfactorily but knew how to cultivate sustaining relationships outside the family it also became clear that the letter writers were increasingly conscious of themselves *as* writers. True, their multiple accounts of Sarah Adams's death and Lizzie's wedding have introduced us to Wilson's experience of having the same events re-created by at least three voices and points of view. Since we know that they wrote without having read each other's letters, the similarities in their accounts is striking. Even though they endeavored to present a united voice to their father and convince him not only of their faithfulness but also of their dependability, the voices in their letters, like their personalities, began to become more and more individual.

Though as modern readers we do not have Wilson's advantage of recognizing the correspondent's handwriting before reading the letters, we can observe each letter writer's style and choice of emphasis becoming more and more distinct. Lizzie, busy with children, writes less frequently, compressing her feelings with unchecked intensity and skilled narrative drive; Annie either entreats her father with unbridled candor or skirts personal issues of love and loss with descriptions of her reactions to public issues. Charlotte continues to be the most consistent and unaffected chronicler of the quotidian. Nonetheless, it is Charlotte who first observed, with her characteristic imaginative projection (and astuteness worthy of a sophisticated critic of narrative): "We are all engaged in writing to you at this time. I think our different styles of writing must be an entertaining study" (Charlotte, 8-3-53). James Wilson unfortunately left his reaction to Charlottes's observation unannotated at the letter's end. But we know that the tale of days in New York and Keene had acquired a new complexity and interest for its writers and, we suspect, for its intended reader as well.

While his children enjoyed New York, engaged in letter writing, and bewailed his living on the frontier, General Wilson had found California exactly to his liking. Enjoying the pleasant climate, Wilson had bought a farm and staked a successful claim at Gold Bluff. But not everything went smoothly. His patron, Daniel Webster, had died, and Franklin Pierce, a fellow New Hampshire man but no political ally of Wilson, was elected president. Most important, Wilson himself had been charged with corruption, and in the fall of 1852 the Senate refused to confirm his appointment to the Land Commission. He had held the post less than a year. Wilson hardly missed a beat. He did what many clear-thinking politicians—then and now—have done; he set up a law practice specializing in pleading cases before that commission.

In fact, since March 1853 was the deadline for filing claims, the commission was designed to have a limited life, so Wilson's position would not have lasted many more months in any case. A historic land case that grew out of his legal work before the commission proved to be much longer-lasting and more exciting. On February 3, 1853, only one month before that deadline for filing land claims, a French trader and adventurer José Yves Limantour, threw a bombshell into the civic life of San Francisco when he filed a claim with the Land Commission. With Wilson acting as his attorney, Limantour requested confirmation of two grants by the Mexican governor of California dated 1843. One was for several islands in San Francisco Bay, including Alcatraz and a small portion of Marin County. The second was for four square leagues, approximately 16,000 acres, not a large grant in a territory where grants commonly ran to eleven square leagues, or 48,712 acres, but these acres included the middle of the city of San Francisco.

In the early 1840s, Limantour, then in his twenties but already a man of fortune, sailed up and down the coast of California under a Mexican flag, trading silks, brocades, brandy, clothing, and perfume from France for cash or hides and tallow from the settlers along that thinly populated coast. One San Francisco banker and printer, Edward Bosqui, described him. "Limantour was a born adventurer, of very striking personal appearance, cool, self-possessed, and as brave as a man could be. He had confronted death in almost every form by land and sea" (Kenneth M. Johnson, *José Yves Limantour vs. the United States* [Los Angeles: Dawson's Book Shop, 1961], 76). He became a firm friend of Micheltorena, the Mexican commanding general and governor of California. In fact, when the Mexican government was slow in sending money to support the army and the local administration, Limantour sometimes lent Micheltorena money to tide the government over. Like Wilson, Limantour had many connections and many friends, particularly in the Mexican government. He claimed that for his service to Mexico, Micheltorena had in 1843 granted him sixteen thousand acres of land. At that time Yerba Buena, which later became San Francisco, consisted of a small mission without a missionary and with fifty

Indians, sixty head of cattle, fifty horses, two hundred sheep, a village of twenty houses belonging to foreigners and used exclusively as warehouses, and a dilapidated fort with a sublieutenant and five soldiers. Even so, the value of San Francisco as a harbor was already recognized by the Hudson's Bay Company and other traders.

By 1853 the Mexicans had lost the territory to the United States. Gold had been discovered, and the land Limantour claimed had erupted into the wealthy port and boom town of San Francisco, with about thirty-seven thousand citizens. Most of them cried fraud, pirate, robber, and charlatan at Limantour's claim that he owned the land on which they had built their city. It was to be the largest land case in the history of California, and General James Wilson was Limantour's primary attorney.

Wilson began preparing a case to argue before the Land Commission based on a letter Limantour had written to Micheltorena applying for these grants, a letter from Micheltorena recommending the application, a grant from Micheltorena, and a confirmation by the Mexican minister of the interior ratifying the grant, all dated 1843. The U.S. government, which opposed the claim, based its case on two facts. First, these grants to Limantour were not noted anywhere else in the records, whereas other established grants were referred to frequently. And second, Limantour had never made any attempt to occupy these lands or made any public statement about them. However, this negative evidence seemed fairly slim to many. By September 1853, when Limantour felt his case was convincing enough, Wilson began collecting quitclaims from the citizens who occupied the property that Limantour claimed, giving his own assurances the claims were valid. Limantour set the quitclaims low enough so that many people paid them to clear their deed once and for all. And of course, anyone who wanted to sell his property was obliged to settle with the Limantour claim first (Johnson, *José Yves Limantour*, 42; Wilson's account books for 1853–56).

For the next five years the Limantour case demanded much of Wilson's attention. His spirits rose and fell with the fortunes of the case and of Limantour, whom a younger, more imaginative, more reckless, and slightly less respectable Wilson might have emulated. In New York his daughters, who had often recommended that he concentrate on law rather than prospecting, struggled to empathize with his deep involvement in the case.

Meanwhile, New York was very gay, and sleighing was all the rage in December and January of 1853–54 (Jamie, 1-4-54). On New Year's Day young Jamie went sleighing with a friend on the Bloomingdale road. Though Lizzie had to forgo society because she was still in mourning for her brother-in-law, Annie and Charlotte went to visit their friend, Mr. Samuel Ruggles, and had a splendid time. On January 11, city dwellers enjoyed "a real New Hampshire snow storm," which enchanted those already "insane over the delights of sleighing" (Annie, 1-11-54). Even Charlotte, who had enjoyed many real New Hampshire snow storms, found the sleighing superb and exhilarating.

In the midst of these pleasures of winter in New York, privately Annie had to look to the summer in Keene and another crisis in their precarious finances that threatened to take away the family's other home. "I beg you not to treat this as a piece of disrespect or impertinence," Annie pleaded when she told her father in October 1853 that their creditors doubted his good faith and threatened foreclosure. But General Wilson ignored her excuses. He was furious. He accused her of doubting his honor and integrity—something he certainly endured from others but wasn't prepared to tolerate from his family. Annie protested that she never intended disrespect, but she did not recant. "In showing you clearly what our position was at Keene and how urgent and impatient *your creditors* were, I but told you the naked truth, and was far from expressing any thought or idea connected with yourself which was in the slightest degree improper or untruthful as an expression of disrespect would have been" (Annie, 1-4-54).

However wounded Wilson was, he came up with a plan to assure that Annie, Charlotte, and Jamie would keep the house. Although he had no intention of diverting any of the thousands of dollars that monthly went through his California businesses to pay off his debts in Keene, he proposed settling the house on his children. If the house belonged to the children, he reasoned, his creditors would not be able to seize it in payment for his debts. He proposed to have his son-in-law John Sherwood act for him in the matter.

Humiliated by every slight and accusing look from her father's creditors, Annie was too desperate about the house to protest against this maneuver, essentially the same one used by Lizzie's old suitor, the discredited Mr. Macalaster. Lizzie too urged Wilson to do it, reassuring him that he would never become a King Lear unwelcome in the house he had given to his children. "I do not think you will ever find an *inhospitable reception* there from your *children*, who live for you and love you more and more" (Lizzie, 1-17-54). Annie and Lizzie resisted having John involved in their father's finances for fear someone might say something to Wilson's "disadvantage" (Lizzie, 1-17-54). "Your proposition to settle the house on us is perhaps well enough. You are the best judge. But your proposition to make John an agent in the affair I don't think quite advisable since he knows nothing about yr affairs and I think the necessity of treating with Uncle Robert would be disagreeable to him and can not think it advisable to mix him up with all those Keene people who know all about you and your embarrassments" (Annie, 1-4-54).

Though Lizzie had been married to John for three years, she and Annie still smarted from the Wilsons' comparative poverty and the instability of their situation: their father's absence, his turbulent career, the scandals that periodically erupted around him. The women, particularly Annie, suffered from the moral and social stigma that fell on them from their father's wheeling and dealing. To be poor was bad, to be in debt was worse, and to be the daughters of a man involved in shady financial dealing was worst of all. The situation wore on Annie's health. John already knew that they were poor and in debt. What would he find if he looked closely into his father-in-law's financial affairs and talked to people who knew of his "embarrassments"? Better an old acquaintance who already knew the worst than to have to sit down to dinner nightly with a censorious brother-in-law. "Have not you some business friend in Boston who would be safe to entrust your business to? I should prefer to entrust any business transactions to him than to introduce John into the unknown region" (Annie, 1-4-54).

Wilson chose Lucius Skinner, his business associate in the East, to look into the problems in Keene. He also sent $559 to Annie and $200 to Lizzie at Annie's suggestion that Lizzie needed things for her house, but he did not pay off the mortgage on the house and give it to his children. By March, Wilson still had not settled things in Keene; and Annie, already tired of having Uncle Robert come to her "with every disagreeable thing," received a disagreeable letter about affairs there. They were especially stricken by Uncle Robert's threats since they expected him to protect them in their father's absence.

* [UNCLE ROBERT]   Keene Feb 27th 1854

Dear Anna,

Your cheque was duly received and applied to the payment of the wood bill. You have got some good wood and I believe enough of it. I have not sent the potatoes yet, as there has been no day when they would not freeze. This month has been remarkable for cold, even in New England. Did you say anything to James Wright about staying another summer? There is also a lad at Peterborough of about 15 who is an excellent boy, if James should not come. . . .

I had a paper from DuBuque last week, and I see that your father has sold his city lots at a great price. They realized above six thousand dollars. I am sorry to learn that he has ordered that money to be sent him at St. Francisco. I cannot believe that your father and my brother will prove himself so ungrateful, and dishonest, as to neglect paying his honest debts. I have been advised by able persons here, and by friends of your father too, to proceed and trustee that fund in DuBuque and pay his debts with it at home. I shall not interfere with it in any way. But what am I to think by and bye if he manages in that way? I have kept this property at his especial request and desire, and managed to the best of my ability, to preserve it as his home. I have deprived myself of much which was my right, for the last fifteen years to aid and benefit him, and no one can ever know mortification, and degradation of feeling, that I have suffered on his account. I confess that this movement looks as if he had forgotten all old friends, and looked for new ones in California. I do not know how much longer my patience and confidence in him may last, but it is growing weaker as time goes on. I have written him several times, and he does not condescend to answer of late. I wish you would write him a good long letter and get a decided answer if possible, that we may know, sometime, what to depend upon.

But Annie had learned better than to relay any such messages to her father. Instead she simply sent Uncle Robert's letter with her own and let it speak for itself.

Money problems notwithstanding, circumstances in the winter of 1854 provided an opportunity for Lizzie, Annie, and Charlotte to further examine and cultivate a society of women. In the nursery in New York, Lizzie's two boy babies commanded the energies of one, three, five, or any number of mothers, aunts, and nursemaids who could afford to devote their attention to them. And father John acknowledged that he was excluded from the world of the nursery. Then in the drawing room appeared a woman (her arrival from California had been mentioned earlier) who did not fit into the social scheme as Lizzie, Annie, and Charlotte conceived it and forced them perhaps not to alter their concept of good and proper behavior but at least to reconsider it. Men played virtually no role in these interactions. Although the women continued to recount and justify to their father what they thought and did, *they* defined and performed the tasks in the nursery; and in the drawing room they observed this perplexing new woman and judged her behavior.

As if to illustrate to his family the exotic charms of his new home, Wilson sent Mrs. Berry, his landlady in San Francisco (who, with her mother, Mrs. Duncan, was visiting in the East), with a large gold "slug" for Jamie. Jamie admired both the gold and Mrs. Berry. "I cannot thank you too much for that splendid great coin that you sent to me. I have had it converted into cash and am going to get some clothes with it. Mrs. Berry came here with Mrs. Duncan and we liked them both very much. I went to call on Mrs. Berry a few days ago, and she told me that as my father had given the largest coin in the world she would give me the smallest, so she gave me a gold twenty-five cent piece. It is the neatest little coin I ever saw.

"They all seem to love you very much, and talk of you with a great deal of respect and affection, and the tears came into Mrs. Berry's eyes as she told us how '*The General*' wanted to see his children. I think that she is a very sweet person indeed. She says that when she goes back she shall make it a point to have a room in her house for you" (Jamie, 1-4-54).

Besides being his landlady, just what Mrs. Berry's relationship to James Wilson was is never very clear, but she must have arrived with glowing recommendations from him, for the daughters strained every social nerve to be cordial to her. Never did the manners of East and West seem less comprehensible to each other, and the sisters' response to her was more measured than Jamie's. Annie assured the General, "I have seen Mrs. Berry and Mrs. Duncan and was as polite to them as I always shall be to your friends. We were delighted to see them," and then added, "How you must miss *real* ladies' society" (Annie, 1-4-54).

Wilson apparently bristled at Annie's ambiguous suggestion that Mrs. Berry might not be a "real lady." In defense of his friend he evidently accused Annie of confusing wealth with good breeding. Gradually, a picture of an interesting new breed of woman emerged. Annie clarified her previous statement in a letter written on her father's birthday and dug a deeper hole for herself. Mrs. Berry might be "ladylike," but clearly she was not a "lady" but a landlady. The letter also provided Wilson, if unintentionally, instruction on the "*real* ladies' society."

✳ [ANNIE]   New York March 18th 1854

My dear Father,

Your letters of 16th February are duly received. We are truly thankful to hear of your restoration to health, as the news of yr illness by the mail before quite alarmed us. I rejoice, too, to hear that you have written to Mr. Skinner about affairs at Keene. I have been quite sure that there was something wrong there for some time and I hope he will find out where the money has all gone to.

Nothing of great interest has occurred here. We are well as usual, and Jamie writes me the same. Wilson and Sam have not been very well having violent colds, but are recovered. Wil is a delicate boy and I think always will be. He is too bright I am afraid, reminding us constantly of dear little Webbie. Yesterday was St. Patrick's day and the streets were full of soldiers to Wil's great delight. You would have laughed to see him march up and down the room like them blowing through one little fist for a trumpet, and holding an imaginary gun in the other. Wasn't that smart for a little seventeen month old?

You misunderstood my remarks relative to "*real* ladies society." I like Mrs. Berry extremely, and consider her a very ladylike, and uncommonly bright woman, and it was in consequence of her conversation concerning you, that I was led to that reflection. I don't think you are one of the men who can live contentedly without the "female influence" (as Thackeray says) about you. When Mrs. Berry told me how many little things she used to like to do for you and about yr talks and books and all I was led to consider how much you would miss her, and then how much you must miss *us* all (of the sex) as she tells me there are comparatively few agreeable women in San Francisco. As to the fallacy that money makes "ladies," I have lived too long for that, and conclude on the contrary, that few women can bear money, with out very soon showing that they are not ladies at all. Prosperity is so much harder to bear, gracefully than adversity.

March 19th

I send you by Mr. Upham of Maine, an uncle of Mrs. Little's two books of Thackeray's. That they are his, will recommend them to you, and you have lived enough in a small village, to enjoy the satire, and to appreciate the truth of his description of the littleness of people's minds when their sphere is narrow, or rather the tendency to littleness. I send you, too, the last "Putnam." It's the best magazine in the country, and some people consider it a good step toward the English reviews. I don't know but you always get it in San Francisco. If you don't, I will send it to you. Tell me what you think of the paper on "The great Cemetery."

I did not know till yesterday afternoon that I could send you anything by private hand. It was Saturday, and a bad day, so I was unable to go to many places to look for some nice handkerchiefs for you. I got these from A. T. Stewarts, all he had and meant to put in two white ones to make up a half dozen. I got three by mistake, so I send them, tho' Charlotte says the odd numbers annoy you. I hope you will like them. I wish I knew what size of gloves you wore. I would send you some nice ones.

. . . You must not despise New York to call it "desert where we can see no green grass," any more for we are going to have a new Park six miles in circumference. What do you think of that?

Little Sam is not well today (Sunday the 19th) and Lizzie herself is suffering from the same influenza and will not be able to write to you. She is a very anxious and devoted Mother and unless she gets more philosophy about her children's little ailments will wear herself out very young. I don't know why I persist in misleading you about the date of Sam's birth. The new family bible says, "Decr. 8th 1853," but I don't know how one can be expected to remember the dates of children's births when there is but fifteen months between them.

I hear no news from Keene or New England generally except that the agitation of the Nebraska question has somewhat reduced the democratic majority. A recent dispatch to President Pierce is going the rounds of the papers, purporting to have come from a friend in New Hamp. to this effect. "The state has gone to ———— ." It's short and pithy, but it doesn't seem true that the State can have experienced any great change to have effected such a result.

We go along from day to day very much in the same way. Charlotte practices her music and reads French every day and improves a good deal. I take care of the children and Lizzie and the house generally and manage to read a little and keep my stockings mended. If ever I get time I mean to study Spanish.

Do take care of yr precious health dear Father and make haste to come home.

Mary Murray and all the family inquire for you always with interest. The Mr. and Mrs. Ruggles whom Charlotte mentioned in a letter to you are Mr. and Mrs. Saml. B. Ruggles cousins of John Sherwood's and very kind friends of ours. Mr. Ruggles is a prominent man here politically and socially. You confounded them with Mr. and Mrs. Wetmore.

I must close my letter to take Master Wil who is crying "Annie" from the top of the stairs. Good bye dear father. God bless you always prays yr loving daughter.

Annie F. Wilson

Charlotte calls Mrs. Berry "a very sensible intelligent woman" (Charlotte, 1-4-54). Lizzie, who is without a nursemaid and still weak from childbirth, postpones meeting Mrs. Berry. However, she reports, "The girls were much pleased with Mrs. Berry. . . . I am to invite Mrs. Berry to dine with me as soon as I get a nurse. I have not yet seen her, but long to do so to thank her for all she has done for you" (Lizzie, 1-17-54).

The sisters searched for words that would fit this woman into some pattern of behavior they understood and approved but succeeded only in sounding patronizing. "Mrs. Berry I like very much. She seems a perfectly sincere, whole-hearted person. I should think you would miss her extremely. One rarely meets such a kind person as she. I know, when I was boarding in Boston, my comfort depended almost entirely upon the lady with whom I lived . . . and all the women were kind to me" (Charlotte,

2-14-54). "We are quite delighted with Mrs. Berry's frank honesty and apparent kindness of heart. Her yankee shrewdness quite delights us" (Annie, 2-17-54). Lizzie, after entertaining her at dinner several times, is franker in her assessment. "I like Mrs. Berry very much. She seems eminently honest, good hearted and *very* funny. Isn't she the strangest mixture of yankee smartness and California never-say-die? Of cultivation and rudeness, polish and unpolish that ever was jumbled together?" (Lizzie, 3-5-54).

After some acquaintance, Charlotte shrewdly perceived that Mrs. Berry represented a new feminine ideal that was gaining general approval. "I admire her greatly. She is so uncommonly sensible and unaffected. Just the sort of woman to succeed in the World. I think gentle, dependent women are 'out of Fashion,' as it were. At least, people, now a days, seem to prefer *strong minded, decided*, sensible women" (Charlotte, 3-5-54).

Charlotte gained further insight into manners of both the east and west coasts at a tea party the three sisters gave late in March. They invited Mrs. Berry and Charles Ladd, scion of an old and aristocratic family from Portsmouth, New Hampshire, whom Charlotte and Lizzie had visited while Charlotte was recuperating from erysipelas. Mr. Ladd turned out to be rather a bore. "He is rather *too* respectable and aristocratic, for he can think or speak of nothing but his possessions, and the antiquity of his family. I don't mean to speak disparagingly of Mr. Ladd, but, merely, to regret the *inevitable* consequence of the *best* and *greatest* Family in a small place" (Charlotte, 4-3-54).

In contrast to the aristocratic Mr. Ladd, Mrs. Berry, the New Woman, was a social lion. Though she missed the tea party because her invitation was mysteriously delayed, her presence at a small party which the three sisters took her to delighted the gathering. "She was very much attended to all the evening, interesting all the quiet, conventional, 'stay at home' people with her accounts of her travels through Mexico and etc. She enjoys the stirring life of California, I suspect, and sighs for it even here. Women, in the present century, write and act like men. They affect masculinity. They must *assert* their rights, and *maintain* them *themselves*. The successful women do it" (Charlotte, 3-5-54). Whether or not she admired the New Woman as wholeheartedly as she affected to, Charlotte made no noticeable effort to fashion her own behavior to fit the new mold. Since Wilson was so taken with her, his daughters were much relieved when Mrs. Berry wrote a favorable account of them to him.

Having lived in the same house with their father, Mrs. Berry knew his little daily habits, and being a woman of insight, she realized that those were the things that his daughters would cherish. "I learned from her much about you. She even told me of the pink and blue coverlid that proved a failure! I never laughed more heartily. How glad I was to hear that you had the surroundings of a gentleman, and were so comfortable" (Lizzie,

3-5-54). Charlotte and her sisters were delighted to hear that he still had a drawer full of toiletries. "She said your washstand drawer was filled with tooth brushes and nice soap. I remember perfectly, when the corner drawer in your bureau at Keene, was filled with nice soap, and tooth brushes, of a 'superior kind.' You also, had a great many bottles of 'Rowland's Kalydor' 'Macassar Oil' and 'Eau Lustrate.' We were comparing notes the other day, and we found that we all suffered in the same way, since you went away. We had never had a good tooth brush since that time" (Charlotte, 2-14-54).

Although Wilson wrote long letters to his children—they often ran to sixteen pages—he did not include many details of his personal habits. Mrs. Berry's accounts of their father focused the details of his intimate life for them, and after three years they once again tried to become a part of it. Since she told them he needed handkerchiefs, Annie searched for some to send him for his birthday but succeeded only in finding red ones with yellow "moons"; then she remembered that he liked blue and brown ones. Charlotte began making a pair of slippers for him, which Annie finished, scrupulously reporting that "Charlotte did most of them and I finished" (Annie, 2-17-54). They sent the slippers by Mrs. Clannon, a former housekeeper of Mrs. Sherwood, who was going to San Francisco to join a sister. Disturbed that Wilson complained of neuralgia in the stomach, Lizzie suggested that he should fly to the woods as soon as possible because he required exercise in the open air, hunting, fishing, and shooting like a "chochtaw Indian" (Lizzie, 3-5-54). She questioned Mrs. Berry about Wilson's burns, acknowledging that Mrs. Berry had taken good care of him.

Since recent visitors from California had reported satisfaction with life there, Annie worried that her father might never want to come home. Completely missing the attraction adventure held for their father, Annie thought California must have the advantages that would please her if Wilson preferred it to the East. Everybody returning from California was "affected with the same fever and now, as a matter of course, we ask if he said it was 'the greatest country in the world, infinitely superior to New York in point of comfort, society, climate, education. In fact every thing" (Annie, 3-5-54). Though Charlotte suspected that Mrs. Berry missed California, Annie reported that she had said of the Wilson daughters, "It's no place for you. It's a hard place to get at, and an expensive place to live comfortably in, and you would not be happy when you got there" (Annie, 3-5-54). No doubt both of those propositions were true.

Although the sisters received their father's western landlady with gracious hospitality and puzzled over her new manner in letters to their father, they continued, as if by contrast, to behave according to the expectations they had inherited and observed in the East. And they continued to write avidly of their traditional manners and commitments.

Taking care of Lizzie's two baby boys proved a demanding task. Their physical needs naturally required much attention, but developing and following a scheme for rearing citizens—male, of course—for the republic was the major task that fell to Lizzie and her sisters. This great undertaking admitted advice from men—fathers or grandfathers—but no real involvement. The three women and various nursemaids bent their energies to taking care of the boys, and Lizzie, with the advice and help of her two sisters, struggled to evolve a theory about child rearing. The arrival of Lizzie's two boys had surprising effects on several lives as the nursery, like the drawing room, attracted some unexpected women and created interesting social dynamics.

Soon after Wil was born, Lizzie hired Margaret, probably one of the thousands of Irish immigrants who landed in New York during the middle of the nineteenth century, to help take care of him. Her first pregnancy and birth dragged Lizzie down, and she never really recovered her strength before she was pregnant again. Samuel's birth only fifteen months after Wilson's seemed, however, to drive away all of the ailments that had plagued Lizzie since the arrival of her first child. Sam was more robust and more precocious in learning the baby skills of turning over and sitting up than Wil had been; Wil tended to be thin and wan. Even so, Samuel, like most second children, could not compete with the perfections of Wil. Lizzie had not written to her father in over two and a half months. In that last letter she had anticipated her second child's birth as one of those "providential things to be regarded with patience and joy." She had also confessed: "I am a constant sufferer and look forward with terror to the struggle that awaits me" (Lizzie, 10-31-53). Child rearing, as Lizzie wrote in the new year, is fraught with unexpected turns, as is life in general.

Deep as they were in domestic affairs, the three women and their friend Charlie March joked about a major scandal involving reparations following the Mexican War that was portentously analogous to the Limantour case in which James Wilson played a role. One stipulation of the treaty of 1848 that ended the war required that Mexico pay the United States $11,000 to reimburse U.S. citizens who had suffered financial losses resulting from the conflict. A commission was established in Washington to distribute the money. Among the chief claimants was Dr. George A. Gardiner. Aided by Edward Curtis, former Whig congressman from New York and envoy to Mexico, and General Waddy Thompson of North Carolina, Gardiner, a longtime resident of Mexico, claimed to have lost a silver mine during the war. Titles were forged, "mines" faked, witnesses assembled, and all was presented to the commission. Gardiner received repayment for the loss of the mine. Part of the money went to Thompson. Curtis may or may not have received part of the ill-gotten gains, but in any case it was he who later suggested to President Fillmore that the claim was false.

* [LIZZIE]   New York Jany 17th 1854

My dear Father,

Your very kind letter of 14th Dec. with its very munificent gift arrived safely. I am more obliged than I can express, for the gift, and hope never again to need it so much or to ask you for anything of the kind. It has more than made me comfortable and I thank you again and again for it.

The "Babies" are both asleep. The new one who rejoices in the very ugly name of Samuel, is a very nice fat homely baby, good and quiet, and named for his Grandpa Sherwood, who is very much pleased with the compliment. He looks like me, having my black hair, high cheek bones and etc. We are very happy in having another perfect little boy, tho' he is not such a *miracle* as Wil. was of course.

We came very near losing our dear little Wilson the other day in a very shocking manner. His nurse had taken him out to walk as she has done every day, nearly, since he was five weeks old, and was knocked down by an omnibus pole and run over, her leg being broken in two places. Imagine my horror when Wil was brought home, screaming, by total strangers! Poor Margaret the nurse was very heroic about it, and threw him out of harm's way, and kept her consciousness thro' the whole. The boy was not hurt in the least, except by fright, and scrambled up on his hands and knees and commenced taking care of himself. Being brought home by strangers however frightened him very much but he has recovered the shock now. The nurse was taken to the hospital where she receives such admirable care that she prefers remaining. She will recover in time. The surgeons think [she will keep] the use of her limb, but cannot move for six weeks. She saw him safe in a woman's arms and made her promise to not leave him until he was safe in his *Mother's* arms. Which promise the woman sacredly fulfilled.

Margaret was a troublesome cross old woman and was to leave in a fortnight, but this accident and the devotion she showed the child has bound us to her very much, and we shall not let her go unrewarded.

Of course it throws us into great confusion, and Annie has to sleep with Wil and take the general charge of him. She has such admirable capacity and such rare devotion to him that I tell her I hate to *change nurses* and wish she would remain in that capacity, but she is rather too much worked down in it as she has been hard at work all winter for me and mine. She is a *first rate girl*. So I sleep with *Samuel* and Annie with *Wil.* and an excellent young woman named Fanny, who has been my chambermaid and waiter helps in the day, and we all work as hard as we can and conclude that however good for the *state* it may be to raise *men*, it is very hard for the immediate friends.

I am in better health than I have been for two years. The birth of this little boy has carried off all the ills caused by the first one and I hope to be strong and hearty once more. . . .

James spent his holidays here. He is really "pitching in" to the Latin and Greek and mathematics. Boston is *the place* for good scholarship. He is quite *vain* of some of his *abstruse* learning and reels off a little occasionally for the benefit of family members. He is a fine gentlemanly unaffected fellow and we are highly pleased with him, and he was *particularly* pleased with the *slug* and the inscription on the back. He turned to me and said, "Now Father likes me, don't he?" I told him I thought you did rather.

Charlotte is quite magnificent and getting quite ambitious. She has got over that suffusion of blood to the head and face, and is developing more and more a talent for society. I suspect she will cut us all out. She is very ambitious to play superbly and has a good foundation for that elegant accomplishment. She too is very devoted to dear Wil. I laughed very much at her writing to you that I did not govern him, while she spoils him to the top of his beat. I gave him a spanking the other day and intend to be a model Mamma.

I am very glad you intend to settle the house at Keene on the children, as in the dire calamity of your decease, or mine, which if not so great a loss would still deprive them of a faithful friend, they would have some certainty. The awful uncertainty of human life presses on me since I have been so ill, and I am glad of any arrangement by which these dear ones may have a home. I do not think you will ever find an *inhospitable reception* there from you *children*, who live for you and love you more and more. If quite as convenient for you I could have Mr. Chamberlain do the business, as John has not much knowledge of how matters stand at Keene and I am anxious he should not be mixed up, if there is any danger that any one should be angry or say anything to your disadvantage. Still you are the best judge. Uncle Robert is very kind and truly attached to us I think, but you know how tempestuous he is and he's apt to say disagreeable things. It has really worn on Annie's health very much. Annie says she shall never be married since she has seen how much trouble I have had, so I suppose we need not trouble ourselves about Mr. Cram. Young ladies are apt to be so *much* in earnest in these things. Mr. Cram is very attentive and matters remain *in status quo*.

Mr. Edward Curtis has gone mad and is in the insane hospital. He wants to give away all his property. Is it uncharitable to suppose that there is a sting of awakened conscience in this.

John remains well and as good as ever. He says he is entirely shut out from his family as all the females are occupied in taking care of babies. I have not had time to read the Limantour pamphlet except the statement at the end, but am entirely satisfied with that. Mr. Sherwood senior has read it and is very much convinced by it. Believe me dear Father, with constant affection your daughter   M.E.W. Sherwood

Raising men for the republic was after all the closest women got to political power. Lizzie took these responsibilities very seriously, especially after the accident, when she did not allow Wilson to go out even for a short walk with the nurse unless she was along. Charlotte observed that Lizzie was exhausted, and she was looking forward to the summer in Keene, when the new mother could regain her strength. She felt that such intensive care was bad for the children as well as for Lizzie; she also feared that Lizzie, unlike their own mother, was overprotective and indulgent with her children. The young aunt approved of whippings and was glad that her mother approved of them, too, though she was convinced that she would be a better person had she been punished more, her father having whipped her only twice. She thought Lizzie did not discipline her children enough. Although the aunts apparently had license to administer the discipline neglected by the mother, she herself felt like a "guilty brute" when she administered corporal punishment to eighteen-month-old Wil.

While General Wilson evidently admonished his eldest daughter about indulging his grandchildren, he indulged young Wilson with a bank account. Lizzie soon defended her child-rearing practices and in doing so wrote a long and engrossing letter about many facets of indulgence and self-control. Appropriately, it was under this rubric that Lizzie made her final observations on the fate of Dr. Gardiner. The Gardiner case was aired first in the House of Representatives and then was tried in court. On March 5 or 6, 1854, Gardiner was sentenced to ten years of hard labor. On the way to jail, he managed to avoid this fate by poisoning himself (*New York Times*, March 7, 1854).

✳ [LIZZIE]   New York, March 5th 1854

My dear Father,
    I have taken time from the very engrossing occupations of the nursery, to write you a few words, altho' I cannot speak very largely of what is going on around here for I seldom leave my post, and *then* accompany my nurse and Wilson for a short walk, only, for since the very narrow escape of that dear little boy will not allow him to go out alone. I am sorry to say I am an over anxious mother and eat, drink, sleep, and live in my nursery. I feel

constantly that no one can do justice to these charming promising boys but myself. They have the splendid inheritance of masculinity, and I wish them to make the most of it. If their Mother's strict attention can give them good constitutions, good hearts, good principles and good thoughts, they will have all these. But God only knows. I only know I cannot stay away from them. I am provoked that the girls should have written you that I did not govern them. Wil. was very nervous and ill from his teeth and I then *would not* punish him, but I hope I am not such a fool as to let him grow up the slave of his own passions. No, I shall punish him and *govern* him or I am very much feebler than I believe myself to be. That I shall ever have the exceeding authority over my children that you had I doubt, for I think *that* is something uncommon, but I shall *prayerfully* try to make my boy learn the necessity of obedience and reverence, for after all what are we thro' Life, but the children of a High and Mighty Father whom we should implicitly obey and revere.

You mention in one of your letters that you suspect you look like Thackeray. There never was a greater mistake. He isn't half so good looking a man. His nose is all over his face, splashed, as it were, like a mud pie that had been thrown at him. He is tall and burly. So far very good, but not good looking. Then you say you resemble Dick Steele. There never was a greater mistake. He is an arrant liar. A dirty drunken loose out-at-elbows chap is not a fitting prototype of my brave and honorable and respectable Father. But Mr. Thackeray is hitting you off in a character that he is just writing about Col. Newcomb, a brave officer who comes home from India and who loves his only son, as you love yours. We will send you it, when it is complete. Or you will find it in Harper's Magazine which I suppose finds its way to California.

. . . I questioned Mrs. Berry much and closely about your health, your burns and etc. She seems to have taken much care of you. How much you have suffered. I have known it and felt it, all the time. How strange that you and I, who supported each other in many trying scenes, who are more alike and more sympathetic than any two people in the world should have been separated during the hardest years of our lives. Perhaps it is best. We should have exaggerated each other's pains. But Heaven only knows how I have missed you. I have nothing but praise, unqualified, to give my husband. I love and know him inexpressibly and he has done all that suggested itself to him to make me comfortable. He is irreproachable, but I have had mortification jealousy "privy conspiracy" and scorn to bear from some of my *dear relatives*. As *your daughter* I was never snubbed, never plotted against, never an object of dislike. Perhaps my position as a young Lady, so successful, so brilliant as it was, unfitted me for what I have come into and would have made any sphere but a brilliant one unhappy. Be that as it may, I have been *put down*, made to feel my *want of money*. Determined they have seemed to make me feel that I need not consider myself *anybody*. I have lived it down somewhat. I have submitted patiently. I don't believe any one knows how or when the arrows hit. I am afraid the scars will always remain, but I pray God to forgive any wrong feeling. I have gone shabbily dressed. I have lived in obscurity. I have borne ill health. I have drunk the bitter cup that has been given me to drink. "But it is always the darkest the hour before day." Since the birth of my last child I feel renewed health and strength of heart to fight the Battle of Life. My only remaining ambition is to do my duty. To make my dear and excellent young husband happy. To raise the boys and to see my own family successful. We *stand together* I assure you, a solid phalanx that is "hard to beat."

"Samuel" was christened on March 2d seventeen days before his Grandfather Wilson will be Fifty seven. His Grandpa Sherwood is 73 and as hale and hearty as possible. He (Samuel) is very large and well formed, *not classically beautiful* but a very fine lump of a baby. Wilson is too fine, too precocious. I fear me much that he is not for this world. He is like those dear little Keene boys too much, but I will enjoy him while I may and thank God for him while he lasts.

. . . John brought me home a very pretty note from Mr. Elijah F. Purdy the other day and a Bank Book for Wilson. I cannot attempt to thank you for all these kindnesses. John had unbeknown to me added enough money to what the *gold* would have come to make $200. and put it in the Delhi Bank which pays nine per cent. So he is going to put Wil's *interest* into the "Sixpenny Savings Bank" and he will thus make money fast.

I must tell you *again* how exceedingly comfortable your present of money made us. I thank you again and again.

As for the Keene business I hope all past debts will be paid and the house secured free of Uncle Robert or any body else to us. For even then should you not wish to live there when you return the children can dispose of it for something and it is a dependance. It galled me so when Roxana was here to have her as she continually delights to do, say what Uncle Robert said we had "got" to do about the place, and what he should cause to be done. I dislike to be a tenant on sufferance or have my brother and sisters. The first money you can spare I pray you effect that discharge you spoke of. Pay old mean Roxana, and let us be free of her patronizing airs forever. She is faithful and attached but plebeian and ignorant. She should be *our* servant, not we her's.

You will see by the papers that that poor little fool Dr. Gardiner has poisoned himself. I hope Waddy Thompson and Lally will be brought to justice. Waddy got *$120,000*. out of that matter and Lally $60,000! Now we are peculated from *all* the time.

I hope your affairs will allow of your coming home sooner than you anticipate after all. I can't help hoping it. I wouldn't have you lose a fortune by it but I would have you try and come. I am sure dear Jamie will love his handsome watch much better if you hear it sometime. Jamie says he ought to know "what's o'clock, for you always promised him your watch, and I gave him *mine*. Which Chardie will take, Annie having a very pretty one Clement March gave her. You ask for a description of Jamie. If a fond sister's pen is to be trusted I shall write you that he is the most charming *boy-man* that I ever saw. He has the dignity of five and thirty, the simplicity of ten. He is very fully developed having very large legs, and arms. He is I should say five feet ten, judging from his superior height to mine. Very long waisted and he cannot be ungraceful if he *tries*. He has fine eyes and uncommonly fine hair which he says he "gets out, with the legs of a chair." It is dark brown and slightly curly. His complexion is ruddy, a trifle freckled under the eyes. His teeth are not as good as yours, more like mine. His feet are very small and I am *afraid* he squeezes them, but as this is a point on which youth is very touchy I don't attempt any further to save him from impending corns. He has a *nascent* moustache, which we laugh at and he says he is afraid to have it shaved for fear of "*taking a severe cold.*" He is very funny, has the simplicity and honesty of a boy and the intelligence and grace of a man. He is so well framed that he never feels badly about his hands and etc and does not seem even to be embarrassed. In short James is a *success*. Whether he will do well in Life I cannot tell. He is *not* communicative nor open in his confidences, but I have *no doubt* he will enter college this coming summer with honor. His ambition is aroused.

How uncommonly well you write! I am so ashamed of my hand writing that I have great mind not to write any more. I write badly. Annie writes worse and Charlotte *worser* still. When I see *sixteen pages* so well written as yours are, I tremble for the answers. You need not be afraid we don't read your letters and like them.

Do not write any answers or questions to my *complaints*. They are between us. It cannot be wrong to confide in one's Father, and a better feeling begins to dawn.

God send you health and prosperity and a speedy return to us.

Believe me ever my dear Father

Affectionately and devotedly yours   M.E.W. Sherwood

To help them with the children after Margaret's accident, Lizzie asked Roxana to come to New York—quite an adventure for an elderly servant from northern New England. Roxana sometimes went as far as Hartford, Connecticut, to visit friends or family or to help the Wilsons as she had during Charlotte's and Lizzie's bouts with the measles in the Christmas of 1851, but she had never ventured as far as New York. And Hartford, with a population of seventeen thousand, was a far cry from New York, with a population of half a million people.

The sight of Roxana in New York at first disconcerted Annie and Charlotte more than the sight of New York disconcerted Roxana. "It seems perfectly impossible that our old Roxana Smith should be here, in this whirlpool. She does not seem as much bewildered as one would suppose she would be. . . . She seems a perfect 'anachronism,' with respect to *place* more than *time*, however" (Charlotte, 2-14-54). However, once Roxana had time to see the city, she too was thoroughly amazed and Charlotte later observed: "I suppose, if her horoscope had been cast in her infancy, and it had been predicted she would come to New York in her lifetime, it would have been considered an immensely extravagant idea, and quite impracticable. I took her to walk in the Fifth Ave. yesterday. She was perfectly bewildered with the magnificence of the houses" (Charlotte, 2-19-54).

But the job of taking care of a house and children, whether in Keene or New York, is always familiar. Houses have to be swept and dusted. Clothes have to be laundered. Meals have to be prepared. Babies have to be diapered and fed and comforted. Within the confines of the house, Roxana soon felt at ease. She took care of Lizzie's babies and was as much at home in Lizzie's house as she was in the cellar kitchen at Keene. The people, after all, were the same. As Roxana told Annie, "where is my home except where *you* are" (Annie, 2-17-54). In spite of the attachment between Roxana and the three sisters, she also brought all of the old tensions from Keene with her to New York.

In the quiet winter of 1854, while Charlotte played the piano and Lizzie nursed her babies, Annie fell in love. After her brief engagement to Robert Sherwood, whom no one but Annie much liked, she weighed the strengths and weaknesses of Mr. Clarence Cram as a husband and even sought advice before committing herself to this suitor. As Lizzie had mentioned earlier, Clarence, son of millionaire brewer Jacob Cram, was not unknown to the family. Writing in the midst of a snowstorm, Annie introduced her father to Clarence Cram and to her feelings toward this young man of uncommon talent and education.

"The case is this. I have known Mr. Cram for three years and more, ever since I was in Washington and for two years have known any time that I could have married him if I chose. I never did think of it at all until last winter when he used to come here a good deal and I saw that he was a young man of uncommon talent and education. He has had the misfortune to be the son of a very rich Father who has indulged him most absurdly and given him no business and no business habits. Still he is I think unspoiled and is only twenty three not too old to begin and is heartily sick of his idle life. I like him more than any of the men about me and think he will make something more worth having. I think he already *is* worth having, but I will not engage myself to any man who has no profession or business if he has a million of dollars.

"Consequently *I am not* engaged to him. His fond old foolish Father has a weak satisfaction in having his son a gentleman (i.e. an idler,) and refuses to establish him in business and Clarence Cram determines if his father continues of the same line to study law, which is a discouraging prospect for him. As long as he chooses to live at home he will have every luxury of life and his Father will continue to indulge him, and if he goes to work at the tedious business of studying law, it will be for me and not for himself alone, which is precisely what his older brother did when about to marry a daughter of John Sargent of Philadelphia, and Henry Cram the elder brother is one of the most brilliant young lawyers at the N. Y. bar as John Sherwood says. This is the precise state of the case. What will come of it I don't know, but be assured my dear Father that my eyes are open and I shall do nothing hastily or unadvisedly. I am in no sort of hurry to be married and shall not do it until I am sure of being much happier than I am now. You may be interested to know that my friend old Mr. Sherwood strongly approves of the connection and for a year has been constantly telling me that few girls would let slip so advantageous an offer still I shall wait till I am satisfied. Perhaps till you come and see for yrself, or rather see for *me*. (Annie, 1-11-54)

To Lizzie, Annie confided that she would never be married because she had seen how much trouble Lizzie had had, presumably referring to her ill health after young Wilson's birth. Nonetheless, she was spending increasing amounts of time with Mr. Cram. Lizzie had reservations but commented approvingly: "If he [Cram] wants spirit and energy his wife will have enough for forty, and he is desperately, dreadfully, fearfully in love. He isn't so good, so unexceptionable a match as John Sherwood and I don't know where such an one is to be found. Perhaps I may be a prejudiced judge, but I think my husband (as John Van Buren said to the Queen, about the lakes and rivers in America) 'hard to beat'" (Lizzie, 6-4-54). Still, she saw advantages in Cram. "I am inclined to believe in Mr. Cram, more and more, as I see Annie place so much confidence in him, tho' his want of a profession did trouble me. He will have a great deal of money, and he is a gentleman" (Lizzie, 6-4-54).

As the spring approached, the daughters could not bend their minds too strenuously to Wilson's struggles in California because they were much involved in Clarence Cram's pursuit of Annie. For several months after she first mentioned it to her father, the courtship remained in limbo. With all the ardor of the young lover, Clarence continued his two-year siege for Annie's hand. Annie was not unwilling, but she needed convincing that her fiancé was a man of business, not a playboy. Five months after she first mentioned her suitor, Clarence met all of her requirements, and she said yes. The twenty-two-year-old Annie announced her engagement in a long and initially circuitous letter to her father.

✳ [ANNIE]   New York May 4th 1854

My dear Father,
   Your letters of the 6th of March and the life like stereoscopic daguerreotype arrived quite safely. We rejoice to hear such good accounts and to see the same.
   . . . We are all well here and the children grow finely. Jamie has not been well at all for the last month. He suffers very much from violent headaches and is at times entirely unable to study. I am going to Boston on my way home on Thursday next and if he is not well enough to study, shall take him home and try to cure him. I have written to Dr. Bowditch about him and Jamie has been to see him. He prescribed light diet, and hard out of door exercise. Jamie is too full of blood to endure confinement. I am earnestly in hopes that he will be able after a little recreation to begin again. He is determined to himself.
   I have not received a word from Mr. Skinner yet. I got a letter from Uncle Robert today in which he says, "Mr. Skinner has been here and I had a talk with him. It is necessary that all shd. be kept quiet as yet. There has been a man here to look at the place. He desires to buy for himself. I have put him off in the hope that yr Father would be able to do something this Spring. I judge from yr letter that Skinner is the man. You had better be hiring soon. The yard looks finely, and Roxana has the house in apple pie order. I will have the painting done as you desire." That's all. He seems to write in a kind spirit enough, and expects us soon. I shall go to Boston next Thursday the 11th and shall see Mr. Skinner.
   I am engaged to Clarence Cram and under all the circumstances I thought it best to acknowledge it, for people had talked about it and prophesied long enough, and situated as I am, I preferred to have it all fair and open. He is at present at work for his Father the management of whose real estate in this city is no small matter, since it is worth from six to eight hundred thousand dollars. He has kept a species of agent and clerk for years. He has dismissed him, and gives Clarence his work, and his pay. Mr. Cram is very old and his mind is very much impaired. His son therefore has a very responsible position as you will see, and the confidence of

his brother who is a distinguished man here and his married sisters, which is no slight matter. His brother advises Clarence to come into his office and study law, but I discourage it, as his present position with his Father gives him experience and knowledge which will fit him for the business of a broker or some thing of that kind sooner. His Father too, wishes him to join a friend of his now in business and he will possibly do that. At any rate he is not idle now, nor will he be. As to his fortune, he will have it before long unquestionably, for his Father can never make another will if he would. More than all the rest, the family wished him to marry me, and I thought it would advance both his interests and mine to acknowledge our engagement, and it made my position satisfactory. I felt the necessity too of looking about me now that I have the chances. I have not acted rashly or thoughtlessly, and I hope you will be satisfied with me. I have certainly done my best. John Sherwood I don't think likes Clarence Cram much. He is too independent. John is very lovely, and as pure and upright a man as ever lived, but a man of singular obstinacy and prejudices, and very fond of his own kind, of his kith and kin. I have no reason to say so, but I don't think he thinks Clarence good enough for me. He thinks nobody good enough for *his* sisters. Old Mr. S. likes him very much and has always encouraged the suit. You will judge for yrself. I shall probably not be married till you return. I am in no hurry. Clarence will write you himself, by the next mail if not by this. Don't write him till you hear from him. He has more talent and brilliancy than all the Sherwoods that ever were born. And now that's enough.

Mrs Berry is very well. I saw her day before yesterday. I hear no news from any where.

Do take good care of yr precious health and hurry to come home. Wil calls yr picture "Umpapa" and calls the glasses to look through "eyes." He calls Chardie and I by our names, and not "Aunt" at all. They are splendid children. Write as usual, and believe that I am always most fondly and dutifully yr child   Annie F. Wilson

When I quote from Uncle R.'s letter "Mr. Skinner is the man" I don't mean, "the man who wanted to buy the house," but the man through whom "your Father would do something." By referring to my letter you will understand.

Charlotte wrote you something about a fancy ball to which we went. Lest you misunderstood her I wanted to tell you that it was a private fancy dress ball *not* a masked ball at a private house, and enclosed, is one of the cards of invitation. If you will look in the January "Putnam," you will see a picture of the house. It is on the corner of the Fifth dr. and 37th St. I think its the January number at any rate. It is the one which has all the gentlemen's houses in it. Did I not send it to you?

Clarence's mother, Mrs. Cram, "a very candid, plain spoken old Lady" (Charlotte, 5-54), came to New York to see Annie and made a very favorable impression on them all. They all trusted and liked her at once; and Mr. Cram, a New Hampshire man who knew the Wilsons, heartily approved of the marriage as well. Unlike Lizzie's engagement to John Sherwood, which was fraught with family obstacles, Annie's engagement seemed headed for plain sailing.

"Annie," Charlotte wrote, "is in excellent spirits. Very happy in her engagement" (Charlotte, 5-54). Reviewing the winter season, Annie affirmed that it had been "in many respects the happiest winter of my life." Certainly, Clarence Cram's courtship and her engagement were responsible for much of her happiness. Though Cram did not write immediately to General Wilson to ask officially for Annie's hand, Annie assured her father that he was only waiting to "offer you something advantageous." Perhaps the wealthy Crams, who approved of Annie, would be willing to improve the Wilsons' family coffers, as the Sherwoods had not. Annie was delighted with Wilson's reception of the news. "How can I thank you dear Father for yr kind and handsome reception of the announcement of my engagement. I *do* thank you dear Sir, from my heart. You will have received a letter from Clarence by this time. I hope you will like him half as much as I do" (Annie, 7-2-54).

"Despite Our Doleful Letters"

Outside Lizzie's nursery and parlor a thousand things caught the attention of the Wilsons during their stay in New York in the winter and early spring of 1854. Annie and Charlotte sometimes wrote about political questions such as slavery or about legal and economic questions such as ownership of property or the Limantour case, and sometimes they struggled with the underlying justice and morality involved. They often asked questions and spoke their opinions diffidently, however, as ladies would who knew nothing about such affairs. On religious and educational matters, they felt on safer ground, thus they held strong opinions on churches and schools. They judged and criticized these institutions without apology, from their private experience and from a public perspective. They also explored with some thoroughness such questions as "What does Jamie need to learn to be what we want him to be?" "Where can he best learn it?" "How well is Mr. Brownell fitting Jamie for Harvard?" and "How well does Harvard fit its students for success in America?"

Their church continued to be a comforting institution for the Wilsons and one whose intellectual stature had a strong effect on their thinking. Writing frequently on Sunday, they reported church attendance to their father and kept him posted on pulpit changes in Keene and New York. Charlotte often wrote of her religious insights and struggled to differentiate duty from natural piety. Keene's small Unitarian congregation succeeded in attracting pastors of stature, providing the Wilson sisters with the opportunity to become acquainted with some of the best teachers and preachers the denomination had to offer. From these pastors the sisters heard stirring new ideas and a heavy dose of abolitionist sentiment.

Annie boldly advocated the values and strengths of Unitarianism, gaining strength herself from her association with it and her defense of it. These passionate feelings spill out because of another issue linked to the church: concern about education, especially for Jamie but also for the young republic, which needed educated men. All of these issues were bound up in the establishment and development of Unitarian and Episcopal colleges. Annie was outraged when Columbia, an Episcopal school chartered by King George but ostensibly free of religious tenets, refused to hire a promising young chemistry professor because he was a Unitarian. Just as Charlotte was sustained by her Unitarian mentors, the Bowditches and the Livermores, Annie too sought advice from like-minded family friends nearby to test ideas she might otherwise have expected a parent to illuminate. In this case it was the Sherwoods' relative, Samuel Ruggles, who informed and affected Annie's thinking. Ruggles had been so offended by the controversy that he had published a pamphlet, titled *The Duty of Columbia College to the Community* (1854), deploring the closed-mindedness of the institution. Religious discrimination, however, was only one issue that Annie saw in this affair. At the heart of the matter was the conflict, widely argued in the nineteenth century, between science and religion.

✳ [ANNIE]   New York February 5th 1854

My dear Father

I have just come from our beloved Mr. Bellows' church as "choke" full of Unitarianism as I can well "hold," and feel as if I must write a sermon instead of a letter. We (Unitarians) are quite up in arms in consequence of an indignity received from Columbia college a few weeks since, and I can write of nothing else. If you want to know news read Charlotte's letter first, and let her tell you. That Columbia college is the institution of this city as you already know, an episcopal college, tho the charter from King George expressly stipulates that any particular religious tenet shall never be allowed to rule supreme to the exclusion of any or all others. In fact that the religious opinion of any man whether teacher or pupil shall never be questioned. In spite of and in the face of all this, the college has always been episcopalian. No man's religious opinion has been questioned because no other than "Churchmen" have come in. Now the college is a poor inactive unknown dying affair, and some of the growing and grown men in this city are disturbed to see Harvard stride along and leave *all* the other colleges behind it, (what is the reason by the way?) and propose new professorships and so infuse a little life into the dormant body. They are enormously rich, and want only new men, so among others is proposed as Professor of *Chemistry* (not theology) Mr. Gibbs of this city the finest young chemist in the country. In fact the only man. People are delighted. Science will look up, and Columbia college shall show the world that an episcopal college can compete with the Unitarian college when lo! a meeting is called by the "Bishop, and other clergy" and they whisper, and look, and nudge each other's elbows, and Mr. Gibbs is *rejected because he is a Uni-*

tarian. 1854 too. Bishop, a wise and wary man did not want to have it go abroad that *that* was the reason, knowing that public opinion would decide, and so proposed that they should *pretend* that it was for some other cause. Ah! the morality of the Scribes and Pharisees! But it would not do. There *was* no other cause, and we know it, and the public know it, and they have done us the greatest service they could do for people begin to say what is this doctrine so dangerous to be feared, and that's all we want and people to begin to see that the educated men in the country are Unitarians, and the men of science are Unitarians and the greatest college in the land is Unitarian, and say why is Trinity college at Hartford obscure and of no account, and why is Columbia college dying and dead and why have we not *our* great men of science, and then comes their answer because "*the church is opposed* to the progress of science, and *always has been,* for men will learn and *will* inquire and [word missing] to that faith which will not survive much study of Knowledge of God's *works* as well as God's word. Now we have an Institution in Ohio—Antioch college—a college which will influence the whole West. Horace Mann is the President. The Professors are mostly Unitarian. It is our college tho' of course no other denomination is *at all* excluded. A *free* college to be supported by *our* churches. At present it is very poor and cramped. The applications for admission are *five* hundred at present, and they can take only *two* hundred. The opening for the spread of liberal christianity through the whole West is enormous. The Boston churchs propose to raise $75000 (seventy five thousand dollars) and our five churches here and in Brooklyn $25000 (twenty five thousand) as a fund for that college. Now is not Mr. Gray's society in San Francisco able to do something in this cause. Can you not put it before him and let him propose it to his people. Let him tell them our position here and see the necessity of strenuous effort in support of our beloved faith. There, I feel relieved. . . . I am ashamed to send you so much paper and hope you will excuse my Unitarian fanaticism.

Take care of yr precious health and hurry to come home. Always believe me yr truly loving daughter.   Annie F. Wilson

Politics, too—in fact, public events of all sorts—occupied the writers' thoughts. Franklin Pierce, the New Hampshire Democrat who had become president, promised to compromise away the deep divisions between North and South that ultimately led to the Civil War. The Nebraska Bill—officially, the Kansas-Nebraska Act—was the latest in the series of those compromises strongly supported by President Pierce. However, Democrat Pierce, who had recently said that New Hampshire had "gone to ———— [hell]," and General Wilson were on opposite sides of the political fence.

Though people talked much about the Nebraska Bill, which once again aimed to head off a confrontation between North and South, Annie and even Charlotte had lost interest in the slavery question. Although Lizzie declared that *"we care nothing for N. H. politics,"* she went on to observe "great triumph of Know nothing-ism" in the state, and "our friend John P.[arker] Hale is right-side-up for Senator." Hale was one of the first abolitionists elected to the Senate and afterward ran for president on the Liberty ticket, an antislavery party. Once a political ally of Franklin Pierce, one of Wilson's arch political opponents, Hale had abandoned the Democrats to take a vocal stand against slavery.

In contrast, the growing conflict between North and South raised Lizzie's hackles, and ten years before the Civil War she passionately took her stand against the South, the place she had found so entertaining five years before, when she was in Washington. "We are all excited about the slave case in Boston where 'Burns' has created such a fever, and the Nebraska bill has stirred up the North, I hope to some purpose, but the miserable doughface spirit has such possession of the North that I fear it will never rise. I hate the south so I can scarcely breathe a *south wind*. I am not at all sympathized with here, for my friends here are all very conservative and order-loving people, and rejoice in the triumph of Law" (Lizzie, 6-4-54).

The burning of the clipper ship *Great Republic* caused much excitement. Jamie sent his father detailed accounts of the burning of this four-thousand-ton, four-masted ship, the largest merchant vessel in the world. He had watched the immense clipper, designed for speed, being launched in Boston before it sailed to New York to pick up a cargo for Liverpool. There Jamie watched as it "burned to the water's edge, . . . the most mournful sight I ever saw. . . . She was as sharp as a knife, and cost over $300,000" (Jamie, 1-4-54).

In January the wreck of the steamship *San Francisco* on its way to California caused general consternation. The papers reported all of the details of the drowning of two hundred people and of the disease, starvation, and fire that threatened the six hundred survivors, reawakening all of the fear the three women felt for their father's welfare during his trip west.

The city of New York flourished. Central Park was being laid out, and the Hippodrome was opened, "where 'Franconi' will have '*Grand Dramatic and Equestian Entertainments.*' It is built of brick and is round, with two little towers on it. . . . It is very much like the old Roman Circus Maximus" (Jamie, 4-54).

At the same time, Barnum's octagonal Crystal Palace—363 square feet—was being built near the Croton Reservoir. When it was finished in May, they all went to it. Charlotte, who scorned P. T. Barnum, betrayed her insecurity about American culture. "Last night we all went to Barnum's

Crystal Palace. It has become quite national, as every thing American does. Its avowed object now is to bring money to its owners. It has become a *vulgar humbug*, and will doubtless succeed. It was originally a very splendid thing, but nearly all the fine statuary and valuable *foreign* things have been removed" (Charlotte, 5-5-54).

In California, like a magician producing rabbits from a hat, José Limantour produced new documents from Mexico to validate his claims to property in San Francisco. Meantime, one of Limantour's agents wrote to another, "Surely dear P. Limantour is considered here like a little boy, and known to be a very bad bed-fellow" and he advised, "Try to humbug Wilson and Chittenden, Dillon and Co., telling them that to do good business the documents are very precious" (Johnson, *José Yves Limantour*, 38).

With each new document his case looked better, and collecting quitclaims became easier. At 10 percent of the assessed value, Wilson finally collected what has been estimated at between $200,000 and $250,000 for Limantour. Wilson, who felt confident about the case at this time, also wrote pamphlets about the case to sway public opinion. He sent copies to his daughters to keep them abreast of what he was doing, and he also sought the opinions of John Sherwood and John Sherwood, Sr.

Unlike Lizzie, Annie read her father's pamphlets with interest and declared, "John and I read the Pamphlets and made up our minds that you must succeed. At any rate yr concluding sentence seems to suggest *you* are firmly convinced of the strength of yr position. John says, 'Your Father is in earnest, isn't he?' I told him you were in the habit of being in earnest when you got started. The evidence is very strong and clear. Old Mr. Sherwood (a cautious old lawyer) had it, and said at once, 'the Genl. is right'" (Annie, 1-11-54).

By the next mail they received more encouraging news about the case, including the hint that it might even bring Wilson to Washington. Responding to that possibility, Charlotte wrote: "We are all rejoiced at your success in your legal labors. *I* think you ought to have all your cases decided in your favor. Particularly the Limantour case. Every one, of any legal ability, who has any knowledge of the case, considers it a perfectly plain and indisputable claim. I don't know any thing about it, I regret to say, for my mind seems almost incapable to comprehend any legal matter. But with all my heart I hope *your* wishes with regard to it will be gratified" (Charlotte, 2-14-54).

Charlotte was much more interested in the strangeness of life in California and the changes it may have wrought in her father than in the Limantour case. She wondered whether her father wouldn't find Keene rather "stupid" when he came home "to live with [her]" after his California experience (Charlotte, 4-18-54). She was puzzled, amused, and scared by the stories she heard about life in San Francisco. "Nothing amuses me so much as the price of eatables there. Turkeys at Thanksgiving or Christmas would be nice things to invest a small fortune in. Mrs. Berry said one gentleman paid twenty five dollars for one turkey. Why one could buy a beautiful set of lace, for that sum, which would last years" (Charlotte, 4-18-54). She also perceived that success in California required a certain recklessness. The daughters learned more about life in California through Mrs. Berry perhaps than through their father's letters, and it did not appeal to them.

In May the daughters, who had not seen their father in three and a half years, were delighted with a daguerreotype of him. They scrutinized it to discover what changes his experience in California have wrought. "There is a look about the right side of your face, (left, as you look at the picture) that seems to me a little unnatural, as if the skin was drawn tighter than it used to be, drawing up the corner of yr mouth a little. Is it the effect of the burn, or a fault of the light and shadow in the picture? Altogether it pleases me tho'. The lines are a little deepened round yr cheeks, and in yr forehead. I am delighted to have it, and thank you for it heartily" (Annie, 5-4-54). "Your hair has lost none of its beauty has it? I wanted to see your *teeth* but of course that was out of the question. I should love to see you laugh and talk, and have you kiss me and be kind to me in the old way" (Charlotte, 5-5-54).

In May also, the threat of foreclosure on their house was lifted, and like migratory birds Annie and Charlotte left New York and the excitement of the Crystal Palace, Central Park, and Clarence Cram to spend the summer in New Hampshire. Annie stopped off in Boston to check on Jamie, who had been complaining of debilitating headaches. She found him sicker than she had expected. Dr. Bowditch recommended a "rough and tumble round Cape Horn," "an entire change of scene and life," which could only mean that Jamie should join his father in California. The advice, perhaps based on Richard Henry Dana's 1840 account in *Two Years Before the Mast* of leaving Harvard to sail around Cape Horn and recover his health, grew out of the assumption that hard work and sea air cured myriad illnesses. Nothing could provide them like working as a sailor on the brutal trip around the tip of South America. Jamie himself thought it a good idea (Jamie, 8-54). Annie did not think that would be necessary. Though she dreaded to take the responsibility, she proposed to take him back with her to Keene and to oversee a violent course of outdoor exercise and horseback riding that would restore his health. Dr. Bowditch consulted another physician, Dr. Jackson, and Mr. Bradford, Jamie's teacher; all agreed this would be a good plan. Jamie's teacher reported that he was a good, attractive, and bright student who was so near ready for college that he could finish preparing himself and join the class in September. Annie planned to get Mr. Torrance or Mr. White in Keene to hear Jamie recite.

During James Wilson's three-year absence, his daughters and their lives had been transformed. Annie and Charlotte had grown up. Among other things their yearly routine included a regular social season in New York rather than in Washington, where Wilson's political cronies spent their winters. Though Wilson knew the Sherwoods and probably the Cram family—Lizzie had visited them in Hartford shortly after Wilson left—in New York and Boston the three women had made a whole new circle of friends whom their father did not know. Among the people they had grown intimate with in Boston was the family of Nathan Hale, the famous American patriot. When they picked up Jamie, they stayed for a few days with these new friends and invited the bright, cultivated, and agreeable family to come to Keene in the summer. Susie Hale, a great friend of Charlotte, promised to come for much of the month of August.

On the May 15, Annie, Charlotte, and Jamie settled in their house on the corner of Main and Emerald, where Lizzie and her two children would join them when the weather got too hot in New York. Here they were surrounded by people who identified the family with the father. "All the old farmers that I meet in the street, always speak to me and ask after the 'General,' want to know if he is ever coming home to live, and end by saying that they had rather see him than any other man in the world" (Jamie, 6-3-54). When people asked Annie when her father would return, she replied flippantly, "I don't know—perhaps on the next Steamer" (Annie, 5-17-54). Her engagement may have made her more relaxed about her father's return, for only two months earlier Annie was much provoked when Mr. Winslow Pierce suggested that Wilson would never come home to live because he preferred California. "I was quite angry when I heard of it. I always say to people, 'Come home to live? Of course he will'" (Annie, 3-5-54).

Though Wilson had not in the end decided to make the house over to them, Mr. Skinner had "adjusted" the business by buying the house for $7,000. Just what scheme he and James Wilson contrived no one knew, but Uncle Robert, who had received an offer of $9,000, settled with Mr. Skinner for $7,000, and Skinner took over the title but not possession of the house. Though it annoyed Annie that people in town constantly greeted her with "your house is sold," Annie, Charlotte, and Jamie were relieved to have their home to live in.

In any case they were happy to have Mr. Skinner in charge of Wilson's affairs and to have the house once again in their possession. Annie began redecorating. She wanted to have the whole house redone but started by having the best parlor repainted and papered. Spring, with the help of gardener James Wright, redecorated their gardens and newly planted orchard. "Our grounds look gloriously. The fence, between garden and yard, has been removed. . . . Keene is as green as it ever was in Spring. That is saying a great deal. We are glad to be home, and truly grateful for our pleasant prospects this Summer, as well as our present comforts" (Charlotte, 5-54). Annie rejoiced in the "profusion of the most superb and large rich wild strawberries," recalling that her father was as fond of them as she was. From her window she could see their young orchard and West Mountain and the meadows between, a picture she would like to send to her father. A family of robins—perhaps "his" robins that had appeared last year—had returned to a large nest in the grapevine. There were only two little worms in this Eden. First, Uncle Robert had torn down a brick wall on the northern boundary, ostensibly under orders from the selectman, who wanted to widen the street by fifty feet. The second was a small brick house, which a blacksmith built nearly in front of their house, blocking their view down the street.

The house was soon overflowing with visitors. Jamie had school friends to visit; Charlotte had one or another of her friends. Clarence Cram came and spent a week early in June. While he was there, Mr. and Mrs. Wheeler came to look him over, and Mr. and Mrs. Hale came to Keene to attend a fair organized to raise money for a new organ for the Unitarian Church. They all expressed their approval of Annie's choice.

Never to be long out of the limelight, Mrs. Berry wasted no time in engaging herself to a Dr. Morrison, of whom her friends heartily approved. In New York, while Lizzie was confined to her room with a sprained foot, the irrepressible Mrs. Berry insisted that Dr. Morrison be allowed to visit her. Making an exception for Mrs. Berry, proper Lizzie allowed him to come upstairs, since "doctors frequently *went into bedrooms*," and while they were there, she invited the couple to Keene. But the engagement proved rocky and was broken off—"by mutual consent." In fact, it was finally Dr. Morrison who broke the engagement. Mrs. Berry could not be hidden behind such a colorless phrase as "mutual consent." Dr. Morrison broke off the engagement because, he confessed to Lizzie, Mrs. Berry "made very extravagant requirements such as 10,000 for a year in Europe, and wished to live in New York more expensively than he could afford." He also foresaw that her family would be a problem: "her Mother gets drunk and the whole family would live on him he thinks. He seemed much attached to her and I was sorry to have her throw away so good a man" (Lizzie, 8-3-54). But Mrs. Berry evidently did not want the good doctor without the year in Europe, and her drunken mother was part of the package. Lizzie had never thought her "over and above *in love* with the Doctor," so Mrs. Berry's heart was probably not broken at losing him. Within a few months she began talking of returning to California.

Late in June, Lizzie, John, their two children, and two maids appeared in Keene and filled the house with noise and playfulness. The influx of grandchildren required some further rearrangements in the house, and Annie feared they would soon need to use the "room in the back chamber," the extension of the house occupied largely by the servants. Mary, the nurse-maid, and Sam took over Roxana's room. When Annie converted James Wilson's office into a nursery to be occupied by Lizzie and his first grand-son, Wil Sherwood, the daughters had tacitly admitted that their father was no longer their first priority and gave their hearts to the new generation.

One of the attractions that the country had for all of these visitors was that they felt life in the country was healthier than in the city. Certainly, Annie and Lizzie considered the summer in Keene would benefit their frail charges, Wil and Jamie. Even his mother's partial eye could not overlook the fact that Wil was delicate. In fact, he weighed the same as Sam, who was fourteen months younger than he. "Wilson is a delicate nervous fellow with too much brain, but we hope to subdue that by country air and much Keene fare. He has great want of appetite and we never dared to give him meat as he is so nervous" (Lizzie, 6-4-54). Dr. Bowditch had suggested that Jamie also give up meat to cure his headaches, but he didn't do well on the diet and returned to "nourishing food" (Annie, 6-3-54). For little Wil, who was pale and nervous and had "too much brain," and Jamie, who had "too much blood" and could not bear to study, the prescription was the same—exercise and nourishing food. Keene provided the opportunity for both.

Although Jamie's headaches abated somewhat under a regimen of good food and lots of outdoor exercise—horseback riding, fishing, hunting, camping, and walking—he was not able to concentrate on his studies and for that got very little sympathy from his sisters. "I go out in the morning and take a long horseback ride, and come in, feeling as fresh as possible, but as sure as I study half an hour, I begin to grow dizzy and am a perfect dead weight all the rest of the day. I don't think that my time ever passed so unpleasantly in the world, for all the girls instead of sympathizing with me, in the least degree, scold me the greater part of the time—that is not true. I exaggerated it very much. (I mean the part I scratched out.)—seem to blame me. They seem to think that I don't study because I don't want to. If this vertigo clings to me, I don't see how I can get along after I *do* get into college, for I certainly can't study enough now, to keep up with a class" (Jamie, 7-3-54). Despite the exercise and the nourishing food, Jamie lost 11 pounds in two months, going from 141 to 130 pounds, which, stretched over his five-foot-eleven-inch frame, must have made him very thin indeed. As the summer passed, it became clear that he would not be ready to take examinations in July or enter Harvard in the fall.

Furthermore, the dreadful heat of that August aggravated his headaches and vertigo. In the midst of the financial crisis, then, Annie began recon-sidering Dr. Bowditch's advice to send Jamie to California. But she still had reservations. After all, Jamie was Annie's biggest responsibility and his absence would leave a big hole in her life. She was worried about him but Annie was also reluctant to acknowledge that Jamie, like his father, might find life on the frontier more attractive than a domestic life in the East. She might lose him as she had lost her father. Lizzie assumed a "head in the sand" posture and insisted that Jamie did not want to go and that he was improving.

Three thousand miles away in California, James Wilson suffered a pang of homesickness. Early in the summer he asked Jamie about the house and the trees at Main and Emerald streets. He loved his new home in California—the warm climate and the dramatic landscapes, desertlike, with scrub pines and cottonwoods, or rainy and damp with gigantic redwoods, all dominated by the Pacific pounding at the base of rugged, bare cliffs. It contrasted shockingly with the landscape in New Hampshire from which he had detached himself, with its frigid winters, deep snow, and warm summers, its forests of evergreens and elms, maples, ash, and oak slashed with the white bark of the birch.

To his father's questions, Jamie replied: "In one of your last letters, you asked me about the trees, about the house. They are all of them magnificent, without a single exception. The most perfectly shaped elm, is the first one on the right-hand, as you come in at the gate. It is a perfect vase. The trees on the side-walk are all, *very* perfect. The two mountain-ash trees, that you expressed so strong an affection for, are the handsomest ones, on the place. They are higher than the ridgepole of the house, and are exactly in the shape of an egg. Their shape is very dense, and the leaves are a splendid dark green" (Jamie, 8-54). Jamie described the trees not in spring, as perhaps his father imagined them, but in late summer when he received the General's letter. And by the time Wilson read Jamie's letter, those dark green leaves would have turned yellow, a reminder again that seasons as well as time and distance separated the father from his children.

If Jamie's description of Keene fanned the flames of Wilson's homesickness, Annie's letters must have blown it right out. While Uncle Robert described lucidly his errant brother's method of handling money, he himself was sinking into drunkenness and relying on advice from the dead on how to handle his own affairs. With rising panic Annie struggled to control expenses. She complained unpleasantly of Charlotte's trip to West Point and Jamie's demand for $45 to pay a debt that he refused to explain to her. Annie never realized that all of the money she could conserve would never bail the family out of debt, for James Wilson's capacity for financial mismanagement on a large scale far exceeded anything her frugality could save. Furthermore, even when her father was flush with money, he shared it with his family only sporadically and seldom in response to her desperate pleas, which mostly tried his patience. Lizzie, who did not hesitate to tell

Wilson what she needed and scolded him for leaving the family strapped for money while lending to the ever impecunious, seventy-eight-year-old Sam Swan, among others, never feared her father's wrath and evidently was seldom the recipient of it. However, threats to the family home in Keene finally drove Lizzie to join the fray. Although she no longer managed the family affairs, Lizzie maintained a strong voice in family matters, particularly since she had to a large extent blended her brother and sisters into her new Sherwood family. Lizzie was loath to stay with her in-laws at Delhi, so Keene remained an important refuge for her in the summer, and she continued to defend it for herself as much as for Annie and Charlotte. Four urgent letters explained the situation.

✻ [LIZZIE]   Keene August 3d 1854

My dear Father,

We are all assembled for the summer at Keene and the family seem all to be doing well. My little son Wilson is not as robust as I wish he were, but care and time will I hope make him all we can hope. His teeth trouble him, those large grinders in the back part of the jaw. The youngest is very splendid, and Wil is no disgrace to his name.

But there are some things going very wrong—some things demanding your attention. Just before we came up Uncle Robert tore down that brick wall on our northern boundary, and has erected a picket fence which is four feet nearer the bank than the wall was, and consequently a very awkward jog is made into our yard at the terminus of the iron fence. This job coming into our yard affords a convenient place for men to come and commit nuisances, and the Emerald House on any public day can come in and run the carts and etc. into our very yard. Uncle Robert says the selectmen named him to enlarge the street to the fifty feet which you proposed as the width of the street. We are convinced this is a lie, because no one has spoken of removing the iron fence. He never would have done it but because the house is being seized out of his rapacious hands and he desires nothing but to overturn us, cheat us, and grow rich himself out of the spoils. Now Father I want you to write me an answer to all these questions.

Has Uncle Robert any right to do this great outrage? Can you not write to him, to the Selectmen and to me, authorizing me to have the fence moved so that it will take a slanting direction from the line of the iron fence down to the carriage house. Such an arrangement will only affect the public a very few inches, and it makes our place less valuable by a thousand dollars, as it at present looks.

Secondly will you answer this. Has Uncle Robert any secret in his possession by which he has any power over you? This of course I do not wish you to answer unless you are perfectly willing.

Thirdly, had he any right or power to seize $5000 belonging to you in Iowa, as he told Mr. Chamberlain he had done, and has he any power to seize your property out there.

Fourthly can the matters between him and you *never* be settled and adjusted? Because if they cannot, I will give up every thing, and never come back to Keene again. If my husband can (and he certainly can while he has health) support me elsewhere I will stay away. If he cannot I will support myself. As for giving myself the pain of coming here and seeing you so abominably cheated I will not. But if it can be settled I do beg of you for God's sake and your children's sake to have it done, to do it yourself. Perhaps it may be inconvenient and disagreeable and require some effort, but believe me you are losing more than you can afford by neglecting it. Uncle Robert is growing rich and has money to loan and lives luxuriously, while Annie and Charlotte have never had money enough to dress respectably since you went away until this winter. They have frequently had to stay away from places in New York because they had not proper dresses and no money to buy them, and James until this winter has suffered for the want of handsome and proper clothes. At this time Annie is without a cent, except some money she borrowed of the Bank and has had to borrow of John.

Now do you think you ought to let matters go on so? Do you think you ought to loan $500 to Sam Swan or any other man who of course never will pay, while your children are so disagreeably placed? I am doing myself a great injury by saying these things I know, and I hate to do it. I love you better than any one in the world except my husband, and I dislike to say anything to hound you but there has been too much saving of feelings in this family and while we have been saving each other's feelings Uncle Robert and others have been stealing our property. Do write me fully how you stand. Write me if you cannot return to this country and settle your affairs. Dr. Morrison tells me if you had chosen to compromise with the claimants against Limantour you might have already been worth $100,000.

My dear Father, there is one fault in your character, and you must forgive your daughter who never allowed that there was a fault in it to any one else, for mentioning it. It is that you are always led on by an ignis fatuus. You always see great things in the future, and in your pursuit of them you are too apt to forget the interests and the happiness of those *whom you sacrifice* in your pursuit of your anticipated good fortune. We have taken and are taking all the disgrace, the inconvenience of the failures of the various schemes you planned and lost up here, and we must take the consequences of all future ones. Now is it not better to pay a little attention to the present to the small things up here in Keene, so that if all your great plans fail, there may be a something of your own to fall back upon.

I am sorry to make myself so disagreeable because I love you and I want you to love me, but this state of things I cannot stand, and to see Uncle Robert coolly invade our place after it has ceased to be an object of interest to him and thus expose us still more to the annoyance of Keene and the Emerald House is an immediate evil which drives me to do it.

You once said that this place founded as it was, by the railroad, was to remain intact and I know that it would have done so if you had been here.

. . . John is here just now and very well and as good as ever. He is indeed one of the excellent of the earth.

I am in poor health. I am not going to have another child, but I fear I have Mother's complaint. I still nurse little Sam tho' scarcely able to do so. Yet having fine nourishment for him I will not deprive him of it, as he so splendid and flourishing. I am in low spirits and bad health. If I have said anything improper and harsh I beg you to forgive me, and I hope you will tell me how matters stand, as the worst truth is less hard to bear than the suspense, the alternatives of hope and despair which have pursued me for many years, and which I feel have made me the wreck I am, and Annie is following in the same line and is an altered person, nervous, pale, disappointed. If you do not come home soon, we shall probably never see each other on the earth.

Ever dear Father in all States
Lovingly yours

Lizzie Sherwood

✳ [ANNIE]   Keene August 3d 1854

My dear Father,

Your short letter dated June 30th came by due course of mail. It found us all well as usual. The little Wilson had been very sick a few days before from the . . . heat and the effects of two back teeth. Jamie is better than he was a fortnight ago, tho' he has not studied at all for that length of time. The unparalleled heat over came him much, as it did every body. We had 109 degrees in the shade and as high as 90 degrees for ten days in the middle of the day. I don't know what to say about Jamie. If the expense were not very great I should allow that he had a tutor or some person to whom he could recite daily for a year or two when I have great confidence that his health will be restored. He is very unwilling to take any steps which will prevent his acquiring an education, and says he dreads nothing so much as becoming an "illiterate merchant." It is possible that the cool autumn may so far revive him that he will be able to enter college, but he has lost eleven pounds with two months. He weighed 141 lbs two months ago, and now today weighed only 130 lbs. Well I think he requires great care and that it is a matter of vital importance and that his future must not be sacrificed to what I firmly believe to be a temporary indisposition.

I have recently had occasion to pay for Jamie forty five dols., I don't know for what, as he refused to tell me, but he will perhaps tell you. If it had been a thousand I should have paid it, if I could, rather than have him accustomed to the idea of being in debt. I had to borrow the money from Mr. Newell and I am now without any. Charlotte's excursion to West Point cost her fifty dollars. I disapproved of it from the first, as I thought it was an unwarrantable extravagance, but all the family insisted upon it Lizzie and John taking very strong ground, the former going so far as to accuse me of gross *selfishness*, and taking the responsibility of engaging a room for Charlotte. I could not do much to prevent it, so she went, and if we could have afforded it I should be very glad, as she has come home vastly improved in manners, and having acquired much self reliance, and power to look out for herself, which long dependence upon us, came near depriving her of, all together. Still the two sums will make a large hole in our limited income and I must beg that you will allow me an extra amount to cover them. I wish I could get along with less dear Father, but as it is I have to preach and scold continually and get the reputation of being very *"mean"* from our very generous and somewhat lavish elder sister, and some times the "younger members" like to repeat it. It's rather a hard position I can assure you. They seem all to think that I buy flour and wood and wine and sugar etc. for my *own* private gratification, agreeing that I am as "mean" about my dress as any "old miser."

I don't know what to say about Uncle R. I don't know what to make of him. If he has a right to all he takes, we shall have precious little left, by and by. He has taken down the brick wall on the north side and put up a wooden fence three feet in, nearer the bank, improving the appearance of the place very much. On the south side I *must* have some trees set, this fall, as we have a long line of windows, and *back buildings*, exposed, on the line of our garden fence. I *must* have something, either trees or a trellis and vines *if I can afford it*.

As usual, dear Father, my letter is disagreeable from beginning to end. I have not time to tell you about a pleasant visit to Bellows Falls to see Mrs. Cram which I had last week, or how very pleasantly I was received. I *must* take an extra piece of paper rather than not tell you Mary White's message to you. As she was going away after a fortnight's visit she turned back and said, "When you write to yr Father, give my warmest love to him, and tell him he has got the *finest family in the United States* and its his bounden duty to come home and see them, for something will certainly happen to them if he don't, and he should see them in *perfection*." I use her own words.

Good Bye dear Father. I wish I could hear that you were getting large fees in the State courts, and had never seen a mine or a Limantour. "A bird in hand" you know.

God bless you, always prays yr loving   Annie

✱   [LIZZIE]   Keene August 18th 1854

My dear Father,

I wrote you a letter last mail in rather an excited frame of mind perhaps an improper letter. I did not tell any one the contents of it. I hope if it was improperly worded you will forgive it. Many and constant aggravations had induced me to mention some subjects on which I have hitherto been silent.

Annie has mentioned her conversation with Uncle Robert. He says you owe him $27,000—that your property here is covered with mortgages that he has no money and had to borrow $1000 at the Bank—that he is here responsible for your debts, and that Mr. Chamberlain has the accounts, saying that he has to devote every cent to the payment of interest and etc.

Under the pressure of these debts he says, that as he must live, as he must pay the interest of these debts, therefore he has stopped that money out West. If his statement is true I think he acts reasonably and properly to do so. He certainly *appears* to feel toward us most kindly, but whether he does or not, it seems to me that our rights should not be in his hands.

The proof of his regard he certainly gave. Mr. Morse of Boston offered him $9500 for this place down to the end of the Orchard, and Mr. Chamberlain advised him to sell it, telling him that if that sum could be raised on any piece of your property it ought to be done, but as Mr. Skinner came up the same day he allowed it to go for $7000. "rather than turn those young women out of doors" was his expression.

Another reason why it should not remain unsettled is *his condition*. He is either drunk or crazy nearly all the time, and has spiritual communications. He told Annie that Grandfather told him that Skinner was a dishonest man and also that he did right to stop that money from Iowa. So you see your property (if yours) is in the hands of a maniac, who knows enough to *get it* and keep it. Your being affectionate and calling him "my brother" will not help you. You must attend to it, and if you are in the right the strong arm of the law will do what is right. Annie said to him, "Uncle Robert, do you think Father intends to cheat you?"—"No, Annie, *not if he has money,* but your Father's policy has always been to spend freely for *every thing he wants* without regard to others. *Then* if he has a superfluity he will use it for others. It is very pleasant for him to be in a foreign country, away from his creditors. You see he won't stay here where they are, but he lives well and lends money where they are *not* and does not trouble himself much about them." Now if a man feels that way, there is no wonder that he seizes all the money he can get, if for nothing more, to pay your debts here. I think it possible that you forget how your matters stand here. Do you know the extent of the mortgages? Either Uncle Robert must tell an egregious lie, or you must be in great error, for you say you left more than enough property to pay him. He says it is so covered by mortgages as to be wholly valueless in the payment of his debt.

Please to write me or Annie on this subject *tangibly* so we may know the absolute facts.

Then again he says you have a great deal of land in Iowa you might sell advantageously and that you have copper stock now saleable to the amount of several hundred dollars. Please tell us if this be true. The other important topic is James. He does not want to go to sea, and we do not want to have him. He is getting better at home. He and Chardie are up making a visit at Judge Gilchrist's at Charlestown with whose daughter they are intimate. They are two very charming young people and very much respected and admired. *Frank Fiske* goes to California next mail steamer and will bring you daguerreotypes of us all. . . . I have done nothing but fret and worry about business so long that I can hardly find heart to tell you that the children are well. Annie and I are both very much out of health, and worried to death. I shall go home the 1st October. Do let me hear from you before that.

Ever under all circumstances affectionately your daughter

Lizzie

✳ [ANNIE]   Keene August 16th 1854

My dear Father,

Your letters of July 15th arrived in due course of mail. The intelligence relative to Uncle Robert's movements in Iowa was not new to us, as Mr. Chamberlain had told John of it a few days before yr letter arrived. I did not know what to do exactly, but after some consideration I determined to ask him myself with regard to it, so today I reminded him of his letter to me last winter, and asked him if he *had* seized that money, (as if for my own information), since I knew that you had not received it. He said yes, he had, and then he went on to say that he had been offered nine thousand dollars for this house and the garden, as far down as the end of the orchard, that he had surrendered not only *that*, but the remainder of the lot, to the railroad, for *seven* thousand, rather than have *us* deprived of our home, and that he thought if you had intended to pay him, you would not have been so anxious to get *this* the most valuable piece of property out of his hands, and you would have also sent the money from Iowa here, instead of having ordered it to be sent to California. As to selling any of the New Hampshire property he says its impossible, as nobody will buy it. He says, however, that all the receipts from the property here, do not much more than pay for taxes, repairs, and the interest on the mortgages, and that he is now liable for a great deal of money which you have borrowed and not he, and that to keep the interest paid takes all he can get, and that he has not had money enough for the last year to go out of town with, that he has never received his portion of Grand Father's estate, and he thinks it time for him to get some money some where and that he shall apply the money in Iowa to paying the Bank debts. I may add that he is a firm believer in "spiritual manifestations" and thinks he has repeated communications from Grand-father Wilson advising him to this course, so you may have more difficulty with him on that account, than you otherwise would. At any rate, I think if you can possibly effect a settlement with him, even if you have to sac-rifice a great deal, you had by all means better do it, for his mind is in a very singular state, and I feel great uneasiness about him. He says you did owe him about twenty (odd) thousand dollars, and that, now, if the bank debts were off his hands, you would owe him about *nine* thousand. This is as I remember his conversation. He seemed very much moved and affected while he talked to me, and shows great affection and consideration to me always, and for all the children. It seems to me that these debts here will kill us, and I beg to know if you have not some property either at Lake Superior, or Iowa or *some where*, which can be sold to pay them.

Uncle Robert wishes me to tell you that the attachment which he held on the personal property here—furniture and etc—has been released in consequence of his having done nothing about it, and that he has been asked twice within two days, if he still held an attachment. Thus he said, yes, but he fears that Dan or some of yr creditors will find out that he has no longer any power, and he wishes you to make out a "bill of sale" to me, or some one, or all of us, and send it as soon as possible, to prevent the sale of the furniture etc. He says you have a very erroneous idea that he intends to cheat you, and he wishes me to send you the accompanying letter, to show you that he has rather made a sacrifice than evinced any desire to take advantage. I give you his words as near as I can remember, without any comments of my own. I think Uncle R. dislikes Mr. Skinner very much, and it seems to me a rather suspicious circumstance that he (S.) did not pay all of the two thousand dollars you had sent, at once, but gave his note for a part of it. This may be all right and probably is, but for many reasons I think it *highly advisable* that the property should be transfered to our names as soon as possible. Could it not be done as soon as you have paid up all but the last mortgages, which could also be given in my name?

Your bill for three hundred $300.00. dollars was received. I have already shown you how a large proportion of it was already appropriated.

I am sorry to tell you that I am not very well. I have got quite "run down" as Roxana expresses it, by the intense heat, and the duties of hospitality. I think of going down to Portland to stay a few days with Mrs. Little to breath[e] the sea air if I don't get better, and if I can afford it.

Lizzie is much better than she was in the early summer, and little Wilson begins to get some color in his face, and to look like this world a little more. Sam. weighs twenty six pounds, and is as jolly and hearty as possible. I asked Wil. yesterday whose money that was in my purse, and expected him to say "Annie's" when to my amazement he said "Ganpa's." He says to yr picture when he goes into the parlor, "How do Ganpa" and turning to *our* grandfathers, he speaks "How do *gate* Ganpa"!

The children will all write you for themselves. I don't know what to do about Jamie and want to hear from you concerning him. I think if he were to go to sea he ought to go as a "Steerage hand" and work, as many gentlemen's sons do, that is, to make it beneficial, but I hardly think it necessary that he should go at all. I think by winter he will be able to study, tho' he will *not* be able to be in college, and be *done* at any certain time, whether or no. What do you think of my proposition of a tutor?

We expect Mrs. Berry in the course of next week. She is now in Peterboro. How foolish she was to give up so good a man as Dr. Morrison.

Take care of yr precious health, my dear Father and keep up yr spirits in spite of my doleful letters.

Believe that I am always devotedly and fondly yr daughter

Annie F. Wilson

Neither Lizzie's scathing letters nor Annie's frustration nor accounts of the perfections of his deserving family caused Wilson to alter his agenda. He did not come home, of course, and his finances went from bad to worse. In August he sent $600, which covered some of the family's ongoing expenses; but as the summer turned torrid, bewildering legal and financial problems plagued the family home they had so happily returned to in the spring. And none of his daughters' pleas for explanations from their father would receive answers until they felt the chilly bite of autumn in New York.

"Times, Prices, and Everything Has Changed, Since You Went Away"

I n 1853, James Wilson received sixty-seven letters from his children describing the rich family life they had invented and maintained for themselves in his absence. In 1854 fifty-five letters continued the developing saga of life in Keene, New York, and Boston as his children constructed a life without father. In 1855 the children's chronicle of that life became sketchier and sketchier. Lizzie's and Annie's letters became not only less frequent but more anxious and urgent in tone and choice of subject matter. Charlotte, unmarried and without the anxiety of managing the family, still wrote as if hardly brushed by worry. In 1855, Wilson saved only eleven letters from his daughters. One major event is nevertheless fully discussed. Annie had finally agreed to send Jamie to California. By spring Jamie had joined his father, and the correspondence reflects the fact that the comfortable routine the family had established had changed yet again.

Lizzie made the point well when she wrote: "Times, prices, and everything has changed since you went away and our anxieties and troubles have nearly destroyed us. Jamie knows the whole story. I hope he will tell it to you. He promised he would, and I trust he has had the courage to do it" (Lizzie, 5-19-55).

The times were changing at home and abroad. John Sherwood, concerned about international affairs, studied the papers for news of the murky and desperate war in the Crimea made famous by Tennyson in his poem "Charge of the Light Brigade." When the war bogged down during the winter of 1855, John studied maps and followed the positions of the armies of Turkey, Sardinia, England, France, Russia, and the Ottoman Empire in the *London Illustrated News*. Florence Nightingale struggled to clean up the field hospitals and reduce the mortality rate among the soldiers. Charlotte read letters from the officers published in the *London News* and developed some opinions on the war. "Has not England behaved shamefully during the whole war? As to the French, I think they have been great. I suppose you read the accounts with interest, don't you? I never read anything but private letters from the officers etc. . . . But I hear the subject so much discussed that I know something about it" (Charlotte, 3-4-55).

She worried more about the fighting on the western frontier of the United States because the young men whom she had met at West Point were being called to fight the Indians. "I only hope *we* shan't engage in any war soon. My friends in the Army are to be all ordered off to the Western Frontier next Autumn to fight the Indians. Poor fellows, they will have a pretty hard time I suspect" (Charlotte, 3-4-55).

Annie was not well during that winter, while she was receiving Clarence Cram's visits and struggling with money problems. She had what Lizzie referred to as a "bunch"—some kind of tumor—that did not disappear until April, and she looked pale and haggard well into spring. She, however, finally made plans for Jamie to go to California. Furthermore, the litany of money problems ran on, what Annie aptly describes as "the same old story."

✳ [ANNIE]   New York, March 18, 1855

My dear Father,
   Your letters bring the money and instructions for Jamie, arrived safely, and we rejoice to hear of your health, and to find you in better spirits.

   It was not possible to have him ready to start by the twentieth of March, as I believe we told you in our last letters. He will therefore start on the fifth of April (God willing.) The fare to California, *today*, is three hundred dollars. The agents of the Express told Jamie that it would be lower by the fifth, as two ships sailed on that day. How much, I don't know, but with our money, Charlotte's and the general fund we shall be able to get him off, I imagine.

   I have told you that of the six hundred dollars you sent me five hundred of it I was obliged to pay for the expenses of last summer. You will remember that I had no money after August through the Autumn months till the middle of January. To come here I was obliged to borrow of Mr. Skinner $350 and that would not more than half pay our bills for the summer, the hardest season we have ever had. We have spent about one hundred and fifty dollars this winter, *all three of us*, for our own necessities. This included everything in the way of clothing, travelling expenses, from Jamie's little jaunts, and pocket money. That is allowing fifty dollars a person for five months and in the city of New York, I don't think you can call that very extravagant, when you consider the position which we of necessity hold. I don't think any one who knows anything of my affairs, will accuse me of extravagance. I wear a shawl which I made myself of one of Mother's, a bonnet I also made myself, and I have two winter dresses that I had last winter, one of which John gave me as a Christmas gift. With this wardrobe I have gone all winter with people of *wealth* and *fashion*, and I don't mention it to complain, for I am satisfied, (Lizzie says I have a way of looking like a lady, and well dressed on no money"). I only mention it, to assure you that my expenditure of money is not wholly for *personal display*. Our establishment at Keene I may have made too expensive, and I will try to retrench. It will be easy to do it if only Charlotte and I are there.

One favor I must ask of you, Dear Father, that you will send to Roxana Smith the money due her, for she is getting altogether too hard a mistress for me to live under. We still owe Mr. Harding fifty dollars which is a debt I feel, and there is an account of Dr. Adams and Dr. Twitchell at Keene that I want to see paid. I pray, therefore, that, as soon as convenient, you will pay those things at Keene, for tho' I have no doubt you feel them, you can't imagine how hard it is to a proud spirit to *live with one's* creditors. The world is not generous or magnanimous at all.

Jamie will sail on the fifth of April, in the "George Law," if nothing occurs to prevent. There is no news. I will send you the Atlas you mention, if I have the money. I hope the California failures don't affect you. We have got our letters yet. God bless you always prays yr loving daughter

Annie F. Wilson

Mrs. Berry says she shall not be able to go out by the fifth of April, if at all.

✳ [ANNIE]   New York May 4th 1855

My dear Father,

. . . We are as well as usual and in statu quo. I have not quite made up my mind when to go home. Charlotte desired to go with Lizzie and John to West Point for a week the first day of June. If she does I shall stay here till she gets back I suppose. If she does not we shall go the last week of May I think to Keene.

Roxana and Daniel Seward are safe enough I imagine without my supervision and I have written to James Wright every direction about the garden and he will superintend the making therof. Roxana writes that "the soap is made," etc etc. She is so in the habit of doing her regular work that each day of the year has its unchanging duty and if the currant jelly was not made on the twenty fifth day of July "it would not be good."

We are greatly in need of money. I have not yet been able to pay James Wright fifty dollars which I owe him and Mr. Skinner I still owe a hundred and seventy five. Mr. Bridgman claims forty more as I wrote you. Mr. Harding always "hangs over my head." It is always the same old story isn't it? We have not been very bad this winter have we? I mean since November. John *must* be paid; he works too hard and has too expensive a family to be made to wait. He is very kind to us always, and it is really a great mortification to me not to be able to pay Mr. Skinner the money he lent me last Fall so kindly, when I was so pressed. However, I suppose you will send it when you can.

I don't know any news. I have been much better and am again not so well, and a great deal of the day I spend on my bed. This must excuse my short letter for I feel particularly ill today.

Do write us fully about Jamie what you think of him and all. Take care of yrselves and get ready to come home.   As ever yr loving daughter
Annie

The "same old story" did not bore James Wilson; it made him angry, and after the first letter he wrote once again to scold Annie. Annie, no longer abject, replied wearily, "I am sorry you thought my letter and advice disrespectful, as nothing was farther from my mind and intention." Then she added without comment at the end of the letter, "I suppose we shall go to Keene about the first of May. I shall not be able to pay John what we shall owe him by that time with my present funds, as a very large proportion of all I had, went to pay for the expenses of last summer" (Annie, 3-4-55). Passionate Annie sounds burned out. She had planned, harried, begged, accused, and shamed, but nothing worked. For the time being she could not devise another strategy for persuading her father to bail them out of debt and seemed to fall into lethargy.

With Annie powerless to construct one more scenario that might persuade Wilson to send money, Lizzie took a turn. Delighting in the news that her father's fortunes have taken a turn for the better, she took the opportunity to provide her father with advice:

"I sincerely rejoice at the change for the better in your fortunes. Heaven knows how I have prayed for it, and now that you feel so happy and cheerful let me beg of you to direct some of the money to the discharge of old debts, which harass and distress us. Roxana first and foremost, who for the last four years has been an incubus which any demon might have fastened on a doomed sinner, and she *should* be paid. Next, do place a small sum in the Suffolk bank for Annie, whose trials, and whose economy, good principles and exertions demand some relief.

"You say very truly dear Father that we must allow you to manage your own business. Heaven knows that I would not willingly let one word of interference or dissatisfaction pass my lips did not the extremity of the circumstances demand it. But you are far away. . . .

". . . Then as to our place at Keene. John says if you will send him power of attorney, he will soon unravel the Uncle Robert business, and I asked you last summer if something could not be done about that fence which he unjustly pushed into our grounds, almost ruining what was not already ruined. James will describe it to you. If you would think about these questions, you would very much relieve your daughters" (Lizzie, 5-19-55).

Amid all this uncertainty about the time and about money, it is no wonder Annie insisted that Clarence Cram establish himself in a responsible profession before they marry. Evidently, Clarence's first job working for his father proved to be unsatisfactory, for during the winter of 1855, while John Sherwood worried over the war in the Crimea and the girls worried about money, Clarence Cram studied the law. In the evenings he visited Annie, who had inspired this rash of ambition. "He says, if [he] were of a mind to study all the time, and give up seeing Annie often, he could be admitted to the Bar by June, but he, *naturally, prefers postponing his admittance to the Bar* to giving up his calls on Annie." He even took an interest in little Wil, giving him a book with pictures of all of the uniforms of the Emperor Napoleon's guard. However, Charlotte opined, "I don't believe they will be married for a year. They are so wise as to have determined not to be married, *till they can afford* to do so" (Charlotte, 3-4-55). Given Clarence's preference for visiting Annie rather than studying law, the "wise" one was probably Annie, who cannot have wanted to jump from her father's house to another house where she would have to pinch pennies. Certainly, Charlotte thought that women were the ones responsible for making these wise decisions. "It seems to me perfectly wicked the way some girls get married, without *knowing how* they are to *buy their bread* in a year. It is unjust to their husbands, as well as to themselves" (Charlotte, 3-4-55). The young couple had been engaged for over a year. Though, according to Charlotte's observations, Annie was "very fond" of Clarence and he was "entirely devoted" to her, the wedding date had not been set.

Charlotte's life, aside from practicing the piano, revolved around Lizzie's children and enjoying herself. With Lizzie and Annie as guides, Charlotte concentrated much of her energies on her social life and thoughtful observation of her family, especially Wil and Sam. Every detail of their activities and development fascinated their aunt. "The babies are glorious. Sam walks all over the room alone. He says 'Nannie' now is very sweet indeed, though not quite as fat and rosy as formerly, on account of 'teething. . . . To think of my telling you about *Sam*, and *not* about *Wil*! I must confess that my forgetfulness was *partly voluntary*, since Wil is always *elsewhere*, remembered, to the *exclusion* of poor Sam. Wil has two new tops, and a 'hoopla,' as he calls a *hoop*. One of the tops *whistles*, and the other *hums*. He is perfectly wild over them. And dances all the time they are 'on the tapis.' He is very sweet in a large straw hat, which he sports at present" (Charlotte to Jamie, 4-4-55).

The rest of the Sherwood family bored her, and she found some of them rather silly. Despite her boredom Charlotte, as usual, observed and censored people's behavior on occasion, especially Louisa Coggeswell's failure to respect the subtleties of behavior that distinguish the way married women treat men in society versus the way unmarried women (i.e., "young women") do. The phrase "receives attention" (would we call it flirting?) suggests how heavy was Louisa's responsibility for the men's behavior as well as her own. "We have been to the Sherwoods this evening to meet Mrs. Dixon's 'Aunt Lois,' and her (Mrs. Dixon's) sister, Louisa Coggeswell. She has been married sometime, but acts like a young lady—receives attention etc. I believe she is a good hearted person. We have such stupid times at the small tea partys the family are in the habit of giving, that it fairly stupefys me for two evenings to go to one. We have been to *two* this *week*." Otherwise in that spring "there are no parties and no gaity" (Charlotte, 4-4-55).

Laughing at her unmarried state, Charlotte wrote: "There are several very young girls in Keene married, and engaged, which state of things occasioned this remark from Mary Dinsmore, (aged *fifteen*), that *now* 'almost all the girls are engaged, and Charlotte Wilson and Susan Adams were nearly all *of the old set* who were left.' *I* think that is *funny*, because I never was called *old* before" (Charlotte, 4-19-55). Although the youngest sister clearly felt ambivalent about the parties that delight her sister, opting not to attend some of them, she looked back on her trip to West Point wistfully. Fanned by visitors' reports of the Point, that visit in 1854 glowed in her memory as the happiest experience of her young life. She worked herself into a frenzy of desire to repeat the experience. Realizing that this might be the last chance she would have to get written permission from her father to make the much-desired trip, Charlotte asked but did not importune in her next letter. "There is *one* other *great extravagance* which I should delight in extremely, going to West Point with Lizzie and John, in June, but as I hardly hope to have that wish fulfilled, I shall readily coincide with your opinion, if it is not favorable to such a plan. I see all the reasons why it should *not* be granted, and should only consider it an *immense indulgence* if it were so. An indulgence that I ought not to ask after having been so leniently treated" (Charlotte to Jamie, 4-27-55). Annie, who opposed her first trip on the grounds of expense, recognized that Charlotte's coy request was a disguise for a hell-bent determination and reconciled herself to the visit without protest.

April was warm and balmy in 1855 in New York. The trees were fresh and green and plentiful. Though the dust from the streets that stung pedestrians' eyes dampened somewhat their pleasure in the spring weather, Broadway was crowded with handsome, beautifully dressed women and "insignificant men" (Charlotte, 4-4-55). Charlotte in a new hat trimmed in green and Annie in a new dress given her by John Sherwood would have fit into that lovely throng. There were few parties. Instead, the three sisters walked sometimes in the evening or went to the theater to see such plays as *Elopements in High Life* and *Bold Dragoons*. The latter appealed to Charlotte, with her weakness for soldiers. She found the leading man, Lester, especially "handsome in soldier's dress."

Not all of these pleasures or concerns—for Jamie, her children, her husband, her father, her sisters, and her large household—distracted energetic Lizzie from "the one great ambition" she had confessed to Susan Colgate (née Colby) in 1849 shortly after her mother's death. Through everything she continued to write. In the spring of 1855, about the same time that Jamie departed for California, Lizzie wrote a poem, "The Lighthouses of the World," which Mr. Bellows published in the *Christian Inquirer*, a small Unitarian newspaper. It was widely admired and copied. Lizzie copied all eight quatrains in a letter to her father and asked his opinion.

* [LIZZIE]   New York, April 19th 1855

My dear Father,

. . . What a year of calamity and discouragement this has been to all of us, yet we have lived and have got to see better times. I too have had a success. I have written a poem which has excited a good deal of admiration, illustrating an eloquent passage in Mr. [Samuel] Ruggles's speech on "Rivers and Harbours." I send it to you, knowing that you do not generally read poetry but believing you will not despise mine. It is called "The Lighthouses of the World." I have also written a story which I shall send Jamie, for which the publishers pay me *fifteen dollars*. This last is a secret, however as I do not wish the *publishers* to know *I* wrote it. But you cannot imagine how happy it makes me to achieve *literary success*. I have always had as you know, a strong taste for writing. John too is very much pleased.

My boys are splendidly healthy, and Jamie will tell you how fine they are. My own health continues very feeble, but I am more able to attend to my duties than I have been. I mean I feel more energy and less fatigue, though I have just had a horrid felon on my finger which has kept me awake several nights. It threatened to be very ugly but I had it opened and it is now well.

I published this in our little Unitarian paper, Mr. Bellows editor, and it has been extensively copied. Write me your opinion.

THE LIGHTHOUSES OF THE WORLD

"Could a Christian community exist and stand erect in the family of civilized nations, and shroud its shores in utter darkness? For what do we see when we look around us? The British Islands, blazing with upwards of three hundred lights; France, with more than one hundred and fifty; the Baltic, the Mediterranean, the Euxine, all illuminated; and even in the frozen North, Imperial Russia lighting the American mariner on his pathway through the White Sea out to the Polar Basin. The whole globe, from North to South, from East to West, is encircled with these living monuments of humanity and civilization." —*Duty of the American Union to Improve its Navigable Waters.*

> Darkness descends, and gives the spirit wings;
>   The eye, emboldened, claims imperial right;
> And, lying grandly at my feet, I see
>   The world at night.
>
> Behold the vision! How sublimely fair!
>   For myriad lights illuminate the sea,
> Encircling continent and ocean vast.
>   In one humanity.
>
> Perchance some habitant of far-off star,
>   Born to the heritage of loftier powers,
> Although we cannot see his glowing world,
>   Yet looks on ours—
>
> May see these patient sentinels of night,
>   May read their language, eloquent and grand,
> As, shining coldly 'neath the Arctic light,
>   They warning stand;
>
> Or, beaming through the still and fragrant air,
>   Where coral reefs the vexed Bermoothes guard,
> O'er freight of human life may see the Lamp
>   Keep watch and ward;
>
> Or, streaming from Leucadia's haunted cliff,
>   Where fiery genius sleeps beneath the wave,
> Touching with light the waters surging o'er
>   A lonely grave;
>
> Or, blazing bright amid Atlantic storm,
>   While bending masts are quivering with fear,
> The guardian Light upheld by sea-girt towers
>   Aloft and clear.
>
> Burn on with inextinguishable fire!
>   Companions of the silent stars above!

Resplendent types, amid a world of strife,
Of deathless Love.   M.E.W.S.

. . . We are going to Delhi this summer to save the girls the cost of our living, though I don't know what the poor things will do then, alone. Living is so immensely high that every ounce of butter is an item worth saving, and I have to study the economical more than I like to, I assure you.

You must think me mean or grasping, but I have made a determination *never* to live above our means, and as I have got our expenses down to the lowest minimum with our family, I must reduce the family, or have an equivalent or rather John must, and the girls can live here cheaper than in Keene.

Best love to dear James. Tell him that I should write him but have seen nothing amusing since he left, but shall write him and send him a book next mail. Tell him Wilson goes about talking of "dear Uncle Bim," and that we all talk and think of him all the time.

Ever most affectionately your daughter,   Lizzie Sherwood.

Lizzie knew she made a breakthrough in her writing career when the *Knickerbocker* published her story. She was twenty-nine and launched on her long-sought literary career. With money scarce, Lizzie quickly planned to make a profit from her newly won skill. "I wrote you that I had been paid for one story. I mean to be paid for more. Poor John has had a hard winter. Our grocer's bill alone has been nearly fifty dollars a month nearly all winter. Provisions are enormously high, and a young family of ten people is considerable for a young lawyer. So I mean to work as long as my brain holds out and try and help him" (Lizzie, 5-19-55).

Annie described Lizzie's poem as "very eloquent and strong" and agreed with Charlotte that it was "very unlike most women's poetry," specifically, Charlotte added, because it had "no sickly sentimentality, in it as there is apt to be in ladies' poetry" (Charlotte, 4-4-55).

However much they admired her work and however much her earnings contributed to the general welfare, her family nonetheless devalued her writing in favor of motherhood. Quick on the heels of her praise, Charlotte declared the "most successful Poem of her life Master Wilson Sherwood is becoming a large rather noisy boy" (Charlotte, 4-5-55). Her facetious comparison of Wil with Lizzie's poem hints at what all of Lizzie's family soon suspected—her writing distracted her from her children. During their infancy she had spent so much time taking care of them, her sisters feared for her health and advised her to take time out from her children to rest. Still, they had little sympathy for her private ambitions, which also required time away from the nursery. By May, Lizzie was defending herself against such suspicions. "Do not be afraid I shall neglect my husband and children. If you could see the stockings of the former and the faces of the latter you would not think them neglected" (Lizzie, 5-19-55). Whether they repeated these sentiments to their father or not, the news of her literary pursuits prompted him also to suspect that Lizzie was spending too much time writing at the expense of her family.

On the other hand, Wilson did not allow his own family's problems to interfere for a minute with his career. A critical moment in the Limantour case loomed. Unfortunately, no other mention of Limantour's important grant could be found in all of the records of California land grants. And Limantour's friend and confidante, Thomas Larking, was prepared to testify that Limantour had never mentioned the grant to him. The opposition further argued that the descriptions of the land were obscure. However, the descriptions were no worse than usual as California land grants went. The signature of Micheltorena, the Mexican governor of California, on the original grant and that of Bocanegra, the minister of the interior, endorsing the grant to Limantour had proved genuine. When Wilson worried that the original petition from Limantour to Micheltorena was missing, a clerk fortuitously produced the document from the county recorder's files.

Wilson became anxious, perhaps partly because the wealthy and formidable Captain Folsom contended against the claim. Wilson described the evidence to John Sherwood and John's father, both of whom assured him that they thought the case airtight, unless, John added, there was a fraud. He also penned a long and fascinating letter to Annie describing the trial. Vivid in detail and full of exuberant self-approbation, Wilson provided a step-by-step account of his performance. And performance it was. Casting himself easily in the role of the leading man, Wilson described with heady, boyish self-confidence and exaggeration the details of his assumed (if mock-heroic) finest hour as a jurist. Addressing Annie as his "associate counsel," he laid out his case with winning confidence. The finest stump speaker thus constructed yet another heroic scenario for himself. A copy of the letter remains, annotated at its end in Wilson's hand.

✳ [JAMES WILSON] San Francisco, March 13, 1855

I have the honor to inform you, (for your professional consideration and mature investigation) that the Limantour claim came on for trial before the Board of Land commissioners on Friday the 9th instant. As counsel for the claimant I opened by a brief statement of the case as I expected to make it appear on the evidence. This occupied but an half hour. I then proceeded to put in the evidence in behalf of the claimant, (*our client Limantour*) much in the same order the Documents stand in the pamphlet as far as that Document contains them. Having finished reading through those papers I put in several additional documents and the testimony of several witnesses taken since the pamphlet was published. They contained much important new matter and a great deal of corroborating evidence. Among other things I proved the genuineness of the signature of "Bocanegra" who certified the approval of the grant, by the Supreme Provisional Government of Mexico, made by Governor Micheltorena to our client. The genuineness of that signature I proved, and to remove all doubt and cavil I provided it by three good competent and truth-ful witnesses which I thought important as that fact is a very strong point in the case. It removes all question about the authority of Micheltorena for by the approval of the grant by "the supreme provisional Government" they make it their grant by adoption. (Is that good law and sound logic?)

It took the whole day on Friday to put in our side of the case which consisted of some 30 Documents and Depositions and I was full of courage and confidence got great advantage of the opposing Counsel in all the by play and ready repartee on the trial and with large steps and lofty bearing I marched right over the Law Agent of Uncle Sam in a manner I should have thought highly creditable to me in the best days of my professional pedestrianship.

This mode of preparing the case and this mode of presenting it for the consideration of the commissioners I hope will meet your approbation.

At about 4 o'clock P.M. of Friday I got our side of the case fully before the Board. The Defence had taken, in all, Eight Depositions. In two of their Depositions they attempted to impeach our witness Prudon but the attempt signally failed as the testimony supported Prudon and proved that he was a capable, truthful person and every way worthy of credit. By two other witnesses they tried the same experiment with exactly the like result. One of their remaining witnesses and the most intelligent one they had sustained and corroborated our side of the case throughout. Their other three witnesses knew nothing about the case and of course could prove nothing. The Law Agent absolutely refused to read his miserable immaterial and irrelevant stuff and putting in the Depositions silently said that the evidence was closed.

On Saturday morning the 10th instant Mr. McKune the Law Agent commenced what he called an argument. He floundered along for some three hours in the most bungling, clumsy, unlawyerlike and boyish manner of any person of position I ever saw. If my son James could not and cannot argue better, even now, he is not the boy I take him to be. McKune's whole effort (I cannot call it an argument or a speech) was nothing but a disconnected, absurd, miserable string of old, childish justice court platitudes, weak as dishwater. There was neither power or sense or genius in it. It fell like a wet blanket on the Commissioners who were obliged to sit under it, while every body else went out of the court room preferring to stand in a pouring fresh rain out of doors.

Mr. Blanding, the associate Law Agent, then tried his mill, but as his head is not great and his reservoir not large his pond run out in a very short time but it was Saturday afternoon and the commissioners refused to let me go on in reply on said evening. There were fatigued and tired and worn out and would take a recess until Monday morning.

On Monday morning the 12th day of March A.D. 1855, I commenced my argument in the Limantour case No. 548 before the Board of Land Commissioners at a few minutes after ten o'clock. 1st I took up McKune's "suspicions" of the genuineness of the title papers in a perfect hurricane—whirled them aloft—stripped them all entirely naked, showed their absurdity and wickedness and exhibited to the Commissioners and every body else their deformity. I then went regularly through a thorough expositions of all the Documentary and other testimony in our case showing the utter impossibility of any fraud or forgery about it. The facts of the case I presented fully and then I went into a full and elaborate discussion of the Law of the case.

Now addressing you, as associate counsel, you must permit me to say that in my argument of the cause I entirely satisfied myself—words never came to me more readily or of a more select character—thoughts never presented themselves to my mind more clearly, distinctly or in better methodical order. The imagination was vigorous and obedient—illustration, comparison and all the graces of eloquence came forth almost unbidden—the rhetoric and ornaments of style the power of antithetic and the force of epigrammatic expression all volunteered their happy assistance—memory seemed determined upon giving me an entertainment and brought forth and presented every thing within my reach, that I had seen or heard or read or thought of before in all my life.

I was clear unembarrassed and conclusive in my logic and exact in its applications. In the days of my best strength I think I never commanded sounder or more irresistible [word missing] Let me repeat and say that I satisfied myself entirely, and the commendations of those who listened to me was and is quite enough to satisfy any reasonable man's vanity. They all say I deserve success whether I get it or no. I spoke until half past four in the afternoon and although I was very tired and much exhausted it was the want of day light rather than the want of good thoughts that induced me to close my argument.

The courtroom is very dark and a thick dark cloud shedding torrents of rain had taken a position between the earth and the sun which it maintained all day. The cause is presented to the Board for consideration. I have prepared it, managed it and argued it "solitary and alone." . . . Whether or no I shall gain it is more than I can say. I have faithfully performed my duty. I believe fully in the justice and equity and legality of the claim and I am therefore confident of success.

If it be rejected it will be a triumph achieved by corruption and power and wrong, over truth and right and justice and law. I cannot conceive such a result quite yet in my country, if I had it for trial before any of the highest courts of judicature in any of the old States of this Union I would not have a fear or a doubt in regard to the result.

What the opponents of the claim may do and accomplish in California is more than I know.

The state judiciary here is truly awful but I must hope to find a purity and honesty of purpose in the District Court which will enable me to get my cause fairly and honestly before the Supreme Court of the United States and if so it will be all I ask. I can, I shall beat them. I do not expect the decision of the Board of Land Commissioners for several months yet to come. Judge Felch, the Chairman, and infinitely the most intelligent member of the Board, will leave here for his home in Michigan in a few weeks. He has enough to occupy every minute of his time until he starts. He will be absent 3 or 4 months. The Limantour claim will not be decided as I think and hope until his return. I shall have much more confidence in his opinion than in that of the other members of the Board although they are very clever men. Judge Felch is a very able lawyer and a man of unquestioned purity and integrity.

While Wilson had marshaled his oratory in a case that was almost as famous on the East Coast as it was on the West, he was not on the popular side. His daughters responded quickly to newspaper accounts of the trial. "Every one we see brings us a complaint on the Limantour *argument*, I am glad it is off your mind. I can hardly believe there is sufficient justice in California to make the decision a righteous one, with Capt. Folsom, that indomitable man, to contend against the claim, and many like him. Still hope does not desert me. I am afraid you found yourself so fresh and young, your mind ought now to be in its prime. Mr. Webster was at his greatest (I think) after sixty. . . . A life of rich experiences ought to facilitate a man's utterance and make the periods flow with a more opulent flood" (Lizzie, 4-19-55).

Annie observed of Wilson's language: "We were charmed to hear of yr brilliant achievement in yr argument in the Limantour case. I know the force of yr *words*, very well, as ever since I was born I have only needed to hear you *say* black was white to be thoroughly convinced of the truth thereof" (Annie, 4-19-55). Having received stunning reproofs from her father from time to time, Annie could testify to her father's powerful language. On the other hand, there is a certain ambiguity in what she says. She may indeed now recognize that how he sees things is not necessarily how she sees them or how many other people see them. Perhaps she was resisting at last his black and his white. Perhaps Annie was too grown up not to be cautious about his boyish confidence.

A month later, Lizzie, more realistic than her father, was thinking of reasons he would fail. "Don't be too sanguine about the Limantour. I don't doubt *you* have done admirable, but with such a corrupt court, with such immense interest against you. I don't believe—I *can't* believe, what I *want* to believe (Lizzie, 5-19-55).

Even in the East there was speculation that regardless of the Land Commission's decision the case would go before the Supreme Court. Charlotte and Annie, not much interested in the case itself, seized on this chance to have their father home for a visit. "We rejoice at yr success in gaining a hearing as the prospect of yr coming home seems nearer. . . . What are the delays before you get to the Supreme Court?" (Annie, 4-19-55). And Charlotte, who had renounced all interest in legal affairs, confined her observations on this critical junction in her father's career to "Come Home, as soon as you can make the Limantour *compel* you to do so" (Charlotte, 4-4-55).

But home was not the popular place for young men. Horace Greeley from Amherst, New Hampshire, less than a hundred miles from Keene, founded the *New York Tribune* and exhorted the generation of the middle of the nineteenth century: "Go west, young man." The phrase was perhaps directed at men like the poor New Hampshire hill farmer who struggled to survive on the thin, granite-ridden soil of New England when there was for the taking land with deep loamy topsoil in Iowa and Nebraska. Hundreds followed Greeley's advice and abandoned their unprofitable farms. The Wilsons were not part of that exodus, but they went west with the same high hopes: Jamie Wilson followed his father to California to search for health, adventure, and fortune. His sisters sent him as a messenger to their father, both to test their father's reception of one of his children and to present their precarious situation in person. They also enjoyed the prospect of hearing what their father thought of their handiwork, this brother they had raised.

While Lizzie was encouraged about the state of Wil's health, Jamie's headaches remained intractable. All through the summer, fall, and winter of 1854 and 1855, in Keene and New York, the three sisters had tried every remedy they could devise. Nothing worked. Though they fretted over Jamie's moral and physical safety in disreputable San Francisco, they also worried that at eighteen he had been idle for over a year. They inched toward the decision to send him to California.

What would happen, they wondered, to such a boy in the Wild West? After all, the three sisters had invested a great deal of time and attention in their brother's development, too much to allow him to go to California to turn into a wastrel. Each sister wrote of the concerns Charlotte summarized: "I feel even *more* alarmed for the safety of his *Soul*, than his *body*. If my *prayers* are answered, he will be preserved through it all. It is because California is *so full* of unprincipled men, that I hope you will *keep* Jamie *with you*. The temptations to 'lower his standard' will be so many, if he is surrounded by bad people" (Charlotte, 3-15-55).

Lizzie had more than a few words of advice on how he should be managed. "I have a few words to say about Jamie which I hope will not seem intrusive. I hope you will when he reaches you, be as much pleased with him as *we* are, and attribute all the good qualities of which he is possessed, but I hope and entreat, that you will keep before him the advantages of an *education* and induce him if possible to study. Do try at least to have him take French or Spanish lessons, and keep alive in him the desire for Knowledge.

"And another thing, to give him some idea of regulating his expenses. Do give him an *allowance*. From never having any regular money he spends foolishly, and without result, any small sums he gets, trusting to luck for more. This, I think, is his greatest fault, and the one most to be guarded against.

"Then he has like most boys a great dislike for going to church, and will I fear get to be careless about the Sabbath, from which springs all manner of evil. I do not believe he has any bad irreligious feelings, but he is careless and needs advice on this point.

"If I were you, I would not keep him in California, more than three months, for if you do I fear his collegiate education will never come off, and I cannot help hoping that he *will* yet go there.

"As for all the rest, you will find out how bright he is, how much use he can make of all his knowledge, and how social and easily influenced he is. I hate to have him go, but still I feel he goes to his best friend, and that he will be thus protected from his worst enemies—his own passions.

"He, of course is very fond of the opposite sex, and cares very much for the set of his clothes etc. Don't let him fall into the snares of designing females if you can help it. Women do more mischief than men, I think" (Lizzie, 3-19-55).

Finally, that spring, despite news of serious business failures, they put

Jamie on a boat for California. Annie found it impossible to prepare him for a sailing on March 20, so he shipped out on April 5, which Mrs. Berry assured them was the best time, since the equinoctial storm occurred about March 20. Thus, nearly a year after leaving school, on a balmy day in April 1855, Jamie followed his father to California instead of his grandfather to Harvard.

The departure of this beloved dependent on whom they had lavished their care, on whose well-being they had centered so much of their attention, left the three women as desolate as had the departure of their father, on whom they felt dependent. Lizzie wrote: "We were quite broken hearted at losing dear Jamie, so long the centre of our hopes, plans, and movements, and were in that condition of discouragement and melancholy where we too often have found ourselves since you left us" (Lizzie, 4-19-55). Annie went to bed.

To ease their sense of loss, his three sisters at once began writing him lively letters that embodied all of the affection, hopes, and concern they had lavished on him in the previous five years. His relationship with each sister was different, however, and the letters they wrote reflected their differences.

Lizzie's first letter to Jamie was a playful and loving account of his departure, as reflected in the myths and images of a young man launched on the sea of life. Full of hope and excitement, she expressed none of the reservations she had mentioned to her father before his departure. As in her correspondence with Susan Colby, Lizzie was chatty, tender, and full of news. Though she had two sons of her own, they clearly did not displace Jamie in her affection.

* [LIZZIE]   April 27, 1855, New York

My dear dear brother Jamie,

There was joy in this house when the George Law was reported off Sandy Hook. Still more when a letter, a real live letter in the well known characters told us that our beloved boy was well and happy. Our eyes grow "very sweaty" as Susan Adams says whenever you are mentioned now and oftener too. We miss you more than I can express. Poor Annie went to bed and staid there. It seemed as if her occupation were gone, like Othello's. But she roused when the *Geo. Law* appeared and has seemed like a new creature.

John says when he thinks of you he can only see that fine figure of Retzch's [picture] "Song of the Bell" where the young man starting out in life first sees the sea! What a splendid allegory it is. (You remember you impersonated it in a tableau once). The sea with its promise of adventure, and what youth always anticipates, success. O! my dear brother, now I hope the allegory will be carried out, and the youth will return a *man* in all high intents and purposes.

How much I long to hear of your meeting with Father. How glad I am you have gone to him. You must persuade him to take exercise and care of himself. I need not ask you to be good and dutiful to him. Father has always inspired his children with that sort of behavior.

... Mrs. Berry came over after you left with her "kinder's" and "sorter's" and was a good humored and queer as ever. Did not feel hurt by your not calling as she said she knew how "kinder busy you must have been." Augustus came from Amherst and took Herman home, very much to the displeasure of everybody as Herman was improving very much. Augustus is growing priggish and conceited all owing to that miserable calvinist college. He however spoke most affectionately of you. Mrs. Murray was here last night. Spoke most kindly of you as always. We have not been to any place of amusement since you were here except once to the opera to hear "William Tell" which is splendid only too long. The Sherwoods are all very much pleased with my poem and seem quite proud of my success. I meant to have sent you a *Knickerbocker* for May with my story in it for which they paid me $15. The first money I ever earned. I feel very much encouraged by it. You must not tell as the publishers don't know who wrote it. I have heard that Mrs. Stoddard that lady you met here, makes $300 a year by writing for California papers. Now you get acquainted with some Editor there and see if I cannot make something. I could write letters about the operas theatres entertainments etc or stories, and if you would see to them you shall have *half the profits*. You know how I need money and how easily I can write, so I think I might make something in California. I cannot send the *Knickerbocker* for it is not out.

Annie was disappointed at not getting some money, as she had spent almost her last dollar on fitting Charlotte for spring, and had not a dress or garment fit to wear herself. John and I insisted on her getting something and John paid for them, but you must ask Father to send her some, as she really needs it very much.

Charlotte is the same as ever and looks beautifully in a new bonnet trimmed with green. She finds her doll stuffed with sawdust occasionally and wishes to enter a convent, but we shall keep her out I guess. The boys are lovely. Sam walks every where and is in immediate danger of stumbling down stairs in consequence. Will has a great number of fables about "big tall Uncle Bim in ships" and loves you very much.

The girls will probably stay here until June now that there is no Jimmy to call them to dismal Keene and I may go there in July if Father has plenty of money.

Charlotte has just appeared with a letter to you and a *note* to Father! That is respectful! I thought the girls were both going to write Father and so *I wrote you* and they thought the same I suppose.

Do write us often and we will keep you advised of our doings. Dear Jimmy how we all love you! Wil says "tell dear Bim Wil has had *a* ear ache but is very better and wants some taffy candy." Give my *best love to Father*. Annie says, tell Bim I haven't forgotten him *yet*. John sends his hearty congratulations and love. Ever affectionately and lovingly your sister

Lizzie

Even when she confessed to her father that she was difficult to get along with, Charlotte sounded a bit disingenuous, perhaps because for him she remained the good little girl. To her brother she sounded different. Though she was older than he, Charlotte was his cohort in the family, and she expected him to understand her desire to go to West Point and her reservations about New York.

✳   [CHARLOTTE]   New York April 4th 1855

My dearest Jamie,

I can't remember that anything has transpired, worth recounting to you, since last week, when I wrote you via Nicaragua.

Lizzie's poem, on "the Lighthouse," has been greatly admired. It is very fine, I think. Did you see it before you went away? She has written a short story for the *Knickerbocker*, which was published therein, this month. *15 dollars* came to her, as pay therefore. Wasn't that nice? You and Father, you know, need not say anything to *her* about *my* telling you, *unless she* writes it, herself, to you.

. . . I am anxiously awaiting the result of our next letters from Father. They will decide whether I go to West Point or not. I can't help wanting to go very much and if he sends a good deal of money, I shall go.

We are pretty poor now, but a better time is surely coming.

. . . There is no news from Keene, . . .

Ottie writes us long letters, expressing her grief at not seeing you again before you went away. She says the garden looks very well. The strawberries alone, were winter killed, this winter.

Frank Fiske is still at Clarendon I suppose. He has not called here for several days.

I had a letter from Mary Dinsmore the other day. She says she saw you on the sidewalk, when she was driving to the Depot here.

I asked Wil what I should say to you for him, and he said "kant on"

Uncle Bim, which means, "thank you,' you know. I thought it was a good reflection upon my own stupidity, in supposing the young innocent creature to *conform* to the *tonalities* of the *letter writing* community. It means as much as "*regards*" or "*respects*" from people one *hates*.

I know you will be a good boy. I hope and pray that you and Father will come Home next Winter. Then—if nothing happens—shan't we be happy people? My darling boy, don't forget us. We think of you a *great deal*, and nobody loves you *better in this world*, than your sister   Charlie

Annie, who had worked hard to get Jamie's things ready for him to go and scraped to find the money for his ticket, could not see Jamie as the mythic young man launched in the world or as a friend in whom she could confide. She remained the loving and responsible mother, and Jamie's departure was a serious and sad occasion on which she looked back with some regret at the way she had handled him. She told him of people they both know from New York society—Mrs. Meiser, Bryan Schott, Mrs. Tighe—whom her father would not know. She spoke with almost the same familiarity of Lord Farintosh and Ethel and Barnes, characters in Thackeray's new novel, *The Newcomers*, in which, according to family legend, the main character was modeled after James Wilson.

✳ [ANNIE]   New York May 4th 1855

My dearest Jamie,

Your nice letter from ship-board arrived nearly a fortnight ago, and I can't tell you how much delighted I was to get it. What a nice letter it was! And what a good boy you were to write it. It was just the thing, and I was made very happy by it and rejoiced to hear that you got along so well. How lucky you were to find yr old "chum" a friend of Father. You will find his friends all over this country, and everywhere they will speak well of him. That's for being a good man.

I don't know any news to tell you. There seems to be none from Keene. Roxana writes me that James and Emily are going to housekeeping "on their own hook" this month. I am sorry to exchange James for Daniel Seward but I am afraid I shall be obliged to. I don't yet know when I shall go home. Charlotte is [going] away about West Point, and if she goes with Lizzie on the first of June it may detain me here later than I care to stay, as I don't feel quite equal to returning to Keene *entirely* solus.

. . . My darling boy I think about you a great deal, and love you dearly always, and I hope you will never forget it. I am afraid I have not always been as kind to you as I ought to have been, but my dearest boy you must never doubt that I love you *more than any other person in the world, without an exception*, and if I ever seem unkind and cross, you must remember that I am so anxious and nervous about you that I don't know any better.

New York only just begins to be green. The Spring is very backward. Today Mrs. Tighe came to take me to ride in her coupe and B/way was very brilliant. I saw Mrs. Mesier in her carriage and Bryan Schott with her.

Clarence has given up his European project. His brother thinks it would be a great interruption to his studies, and so he stays, and will be admitted by about the first of July. He is as good and generous and kind and handsome as ever. He is very fond of you and asks a great deal about you and wishes you would write to him.

We went to a brilliant wedding the other day, and you will be gratified to hear that I had a new dress. The family said they were ashamed of me and would not go with me in my old clothes any longer and would not let me stay at home and so I went and got a blue silk with flounces, and I have not paid for it yet!

Willie and I talk about 'dear Bim" a great deal, and Wil always says "Will come back, Annie" when he sees me look downcast. I hope you see the Newcomes. Isn't it a comfort to see Barnes on the ground? And isn't it a good scene between Ethel and Lord Farintosh? Read all the new books you can Darling, and try not to get behind the times. Read Lunt Straines journal in Harper March, April, and May. Be a good boy and don't forget you are to come home next Fall. Write always and never forget yr sister

Annie

When Annie writes, "Be a good boy and don't forget you are to come home next Fall. Write always and never forget yr sister," we suspect a subtext. Her father had, after all, been a faithful correspondent and yet had not come home for four years. Times, prices, and everything, as Lizzie had written, had changed. And marshaling her considerable rhetorical arsenal, Lizzie had reiterated the daughters' litany that their anxieties and troubles had nearly destroyed them.

The letters do not answer the question of whether Jamie faithfully fulfilled his sisters' charge to "tell the whole story." At any rate, Wilson did not race back to his daughters and end their long wait. In fact, according to Charlotte, he occasionally even berated them for the inconstancy of their correspondence. "Don't imagine," she urged, "that you have a family of heartless neglectful children, that we are 'Regans and Gonerils,' for we are more like Cordelia, I think, although we did miss that mail" (Charlotte, 9-3-55). In the end the letters of this three-year period of relatively harmonious relationships among the children are laced with the bitter herb of unfulfilled expectation. Annie's reminder says it all: "Oh, Father! do come home. The other night a lady asked me if I had 'any Father,' and it gave me such a shock, that I could hardly answer her, and yet, it was a very natural question" (Annie, 4-19-55).

General James Wilson, Jr., from a painting by P. Prescott (1879), now at the Historical Society of Cheshire County.

Two views of the residence of General James Wilson, Jr., corner of Main and Emerald streets, Keene, New Hampshire. In the larger picture, note the man (General Wilson?) standing on the steps, a woman (Charlotte?) at the right side of the house, and another woman and man (Annie with Frank Fiske?) on the front lawn. Courtesy of Jane Leahy Fiske. The smaller photo, taken at a later date, is courtesy the Historical Society of Cheshire County.

Mary Elizabeth Wilson Sherwood, from a painting by Stephen Hills Parker.

Annie Wilson Fiske and Frank Fiske, from a photograph courtesy of Jane Leahy Fiske.

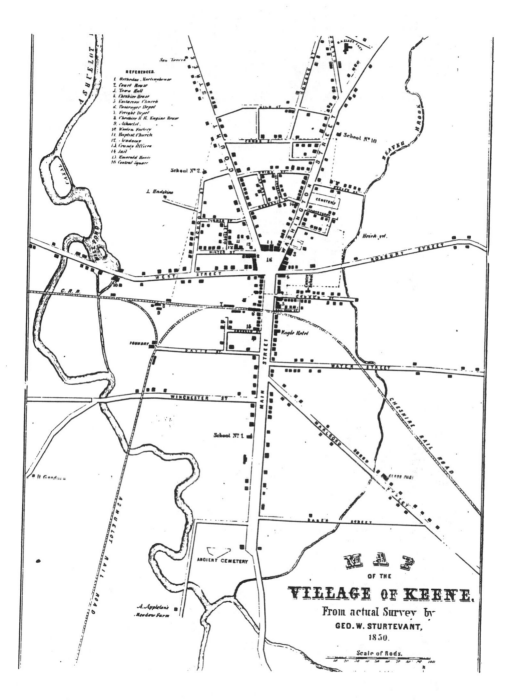

MAP
OF THE
VILLAGE OF KEENE.
From actual Survey by
GEO. W. STURTEVANT,
1850.
Scale of Rods.

Map of the Village of Keene, 1850.

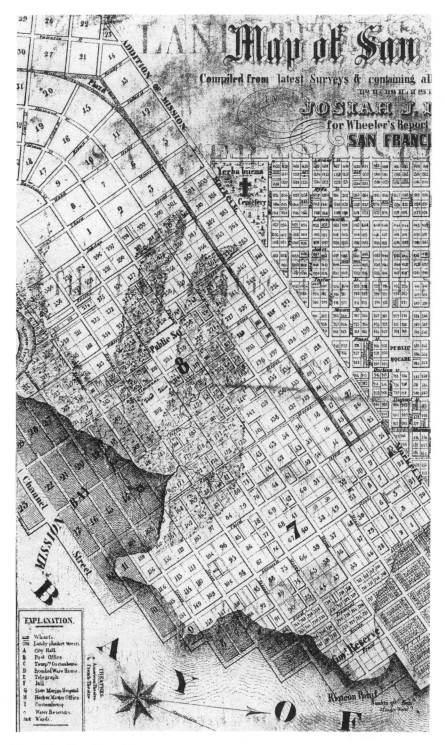

Map of San Francisco, 1848.

Francisco,
l late extensions & Division of Wards.

COUN.
on Land Titles in
SCO CAL.

Line of Larkins or Presidio Ranch.

Lagoon

PUBLIC SQUARE

North Point

SAN FRANCISCO

PLACES of WORSHIP.
a First Baptist Church
b Presbyterian Ch.
c Congregational Chu.
d Trinity Church
e Methodist Episcopal Ch.
f Grace Chapel
g Roman Cath. Church
h New Court? Church
k Baptist Church
l Catholic Church
Presbyterian Church
m Methodist Epl Ch.

The Blocks inclosed in
dotted lines indicate
Grants, outside Historie
Boundaries, as found
in Wheeler's report.

Scale   Varas

1848

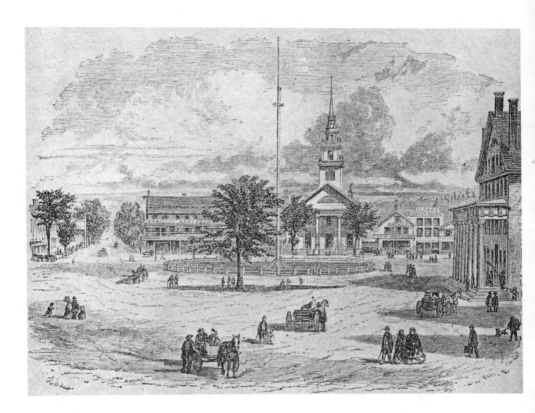

Central Square in Keene, 1858.

PART THREE

"Where Is Father?"

(1855-1864)

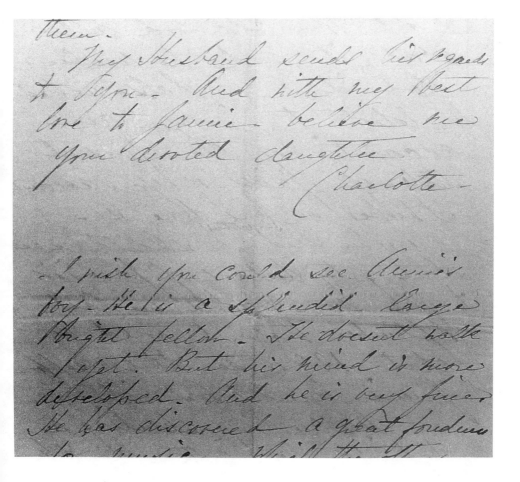

"Annie Has Done the Best Thing"

·

In 1855, Walt Whitman published *Leaves of Grass*. Irish immigrants, still pouring through the port of New York to escape the potato famine, exceeded one million. Abolitionist John Brown and proslavery forces clashed in "bleeding Kansas," and Asa White, who had emigrated to Kansas from Keene, came back to visit and brought an eyewitness account of the violence to his hometown (Keene History Committee, *Upper Ashuelot*, ed. Kay Fox [Keene, N.H.: 1968] 107).

James Wilson was wrapped up in the Limantour case. The same month that Jamie left for California the Limantour claims were submitted to the Land Commission. The commission took its time with the case, sending several times for more testimony and keeping Wilson on tenterhooks.

Annie and Charlotte were deeply in debt. John Sherwood also was short of money, no doubt partly because of the economic depression that had begun in 1853. Lizzie was delighted that her writing had been rewarded with some success, which encouraged her to hope that she could earn more money with her pen. Annie concentrated most of her energy on managing the house and garden in Keene rather than planning an early wedding to Clarence Cram. Although Charlotte was wrapped up in Wil and Sam, she seemed restless and depressed. To cheer herself up, she longed to go with Lizzie and John to West Point before the young officers of her acquaintance departed to fight Indians in the West.

Although readers accustomed to fictional narratives naturally expect to find out what happens next to the characters, a collection of letters does not promise to answer that question. Though, as Annie acknowledged, they felt a strong impulse to tell their story, the survival of the letters and therefore of their story depended on good luck. That there are gaps in the story should not be surprising.

A major gap occurs between June 1855 and April 1858. We have no letters from the three women to their father during that period. Though we know from John Sherwood's correspondence with Wilson that his daughters wrote to him, we do not have those letters. Nearly two years pass. In Keene, 1857 was the coldest winter on record, and the summer was the coolest. The Wilsons may have missed the winter, but they probably were there, huddled around the fire in the back parlor, during the disappointing summer. Springs, falls, and summers were spent in Keene and winters in New York, or so we presume if they followed their established routine. One historian has observed that learning to cover up what you don't know is the mark of a successful historian, and certainly we can make some good and fairly informed guesses about some things that happened to the Wilsons during those many months. In this instance, however, the best guess *about* the Wilsons is not half so satisfying as what the Wilsons write about themselves. And some of the most compelling questions about what happened to them between 1855 and 1858 cannot be answered at all.

In fact, when the narrative is interrupted in May 1855, readers may begin to construct their own narrative about the letters themselves. But the question of whether the letters were lost, burned, or eaten by rats is not so compelling as the questions hanging fire in May 1855. Did Lizzie's writing career flourish? Did Charlotte go to West Point? How well did Wilson succeed in his gold-mining operation, and what did the Land Commission decide about the Limantour case? Did he send some of his newfound wealth home to his needy daughters? What happened to Jamie on his trip to California, and did he return to Keene?

With no letters from the women to Wilson to claim our attention, we can focus on the story of Jamie and his father in California. In fact, for a time Jamie linked the stories of the father and the daughters as he became an actor in James Wilson's story in the West. He took over the operation of the mine at Gold Bluff, about which he writes a neat description to his father, giving us some clearer ideas about the workings of his father's mining and panning operation and of their relationship with Maxwell (Mac), Wilson's mining partner.

✳ [JAMIE]   Gold Bluff Sep 19 [1855]

My darling Father,

Your last package arrived safely, and met with a cordial welcome from me. The letters from the girls are splendid.

We are still packing sand, and there being on hand about 800 (eight hundred) tons. . . .

Mac sends down a small nugget, the result of three days washing which we have washed on days when there has been a heavy surf on. The number of tons washed is 86 and the lump will probably yield about $817.00, not quite up to scratch, but the sand was taken off in a layer, and is probably the poorest in the pile. We have nothing here, that I can retort a neat shapped nugget for Annie in, but perhaps you can have a slice cut off of this lump, and have it [made] over into some . . . shape. I think it would be a very nice present.

Johnson the *last* partner in the Gondolier claim, [was] down here yesterday, and Mac bought his share, for two hundred dollars, so that you and he own the entire claim together now, and I think it will pay splendidly. Perhaps you may recollect, that right in the gulch there is a long broad bank of sand which the surf never troubles. That sand will all pay a good profit, and it is situated in such a manner that it can be shoveled, directly into the machine without wheeling. There is a years work there. Mac has a machine all built and when we get through with the present work, shall probably commence down there. Mac was prospecting there the other day, and found spots where the sand was worth from *ten* to *fifteen* dollars per ton. We shall probably wash in the neighborhood of twenty tons per day.

We have been so busy, that I have not had time to go fishing, read the papers or anything. As the Indians say that is 'tenar work.' . . .

Your devoted, loving boy
Jamie

Wilson saved one of Jamie's letters from a later period, giving more insight into the hazards, excitement, and optimism that fueled the men's fantasy. Jamie, writing from Trinidad, California, where he was stranded by a flood, recounted the progress he was making at Gold Bluff and looked forward with a swagger to swimming home on his horse, Old Bess. "I am happy to be able to inform you that the digging seems to have commenced at the Bluff. . . . Some of the sand has been quite fair and some *beau* quality. But it all helps and the appearance of it has put us all in good humor. The beach is in magnificant order and there is every prospect of a fine run. Up to the time that I started down here the surf had been quite low, that is *comparatively* so. At high-tide during the night, the water would not much more than strike the bluffs, but even with that light force, would wash us out fair sand for the next day. That will give you an idea of how much gold there is on the beach. (Jamie, 2-15-62)

". . . It has rained and hailed furiously now, for seven days, and the winds and seas have been the heaviest ever known here. The sea, three days ago, was the most magnificent sight imaginable. The whole roadstead was a mass of breakers. They commenced way out at sea, outside the head, and came in in long lines reaching half-way to Mad river, breaking entirely over Pilot Rock. What it has been doing at the Bluff, I do not know, but I suppose that it has been the means of opening both the Big and the Stone Lagoons for me, and will give me some pretty tall swimming on my way home. However Old Bess and I are good for almost any trail, and I think we shall '*have souc-cess*,' . . . I send you the disbursements I have made for the Bluff together with the Nett Amount spent to Maxwell and the notes held by the boys. I should have sent it before but the boys' papers were all down here locked up in the safe and I could not make it out" (Jamie, 2-19-62).

Like his father, Jamie threw himself into life in California, finding time to shoot an elk and fight the Indians as well as mine gold at Gold Bluff. As Dr. Bowditch predicted, his headaches ceased.

Jamie's absence provided the occasion for his sister Annie and his father to write two letters to him which bare the bones of the conflict of the two narratives—one of his sisters in the East and the other of his father in the West. Ironically, his sister's letter was delayed by trouble in Panama, so his father's letter from San Francisco reached him at Gold Bluff first. Just as his daughters sometimes borrow conventions from popular literature, Wilson fashions his experience into the mold of a different strain of popular writing.

*   [WILSON]   San Francisco Saturday May 17th 1856

My darling Jamie,

Your exceedingly good letter of the 30th ulto came to hand a few days ago and greatly delighted me in every way and everything—first your health was good, your business successful, prosperous and promising, your courage and confidence unwavering, and last, not least, you had shot an Elk plum through the heart. Bravo, Jamie my boy! I wanted a little more circumstantial account of that noble feat—how you *sneaked* up on the fellow, how your nerves were, how the game stood, which side he stood towards you right or left, how far you had to shoot, which way his head was—north, south, east, west or quartering—was it young or old bull or cow or calf elk, had it horns, how big was it, have you saved the skin or horns or teeth or hoof or any trophy of that victory. Now I think a pretty long and very interesting Letter might be worked up out of those materials fit to fill a column in the "Spirit of the Times" or of "Bells Life in London." But I trow you will have carefully simmered every circumstance through your brain, over and over again and oft, that you may interest and delight me with the eloquent description, *viva voce*, when you come down to visit me. Very good. I can wait and enjoy as great pleasure by anticipation. Really, My Darling, I am greatly delighted that you have dropped an Elk with your Rifle. It is a manly feat and I am proud of it and you. It requires one

of the essential elements of greatness to shoot an Elk—vis. Self possession—the power of perfect self control under the pressure of sudden and
intense excitement. I could deliver a pretty good lecture on that before any
Lyceum.

Your account of the Works and the results and the prospects at the Bluffs
is very full, circumstantial and intelligible, which delights me again, and I
thank you for it. To have you able to do that was one of my objects and
motives in having you go to Gold Bluffs. I have had confident hope, an
unshaken faith, in Gold Bluff ever since I first saw it in the winter of 1850–
1851. I have always thought it a sure thing for me and you and the Dear
Girls at home if we could only take care of it properly, and understand it
thoroughly, and keep it securely. I am full in that opinion now and here
express it to you that it may have with you such influence as it deserves.
Time may show that I am mistaken, but do not give it up lightly or incon-
siderately or without perservering trial. I tell you, My Darling only Son,
that a fixed estate which pays a continuous revenue of some ten or twelve
hundred dollars a month clear is not a thing to be despised or neglected by
any man in this country. Gold Bluff has done and is doing more than that
for our house—*But this is all to be kept to ourselves.*

. . . The Eastern Mail which left New York on the 20th of April ulto is
not in yet. There is a good deal of apprehension here that there is difficulty
at Panama and with the rail road. There was a fight with the last gang of
Passengers that came up and some 20 or 30 of the passengers were killed
by the natives at Panama. The Mail Boat with the Mails of 20th of April is
now overdue and it is feared that there is serious trouble on the Isthmus.

You will see, by the papers which I send you and Maxwell, that San
Francisco is all in a storm of excitement occasioned by a most outrageous
attempt to assassinate a worthy citizen in broad day on the most frequented
street in the city. Jim Casey (or James P. Casey as he calls himself) is a felon
convicted in the city of New York in 1849 of Grand Larceny and served
therefor Two Years in the Sing Sing penitentiary. I cannot say what will be
the result. As a politician Jim Casey has been a man of power here for the
past two or three years. In that capacity he has given effectual aid in the
Election of the present Mayor and High Sheriff and all the other officers
in power here now. Those officers will go in for getting him off. No body
can see the end of this mess. It is a serious business.

Monday May 19th 1856

Our Town is in a State of Revolution. Casey the felon is in the hands
of the vigilance committee and I expect will be hung. So is Cora the murderer of Richardson. He I think will be hung. I never saw such a Sunday
in my life as yesterday—3000 armed citizens taking upon themselves the

Government of this great city as still and quiet and as orderly as a funeral prosession. The Solemnity of the scene was intensely impressive. But my solemn conviction is that "*it is all right*." Had there been a fight I should have promptly taken part with the Vigilance Committee and done what I could to have sustained them in their efforts. I am clear in the opinion that the time has come when the people must assume the position of asserting directly their great right of Sovereignty in California. This is a great question and demands the serious consideration of every good citizen. I must talk a good deal with you, My Darling only Son, upon this subject as you will soon be a citizen and must study how to perform its duties correctly and properly.

I send you and Maxwell the papers.

May God preserve and Bless and prosper you ever prays

Your devoted and Affectionate Father   James Wilson

Five days later Wilson reported with some relish that "Casey the Murderer of James King . . . was hung today by the people. Cora who shot Richardson . . . was hung at the same time. We have exciting times here and everything is at a stand still. It will all come out right I think. Those wretches deserved hanging richly."

The enthusiastic tales of the vigilantism (the formidable Captain Folsom was head of the Vigilance Committee) that passed for law enforcement in San Francisco, the honors he heaped on Jamie for killing an elk, his delight in the success of Gold Bluff diverge so completely from the stories his daughters admire that we might wonder how these correspondents communicated at all. No doubt he tailored his material to his audience and wrote to each in a different vein. If his daughters were not sympathetic to these tales, he knew there was an audience for the kind of stories he and Jamie were sharing. Wilson recognized at once in Jamie's manly achievement in killing the elk a potential story for a lyceum or for a popular eastern or English sporting journal, the sort of journal that retailed masculine adventure fantasies in the West for the eastern market. In fact, Wilson transformed his experience into art almost before it was lived. Felons and assassins, murders and lynchings were "immensely impressive" and "exciting," but he was confident they would "all come out right," just as in all good adventure stories.

The daughters struggled to drag their father and Jamie back from these headlong adventures in California to domestic life in the East. Jamie was responsible for preserving the family's social status. The qualifications Jamie needed to gratify her ambitions, Annie reminded him, were to be acquired at Harvard College, not at Gold Bluff.

✻ [ANNIE]   New York April 20th 1856

My darling Jamie,

I was very much disappointed not to get a letter from you in this last
mail as I always am when that happens, and it seems to be the rule now,
rather than the exception. I had hoped, too, that by this time both you and
Father would be thinking of your return, for which I am so anxious that
when people ask me if you are contented, I say, 'I am sorry to say that he
is.' I got quite angry with John the other day because he repeated his old
remark, 'I gave up all hope of Jamie's ever going thro' college when he left
this Port.'

Oh Jamie prove to him and every body else that you are no common
boy by coming back with all yr man's strength and going to work at your
education as seriously as you have attacked the sands of the shores of the
Pacific. Oh that would be manly indeed Jamie, not the manliness of strong
arm and back but the manliness of a strong head and will, the strength of
a gentleman, both gentle refined and manly in its finest acceptation. My
darling Boy we have been proud of you ever since you were born. We have
been gratified by everything you have ever done. I have always expected to
hear and have heard strangers who saw you for the first time say, what a
beautiful boy! what a gentlemanly boy. What a refined face what a manly
young fellow! And now darling I am ambitious to have you always superior to all the others as you have been. The time is coming when you are
no longer a boy, and when you are a man. These good points will not be
remarked, because they are expected in a gentleman. Then will come the
time when to excel you must be cultivated, educated. In those times when
free schools and free colleges are covering the land and the blacksmiths
boy can learn Greek and Belle letters. Not to have cultivated your head
will be a disgrace since it is in the power of everyone in this country. My
only brother, the last of the name, you will not disappoint me! Know more
than any body else! Not only be better, and do better, but *know more*. My
dearest Jim I beg of you.

Now that is all.

We shall send you out a photograph by the next mail of a drawing which
Mr. Bailey made of me. I hope you will think it like me, for it is a beautiful
work of art. You must not think that I 'got myself up' to sit for it. I had a
wreath on my head the night of Mrs. Mundy's tableau and he asked me to
let him sketch it. It was a wreath made for Amelia to wear and they put it
on me for fun, but it produces a very classic effect.

. . . I don't have any body to walk home with, and often I want to tell
people that I have got a 'big brother' only he won't come home.

. . . Good bye dear Jim. Write soon to yr loving sister   Annie

In truth, the blacksmith had already built a house so close to theirs that it blocked their view. He considered public education a fair opportunity to go a step further and acquire Greek and Latin that would qualify him, if he felt so inclined, to identify himself with his upper-middle-class neighbors. From Annie's point of view the Wilsons would have to be even better educated to maintain that distinction. Shooting an elk failed to demonstrate that Jamie was more than a "common boy." Other paths to social advancement—acquiring land, marrying into a wealthy or prestigious family, making a fortune in the West, building a railroad, inventing a widget—did not occur to Annie. Education and a respectable profession were the protection a gentleman needed from the social climbing of the blacksmith's son.

General Wilson did not disapprove of his daughters' social ambitions or deny his responsibility to help them. He simply melted all of their domestic complications and social ambitions in the golden haze of his masculine fantasy. Everything he did, according to his journals, he did for them. Their financial problems, he told Jamie, would be solved by his mine at Gold Bluff—a "sure thing." The more they bewailed his absence and their poverty, the more he resolved that his stay in California was the solution, not the problem. Deeply as the modern reader may sympathize with the women's ambitions, frustrations, and constraints, Wilson's account of life in California is a little like seeing *Red River* after a steady diet of *Gaslight* and *Yellow Wallpaper*. The life-and-death struggles in Wilson's letter engage us in an expansive, untortured narrative of freedom and action, refreshing after the women's domestic perplexities of families, gossip, courtships, servants, mortgages, and babies. Wilson wanted to talk to Jamie about "great questions" that demand "serious consideration." Shooting an elk. Finding gold. Hanging a murderer. Manly, brave, and simple problems unlike the vagaries of Uncle Robert, mortgages on the house, the demands of Roxana and other creditors, Charlotte's poor health, Annie's unhappy love affairs, the conflict between Lizzie and the Sherwoods, Jamie's headaches—these intricate problems haunted the house in Keene for years and years until everybody was sick of thinking about them.

In this conflict between daughters and father, if we define the sisters' goal as having Jamie come home and go to Harvard and Wilson's as having him remain in California panning for gold, then the women won. Jamie returned home sometime during the gap in the correspondence. When we pick up the story again in the summer of 1858, he was entering his junior year at Harvard.

His father, meantime, was far too preoccupied with the Limantour case to concern himself with his children's domestic problems, much less to leave California for Keene. During the two years of silence from the women, his story proceeded as the case to which Wilson had hitched his wagon drew to a climax. The wheels of justice ground exceeding slow. Not until January 22, 1856, did the California Land Commission finally issue its decision. Then, in two separate and sweeping decisions, they upheld all of Limantour's claims to the land on which San Francisco was built. James Wilson's years of work seemed at last to be vindicated. Lizzie sent her father John Sherwood's congratulations on the victory (Lizzie, 4-19-55).

However, long before the commission validated Limantour's claim, it was clear that the U.S. government would not accept the decision as final. The military considered much of the coastland in his claim vital to the defense of the territory. The government pursued the case in the civil and criminal courts.

The case was expanding in all directions. When Limantour was indicted for fraud and perjury, Wilson called in an eloquent lawyer named John B. Felton, known to be "equally potent to obscure a good title as to mend a bad one" (Johnson, *José Yves Limantour*, 46) The government lawyers had searched the archives of California again and again, scrutinized the papers Limantour presented to validate his claim, and interviewed myriad witnesses time and again but remained unsure of their case and were seeking further testimony in Mexico. The case became more and more convoluted. Having published in 1853 a pamphlet outlining Limantour's claim, Wilson hired a professional writer, who produced a masterful pamphlet stating Limantour's position. A counterargument was presented in a pamphlet for which the writer was rewarded with a job in the office of the U.S. Attorney. One of Limantour's star witnesses who seemed about to crack was attacked with his own knife. Whether the wound was self-inflicted or one of Limantour's agents or a member of the anti-Limantour forces tried to kill the man never became clear.

Finally, the day came when the court convened to hear all of the evidence in the case. Wilson introduced the sheaf of documents from California and Mexico affirming Limantour's claim, supported by testimony of Limantour's witnesses. Then Limantour and his witnesses departed, and the government began producing its evidence.

The end of this epic case was remarkably simple and dramatic. The seal of the Mexican government on the Limantour papers ultimately validated his claim. Although to the casual observer the seals on the Limantour papers seemed identical with seals on other unimpeachable papers, the infant technology of photography proved otherwise. In the late fall of 1857 a young photographer named George Davidson blew up a picture of the seals on the Limantour documents and showed that there were significant differences between the official one used in California in 1843, the date of Limantour's claim, and the seals on the Limantour documents, which proved the seal on Limantour's papers to be from a later date than Limantour had claimed. So convincing was the evidence that neither Wilson nor Felton even bothered to cross-examine the photographer.

This dramatic piece of evidence pretty well put paid to the claim. There was more to come, however. In fact, the case was finished in 1858, about the same time that correspondence between the women and their father is available again.

Exciting as this story and the story of Jamie's and his father's adventures in the Wild West are, they are perhaps not so compelling as the unresolved love story of Annie and Clarence Cram. Annie, the beautiful sister who "flirted with fools," had broken one engagement that Lizzie didn't approve of and entered into another that neither Lizzie nor John completely endorsed. In that second engagement she had persisted despite their disapproval. Did the beautiful Annie, like the heroine of every good fairy story, finally get married and live happily ever after to the man who had for one winter made her happier than she had ever been? The simple but highly unsatisfactory answer is no. The engagement collapsed during the gap in the correspondence in 1856–1857. What the reader wants to know is the story, and of that we only have the barest shards.

In May 1855, Annie told Jamie that "Clarence has given up his European project. His brother thinks it would be a great interruption to his studies, and so he stays, and will be admitted [to the bar] by about the first of July" (Annie, 5-4-55). Charlotte wrote to Jamie on April 20, 1856, nearly a year later, that Clarence was away in England and had been there some time. "I suppose Clarence will come home very soon. He is meeting with success now. Has been having the "Patent Gas Regulator" put into the Houses of Parliament. Which is beginning at headquarters you know. . . . Annie's endurance is almost exhausted. She says she won't pretend any longer that she wants him to stay. Just think, Jamie, what a long lonely winter this has been for her. Constantly expecting Clarence, and constantly being disappointed.

"Nevertheless she has had the proof that Clarence has perseverance and decision of character. He only needed an occasion to call it out to prove that. He wrote me a very funny letter advising me to marry a rich man. His arguments were good. But it was funny that he preferred not to *practice* them himself, but *chose* to be an *awful example* for others" (Charlotte, 4-20-56).

From public sources we can find out that nearly a hundred buildings were built in Keene during this period, and from later family letters we learn that Jamie became the billiard champion at Harvard; but we can't find an answer to the most interesting question, what happened to Annie's love affair with Clarence Cram?

Our only clues to the aftermath are in two letters from John Sherwood.

He observed, on December 23 of an unspecified year, maybe 1856, "Of course our poor Annie is much castdown and depressed but we think very much relieved that the unfortunate affair with Clarence Cram is terminated. She was in very great doubt about him latterly and her fears were not allayed as she learned more—We are all heartily rejoiced—Now that it is all over Sir, I must say he was not her equal in any respect—that he was entirely undeserving of her. . . ." On January 5 of perhaps 1857, he observed, ". . . we feel that our Dear Annie is recovering her spirits after the terrible blow she has had." If the date of 1857 is correct, and it is hard to be sure, then Annie's engagement went on for perhaps two or three years before it was broken off. What did Annie learn more about? How was he undeserving of her? What happened to Cram? In 1858, when the correspondence picks up again, Clarence's name has vanished from the letters. The only thing we know is that sometime between April 1856 and January 1857 the engagement ended and Annie was very unhappy for a time.

It might be interesting to speculate that Annie herself destroyed letters about the engagement. Perhaps after her father's death, when she was forty-nine, still smarting from her disappointment, she sorted through the collection and removed the letters recounting her broken engagement. If so, then Annie chose to edit what she and her sisters had written earlier about her private misadventure before she left her narrative to our mercy. Such speculation stimulates us to create a new narrative of our own which, however tempting, does not answer our questions. It is more useful to recall how devastating would be a broken engagement of long standing, publicly announced. Not quite like a divorce but certainly harrowing and humiliating.

When the mysterious silence in the correspondence is broken, the damage has been done, and we hear no more of Cram. Instead Lizzie, who was so often thwarted by the time and distance that separated her from her father, pondered the advantage of swifter communication via telegraph. "Is not this great news about the Telegraph? Query. Do the human race enjoy life anymore for this annihilation of Time and Space?" (Lizzie, 8-18-58).

In April 1858 the gap in the women's correspondence ends. But time and space have wrought changes uncorrectable by the telegraph. By 1858, when their story resumes, much of the day-to-day quality of the early letters is gone. Annie and Lizzie, both married, occasionally mention that someone Wilson knew had died or gotten married, but they don't spend their time writing amusing stories that do not apply to the family and its situation. They seldom tell him their thoughts on the news of the day. No more long missives about the state of universities or the Kansas-Nebraska Act or slavery. Most surprising is the absence of commentary by any of the daughters on the growing crisis between the North and South. In fact, not until the Civil War actually began did the women write about it. If they discussed such matters, it was not with their father. Only Charlotte, who was still dependent on him, kept him abreast of the dailiness of their lives. After 1858, Annie and Lizzie wrote long and serious letters about important family problems or events—and there were plenty of those—but when there was nothing pressing to communicate, they often settled for a perfunctory page about the charms of Jamie or Lizzie's children and a note about their plans. Although the story is often intense, much of the expansiveness of the communication is gone.

Where are we now in the narrative? Lizzie is thirty-two. Annie is twenty-six. Charlotte is twenty-three. The cast of main characters remains the same, but there have been some major developments, and we are on the brink of even more dramatic events. But some things stayed the same—only more so. Again Lizzie was in Keene for the summer with her three children and four servants, and John was a frequent visitor. Again there was the flood of other visitors as well. Annie, who still assumed responsibility for Jamie and Charlotte, was exhausted, and her budget was, as always, devastated.

Jamie, who had returned from California, was at Lake Saranac in the Adirondacks, camping in the woods. Far from Gold Bluff, he enjoyed the summer in Keene, where he walked and danced and picnicked with some nice young women from New York and occasionally received letters from Max, his old companion at Gold Bluff, about production at the mine. More important, he had already completed two years at Harvard and would return in September to start his junior year. Although as a token of his independence Jamie now received his allowance directly from his father, he frequently overspent and turned to Annie to help him out. Annie, of course, could not say no and justified her brother's extravagance to her father. Her letter was followed by several from Jamie along the same line.

Following Annie's broken engagement, she and Charlotte spent the winter in Keene rather than New York. But the following summer, when they went to the Isles of Shoals off the coast of New Hampshire, it was not to distract Annie from her broken heart but to cure some inexplicable malaise that plagued Charlotte by bathing in the cold North Atlantic and breathing the sea air. Although exercise remedied Charlotte's bout of headaches, this time the doctor recommended quiet and rest.

✳ [ANNIE]   Keene September 2nd 1858

My dearest Father,

 . . . We returned from the Isles of Shoals on the next Tuesday after we wrote you, two weeks ago. We thought Charlotte was benefited by the change, and tho' she was very tired and worn out by the journey home I think she is now really better. There seems no reason why she should not be perfectly well, and yet she is not strong. We saw Dr. Bowditch at the Shoals who said he could not see that anything was wrong, and yet such debility, and disinclination to exercise must have a cause, and he suggested, as a possibility, that she had suffered some strain either from too much walking, or skating *imprudently*. He recommended quiet, which she is now getting, most emphatically. She looks in perfect health, and says she very much enjoys being "made much of." Our darling Jamie left us the day before yesterday. I can never tell you what a source of pleasure and comfort to us he is. I don't know what impression any informant of yrs. might intend to convey by describing Jamie as a "lady's man," but if he meant by that, the most amiable, obliging, chivalrous, honorable, and hence, most popular of young men, he said the truth. Jamie is a very great favorite in ladies society, and he likes it. Thank God! he *prefers* it to barrooms, stables, or gambling houses. He prefers, too, . . . the society of his peers, and those to whom he must look up, to that of his inferiors who will adore him. John Sherwood says he has never seen so high toned and satisfactory a young man, that he can not discover a single bad habit. He is a Wilson—root and branch—and that means, a generous somewhat reckless fellow with money, sought after always, and loving approbation and popularity, never being able to receive anything without returning the same, born to a prominent position, and with a popular Father's reputation to back all the rest. It is hard to learn thrift and method and above all how to say "no," but he is trying, and the harder it is the more praise is due him. Oh Father rejoice in yr son—! and thank God for him . . . even if in these young and prodigal days, he does spend yr money, he will reward you yet.

I am sorry you did not approve of my sending to Mr. Skinner for money. You were displeased last winter that I did not do so, rather than write to you constantly of my wants. I could not know that you were about to send us a large amount. I don't wonder you are discouraged that we should exceed yr most generous supplys, but I can't do any better while your generosity supports so large a family—Charlotte's and mine—and Jamie's grocer's bills for Decr. Jany. Feby. and March all told, was $37.53. Our bill for June and July, (principally July) has been $64.53. . . .

I am glad, Dear Father, that your farm is such a source of pleasure to you. I only wish it lay a little nearer to your children. . . .   Yr loving
                                                                          Annie

Wil at six and Sam at five seem much the same as when we last saw them in 1855. Lizzie sent pictures. "Here are my two oldest boys, which I send you. Are they not nice ones. Sam you observe does his thinking very *hard* as Webbie used, but it is very good thinking when done. Wil is full of genius and beauty but Sam is the strongest. . . . My dear boys are flourishing finely in Keene. On intimate terms with Daniel, fond of green apples and subject to whippings" (Lizzie, 8-18-58). Lizzie had also had a third son, Arthur, "interesting and bright," who arrived in the world to less thunderous applause than had his two older brothers. She did not even send her father a picture of Arthur. "Dear little Arthur has been daguerreotyped but I have never sent you a picture, for he looks exactly as Wil did" (Lizzie, 8-18-58). In fact, children, who had begun to all look alike, had lost a lot of their charm. "I fear Grandchildren are ceasing to be a rarity to you, as I have rather run the matter into the ground" (Lizzie, 8-18-58). They are also ceasing to be a rarity to Lizzie, who was pregnant again.

In September, Lizzie had her fourth son. By this time even this patriarchial family would have preferred a girl—all except Lizzie herself. Though the letters from the women tended to be sketchy during the spring and summer of 1858, Annie instructed her father on Lizzie's courageous behavior during the "illness" of childbirth as one might praise a soldier who fought bravely and endured his wounds stoically.

✱ [ANNIE]   Keene September 17th 1858

My dearest Father,

You will be glad to hear of the safe arrival of a fourth son, to your daughter Lizzie. He was born on Wednesday night the 15th of Septr at a quarter before twelve. Lizzie is very comfortable and was not very ill more than three hours. . . . But I must tell you how splendidly Lizzie behaved. Her Nurse was not here and not expected till the 20th. She asked me to send for Mrs. Reed (in the morning) to come and spend the night and to send word to Dr. Twitchell that she hoped he would be at home. Then she sat down to her sewing, came down to breakfast, dinner, and tea, and nothing but an occasional flush of color showed that she was suffering. She asked me to telegraph for the Nurse, and her husband, and at nine o'clock in the eve/g went to bed, as calmly, and self possessed as ever. She was very ill for three hours, and after that, as comfortable as only a woman of her strong constitution, and *courage* can be. I never knew a woman to behave so well. We don't know what to name the boy, as we had got "Mary Rosalie" all ready for a girl, but Lizzie thinks of "Philip." What do you suggest?

I am sorry Dearest Father that our expenditures are so heavy, and that you are distressed about your affairs. . . . I can not reduce the expenses as long as we keep this house open, and I think this is the last season of it, for Lizzie says she will never bring such a retinue here again, and Charlotte and I may be elsewhere before another Summer Heaven knows. Wherever I am she will be. . . .

I am yr loving
Annie

Wilson needed some of Lizzie's endurance and stoicism to face the last scene in the Limantour case. In April of the year that Lizzie's fourth son was born, the prosecution shredded the remains of Wilson's case. The attorney for the United States had discovered that Micheltorena, the last Mexican governor of California, had no official seal paper during the early part of 1843. It would have been impossible for him to write an official document, such as Limantour's claim, for the simple reason that his supply of the kind of paper on which the document was written had run out. Though the prosecution kept this bit of incriminating evidence secret from Wilson and Felton until a hearing in July, Felton told Wilson he thought fraud had been proved and that he and Wilson would be tarred with the same brush if they continued to defend Limantour. He withdrew from the case. Having fought Limantour's battle for five years and "staked his character and reputation upon their honesty and validity," according to historian Theodore H. Hittel (*History of California* [San Francisco, 1897], 698), Wilson declared he would see the case through even if it ended badly.

In November 1858, a brilliant legal orator named Edwin Stanton delivered a three-and-a-half-hour summation for the U.S. government that demolished the last of Limantour's case. Despite Felton's warning, Wilson was unprepared for this final defeat. So devastated was Wilson that he appeared to be in a state of shock, and when called on to reply to this final barrage, he could say nothing (Johnson, *José Yves Limantour*, 68). When Judge Ogden Hoffman rejected the case on appeal, Wilson had finally lost.

The bold adventurer for whom Wilson had fought his most famous legal battle left the country, still protesting that his claim was legitimate. Wilson was denied even the fame of defeat, for when the government printed the opinion, no names appeared as counsel for Limantour. The name of Limantour disappeared from the letters a great deal more easily than the sting of the defeat and disgrace disappeared from Wilson's heart.

Under the strain of the final months of this debacle, Wilson evidently wrote a cryptic account of his situation and a brutal attack on his family, especially Annie, whose disastrous engagement to Cram may have paralleled too closely his own recent failure. Of course, whoever was in charge of family finances would probably have received the brunt of his wrath. Lizzie responded with an outraged, eloquent, touching, and carefully reasoned summary of his daughters' situation during his absence. This letter, with which we introduced their story, is worth reading more closely now in its chronological place in the narrative of the Wilsons.

✷ [LIZZIE]   New York Nov 5th 1858

My dear Father,

Eight years ago on the twelfth of Sept. I stood on the wharf at New York (as the carriage was conveying us on our way to the depot) and saw you leaving the port on the Steamship *Georgia* (was it not?). The feeling of gloom and despondency which settled down on my heart *then* comes on me again tonight as I remember it. What power could have sustained me had I seen how long that separation was to be? As it was I felt it enough. One poor girl, with three younger sisters and brother to sustain and counsel and our only support and hope gone gone on that terrible journey. Eight long years away from your young and unprotected daughters. Does it not strike you as an unparalleled fact. What should we think of it, if Mr. Sumner Wheeler or any other man should do so? Does it not strike you, looking at it from a *common* point of view as an eccentric and curious thing?

Since then a veil has fallen between you and me. Before we were inti-mate. I used to know something of what you meant, what motives activated you, but now I know nothing of you. I write to you begging for a reply. You never make it. I ask for an explanation. You never give it. I entreat it of you. It does not move you. You write of everything else, your farm, your reading, the climate, etc. All very fine letters, but not what I want to know. I want ten minutes *confidence* from you such as your daughter should receive, such as you ought to give her, such as you used to give her. Here is a mystery which I wish you would clear up. You write sometimes happily, sometimes depressed. You never say why. We *presume* the Limantour case has proved a failure, but is that all that we ought to know? should we not, who are so much interested, know the *truth*?

Then I am astonished at the way you seem to feel toward Annie and Charlotte. The tone of your last letters to them was that of a person writing to some enemy, some hated enemy who had tried to injure him. You not only hint at their probable destitution, which one would think a sufficiently sad thing but you *taunt them* with their inability to work, and their idea of its disgrace. When that letter arrived Annie and Charlotte had been turned out of their own room by my illness. They had had company unexpect-edly arrive. Roxana as usual had refused to do anything and they had been working night and day. Annie's hands and face were red with the exertions she had been making. Charlotte was looking over the week's mending. I went in to their crowded room and found them both crying over your letter. "Now Lizzie," said Annie, "won't you read this letter and tell me what I can do. What does Father *mean* by treating me so. I, who am slaving my life out to please him, to manage this place, to economize to work, to think, to worry, until my life has no pleasure in it." I could only tell her I did not know, that you seemed changed most radically since you went away, that you were always kind and lovely to me. Never did Father treat daughter better, but why you feel so toward these poor dear girls who are much better than ever I was, I don't know. *I should like to know* I assure you.

If you were to ask any man in Keene from Mr. Crossfield the carpenter up to Mr. White the clergyman who was the best girl in Keene, they would both tell you Annie Wilson. If you were to ask the poor Irish woman who would have starved but for her who was the best girl in Keene she would say the same. If you want to see a model housekeeper, neat, energetic, economical, you have only to look at her, and yet what an opinion you seem to have of her! If the public could know what *you* seem to think of her they would say there was a new chapter in this most eccentric history of the Wilson family. But God forbid. Let this sad secret be always locked within our own hearts. Now as to the question of spending too much, do you not see that if anyone is to blame, I am the one? The housekeeping of those two girls would not be very expensive if they had not us there all summer. Therefore you should have written to me that it would not be convenient and agreeable for you to have me there this summer, and I should not have taken it amiss. I have long been sensible of the great additional expense it must be to you, but as you cordially told me to go, I went, thinking it gave you pleasure to have me. Hence the large bills. Annie has to be responsible for all these and really gets the advantage of none of it except the gratification of having her nephews with her. I can offer her the shelter of my roof in return, and that she shall have as long as I have one. God bless her for all her unselfish devotion to me! Poor girl. She has had trouble enough without having her Father turn against her. If she had been a bad undutiful daughter I would not say a word, but she is a religious, hard working loving soul devoting her life like a sister of charity to the poor, to my children and to you, and I cannot stand it. I must speak.

Now Father, do if you can raise money enough to pay your passage, come home, don't stay any longer. You said in a letter of June to John that you would certainly come to attend to that business of Uncle Robert's, and honor demands that you should. Have you no yearnings to see us? Do you not love us better than any one. Don't you want to see your *four grandsons*? Oh do come dear Father. We have not many years to be together on this earth. Do let us have the rest of your life, no matter for fortune. You can always make a handsome living here. If the *Limantour* is used up 'Jim

Wilson' *isn't*, and the recuperative powers which have always distinguished you will do so still longer. We will economize, only let us have our Father within our grasp. If you would only go in partnership with John it would be a good thing for him and for you too. You have eloquence and genius, he has industry and judgement.

If by any horrible necessity or determination you don't intend to come home write to the girls what you want to spend and they will conform. They can give up housekeeping, which with them involves some hospitality and I can refrain from going there. That you will find makes all the difference.

As for Jamie, he is one of the noblest and most satisfactory of young men. Every one speaks well of him. If he gives way to some temptations they are nothing to what he resists. He is not perfect, but he is very good. Surrounded by every temptation I believe he makes a pretty good fight and will make an admirable man. Don't be discouraged or disgusted with him. Let us all try to get him thro' college. He is as handsome as he can be, witty, manly modest and truthful. I dare say he has his little fun now and then, but what fellow that is worth anything don't, at 20? As Thackeray says, 'Glorious youth, it never comes again, let us be fools and enjoy ourselves once in our lives.' But Jimmy is no fool. He has no despicable amount of caution, I can tell you particularly with the young ladies who are all after him.

Charlotte has been miserably this summer but she is better. I felt very much alarmed about her. Charlotte has not much constitution.

You knew I have my fourth son. I am sorry for the other boys that he is not a girl. For my own sake I am glad and for his. I am quite well and strong. Came down to town less than five weeks, and have been quite well all the time. The baby looks exactly like you, has curling black hair, and is very fat and healthy.

We don't know what to call him. Possibly 'John Phillip.' Wil and Sam are up at Keene, very splendid indeed, sucking sweet cider *thro' a straw*, and being very big and boyish. Charlotte teaches them to read and works very hard with them. You knew they have just been up to Fairfax to see Aunt Nancy and she was delighted with their visit.

My dear husband, than whom none more worthy ever lived, has an excellent business, works very hard, is very successful, but our expenses are enormous. I sometimes fear he will break down, but he is patient and courageous. Need I say that I love him dearly, try to make him happy, and to help him bear his burdens.

Do write me soon and tell me that you are coming home. Come to my little house and see how I manage an establishment. Let us read in the next letter, "expect me by the next steamer." Then face to face all misunderstandings will vanish away and we shall find that we love each other, all of us as well as ever. . . .

Farewell, dear Father. don't be angry with me. You know I love you as well as a daughter can love a Father and as poor Queen Katherine wrote to Henry the Eighth, "mine eyes do desire you of all things."

Farewell. God bless you

Your loving daughter   Lizzie

Doubtless, Lizzie's position—her more equal relationship with Wilson and her independence as a married woman—as well as her confidence in her relationship to her father allowed her to defend her sisters and demand accountability from him in this dark tone. Certainly, neither of the other sisters risked writing such a letter.

Lizzie could have added that his criticism of his daughters' reluctance to work for pay was particularly hypocritical since he criticized Lizzie for doing just that. His assumption that they don't work reveals how little he understood how taxing was the work of managing a large house full of people and taking care of four young children, with or without servants. Doubtless part of the misunderstanding resulted from the sisters' reluctance to complain about the work they did, especially when they had to complain so often about the lack of money they had to live on. In the vivid description of the scene in their bedroom, Lizzie stripped away the veil of grace that they had cast over Annie's red hands and face and Charlotte's work on the week's mending to tell her father some hard truths about women's lives.

The qualities required for this kind of work—charity, energy, religious faith, unselfishness, frugality, neatness—were the qualities Annie had, as even notable men like the carpenter and the clergymen would attest. Interestingly, this description contrasts nicely with the disapproving one Wilson gives of California women in general, who are "showy and extravagant" and of one in particular who is a "queer, unprincipled, lying devil but smart and scheming" (Notebooks, 1-2-56, 1-5-56) It was, Lizzie insisted, Wilson's doubt of his daughter's worth that would create a scandal among responsible men.

In a flash of insight into what this correspondence was doing, Lizzie called Wilson's attack on Annie a "new chapter in the eccentric history of the Wilson family."

Almost as violent as Lizzie's stormy letter in the fall of 1858 were two meteorlogical events of the season: a storm that struck Keene during the equinox and the sighting of the Great Comet. They were "all gazing nightly at the most magnificent comet that has graced the skies in *our* days" (Annie, 10-3-58). These meteorlogical disorders Charlotte found "almost alarming" and supposed that her father saw the brilliant comet in California, which indeed he did and noted in his diary. The comet might have marked the Lincoln–Douglas debates that occurred that fall or portended John Brown's raid on Harper's Ferry, which was only twelve months away as the clouds of civil war blackened over the nation. For the Wilsons the comet and the storm marked the end of one chapter of family history and the beginning of another.

Unlike the heroines of sentimental fiction, Annie did not pine away with her broken heart or join a convent or throw herself off a bridge. At twenty-six she dismissed her broken heart and accepted a marriage proposal from a longtime suitor, Frank Fiske, an old friend of the family. Although Annie seemed happy, the engagement, wedding, and aftermath were dogged by dissension and accidents. Wilson had evidently been informed of the engagement sometime before September, when we first hear of it in the correspondence. Then Charlotte broached the subject through a gentle reminder of a wedding present.

"What can we do for Annie on this important occasion? I think, instead of giving her a present as we did Lizzie, we had better give her some money, to invest as she thinks best.

"She has made so many sacrifices for us that we should be willing to make some for her. Of course I leave the matter entirely to you, simply expressing my desire to do something for her, and my belief that *she* is the best judge of what she *needs*" (Charlotte, 9-17-58).

How different is this tentative tone from the positive and assertive one Annie took when planning the purchase and engraving of the grand silver tea service the family presented to Lizzie! Evidently, money was what Annie wanted and needed, but Charlotte was far too eager to please to push her father very hard on money matters.

In a November letter in which we learn that Annie's fiancé is Frank Fiske, we also learn the news was not altogether well received in the Wilson family. Though Charlotte and Jamie liked Frank and thought he would make a good husband for Annie, they felt lost. She who had devoted herself to them was now devoted to someone else. Charlotte complained of being very lonely even before the wedding took place. Though both Lizzie and the General were friendly with Frank, Lizzie thoroughly disapproved of the match, and Wilson evidently was not delighted.

Frank was no John Sherwood. Though the Fiskes were wealthy, Frank was not. Thirty-two-year-old Frank had attended Harvard law school, but his career thus far had consisted of translating a book from Spanish to

English. He had some pretensions to being a writer but had had little success. He had traveled to Spain and then to California, where he spent time with Wilson; but if he had sought his fortune on these trips, it had eluded him. Jamie, who liked him very much, nevertheless found him "fearfully fussy and old bachelor-like" (Jamie 2-20-?). Sometimes pretentious—he affected an exotic Spanish beard—but always intense, his devotion to Annie had not wavered through his own travels and her engagement to Cram.

Although Frank's fortune was far smaller than John Sherwood's, there was no expectation that Wilson would provide a dowry of $15,000 or even $5,000 for his second daughter, as Lizzie had requested. He finally sent Annie $150 before the wedding and another $400 afterward. Annie had no ambitions or expectations that she would cut a figure in the social world. When she assured her father that the money she received would be the last she would ask of him, she characterized not only her relationship with her father but also his reduced financial position.

In any case, Wilson and his eldest daughter effectively robbed Annie of most of the joy of her modest wedding. Annie wrote in a melancholy, even bitter mood of her unhappy experience with Cram, her new engagement, and her prospects as she prepared to leave home without her father's approval.

✳ [ANNIE]   Keene Novr 1st 1858

My dearest Father,

. . . Charlotte and I have just returned from a visit to Aunt Farnsworth, where we went, taking Wil. and Sam. with us, a week ago. We found her much better in health and spirits than last year. And she has a Minister's family living in part of her house, so she is no longer so miserably alone.

. . . I have had a picture, a large Ambrotype, of them and Charlotte and me all tied up to send you, by Mr. Weston, for several days, but he has not called for it yet. . . .

You were right in yr supposition expressed in yr letter of Sept. 20th that Frank had never made any proposition relative to any assistance from you. He on the contrary urges me not to delay our marriage even to procure the ordinary wardrobe of a bride, and will insist upon *settling* Five Thousand dollars upon his wife, which is a larger proportion of his whole small fortune than most men give their wives outright. He has gone to New York to see about the publication of a french translation he has recently made for the Evening Post, and will possibly connect himself with that paper in some way. Nothing can exceed the disinterestedness and dignity of his character and you need never fear or believe anything else of him. He begs me not to postpone the marriage beyond next month, but I really think you will not wish me to go quite empty handed at least without suitable clothing now. So I shall wait to hear from you at least. I am very sorry that proposition made to you offended you so much. It was made half in joke quite carelessly.

I have tried to do my duty toward you Dear Father and toward my brother and sisters since I have been left in charge of the family affairs. In giving them up now, I can not see many things which I could well alter tho' there are many that I *would*. I am sorry I have failed to gratify you all in my marriage and that my most unhappy experience which has cut down deeper than any of you know, or will ever know, I hope, has so sadly mortified you. You must allow me to say in my own justification that I think I should have sometimes done myself greater service if I had neglected my duties at home a little more. However, I don't regret that, but I am sorry not to have gratified you, all, in every way.

Frank loves me much more than I deserve, more than I ever believed any man could love any woman, and I should be strong hearted indeed if I did not return it which I do, sincerely. He will take care of me as long as he lives, and I shall have some home somewhere I suppose, very small, and very modest. But Dear Father, I hope it will be large enough to make you comfortable and that I shall be able to give you my pleasure in it which I have always hoped to have been able to give you in yr own house.

Lizzie feels so strongly opposed to this that we don't mention it at all and I shall feel obliged to you if you will not allude to it to her, and to *no one else* except Charlotte or Jamie who like Frank. Lizzie had her heart set upon a great match for me. Neither my taste or conscience will permit me to gratify her. I shall need about Three Hundred dollars to pay all the bills, of the last year, and that is all I shall ask of you henceforth. If you feel inclined to send me any 'wedding present' as the phrase is, let it be no article of luxury. I have nothing more to do with luxury. Whatever sum of money you choose to give me, I shall prefer to invest in eminently useful articles. If there is any chance of your being here within three or four months, do let me know that I may have the great happiness of yr presence at my wedding.

You must forgive me if I can write of nothing but myself. I feel absurdly tear-y and heavy hearted tonight and realize too clearly, how lonely I am without my dear Mother or Father now, as I go out alone, from these familiar walls, where I have played, and worked (and suffered, God knows). Do try to come, now, Dearest Father, if you can. This is a foolish letter, but it must go. . . We go to New York in two weeks or three, I suppose. . . .
God bless you, ever prays yr loving daughter   Annie

Both this letter and the dark letter from Lizzie that followed it by four days must have been written during the sharp disagreement between the two sisters about Annie's plan to marry Frank. Why go to New York, where Lizzie might try to disrupt this engagement as she had the one to Robert Sherwood? In such gloom did Annie decide there was no point to waiting to be married. Less than three weeks later she described her plans for herself and her brother and sister in a breathless letter.

✱ [ANNIE]   Keene November 18th 1858

My dearest Father,

Since I wrote you, Frank and I have changed our plans, or rather Frank, has triumphed, and I have consented to be married on the 14th day of next month, (December).

The ostensible reason is that there is no necessity for waiting—the real reason that Frank *won't* wait.

He *says* that he can do no work and is good for nothing till this matter which has 'harrassed' him for the last six or eight years, is settled. So I in the most dutiful manner consent to put him out of his misery.

I should prefer to wait on many accounts, but he takes it so very much to heart that I can not be obdurate, as it is now only a question of time.

I have taken the liberty to ask a loan of five Hundred dollars from Mr. Skinner to pay up the family bills here, as I can not leave them in my name.

If I have anything over, I shall get a few necessary things for myself, and I *must* do a little to the house. At the request of the other children I mean my sisters and brother, I shall stay in the house here till Spring, when Frank proposes to hire it of you, or some other place. In either case my home will be Chardie's and Jamie's always. But Frank will not consent to stay here as your pensioner, as he has a very strong inclination to be master, and to offer, rather than receive. I suppose I shall receive a remittance from you before long. I hope so, as I promised to pay Mr. Skinner within two months, and I would not have borrowed it but that I could not bear to run the risk of leaving unpaid bills after I was married as *Lizzie* did, for Charlotte to worry about.

I did hope you would be here at my wedding, Dear Father, and I still hope that you will be my first guest. A good many of my friends, I believe, think I should have 'married money' but I hope and think that you and I will be satisfied.

I am going to New York to take dear Wil. and Sam. home next week, after Thanksgiving, and to get a carpet, etc. I never thought any body *could* be married with so little fuss. I shall only get a wedding dress, and every thing else, as if I were not going to do anything extraordinary. I don't mean to invite any body out of Keene, to my wedding as I can't afford it, and don't desire a "brilliant wedding." Jamie and Lizzie and John will come to "give me away," and we mean to go to Montreal and Quebec for a little while, to be back at Christmas. Now my Dear Father I hope you will be satisfied with my conduct in this matter. I must confess, I feel pretty nervous and very much alone in the world, as if I should like a Father's or Mother's face to look into, and your good strong arm to lean on, but God will sustain me, now, as always before.

Next Thursday Nov. 26th is our Thanksgiving day. Jamie has a week's vacation, and is coming home, and we shall have our darling little boy with us. How I wish you were going to be here.

Chardie will go to New York after I am married for a few weeks, and come back to me whenever she gets ready. Frank will write you himself by this mail.

Roxana and Daniel will stay with me much as if nothing had happened.

Good bye. Yr loving

Annie

✳ [FRANK FISKE]   Keene 18 Nov 1858

My dear Sir,

I have sought and obtained the promise of your daughter Annie's hand in marriage.

I hope that the long time necessary to communicate with you and the absolute control which Annie has exercised over her own actions will be a sufficient apology for my having done so without first obtaining your permission.

I have loved Annie a long time and before I took so important a step as seeking her hand I felt that she was the only lady to whom I could offer a true, enduring and devoted love. Yet loving her as I do I could never have asked her to marry me without the conviction that I could devote myself earnestly and persistently to securing her comfort and happiness.

I assure you, sir, that all the energies and faculties which I possess shall be employed to make your daughter what you most desire,—a happy wife.

You have always manifested so much kindness and friendship for me that I venture to hope that you will accept me as your son in law with approval and a continuance of your esteem.

I have respected and loved you so long, that in assuming new relations to you, I can only say that with the privilege of becoming a member of your family I claim that of showing you the affection of a son which I shall always faithfully render you and hope that you will permit me to remain

Dutifully and affectionately your friend   Frank L. Fiske

✳ [CHARLOTTE]   Keene November 18th 58

My dearest Father,

You will probably be surprized to learn by this mail that Annie is to be married this coming month.

Since she expects to be married about the 14th or 15th of December, she may be married when you receive this.

It seems perfectly absurd that they should wait till Spring, when they are both quite absorbed in one another, and (*on my opinion*) good for nothing now.

You can imagine that I have had time to accustom myself to this idea, as Frank has always been in love with her, was before she was engaged to Clarence.

He is a good manly honorable man I am convinced. And has it in his power to make her happy.

They are a very attached couple, and I assure you are not very *good company* for me, being oblivious to the existence of any one but themselves. If it were not for Lizzie's children I should be forlorn indeed, but they are engrossing both my time and thoughts. There is a good deal to be done to keep them morally, mentally and *physically* right. . . .

I am very fond of Frank, and believe Annie has done the best thing, she could do, in marrying the man she loves.

They mean to be married in Church, have a few friends at Home. After that go to Montreal.

I am to stay here till after they return from Montreal.

We have cold weather here now, and skating. I take the children with me on the ice. We always have an experienced gentleman skater with us, who tries the ice beforehand, so there is no danger. Will cannot stand a minute on the ice. Sam is more successful, but they are so ignorant of the ways of country children. We amuse ourselves vastly with a sled you gave Jamie once, "Gen/l Putnam" by name. I must say good bye. Your truly loving child   Charlotte

Where would the young couple live? Frank lived in Keene but evidently had no house to which he wanted to take his new wife. Annie, who had served as head of the family for five years, could not abandon Charlotte and Jamie, particularly Charlotte. Furthermore, the young couple were short of money, and Annie loved the family house, which would under ordinary circumstances remain vacant during the winter. The answer that Charlotte proposed to her father seemed obvious.

"Frank and Annie are going to stay in our house this Winter, the only change being that Frank takes the responsibility of the whole thing.

"But he only consents, at Annie's earnest solicitation, to stay in the house this Winter, and, I know, will not consent to stay there any longer, except you suggest it yourself. Of course I only suggest this, as I know you will be happy to do it, if you only believe it necessary.

"Jamie and I shall always feel as much at Home as possible there, as we are both delighted with the arrangement. Frank has begged us to consider their Home always ours, wherever it may be" (Charlotte, 12-3-58).

Despite this convenient arrangement, as preparations for Annie's simple wedding went forward, Charlotte worried about her own situation.. At twenty-three she had been more sheltered than either of her sisters. While Jamie's finances were now directly under the supervision of his father, Charlotte would have to manage the money her father sent her. The house-keeping in Keene would certainly fall on her shoulders unless Annie and Frank lived in the house.

Perhaps more disturbing was the prospect of being the last of the sisters to become what Frank said was Wilson's goal for all of his daughters— a happy wife. Until then she would have to brave the world as a single woman, and Charlotte was no Mrs. Berry. Though she and Annie had had some difficulty getting along after Lizzie's marriage, she now felt desolate that her second sister would be leaving her. Since their father left them, they had spent eight eventful years depending on each other. Annie was not a surrogate mother like Lizzie, but a true sister, very close in age, with whom she shared all of the complexities of that relationship intensified by their more or less orphaned state. The strong bond between them would be loosened by her sister's marriage. Nevertheless, she tried hard not to contribute to the gloom that Lizzie and James Wilson had cast over the af-fair. "I say it to no one, but I am lonely indeed in the thought that I have *lost* my Sister. People may say as much as they please about *not* losing a Sister, but gaining a Brother, its not altogether true, and *should* not be so either" (Charlotte, 11-18-58). "Annie will come Home tomorrow I think, and it is only a little more than a week that she will be *my* property" (Charlotte, 12-3-58).

Meantime another plot was brewing that might rescue her from her lonely state.

✳ [CHARLOTTE]   Keene, October 1st 1858

My dearest Father,

. . . Do you remember my writing you about a very delightful young man who had been here this Summer? He came again last Saturday, and stayed till the next Tuesday, at John's invitation, consequently ours. He is a very fine, manly, reliable man I assure you, and I am sure is very fond of me, as I certainly am of him. Mr. Carter is his name, and he is from Lancaster, Massachusetts. He remembers hearing you speak there, during the Harrison Campaign, and, evidently, has a most agreeable recollection of you. Every one who knows him respects him highly. John, who knows his character well as a Lawyer, admires him very much. We have known him a little in society, (which by the way) he does not care much for, for three or four years. I am *only* sure he is fond of me, as no more definite conclusions have been suggested, and my experience of life has led me to realize, early, the mutability of all human affairs. Nevertheless, I am looking forward with impatience to the time when I shall go to New York, as then, we shall meet again.

Annie and I are both anxious to go there early, this year—that is, as near Thanksgiving as possible. Both on our own account, and on Lizzie's, who will need our care and attention. . . .

Please don't mention to the girls all I have written to you about my friend Mr. Carter. And believe me, dearest Father, your truly Loving child

Charlotte J. Wilson

When Annie decided to be married on December 14, there was no reason to move to New York. Instead, Charlotte and Mr. Carter wrote to each other, and Charlotte continued to tell her father of the romance. "I am glad . . . that you speak so highly of Mr. Carter's family.

"I have heard twice from him since he was here in September, but you must not think we are engaged to each other, for we are not at all, and I have lived long enough to appreciate the fickleness of men. I was mistaken in thinking he had a Mother, for he has neither Father or Mother. Several Brothers, and married Sisters, are all who remain of his family. He certainly is a delightful and good man, and I shall be a fortunate young woman, if I interest him permanently.

"You need never be afraid that my conduct will be careless with any young man. I have always been *very particular* in my conduct and can attribute my own fastidiousness to *good sense*, as well as good principles" (Charlotte, 12-3-58).

With this cautious romance brewing in the background, Annie's marriage approached. Still ignorant of the date of the event, Wilson fortu-itously sent her $150 for spending money. With that and the $500 she bor-rowed from Mr. Skinner she bought some things for her wedding while taking the grandchildren back to Lizzie in New York.

The wedding was not complete until it was recounted to General Wil-son. Frank Fiske, himself an aspiring writer, appreciated the Wilsons' facility for storytelling, which we see manifested in these letters. He ob-served they were "all alike . . . in that faculty for making people listen to [their] stories," a compliment Annie sent along to her father. Important stories like that of Annie's wedding, like the accounts of Lizzie's marriage seven years earlier, had to be told by each member of the family.

Unfortunately, Annie's quiet wedding, like many major events, was almost overshadowed by other minor events that seemed major at the time. And so the tellers incorporated the story of a small accident that happened to the beloved Jamie and the presence of Lizzie's new baby, which nearly upstaged Annie on her big day.

✳ [ANNIE]   Springfield Mass December 16th 1858

My dearest Father,

You know I was married on the 14th. Of course I can't begin my let-ter with any other announcement or item. That over, I want to explain to you that I did not write to you by the last mail, owing to the fact that the 5th occurred just at the end of a very busy and hurried week that I was in New York making preparations for my wedding, and I did not know of the date. We were married in church at one o'clock, and then gave our relations a little collation at home Frank and I leaving them all at half past two to come to this place where we shall stay a day or two longer (before continuing our trip to Niagara or some other resort,) as we find ourselves so exceedingly comfortably and pleasantly placed here—not at "Warners" of ancient fame, but at the "Massasoit" which you remember, which has borne away the palm from all the other hotels.

I wish I could tell you Dearest Father, how happy I am, how kind, and considerate my husband is, and all my satisfaction. But you know what a good fellow Frank is, and I need not enlarge upon that subject. The great drawback to the satisfactoriness of my wedding, was, as it is of most occa-sions to us, your absence. Another, was the fact that poor dear Jim came home with a sprained ankle, the day before the wedding, and had to go up the aisle on crutches, and *sit* by the pulpit, to "give me away." I hope it is not going to be serious, as there seems no reason to fear now. He is at home with Chardie and Roxana. . . . In fact, if I should begin to tell you all the good effects which seem to me to result from my marriage I dare say you would laugh at the enthusiasm of a bride of three days.

I have to thank you for a bill of exchange of One Hundred and fifty Dollars, by the last mail but one. I wrote you of my draft on Mr. Skinner for Five Hundred Dollars for my wedding expenses, to pay the outstanding family bills, etc. I did not spend one third of it on my own personal indulgence. I bought only three dresses a bonnet and cloak and a few little things. Not a spoon or fork or single piece of silver, and I don't believe a young lady ever tried more to be economical or was ever married on a less 'extravagant' outlay.

I was obliged to buy two carpets for the house which must have been bought any way.

Charlotte will want her money during the winter, and I shall keep any that may remain after paying everything at Keene till I hear from you. Otherwise, I should send it at once to Mr. Skinner as part payment of my obligation to him. I mean, my One Hundred and Fifty.

Now you will have occasion to see how very small a proportion of the large sums you have sent to us the establishment at Keene has eaten up, now that you are relieved of it. The children desire it, and I know you will not object, so we shall stay in your house—"home," I shall always say—thro' the winter, and then Frank hopes to make some arrangement either with you for that place, or some where, for a permanency.

When I have settled every thing at Keene, I shall write you the result.

We still encourage the hopes that you will be with us before many months. . . . I begin to think anxiously what Jamie is to do for a living. I shall tell you of my wedding presents in my next. Frank sends his warmest and most respectful regards to you, and I am, as always, Dearest Papa, Yr loving daughter   Annie F. W. Fiske

Usually the most detailed observer, Charlotte was so distracted by her new responsibilities, Lizzie's new baby, and Jamie's sprained ankle that her observations on the wedding are disappointingly brief.

✳ [CHARLOTTE]   Keene Dec. 18th [1858]

My dearest Father,

We have had a wedding and an accident since I wrote you last. Annie's wedding was delightful.

Jamie's sprained ankle was a great drawback to our thorough enjoyment of the occasion. He writes you a full account of his accident by this Mail.

Annie was a happy and beautiful Bride. She was married in Church at quarter before one o'clock (Tuesday Dec. 14th). After the wedding in Church, we came Home, and had about twenty five people here at breakfast, which was a delicious repast. Mr. and Mrs. Frank Skinner, and Mr. and Mrs. Bigelow Lawrence from Boston were here. Mrs. Murray, and Mr. and Mrs. John Sherwood from New York. John only arrived an hour before the wedding and went back to New York the same day. Lizzie, her Nurse and baby, went back the next day. Her baby looks just like you. He really does. He has just such a mouth, and dark hair, and a dimple in his cheek, which I believe you have not. He is a nice fat baby.

Jamie and I are here alone. We have been made happy several times this week by receiving *very happy* letters from our new Brother and *Mrs. Fiske.* Annie seems truly perfectly happy. They are still at Springfield, to which place they went the day they were married. I think they will come Home by the middle of next week.

We are rather lonely. Jamie must be so I think, although I have so much to do, amusing and taking care of him, as well as arranging the house, that I have no time to be so.

Jamie's ankle is getting better slowly, but it is the sort of injury which requires time for its cure. Perfect quiet is ordered too. I am now allowed to bathe it with liniment, but for several days I have not been authorized to take any active *steps* (any more than he) with regard to it.

I must say good bye. Your devoted   Charlotte

Confined to his chair with a sprained ankle, Jamie, usually the most perfunctory writer, treated his father to a detailed account of his injury and a vivid account of the wedding.

✳   [JAMIE]   Keene Dec 18th /58

My darling Father,

Since I wrote you last, I have met with quite a severe accident in the shape of a severely sprained ancle. I did it in Cambridge about ten days ago. I was "fooling" with a fellow in a College room, and he suddenly stepping backward, expecting me to hold him up, we both tripped and fell, he on my ankle. It is nothing dangerous, at all, but is a pretty severe case of sprain, and the Dr. says will probably confine me for three weeks or so at the least.

It happened at the most inopportune time possible, viz the Wednesday before Annie's wedding (which took place the Tuesday following). For two or three days I had a good deal of pain, and was unable to bear the slightest motion, but as the inflamation had gone down a good deal on Monday, the Dr. told me that I had better try to get to Keene, where I should have no temptation to move about. So I started off in the 11 oclk train, with my chum Bradlee to take care of me, and reached home in the afternoon as comfortably as could be expected. I hadn't the faintest idea that I should be able to take any part in Annie's wedding, but as she was very anxious that I should "give her away," I went up the aisle on crutches and sat in a chair with my foot on an ottoman, and when the passage came, "who gives this woman to this man," I waved my hand and bowed. The wedding ceremony was *very affecting*, and I found myself on the verge of *crying* several times. Annie's voice was inexpressively sweet and impressive, and it all went off charmingly.

The bridesmaids were Chardie and Katie Wheeler, and the groomsmen, Herbert Bellows and George Hale. After the service in the Church, the "relations" only, repaired to the house, where a very nice wedding breakfast was in waiting, and where all was as jolly and cheerful as possible. I reclined on a sofa, and instead of waiting on other people, was waited upon and thought it was rather an agreeable change.

At a quarter to two P. M. Annie and Frank (*Mr. and Mrs. Fiske!*) went to Springfield, from which place we have heard from them twice. I think they are the two happiest people I ever met with, and it is really delightful to see Annie so cheerful and contented. Frank is a fine, manly gentleman, and I don't know any one, whom I would have preferred to give Annie to. Just after the engagement came out, he wrote me a very nice note, telling me that he should devote his life to making Annie happy, and assuring me that instead of losing a sister, I should gain a brother. To be sure that is very loverlike-talk, but yet was a good thing to say.

There is very little new or interesting to tell you, outside of family matters. The papers are full of the visit of the English officers to the Am. Steamer Washington at San Juan, and every one feels very much outraged at it, except the President [James Buchanan], who seems inclined to consider it an excellent joke. I do think that the government of this country is perfectly disreputable and hardly a day passes, but that some deed comes to light calculated to make any honest man, ashamed of his nation.

I hope this letter will find you, enjoying good health, and in prosperous circumstances. I suppose you will spend the rainy season in San Francisco, as I should think you would find it rather lonely at San Matir during that season. . . .

Hoping to hear from you soon, dear Father, and with many thanks for the check you sent me, I remain, Your devoted boy,

Jamie

I forgot to say that Lizzie brought up her *last* baby, when she came to the wedding, and we were all astounded at the remarkable resemblance to *you*. It was really astonishing. J. H. W.

There were interesting parallels with Lizzie's wedding. The sisters were both married at one o'clock and had receptions at home afterward. They both went to Springfield for their wedding night. And they were both twenty-six years old. There were even more striking differences. Everything about Annie's wedding was quiet and familiar. Frank's ushers had attended the gypsy picnic at Beach Stile with Annie and Frank a few days after Wilson left, when Annie was eighteen. Chardie and Katie Wheeler, daughter of their next-door neighbor, were bridesmaids. There was no bishop, no white watered silk wedding dress, no caterers from Boston, nothing that Mrs. Sherwood would say was as handsome as any entertainment she had seen in New York. Nevertheless, in the history of the family, Annie's marriage was as significant as her sister's.

Lizzie did not compare the occasions. Disappointed in but reconciled to Annie's bad bargain and distracted by three children and a new baby, Lizzie recounted the wedding without too much detail before she went on to other matters.

✳ [LIZZIE] January 5th 1859

My dear Father,

Since last writing you I have been up to Annie's wedding. I felt at first disappointed in her choosing a lot so disproportioned in a worldly point of view of what she *might* have done, and should have done with her beauty and merit, but I am satisfied with it now since I see how devoted to her Frank is, how noble and true he is, and how much happier she is than I have ever seen her. She has felt the need of protection and friends and now she has one who is able and willing to do both. It gave a sad [air] to the beautiful little wedding in church, to see dear Jim come up the aisle on crutches with his broken ankle, but that was *nothing* to his expression, when he turned to Mr. White when he said "who giveth this woman to be married to this man" James bowed from his seat, and waved his hand with all the dignity and beauty of the *young Augustus*. Oh, that boy is too much. He does every thing well and nobly. He *almost cried*, for Annie is his all in all, and she really enjoys having him a little lame and under her charge now. Dear Annie had all sorts of valuable presents from everywhere proving how much she has been loved and respected. She looked splendidly. She never was so handsome, and Frank has attained the object of his long devotion. Jamie and she will have written you fully about it all, and his accident and improvement since.

Charlotte is with me. Very delighted and happy, very good to me and the boys. I am some such friend with *four boys*, and not very good health. We had the baby christened last Thursday "John Phillip." Phillip he is to be called. He looks very much like you, more than any of your own children. My children have all looked like you. I got your letter of the 5th of Dec. I was aware that my letter of Nov. would offend you but I felt it a duty to write it, and am sure the time will come when you will agree that I am right and that I had no wrong motives, but was actuated by real love for you and desire for your good name. I have no recollection of any childish fancies of mine in regard to a "mystery." I only remember I was very fond of you and very much excited if you were spoken against. . . .

Oh! how I hope you will come home this winter! How I hope you are already taking your passage in a steamer say for next month! and will come to your daughter Lizzie who is not so ugly a daughter after all. We are growing more prosperous. John does a very fine business, and is a model man in every respect.

Good night dear Father,
Your affectionate,
Lizzie

✳ [ANNIE] Keene January 3d 1859

My dearest Father,

I received today your very kind letter dated Dec. 4th enclosing a bill for Four Hundred Dollars. Thank you for both. That sum is more than I spent or wanted for myself, but I am sorry to say that the 150. you sent me, and $500 I borrowed from Mr. Skinner did not pay all the bills of family expenses after I took expense for myself. I must therefore encroach upon this 400. to settle *all* the bills which Charlotte now considers herself responsible for, and I will send all that remains to Mr. Skinner. For myself, I shall do very well with what I have. We have started on very economical principles, and If I get into a very "tight place" I shall not be afraid to ask you for a little "lift." . . .

I can not refrain from telling you again, Dear Father, what a good husband Frank is, and what a happy wife I am.

Last week I stayed at home every day from 1. to 4. o'clock, to see my neighbors who came to wish me well. I gave them some oysters and chocolate, and wedding cake, and I am sure no two people ever received more hearty congratulations and God speeds. There were wet eyes all thro' the week. As I sat there, in the parlors, some time alone, I often looked from your picture to my Mother's, and imagined you both approved of what I had done. . . .

I said I should tell you about my wedding and my presents but I am afraid it would not interest you except to say that we were married in church. We asked nobody out of the family, but Mr. and Mrs. Bigelow Lawrence and Mr. and Mrs. Frank Kenner came without invitations and Mrs. Murray, and they, with all Frank's friends came back here for a nice collation. A Mr. Cheney (of the Express,) sent me a diamond ring, in token of his 'high regard for Genl. Wilson.' I have never seen him. Lizzie and John gave me a set of silver knives, Mrs. Bigelow Lawrence a silver tankard, Mrs. James, a camels hair shawl, Mrs. Murray a very valuable lace shawl and Robert Bellows a silver salver and goblet. George Hale, Mary Dinsmoor Mrs. Edwards and Mrs. Phin Fiske each a small piece of silver and many more tasteful things there were.

Good Bye Dear Father, God Bless and keep you ever prays yr loving daughter   Annie

Annie sat waiting for her neighbors to affirm her status as a married woman, seeking the approval from the pictures of her mother and father that she could not get from her absent parents. It was a far cry from the glittering reception into New York society that Mrs. Sherwood had arranged for Lizzie. However, with a husband for company the quiet life in Keene became much more attractive for Annie. Ironically, marriage released her from responsibilities and provided a sense of security that gave Annie a chance to recapture some of the carefree youth that her father's absence and life in the city had deprived her of. "I am living such a quiet life that I can give you very little news of interest. . . . I hardly recognise myself when I look back to the turmoil and distractions of my New York life and sometimes can hardly realize that the fitful fever of care and responsibility is so much over, and that a true loving heart, a strong heart, and willing and effective arms will shield me for all the future" (Annie, 3-3-59).

"A Home Is a
Peculiarly Desirable Institution"

After Annie married, the family needed a new modus operandi. No doubt at twenty-one and twenty-three years old, Charlotte and Jamie were old enough to take care of themselves, but they still were not eager for independence. Though she was glad to escape some of the responsibilities of taking care of her siblings, she was also wistful at losing the special relationship she had had with them. "Charlotte is with Lizzie. I hated to have her go, but Lizzie was very anxious for her to come. And I know the dear boys need her. It does not seem as if I could trust the dear little girl to go and buy all her own clothes, but I suppose I must. I have not quite got over my heart aches at the separation with those others whom I love so. I mean to hold Master Jim pretty firmly" (Annie, 1-3-59).

They agreed on an arrangement that would maintain the structure and routine of the family as much as possible. Annie wrote asking if it would be all right for her and Frank to stay in the house for the winter. Jamie and Charlotte provided an enthusiastic second to this motion. Looking at it from a "common point of view," to use Lizzie's phrase, this arrangement seemed ideal. It provided the impecunious newlyweds with a home, one to which Annie was fiercely attached, as partial repayment for Annie's years of service to the family; and it continued to provide a home for Charlotte and Jamie, where they could live, as always, alternately with Lizzie's house in New York.

Since Wilson didn't answer very straightforwardly Annie's and Frank's questions about the use of the house, Frank reluctantly took up residence uncertain of Wilson's feelings on the matter. He could not afford a house nearly so grand; and Charlotte, Jamie, and Annie insisted that he move in. While Frank benefited from living in the Wilsons' elegant house, he struggled against being discreetly subsumed into the family. He changed the house and objected to the routine.

However, Jamie reaped an immediate benefit from this plan: Annie and Frank took care of him while his ankle healed. "Both Frank and I are delighted of an excuse to keep him here. I believe he does not find us very satisfactory companions. He complains that our conversation is of too 'personal' a nature and thinks that our interest in life generally, is confined rather too much to each other. Still, he enjoys himself pretty well, *betting* against Frank on every conceivable chance, playing chess, cribbage and Solitaire, while Frank rubs his foot and laughs at his stories and jokes to their mutual satisfaction" (Annie, 1-3-59).

* [JAMIE]   Keene Jan 3rd/59

My darling Father,

. . . Annie has returned from her trip with her *husband*(!) (if it can be called a "*trip*," for they stayed all the time at Springfield), and you don't know how cosy it is here. I think that Annie and Frank are the two happiest people I ever saw, and the most in love with one another. Annie's qualities are too well known and appreciated by you, to need any eulogies from me, and as to Frank, the longer I know him, and the more intimately I see him, the more convinced I am of his upright, honorable, manly character, and his kind, affectionate disposition. He is entirely devoted to Annie, and I know will make her life as comfortable and happy, as is in his power.

And I believe it will not be out of place here, dear Father, to ask you to write to Frank, something about the house here. He is as proud as Lucifer, about being dependent on any one, and I know will not consent to live here, unless he can *pay rent*. Now you know it would be forlorn for Annie to live in any other house in Keene, than the one we were born in, and besides that Chardie and I should have no place to go to, and I wish you would write to Frank, and make some arrangement with him, by which he might live [in] the house and consider it his, as long as he lives here. I think it is a very commendable feeling in him, and shows great delicacy, and I know that you will agree with me in considering that it ought to be respected.

My ankle is much better, and I am able to walk across the room, *without a crutch*. . . .

The term will be over on the 20th of Jan. and I shall probably be in Cambridge before it closes. After that comes the seven weeks vacation, which I shall spend partly here, and partly in New York with Lizzie. The time flies so quickly that I can hardly realize that I am finishing my first term Junior, and that College is more than half over. . . .

I remain as ever   Your devoted boy
                                                               Jamie

Meantime Jamie and Charlotte had financial problems with no Annie to run interference for them with their father. Jamie lashed around a fair amount of money keeping up the social position Annie had taught him to expect, and he explained his expenditures to his father with incontrovertible logic:

". . . there are a great many expenses, which amount in the aggregate to a large sum, which at first sight seem useless, but which are *absolutely indispensible* to a young man. Now I know that you would not have me give up my social position for anything. You know just at this time of a young man's live, 'he reaches or comes to his level,' and the position which he takes at twenty, and the friends he makes, last him for life. This is particularly true of Cambridge, and the station that a young fellow has then, *he never loses*. Whatever else happens to him whatever troubles he meets with or whatever he does, as long as he is honest, *his place is fixed*, and he takes it as a gentleman, and moves with gentlemen all his life. Now, I hold that position here, as your son should, and I know that you wish me to do so. I belong to . . . the Porcellian and Hasty Pudding and insignificant as that may seem to you, I can assure you that it draws just as distinct a line, as could be made. *But it all costs a heap of money . . .*" (Jamie, 3-19-59).

In response to his father's repeated scoldings about his expenditures, he promised exuberantly that in return for his father's "universal kindness, indulgence, tenderness, generosity and devotion, . . . I consider myself bound to you for life and shall shape any course which I may take, with sole reference to your comfort and good. . . . The girls, you know, will all be married and their husbands will take [care] of them. You and I will be alone, and we must be *partners*. . . . Shall we be known to the world as Wilson and Son? What a stir we should make! All we got over and above expenses, you know, we could give to the girls" (Jamie, 3-19-59).

Who could resist such engaging exuberance? Certainly not the lovesick young women who embroidered handkerchiefs for him.

In the fall of his last year in college, Jamie led Harvard to victory over Yale in a billiards match—justification at last for the time he spent at billiards when Annie thought he should be studying.

"In all modesty and in the *strictest confidence* I will tell you that the success of the match was principally due to me. My partner was entirely '*flabbergasted*,' while I was a cool as a cucumber and I made nearly the whole of the first 300 points, myself. . . . I never played a stronger game in my life, than I did that night. (Now this is not 'blowing,' and you mustn't tell any body that I talk in this way about myself.)" (Jamie, 10-4-59).

Charlotte found the new arrangements after Annie's marriage less immediately satisfactory than Jamie did. Just as Lizzie left debts from her wedding for Annie to pay, so Charlotte had to cope with the debts that accrued from Annie's wedding. Unlike her brother, Charlotte could not assure her father that family pride demanded that he spend money on her now for which she would repay him in the future. For the first time Charlotte joined her sisters in complaining of her desperate need for more money.

Single, dependent, and sickly, Charlotte took some puritanical satisfaction in flatly refusing to go to balls and being virtuously asleep before Lizzie returned from her merrymaking. "My ideas are few and poor today, owing to my having been up late every night since I came here. I came with the intention of not going any where, evenings, that would oblige me to sit up late. But several people have urged me to go on, first, *one special* occasion, then another. Not to Balls, because I decline those positively. Lizzie went to Mr. Bancroft's last evening to a Ball. I am happy to say I was in my bed before she came, but it was twelve before I lost myself in sleep" (Charlotte, 1-4-59).

James Wilson evidently suggested in 1857 that perhaps Charlotte could take over the management of Lizzie's household since Lizzie was busy with her writing and her social engagements. Though Lizzie advised Annie to be a "good wife" against all odds, she hardly had time to play the Angel of the House. She hired a governess to teach her children and spent much of her time working with Miss Hamilton, granddaughter of Alexander Hamilton, on the Standing Committee for Buying Mount Vernon, a famous philanthropic project undertaken by leading society women from all over the country. John's law practice also flourished, giving Lizzie more latitude in her spending. The family's style, however, required ever more income. Despite these worldly distractions, when Charlotte suggested to her father that Lizzie was too busy to attend to her duties at home, John Sherwood wrote of Charlotte and Lizzie, "By the way Sir you have been, I think in some way misinformed in relation to Lizzie's management of the children and her domestic qualities generally. . . . You know that your eldest daughter is a woman of remarkable ability and more than that of the warmest and most affectionate nature. Without in any way detracting from Dear Chardie's qualities we should as soon think of taking the command from the General in Chief and giving it to the Ensign as transferring our little battalion from their Mother to Chardie" (John Sherwood, 6-5-57).

Nevertheless, two years later Charlotte assumed the task of teaching Wil, six, and Sam, five, to read—a task she felt ill-suited for, one that smacked of the role of unpaid governess so frequently assigned to a poor spinster in her sister's household. "I began yesterday to teach the children. They are being splendid children, and always bright and satisfactory when they *try*. But, like all other children, they hate learning to read, and it tries me very much to teach them. But I shall do it as long as I am here" (Charlotte, 1-4-59). "I don't think I have a talent for teaching" (Charlotte, 2-20-59). Evidently, Lizzie agreed, for she soon hired a governess to take over the job of teaching "polite literature." Despite their doubts about Chardie's skill at teaching the boys, the Wilsons believed that child rearing was a family task and that this move cast more doubts on Lizzie's credentials as the good mother. Nevertheless, Charlotte hastened to assure her father that Lizzie "is a very good Mother, and doesn't neglect her duties at Home"—the capital *H* may be significant—"but her health, I am afraid will hardly last, if she continues to overwork herself as she does now" (Charlotte, 1-4-59). Since the governess taught the older boys only two hours a day, plenty of time remained for Charlotte to take care of them when they had finished their lessons.

Mr. Carter's attentions lent her hope for a while that she might be married and have a family of her own. Her father approved of the Carter family, and she and Mr. Carter shared a dislike of society, but Charlotte was cautious. "I have seen Mr. Carter almost every evening since I came here. Although he has several rivals he is the one preferred. I am not engaged, however, and consequently please don't speak continuously of him as a friend of mine. He is an excellent man, apart from being attractive" (Charlotte, 1-4-59). A month later her caution but not her hopes paid off. That romance flickered out. "As for me I am not engaged or married, or like to be. I hope you are not disappointed" (Charlotte, 2-2-59).

Not having been formally engaged, Charlotte's flirtation received no public attention, but her letters took on a new tone as she struggled with her disappointment. Imaginative and curious, Charlotte, more than her sisters, wanted to understand her father's life in California. Finally, though she was not bold or adventurous, dread of her uncertain position in the East overcame her dread of the distance and strangeness of California. At least in San Francisco she would have a position as her father's daughter, which might be an improvement over being her sister's nanny. She pleaded, "I wish you would come and take me some where. I should like to go with you very much. I should like to *make your acquaintance*" (Charlotte, 2-2-59). "I [renew] my offer to go with you to California" (Charlotte, 3-18-59). "If I shall not be very much in your way there, I should like to go too? You were quite right when you said I should perhaps never be married. I never shall, *unless I meet a sort of Angel*. And I do long to be with you, under your care, and to have you under mine" (Charlotte, 2-4-59). Two weeks later she changed her mind. "I felt so lonely at Keene without Jamie that I thought I would go any where with him and you. But I think, after all, California is not the place for me" (Charlotte, 2-19-60).

Meantime, Charlotte strained her budget to comfort herself with a visit to her friend (Lilly Fay) and her friend's elegant and very fashionable family in Boston, where she was admired and entertained to her satisfaction. Since Charlotte did not have "brilliant qualities," Lizzie did not harbor the same ambitions for her that she had had for the beautiful Annie; but she was pretty and agreeable and loved having a good time, though not in large parties. She also enjoyed having Jamie's arm to lean on when he was in New York. Mostly, though, she awaited her father's return, which he had once again assured them was imminent.

If Charlotte was disappointed in the East, Wilson was desperate in California. Troubles fell like hailstones after he lost the Limantour case. No doubt Judge Ogden Hoffman's observation that "the unscrupulous and pertinacious obstinacy with which [the Limantour claims] had been persisted in [was] without parallel in the judicial history of the country" (Hittell, *History of California*, 699) left a serious black mark against Wilson's professional reputation. He was sick; Gold Bluff had petered out, producing just enough gold to fan a flickering hope; debts swamped him. He was so depressed and broke that his children were alarmed.

"I am very much troubled at your account of your health. Dysentery, is no slight thing. It was a month ago you wrote and it will be another month before you get this. I hope sincerely and most fervently that you will be quite well before then. I shall be anxious to hear, and sympathized with Jamie fully when he said on reading your letter, 'I wish I was with him' Oh! Father I hope you will come soon. Do be very careful of your health. That farm ought to save it. I am very sorry you feel so depressed about your affairs. I know you were disappointed and troubled, but I hope it will come out right yet. Your California property must be very valuable. If your debts here, were only off your mind, there would seem to be no cause for uneasiness" (Annie, 1-3-59). "I am troubled . . . about your health, and wait anxiously to hear that you have recovered from that alarming complaint" (Annie, 1-18-59).

"I hope you will write us all about the Limantour. We hear from the papers that the paper on which the deeds were drawn had testified against you. Is it true. After all I cannot understand why you are so surprized and disappointed at its being decided adversely when you have always said you expected Bribery and Corruption to do their work with the not one scrupulous judiciary of California. Then you own nearly all Gold Bluff. You own a Ranch which every one says is valuable. But there I am again. I don't know what to sympathize with, for I know no more of your business than the man in the moon" (Lizzie, 1-5-58).

By the time he received this letter, Wilson no longer owned the valuable ranch that he loved. He had sacrificed Burri Burri to satisfy some of his creditors. Annie's reaction must have rubbed salt in his wounds.

"I am glad of any arrangement of your affairs that will make you to come home, and should welcome a sacrifice of property, even, which would bring you back to us. Under any other circumstances I should feel inclined to retain the 'Burri Burri' as my passion for real estate investment has always led me to congratulate you on that possession. I have always thought it the best piece of property you have ever owned. I am glad if it will bring you a good price and relieve you of your anxieties. I shall rejoice to know that your debts are paid, and you are free from all that annoyance" (Annie, 1-18-59).

Burri Burri, however, did not bring enough to pay Wilson's debts. His affairs were in such a dreadful state that he began to write reluctantly of coming home. His children were delighted. Though they tried to comfort him in his disappointment, they were naturally a little offended that he showed so little eagerness to come home to see them.

While Wilson struggled with financial problems in California, the family created for itself a delicate and intricate problem in Keene. Unlike Charlotte and Jamie, Lizzie was not at all pleased when Frank moved into the house in Keene. When Wilson expressed his indignation over her demanding questions about the house, she hardly cared. Her questions only increased and became more pressing.

"I should like to know in whose name our house up at Keene stands and *whose it is*. Does Mr. Skinner own it? Do you? Frank Fiske has moved into it, and I suppose I shall not go there again until he is ready to move out. I do not wish to. I wish my dear Sister Annie to have every advantage that I have had, but I should like to know whose house it is, how much of it is paid for, if you have no objection" (Lizzie, 1-5-59).

Of course, with Frank living there, it most certainly was not the same.

"The house is made very comfortable by an entry stove. We use the upper kitchen, thus getting the good of *that* fire and we use the dining room altogether. Jamie sleeps in the 'office,' or Nursery, as Lizzie's children have caused it to be called. I have an air tight stove in my room, which is made the prettiest room in the house by the introduction of the most beautiful suit of furniture I ever saw, placed there by my loving husband while we were away. The house is full of the beautiful engravings he brought home from Spain and altogether, it has quite a new look, with the dear familiar features still not concealed" (Annie, 1-3-59).

Even though the familiar features of the Keene house were not concealed and though Frank begged Charlotte and Jamie to consider his and Annie's house as their own, Annie observed, "Frank has, a not un-natural inclination to be the 'Master of the house he lives in'" (Annie, 1-8-59). The family imagined they were "lending" the house to Annie, when, in fact, they were lending it to Frank. Frank, who was very attached to the Monadnock region, was less attached to the Wilson homestead. Understandably, he wanted to live in a house that reflected his own taste. He was also quite naturally more concerned about the comfort of his new wife and the welfare of the family they had just formed than he was about maintaining the status quo among the Wilsons, which had been that family's first priority for so long. In fact, Annie's husband could not fit himself into the delicate fabric of their domestic arrangements. Perhaps no man could have. For the time being, however, they held the problem in abeyance. James Wilson decided to come home during the winter and spring of 1859 and play the deus ex machina in their complicated drama.

* [ANNIE]   Keene February 2nd 1859

My dearest Father,

I was greatly relieved to know thro' your last letter of date January 5th that you were well again, as your previous letter had alarmed me a good deal. I congratulate you, too, on the sale of your farm. It relieves you of one care, and I hope you will feel satisfied with it. I know of no more unsatisfactory state of mind than that in which we regret what is inevitable. I think we are all rather "given to" that.

I am here alone with my husband, Charlotte and Jamie both being in New York. The latter returned here from Cambridge last week, got his clothes all washed and mended, and went to N. Y. on Thursday last. I hope they will both return to make us a visit during this month, but I don't much expect it, as Lizzie, and New York will be powerful lode-stones.

I am rejoiced as the probabilities of your coming home during the next summer, strengthen. I do most sincerely hope that we shall have no more disappointments. I am sorry you feel so little anticipation of pleasure from it, but I think you will find the cordial welcome of many good friends, the happiness of your children, and the familiar look of many of the scenes of your youth will compensate for the genial climate and other attractions of California. You know there are two homes awaiting you, and when the rigors of New Hampshire climate are too severe for you, New York is always accessible. As to your to be lamented debts, I do hope you will be able to arrange in some way to relieve yourself of them.

. . . Mrs. Hale was here this morning endeavoring to arouse our patriotism on the subject of Washington's birthday ball, all for the great cause of the purchase of Mount Vernon. . . .

You do not say whether you approve of my availing myself of this house or not. Or whether you will rent it to Frank after the first of March. I wish if you have not already done so, that you would be so good as to say something definite on the subject in your next letter after the receipt of this, as Frank is anxious to know what arrangements to make. I do not feel certain that we shall spend all our days here, but Frank's attachment to these hills is very strong, and if his contributions to the journals of the day, and translations, should prove sufficiently remunerative I think he would be strongly tempted to establish himself here. For myself, to help him in every possible way is now my object and pleasure, and so it does not matter much where I live. I should regret very much a prolonged separation from my sisters and Jamie, and there is, pretty much, the whole statement of the case. I confess I think Frank would earn a living faster "in the world," but Providence will perhaps lead us right. Frank's disinclination for all compulsory contact with people at large, amounts to a mania, and I fear will stand in the way of his success. Politics seem to stand open to him, but I can't say I take very kindly to that. . . .

Frank sends his warmest and most respectful remembrances. Do not disappoint us of seeing you. I can't realize that such a happiness can ever be vouchsafed to me. Good Bye Dear Father. My God bless and keep you ever prays yr loving daughter   Annie F. W. Fiske

Annie's attachment to the house in Keene, Frank's inclination to be master, and James Wilson's financial straits combined to produce a complicated misunderstanding that aggravated the quarrel. For some unknown reason Annie and Frank fancied that Wilson might sell the house to Frank for the price of the note at the savings bank—$4,929—far less than the house was worth. It was, however, about as much as Frank could afford.

Frank and Annie were hopeful and doubtful at the same time. When Mr. Skinner wrote, "I shall be pleased to make such conveyance of the estate as you shall direct, upon the surrender of my Note held by the Savings Bank" (Annie, 2-19-59), their hopes soared. Wilson himself evidently hinted at some such deal. In a fit of euphoria, Annie, who had renounced luxury, declared that she not only wanted to have this house but that she still had hopes that she and Frank could one day buy her grandfather's yet grander house. Still, as they say in their letters to Wilson, they were quite aware that they would be getting more of a bargain than they could hope for. Did he really mean they could have it for $4,929? With some trepidation Frank wrote offering to buy the house for that price.

The proposal produced a storm of alarmed protest from the rest of the children.

"In regard to the house at Keene Frank Fiske has no money to buy it with. Neither do we want him to buy it. We want it ourselves and I hope you will pay Mr. Skinner, and the Savings Bank for it, and settle it on us four, *as you said you would five years ago*, allowing Annie to live there for a few years at a small rent with the proviso that we children may always return there. We are all attached to it and it is a *certainty*. Furnished as it is, it gives us a roof over our heads if the worst comes to the worst, and if we ever have *anything*, we would rather have that. Jamie and Charlotte agree with me. I want to be able to go there with my children by paying for my keeping. There is no place so good for them and me, and nothing so melancholy as a family turned out of house and home by poverty as the Adams's were. Do secure the old place to us" (Lizzie, 2-20-59).

"I hope you will wholly abandon the idea of selling the house at Keene. I think it ought not to go out of the family, as you and Chardie and I should have no home at all, if we should lose that. . . . we all have a great deal of feeling about it. For the first time I begin to be troubled about my summer arrangements. But God has always taken care of me in a singular manner, and I no longer borrow trouble, for I have borrowed enough, at a large rate of interest, paying in health and happiness" (Lizzie, 2-20-59).

"I want you to buy the Keene house now, and then Jamie and I shall always feel that we have a Home. Otherwise, I shall never feel at liberty to go to Keene. . . . I am sure you can forgive me if my first thought is for my solitary lonely self" (Charlotte, 2-20-59). What Charlotte was not prepared to do was to make a home for herself and a second home for Lizzie, as Annie had done, with all the complications that would involve.

The house, the source of so much solace and so much grief, became the object of the first serious family quarrel, occasioned by the introduction of Frank Fiske into that family space. Perhaps no man except John Sherwood could have refrained from interfering in their affairs. Since Annie, who never wrote to her father about the quarrel, still insisted on Frank's living in the family house in Keene, it may not have been altogether her husband's fault. Thus, within months after her wedding the family was engaged in such a serious and divisive quarrel as would have seemed inconceivable only a year before. The depth of this division can best be judged by the letter writers' occasional injunctions to their father not to tell the other members of the family what they say. The three voices that Charlotte thought must be very entertaining clamored very distinctly indeed, as they pleaded their cause.

Wrapped up in his own problems, Wilson ignored this dissension. Full of self-pity, he asked Lizzie if she was prepared to take care of him in his old age; he was sixty-three. How often had Lizzie begged him to come home to take care of her and her sisters? But Lizzie generously resisted any impulse to remind him of that now.

✳ [LIZZIE]   New York Feb 4th 1859

My dear Father,

I am so delighted to hear that you are really coming home, that I can bear with composure the disagreeable epithets you choose to apply to Annie and myself.

I would much rather lose all *my future inheritance* in Burri Burri, than to not see you this summer. When you say you are too old to manage it that you feel so, that its value depends on your being devoted to it ten years, is not that reason enough why it should be sold.

Undoubtedly we have "teased" you, undoubtedly we have been instigated by a base desire to see our own Father, now absent eight years from us. We or rather, I plead guilty to a strong taint on that question, but far above all, I have thought of your honor. That is pledged. Three times now, the cause has been put off on assurances from you that you would be here. Now undoubtedly you, who alone see and know about that cause, know you are doing right but the world don't think so. It is important to *seem*, as well as to be, *right*, and rather than have anybody have the power to ever *look* askance when your name is mentioned, *I* would rather sacrifice all the gold of California. I hope you will keep Gold Bluff, because Jamie thinks with you that it is of greatest value. What your debts are, and how near jail you are I have no means of knowing. I hope that was a figure of speech. The Climate we will try to make endurable by good friends and warm affections. I think your *four grandsons* may temper the wind to you. . . .

John has just been to the Supreme Court for the first time. Much to his delight acquitted himself remarkably well.

Now I shall build confidently on seeing you this summer, say June. So we can have much enjoyment before you feel the cold, we could all be at Keene together for two or three months, then come here, and make the climate of Italy, if we choose.

Oh dear! if you knew how much I desired it!

Your ever loving daughter
Lizzie

General Wilson was too self-absorbed to pretend that he was looking forward to seeing his children and grandchildren, and he whined about leaving the pleasures of California. Forgetting their differences over the house, Lizzie and Annie mollified him as they would Sam when they had to take him home from the zoo. When her father was in a better temper about returning, Annie slipped into the rhetoric of the *Book of Common Prayer*. "Your last letter was especially welcome from its cheerful tone and the desired appearance of your intention to show us the light of your countenance ere many months" (Annie, 3-3-59).

Meanwhile Wilson's affairs in Keene were so irregular that he asked Frank to find out whether the local police might arrest him for some of his financial peccadillos if he came to Keene.

"The idea of taking your person was as repugnant to Mr. Wheeler as it could be to any one of our warmest friends among whom he certainly should be counted. He said in the first conversation which I had with him that nothing could compel him to take such a step. At a second conversation he said that he did not believe that any body would or could require him to levy the execution upon your body. And that if anyone did, he should not comply unless his lawyers should tell him that he must do it and those interested in the estate should compel him to or make him liable. He has no expectation that they would do so.

"I give you the result of the conversation as it took place, and, as you expected I find it a very disagreeable subject to talk or write about. I think it impossible almost to an impossibility that there would be any cause for your apprehension. I think you might come here and spend the rest of your life without being annoyed as you fear you might be. You are very popular here and even if someone should be found who would wish to incarcerate you, I do not think that he would have sufficient courage to do so against the universal indignation which such a proceeding would arouse. There is only one feeling of kindness and affection towards you and I sincerely hope you will come home in the summer and enjoy it . . ." (Frank, 3-30-59).

Frank's tortuous and circumlocutory reassurances that his father-in-law would not be arrested failed to convince Wilson that it was safe to come home. "Impossible almost to an impossibility" was not good enough, and James Wilson did not come home to face his creditors. So confident were his daughters that he had left California that they ceased to write to him, but week after week passed and he did not sail. The summer passed and his daughters' hopes collapsed. Fall was not a good time to make the journey, and so it was too late.

"The trees are almost stripped of their leaves, and we are rapidly making up our minds to winter—sleigh bells, and baked apples and cream. The frequent appearance of these latter on our table may account for the fact that Miss Charlotte Wilson weighs at this moment the respectable amount of 140. pounds" (Annie, 10-19-59).

After the summer, when Wilson had failed once again to come home, Frank picked up the pieces of the correspondence and sent General Wilson some snuff packed in a bottle designed to keep it moist, some handkerchiefs, and a copy of *Mississippi Bubble*, a book he had translated to favorable notices. He went job hunting in New York. Without mentioning her father's failure to come home, Charlotte, who was reading *Martin Chuzzlewit*, admired Dickens's wit in describing the hypocrite, Pecksniff.

But these cheery little tokens could not disguise the profound disappointment that the children felt at their father's failure to return home or the profound dissension in the family. Wilson neglected to take any action regarding the house, leaving his daughter and son-in-law in residence with very uneasy tenure. Wilson did not commit himself to selling or renting the house to them. He did not pay Mr. Skinner or the bank for it. He did not give it to his children or tell them how he wanted it to be used.

Annie did not let her father off so lightly for not coming home. She was pregnant and more worried than ever about having a house. "I am disappointed and grieved by your deciding not to come home, as I could be by nothing else. I had so confidently hoped to see you before my time of trial came on, which I can not help anticipating with some anxiety, and I can only submit, as so often before, in believing that you know best, and in the established conviction that the Autumn is the worst time for you to select in which to arrive" (Annie, 9-3-59). Though Frank wanted a daughter for her "elevating and subduing influence" (Annie, 1-3-60), Annie was eager to have a boy.

Annie, who did not admit that her brother and sisters were opposed to Frank's owning the house, was eager to make some decisions about the upkeep of the place. Gas lines that were being laid in the street could provide them with heat and light that would make the old house far more comfortable and convenient.

✳ [ANNIE]   Keene September 16th 1859

My dearest Father,

. . . I was particularly glad to receive a few words from you on the subject of my present condition and future prospects. It seemed to make everything all right, at once. I am glad you think I may, sometime raise up some goodish boys. I certainly owe it to you to do so, and, if it please God to give me some, I shall certainly do by best. I feel inclined to say with Mr. Osgood of New York, who, after the birth of several daughters, and an interval of many years, looked forward to the birth of another child. "If it is a nice girl baby, I shall be the happiest man in New York, but if it is a good boy!!, I shall be willing to go without meat and drink the rest of my life." I am, at present, very well, only rather given to laziness.

Charlotte has gone to Fairfax to see Aunt Nancy. She meant to have been at home yesterday, but wrote, instead, that Aunt N. was so "heart break-ingly happy" that she could not make up her mind to leave her before this week. Mother's children seem to be about all she cares for, in this world.

We received intelligence from our splendid boy yesterday in the form of some nice ducks and plover, which he sent as a present to Frank and me. You will have seen that he beat Yale, at Billiards, all to bits—as, of course, he would at any thing he undertook and I hope he told you (in strictest confidence of course) that *he* did it, *personally*, as his associate, tho' consid-ered the best player, "lost his head" at the outset, and Jim made all the first, and telling counts. . . .

We have not heard from Lizzie for over a fortnight. They are all at Delhi, and I hope well. . . .

Frank received, sometime in July, a letter from Mr. Skinner informing him that the interest, on mortgage of this house, was due the Savings Bank to the amount of $279., and asking Frank if he could "adjust it," till your return, which was confidently expected in July. . . . To which Frank replied that he would speak to the Managers of the Savings Bank, to let it lie till your return, and did so. Yesterday Mr. Skinner wrote again saying he had paid the interest, now amounting to $282 57/100, and asking if he should look to Frank for it, "as Genl. Wilson has not provided for it, and may expect that the rent of the house will do it."

I have no idea that you have any such intention and am particularly sorry to have Mr. Skinner suggest it, as Frank has, all the time, felt very uncomfortably about the indefinite nature of our arrangements here, and has been very anxious to buy or hire a cheaper house, and only prevented from doing so by my very strong desire to stay here as long as we remain in this village.

He is very unwilling to write you again on the subject, lest you should think him intrusive or importunate, and constantly suggests the propriety of our taking another and smaller house. I determined, therefore, to say to you that it would greatly add to my comfort and happiness if you would make some definite arrangements concerning the house. I should be very glad to have Frank buy the place, if you still approve that, and I think the other children would, which he would do, if the price came within his means. . . .

A company is just beginning the work of laying Gas pipes in the streets, and that would be a considerable and much needed outlay, in its intro-duction into the house. There is no Barn on the premises, as you will remember, and Uncle Robert so injured the Carriage House in removing the adjoining building that its foundation is insecure, and a new one, if we retain any, must soon be added. . . .

I hope you will write fully in your next, Dear Father, what you conclude on this subject. I did hope we should be able to talk it over before this. . . . Frank sends you his best love, and I am now, as always, your loving daughter   Annie

Had Frank not insisted on playing king of the castle—especially to the exclusion of Lizzie—the children might have worked out a compromise that pleased everybody, more or less. As it was, the dispute finally erupted in a nasty quarrel between Lizzie and Frank. In 1851, Lizzie found Frank a "fine manly fellow" whom she could recommend for the position of secretary to the Land Commission. Eight years later she took quite a different view of him as a brother-in-law who had married the sister for whom she had had such high ambitions. He had encroached on her territory—the family house—and thought himself master of it. Although Frank, for his part, claimed that he wanted to leave the house and move into his own small house, where he could be as domineering as he liked, he certainly seemed to enjoy living in the Wilson's big house, and he transformed it into his own domain.

As Lizzie worked to cultivate the public image appropriate to her social ambitions, she shifted her priorities, creating some comical and some grave misunderstandings. She no longer remembered with pleasure the White Mountains, where she had gone with the Sherwoods when she and John were engaged. Her estimation of the Sherwood estate had dropped considerably since her first visit, when she admired the view of the Delaware River at Delhi and the perfections of the old house. Then she enjoyed driving over the hundreds of acres with John and was grateful that the Sherwoods treated her kindly. Now at Delhi once again, she harbored other ambitions. "I am treated very kindly here, but I hate it. I don't like the country. It is rough and lonely. Like living up at the White Mountains. I like Newport. I hope someday I may have a cottage there, where in addition to a fine climate I may have the best society this country affords instead of this small village gentry and country rustics who have none of the intelligence of New Englanders" (Lizzie, 9-29-59).

She also became faintly paranoid about small slights. Mrs. Berry, who had reappeared in New York—if she ever left—tried Lizzie's patience. Having once found Mrs. Berry merely unconventional and even amusing, Lizzie now saw an insult and even chicanery in Mrs. Berry's ill-advised offer of some lace. She complained of the affront to her father.

"Mrs. Berry came here the other day and made herself disagreeable as usual. She wants me to borrow some lace of hers to wear to parties. I told her I never wore other people's things that what I wore I owned, and what I didn't own I went without, but she urged and urged, saying her handsome lace flounces would be so becoming. I was firm and did *not* take the lace. *How she came* by it is a question to me, and I have wondered ever since whether she offered it out of kindness, or from a desire to get an advantage over me. I will give her the benefit of the doubt" (Lizzie, 1-15-59).

Lizzie should perhaps have known better than to recount this distinctly feminine disagreement to her father. Nevertheless, to California, three thousand miles away, went this little anecdote, which Wilson promptly repeated to the wrong person, Mrs. Berry's mother, Mrs. Duncan. Lizzie was dismayed as the story became common gossip and she was made to look ridiculous. Discretion is a difficult thing to request after the fact, but Lizzie tried.

"I was very foolish to write you all that about Mrs. Berry's lace, because it perhaps was nothing but a good natured request, which I with the natural dignity of a lady declined. I am sorry you told that Mrs. Duncan, because she will write it to Mrs. Berry and I shall have to talk about it. However it is no matter. Don't however say any more about it to anyone.

"Things seem of so much more importance after they are written and sent to California than they really are, that I am always sorry when I write under the influence of any particular feeling. The feeling passes away, the letter remains" (Lizzie, 3-20-59).

This amusing little incident reminded Lizzie of the minefield of misunderstanding that threatens communication. It alerted her to the power of letters to reify and codify experience as they create the story of the past and help shape the future of the family. But those insights did not prevent her from writing another letter a few months later, attacking Frank Fiske once again.

When Frank flatly refused to stay in the house with her the summer of 1859, Lizzie awaited the arrival of her father at a hotel in her hometown. She put her case to Wilson.

＊ [LIZZIE]   Delhi Delaware Co. N. Y. Sept 29th [1859]

My dear Father,

It is a long time since I wrote you, and now I do it without having heard anything from you for several months. It was so severe a disappointment that you did not come home that I felt as if I never could write you again. I felt as if you cared for us no longer. Your reasons for not coming were so vague and unsatisfactory. The business at Keene is in such an undetermined state,—I wish you would explain to us a little of the business, position, and intentions of our Father. When I wrote you that foolish lace story of Mrs. Berry, you wrote me immediately and with the greatest of particularity about it, answering all my questions and devoting time and attention to a very unimportant matter. Now why do you object to answer other questions of greatest moment. Why don't you tell us what you are doing. What is the present aspect of that important Limantour Case that you used to write and talk about, and let us know something of your real history instead of always evading it. In your letter of February 19th you write me that you wish Frank to hire our house at Keene "of Mr. Skinner, who will let him have it at a moderate rent." Now Mr. Skinner told me that the house at Keene was not his. That you had paid him for it, and that there only remained the mortgage to the Savings bank. What has occurred since to alter this fact? Have we been living in Mr. Skinner's house all this time without paying any rent?

In regard to the house at Keene I think you ought to remember a remark you made in a letter two years ago, which I have now stating that you gave that house to your four children equally. How can you now retract that? Have not Charlotte and Jamie and myself just as good a right to it as Annie. Supposing John were to die and I wanted the shelter of that roof have I not a right to it? Now I ask you by the long years we have known each other, by the memory of the deathbeds of Mother, and Webbie, when we ministered together, by the affection I bear you. I confine you to answer me these questions. "What is the exact position of the house at Keene, and what are my rights there, and what are your instructions in regard to it. Do you mean that it shall go as all the property up there has gone by default, seized for half its value, the house where so many births and deaths have occurred—is it to go the way of the Emerald House and all the rest of your property. Oh! my Father! What are you thinking of, that you have left your daughters so many years in suspense, when one page would tell us all. Why will you not pay off the encumbrances off that house settle it legally on us four, and then let us rent it to Frank, instead of this uncertainty and misery. No matter what the story is, do tell it rather than not answer my questions. If I have never to go to Keene as my home again I want to know it. If I won't I want to know that.

I went to Keene this summer as you wrote me to do, and intended to go to our house of course. I knew there was plenty of room there, but Annie wrote me that she must move out if I came there and that she would willingly. Of course I would not allow her to do that, so I took lodgings over the Dunbar house. From the first Frank behaved very badly to me, scarcely speaking. I went to him and said that I did not wish him to move out, that there was no bad feeling on my part and I wished him to know it, that if I had thought it would *make* him feel unpleasantly to see me I would not have come to Keene. The polite and friendly answer I got was this. 'I thought you knew we did not want you to come to Keene.' I then told him your last message to me was to come to meet you there and that I had done so, that the only feeling I had was that they should not be willing to have me come and stay one month under the same roof, paying my own share of the expenses, with them. Frank informed me that that could not be done, that he would move out at any moment, willingly but would not live there with anyone else. Of course he knew very well that I would not insist upon his moving out. Poor Annie sat there trembling and crying, and is perfectly broken down by his terrible and quick ungovernable temper. He behaves like a madman, so jealous and so unreasonable, a domestic tyrant, and altho' he loves Annie he makes her miserable by it. She talked very freely with me about his temper which she had no idea of, and said some pretty fearful things. I told her to bear everything and be a good wife, that he might mend. He is so jealous of her affection for my children as to behave very queerly almost insane in fact. But this is a secret. Don't tell it to Mrs. Berry or any one. Don't write to them about it. Treat Annie with every kindness for she is born to trouble, and she is denied the consolation of having me with her when she is confined because Frank is so jealous of me even, that he don't want me there. Poor girl! Frank's enmity stops before it reaches Charlotte, and he will allow her to be in the house I believe.

Oh! if you only knew how much we hoped you would come back! How we long to see you, to have you with us! If you knew how kindly we would treat you, anticipate your wants, make your days pass pleasantly, you would come home I am sure. . . .

While at Keene my little son Phillip was very sick, so ill that we thought he must die. He had cholera infantum. When he was able to travel we took him to Newport, in which delightful climate he rapidly recovered. We staid three weeks there enjoying it very much, except that I wanted James and Charlotte there, but they wrote that they had not money enough to come. They took my three eldest and came out here with them, very kindly. We paid Charlotte's expenses of course. Jamie would not let us pay his. . . .

The two older boys are perfectly well and enjoy this place of their grandfather's very much.

Wil is able to read quite well in the Rollo books. Sam takes it very hard, but has a strong congenial mind, which is very amusing in its demonstrations. Arthur is a queer, little, intensely *smart* child, very precocious. Phillip is a beautiful baby with a dimple in his cheek, and seems to have a fine constitution as his bearing this heavy sickness proves.

Old Mr. Sherwood is a fine old man of eighty, vigorous and bright as ever. His health suffers some however. He loves my boys very much. . . .

Dearest Father, do not be angry with me. I feel that the only right thing for me is to ask you to tell me the truth in all things. Do write and tell me if you never mean to come home.

I am as always your affectionate and loyal daughter.   Lizzie

Wilson noted at the end of this letter: "Letter from My Daughter Mary Elizabeth, Delhi NY Septr 29th 1859. N. B. Private and confidential relating to family affairs."

While Lizzie was in Delhi licking her wounds, Annie, in the last days of her pregnancy, was nursing a famous houseguest. Abigail Hopper Gibbons, who had fallen off the gallery (the southern name for the porches under the colonnades) and sprained both of her ankles, was an influential political activist and philanthropist, who not only headed the German Poor School and visited prisons in New York but was also an important abolitionist and temperance leader (*Notable American Women*). Though she worked with women who were released from prison, she never took up the cause of women's rights. She persuaded Annie and Frank to adopt a "colored orphan," a little girl whom Charlotte said they would bring up with the "*purest white* principles." However, when the philanthropist's ankles healed, she moved on. The humanitarian impulse flickered out, and we hear no more about Frank and Annie's adopting a "colored orphan."

On November 15, Annie had a baby girl—seven pounds, twelve ounces—named Mary after Annie's mother. "I have gone through 'the perils of childbirth,' as the English Prayer Book says, since I wrote to you, and live to tell the story, and a pretty doleful story, I think it is" (Annie, 1-3-60). She was so pleased with her daughter, however, that she said she would not trade her for all of the boys in New Hampshire and California, and Frank was ecstatic. Roxana was astonished that she had lived to hold Annie's baby. Everyone, even Frank, agreed, as they had with each of Lizzie's four boys, that Mary looked exactly like her grandfather, James Wilson, Jr. Frank cut a lock of her baby hair and sent it to Wilson to show that in color and texture it was like her grandfather's. Her chin had a deep hollow in it like his, Annie's, and Jamie's. Her hair was very dark, and they thought her blue eyes would turn dark (Charlotte, 12-18-59). Charlotte particularly admired this new baby. "I am sure you will be delighted with your Grand-daughter when you see her, for she is very beautiful and uncommonly bright. She is the *handsomest* child in the family, (you needn't mention this to *Lizzie*!). Her children are splendid, and as dear to me as anything in the world, but this child is certainly brighter, *for her days*, than they were" (Charlotte, 1-18-

60). Jamie was glad it was a girl because "his sisters have been so much to him, that if Annie has any sons they will lean on their older Sisters," adding that "the glory of the Wilson family has come from its women" (Charlotte, 11-2-59).

The arrival of the baby placed additional pressure on Frank and Annie to become independent and solvent. Frank traveled again and again to New York, trying to find work. Annie pressed her father to regularize their occupation of the house. While Lizzie and Frank quarreled most violently about the family place, Charlotte had a strong stake in the outcome of the dispute. Since Jamie had decided to go to California after he graduated, she was the only child left who needed a home, so she felt she must speak directly for her own benefit, something she seldom did.

*   [CHARLOTTE]   Keene January 18th 1860

My dearest Father,

. . . I wish I could have a good talk with you, Father, about several things, of which the principal is the disposition of the House this next Summer.

Annie doesn't know I am writing, or *even thinking* anything about it. But she said to me several weeks ago that she wondered what *I* should do next Summer about the House, as Frank and she should leave it in the Spring, unless you said you wanted her to stay.

I want Frank and Annie to stay here. They are poor, and Annie is happier here than she would be anywhere, but Frank *hates* to stay. He thinks you don't want him to stay, and, in fact, he thinks you mistrust his motives and actions. I am afraid you do, so nothing under Heaven will induce him to stay except your request. We—Annie and I—have *insisted* upon his staying till Annie's confinement was over. It was so necessary to her happiness to be here. Then another great reason why I want them to stay is that *I* feel at Home here. I can't afford to keep House, as Annie and I did, and support John's and Lizzie's family. I should have to spend money at the rate of two or three thousand dollars a year. I don't think it is right. It is asking too much of you.

Jamie and I have a delightful Home now, as it is. Of course the case rests with you, and do please give us your opinion.

John and Lizzie have had the house and all its appurtenances under their control for many years, and, although I love them dearly, and like to have them here with the children, I really think it only just that it should be at Annie's service as well.

Annie and I were always dreadfully poor when we kept the house open. The family was too large.

You will be amused that my final argument for wishing them to stay here is that *I* have a certain and pleasant Home here.

As you said in your last letter, I shall probably never be married, so that a Home is a peculiarly desirable institution for me.

This letter is strictly private between us, as I shall never let *anyone* know I have written it. If you decide to ask them to stay here, I shall wish the request to come *directly from you*. They wouldn't take it as such if they knew I had written. If you decide *not* to ask them to stay, I am sure I shan't want them to know I have written. If I could *talk* to you, you would do Frank justice. He is the most perfectly honorable Creature. He has always been anxious to gain your affection, and deserves it, and he has felt very badly all Summer because some of us wrote you that there was a "hard feeling about the House." There was *more* on *his part*, his only wish being to go out, and leave it to John and Lizzie, but Annie could not bear to leave it. Please forgive me if I have bored you. And believe me your devoted daughter

Charlotte

The controversy over the house was out in the open. When Lizzie told Charlotte about the letter she had written, Charlotte defended Frank even more vigorously. As in the plot of a comic opera Lizzie created a family crisis over an invitation to a ball.

✳ [CHARLOTTE]   Keene February 4th 1859 [1860]

My dearest Father,

. . . I was sorry to learn from Lizzie that she had written you by the last mail such a letter about Frank.

Frank has never said anything against Lizzie in his life I know to any person out of the family. Never. Lizzie thought he had, because *she did not receive* an *invitation* to a *Ball* when she expected to be invited, and as the lady who gave the Ball was a friend of Frank's friends, she jumped at the conclusion that he had maligned her. As it turns out she was invited, but her invitation went to the wrong person.

Frank dislikes Lizzie, and I cannot wonder at it. I know it is wrong. As he is married to Annie he ought to try to like her sister, but Lizzie has behaved with so little delicacy, and she has changed so lately, that it surprises us all. Her letters are exclusively about fashion. She hasn't even mentioned the children in her last two or three letters. I know it is only the effect of New York Society. Her heart is as warm as ever, and her devotion to us is very great.

Success in Society hurts some characters, and I dislike to think that it is hurting Lizzie's. Pray don't say anything to Lizzie about this. Any written rebuke hurts her feelings horribly. When I go on *I* can give one or two *hints* that may do her good.

Here is Annie, who 'has been tried in the furnace.' She grows better and better every day. Dear good girl.

You will say 'this is a cool criticism of character,' and I think you may, with some justice, think me uncharitable. But I feel free to tell you just the Truth.

Jamie seems sure of going to California next August. . . .

Good bye. Your devoted   Charlotte

It was in January 1860, less than a year before the opening salvo of the Civil War, that the quarrel over the house raged. The daughters worried over what would happen in the summer when Lizzie would again wish to come to Keene. There were once again hints that Wilson might return soon, but in the spring, when Jamie graduated from Harvard, his father was not present to congratulate him. Instead, Jamie immediately sailed for California to join General Wilson.

"Sir, It Is All Yours"

With politicians and newspapers threatening secession and Wilson's children quarreling with almost as much bitterness over their home place in Keene, James Wilson, Jr., boarded *The Golden Age* in February 1861, a year after his son Jamie had sailed for California, and returned home. The expectation of his children that the eleven winters of their discontent would be made glorious by his return seemed imminently real at last. Why he returned this particular year remains a mystery. That he chose the spring of 1861 for no obvious reason, when he had already missed Lizzie's wedding in 1851, Annie's wedding in 1859, the births of five grandchildren, and Jamie's commencement only a year earlier, only points again to Wilson's disengagement from his family.

A curious entry in Wilson's journal also reveals that he went at Jamie's urging. "Monday, February 4, 1861: Lovely weather continues. I am satisfied by sundry and various hints that my son Jim wants me to abdicate on the next steamer, via, the *Golden Age* on Monday the 11th instant and I will go although against my will. So is the way of the world and as it is in the order of Providence I must assume it is all right—The old folks are terribly in the way of their children when the children are grown to manhood and womanhood. Thank God I am not conscious of ever having said a word to annoy or irritate my father in his old age—that I did or neglected to do a thousand things that he disapproved may be true but never a thing designedly to cross his purpose." Jamie may not have pleased Wilson quite so thoroughly as he did his sisters. Although Wilson trusted his son not to mishandle his affairs deliberately, he had reservations about his resourcefulness as he confides to his journal. "Saturday 26 Jan. 1861: Jim is off on steamer business. Jim is no great shakes on these emergencies. He goes it on billiards and them fixings—*but—but*—he may wench. We don't find fault with my only son. I am on the downhill side—he is going up and I pray God to aid him in his ascent." Perhaps Wilson left his son in charge to "aid him in his ascent."

Whatever Wilson's purpose, he remained in the East for about eight months, during which he was reunited with his children and grandchildren and watched his country crumble into civil war.

Wilson's journal of 1861 continues to provide the details of his return: "Monday, February 11, 1861: Started on *Golden Age* from San Francisco for New York. Memo of funds—

Parrotts' letter of credit	$10,000
and Bill of Exchange	4,600
Cash in Sack Trunk	700
In Wallet Pocket etc. say	$15,475.00

Rough weather. Heavy sea. Stormy night."

A little over three weeks later Wilson described his arrival in New York after his eleven-year absence without a spark of the excitement he displayed over Jamie's shooting the elk:

"Tuesday, March 5, 1861: Arrived at New York at 2 o'clock PM, lame with rheumatism—Met my son in law Mr. John Sherwood on the steamer. Went directly to his house found my daughters Mary Lizzie and Chardie there and my four dear little grandsons all well and beautiful and happy.

Note of funds—Letters of credit	$10,000
Parrots' Bill	4,600
Cash say	750
	$15,350"

Wilson was home. The country was dividing. Just the day before, in words carefully chosen to be both firm and conciliatory, Abraham Lincoln closed his first Inaugural Address with the words labeled "moderate yet firm" by Republicans and a "declaration of war" by the Confederates. "We are not enemies, but friends. Though passion may have strained, it must not break our bonds of affection. The mystic chords of memory, stretching from every battlefield, and patriot grave, to every living heart and hearthstone, all over this broad land, will yet swell the chorus of the Union, when again touched, as surely they will be, by the better angels of our nature" (James M. McPherson, *The Battle Cry of Freedom: The Civil War Era* [New York: Oxford University Press, 1988], 263).

Annie and her family were temporarily staying in Boston, and she had family duties that prevented her from getting to New York to greet her father in person. But her letter of welcome exuded far more excitement than did her father's diary notation.

✳ [ANNIE]   Boston March 3d 1861

Dearest Father,

You must accept such a poor welcome as I can give you on this sheet of paper, on your first arrival, at home, after eleven years. Frank and I *could* not meet you in New York, you know owing to our "incumbrances," but you know that our "hearts go out to meet you" as thoroughly as children's ever did, and I shall only be patient till you have taken a good look at Lizzie's troup, when you must come right straight to Boston and see what a matronly old woman your daughter Annie is, whom you left seventeen years old, and what a kissing she will give you. Frank and I feel now more than ever, at your arrival, our homeless condition but we will have some Baked Beans in Keene, yet, and that is the *real* home, and always will be.

How do you like Charlotte? Do you think she is, as Jim says "about as good as they make 'em?" I want you to begin to make her behave herself, at once. Frank sends his best love to you and wants me to remind you that, of course, the house at Keene is entirely at your disposition and until we can do it ourselves we will tell Charlotte . . . and others how to take care of you there, just as long as you find it convenient to be there, and a great [deal] longer.

I must wait till I see you now to tell you how I have meant to thank you for my New Years present and to write you a great many letters.

Good Bye till then. Always yr loving daughter   Annie

Perhaps she did write a great many letters; but in the collection of letters that we have, Annie's welcome to her father is her farewell to the modern reader. With the return of her father the frustration of separation that occasioned her letterwriting was past. We learn that she saw him because Lizzie and Charlotte tell of Wilson's being in Keene with Annie during the next few months, but whether the reunion fulfilled Annie's dreams or not she does not say. He had at last shown her the light of his countenance, and her voice is still.

For the next eight months, whenever their father was not with them, Charlotte and Lizzie kept him abreast of family affairs. They also recounted eyewitness experiences of the early days of the Civil War. Since Wilson spent most of his time in Keene, Lizzie, lamenting his reluctance to come to New York, wrote to him most often.

On Friday, five days after the raising of the Confederate flag over Fort Sumter, South Carolina, and four days after Lincoln called for seventy-five thousand militiamen, Lizzie exuded patriotic fervor. Her effusions about the redemptive value of suffering and bloodletting may ring a little hollow considering her own comfortable life and the safety of her brother, father, husband, and sons; but patriotism was the fashion, and love of the military was a Wilson tradition. While he was in the East, General Wilson lent his oratorical skills to the cause.

* [LIZZIE]   Friday Evening April 19th

My dear Father,

Today I have returned from the most glorious spectacle my eyes have ever seen. The Seventh Regiment, comprising the flower of New York youth, marched today through a dense mass of sympathizing, cheering, weeping, excited citizens to the defence of the federal Capitol. As I looked and my eyes were *not* dry, on this noble company composed of the young men of the most fashionable circles, the young clerks, and young mechanics, and saw how manly, how noble and how loyal they all looked, I thought we were not to degenerate after all, and that a country possessed of such sons need not tremble for its perpetuity or its honor. Our friend and cousin James Ruggles was fine, and I went up to bid him good bye. His Father and Mother were very much affected but perfectly firm and determined to give him up. He was very gay and bright, but we feel very sadly about him. The drum and fife are the last sounds we hear at night and the first in the morning. War is upon us, and thank God, it does not find the North wanting. Major Anderson has been received with enthusiasm and tomorrow an immense Union meeting in Union Square is to assemble, under a banner bearing Genl Dix's words,

"If any man attempts to take down the American flag shoot him on the spot."

My three boys have badges of the Red, white, and blue, and are full of love of country, and *fight*.

Trinity Church for the first time in a hundred years hangs out a flag, and at three o'clock played on the chimes Hail! Columbia and Yankee Doodle.

I hear dear old New Hampshire has voted twenty thousand men. And Massachusetts has shed the first blood. Is not Major Anderson's letter glorious.

. . . It is stirring to one's blood I assure you, to see such enthusiasm. I cannot but feel that it is wisely sent to ventilate this country, so debauched as it has been by unlimited prosperity, and that it will restore us to the values as well as to the trials of our Ancestors. May we be equal to the emergency!

Prays your loving daughter   Lizzie

John sends his regards and best wishes to you and Charlotte, and wants you to come back and help us be *enthusiastic*.

He says tell you Father we are all sound here.

Lizzie's enthusiasm for the war colored the family life of the Sherwoods. Lizzie soldiered on by nursing Sam through a fever and saving him for the republic. When Charlotte arrived to help her, she noted that the effort had taken its toll on Lizzie. "Lizzie looks very tired. She has been with him four nights and days incessantly. I am very glad I could come to relieve her" (Charlotte, 5-?-61).

✱ [LIZZIE]   Wednesday evening

My dear Father,

Sam is pronounced on the high road to recovery by the Dr. . . . Sam is very feeble of course and needs the most careful nursing. He has been very sick. I thought several times that his little boat would swamp, but thanks to God and under him to Dr. Crane he is doing very well, and will live. I hope no drawback will occur now. I cannot imagine life without Sam. I want to preserve that clear head and fine physique for future usefulness. They say *War* degenerates a race. All the fine men get killed off and only the puny ones remain at home, so if we have a very extenuating war there will be few boys as fine as yours is, or mine are over the next thirty years. But I don't believe anybody is going to be killed. It all reminds me of the anecdote of Preston King's saying after two men talked so vigorously about fighting a duel that they got themselves arrested—"Mr. Speaker, if there is so much talking here I fear *somebody* will get *hurt*." Don't you think the South is going to back very much down?

. . . Wil will write you when the duties of a soldier will permit, but he has joined a Zouave regiment and has red trousers on prospect and drills all the time [he] is not studying. Arthur shows an immense proficiency in French, and astonishes us all. . . . You should see John! He thinks of nothing but military matters and drills every evening. He comes home to dinner and that is about all. . . . A work called the "Partizan Leader" is attracting much attention and Dr. Crane has bought it to attest what you told him about Secession being an old idea. . . .

* [LIZZIE]

Dearest Father,

. . . Sam has been very sick. He is improving. . . . I promised him last night that when he got well I would take him to West Point to see the nice Cadets. He said "Let's ask Grandpa to go to." He has an idea that his Grandpa knows "considerable" about politics and military matters, and is rather a clever fellow to be with. You know children will have these exaggerated notions. Wil got your beautiful letter and reads it two or three times a day. He was very much pleased with the attention, and will keep it undoubtedly as I did the first letter you ever wrote me from Washington, describing the East Room and *Mrs. Florida White*. I remember every word of it now, tho' it was written twenty-five years ago.

. . . The Doctor has become the most furious of anti-Southerners. Of course I crow and quote his sentiments of last fall. The feeling here is much more cheerful. There is a Committee here, really carrying on the war I think, spending millions and ordering cannon, rifles, ships and stores to an incredible amount. If we are beaten for a year, to suppose a very probable case, we should be better able to fight a second year than we were the first. Jeff Davis has waked up the wrong passenger. I *wish* you were here. As soon as Sam gets well, say next week can't you come down. You would be very much interested. As for your going to war, I hope not. You are so tall that they would pick you out at once, and are too good looking a man to be shot by a scoundrelly bilious southerner. You can do more good to the cause by your advice and money I am sure.

I send you a record of the Rebellion published by Frank Moore. I think it will be an interesting thing to keep.

We hear that the soldiers are much pleased with the Havelocks. I hope the ladies of Keene will make some.

The Doctor has heard from a person in Charleston that Beauregard was shot at Morris Island. He says he does not doubt that a thousand men were killed there. Something has happened to Jeff Davis to paralyze his energies for a time or he would be making more demonstration.

The Maple Sugar and flowers arrived safely tell Annie, and the boys are much pleased with Sarah's checkerberries. Wil says "these are hot shot and my stomach is Fort Sumpter" so he poured them in relentlessly. . . .

Write us as often as your are able, and give my love to Annie.
Affectionately your daughter   Lizzie

Wilson joined this rising tide of nationalism. In our age of speeches amplified through microphones, radios, and televisions, it is difficult to imagine how valuable a loud voice was to a politician in the middle of the nineteenth century. Wilson lent his to the Union cause as early as April, to be followed by speeches in Concord and Rutland, Vermont, and Lizzie wanted him to take a stand as bold and aggressive as his voice was loud in a letter to President Lincoln.

"Charlotte writes me today about your speech. I am delighted to hear that you were well enough, and felt like it, enough to make an old fashioned stump speech. How it must have carried you back to old times. How I wish I had been there to see you escorted up, and to have heard your clarion voice re-echo from the hills.

"You would have been invited to speak here had you been here at the great Union meeting, and I thought with regret that you were not, when I heard the other men painfully fail of making themselves heard by that vast crowd. However the North looks proudly up today, for Washington is safe, the Potomac open and our hands are on their dastardly throats, the Miscreants. The Government seems weak. I hope you will write to the President urging a war policy, and telling him the feeling of the North" (Lizzie, 1861?).

At the death of Ellsworth, Lincoln's young law clerk, Lizzie's rhetoric became as stirring as any her father could have commanded. Shot by a hotel proprietor in Alexandria, Virginia, whose Confederate flag Ellsworth was personally removing from a building, his death evoked a bloodthirsty eulogy from Lizzie. " 'The blood of the martyrs is the seed of the church' and the blood of Col. Ellsworth has roused to fury a set of men who do not stand upon trifles. It seems providential that this brave and beloved young officer . . . should fall at the very outset of the battle, thus nerving every heart and hand to pitiless warfare against those bloodthirsty slave holders. I trust it will be war to the knife, and that a thousand lives may be offered up as an expiatory sacrifice for this brave young man, who was doing only his duty and harming no one. He is the Nathan Hale of the present crisis and has passed into a glorious immortality on the pages of History, and let us hope into the immortality of the brave and just" (Lizzie, 1861).

✳ [LIZZIE]   New York Friday May 17 1861

My dear Father,
. . . The Maine Regiment passes today with green sprigs in their hats. This little sprig of hemlock is as romantic and eloquent as the white plume of Henry of Navarre and will like that famous adornment undoubtedly wave in the thickest of the fight. The great trouble seems to be that these men get nothing to eat on their journeys, a very wrong thing. . . .

Mr. Hamilton came to ask you and us to spend some days at his place in the country and wished me to let him know when you came. He was full of interesting anecdotes of the early days of the republic and says South Carolina tried to secede in 1791, at the passage of the first Tariff. "What this pestilent little d——d state was ever *in* the Union for I don't know" he said getting rather excited, and asking my pardon. He says we are going to have a war of Conquest, we northerners.

Lawrence Williams has been made a Major, under Genl McClelland of Ohio with $4000 a year, and *three horses. Loyalty pays.* . . .

What am I to do with a dozen night shirts I have had made for you. They are large enough for the Vermont and Maine Regiments both, so if you don't want them you can present them to the volunteers.

Charlotte will rejoin you in a few days. Are you not coming back to us at all? I hope so, and I want you to go to Delhi. . . .

Ever yours affectionately
Lizzie

War fever infected Charlotte as well when she was in New York, and she was much embarrassed at New Hampshire's laggardly contribution to the war effort. She wrote several letters full of sensitive and wide-ranging observations, similiar to the ones she wrote during her last year in school in Boston and providing us with some specific details of women's activities in the early days of the conflict. She was proud of the newly founded United States Sanitary Commission, founded by Dr. Henry Bellows, which raised money to send bandages, medicine, food, clothing, and volunteer nurses to army camps and hospitals.

* [CHARLOTTE]   New York Wednesday May 15 [1861]

My dearest Father,

Sam is almost well. He lies on the sofa, in his dressing gown, nearly all the time and is in pretty good spirits always, except when he gets a little tired, when he *droops*, of course, or is very cross, which shows that, he *has been very sick*, and that he is very weak.

One of us stays with him all the time, to keep him company and prevent his *reading* or getting tired. But our active duties are ended.

And I think Lizzie can spare me by the first of next week perfectly well, so if you would like me to join you at Keene . . . I shall be most happy to return. . . .

And if you wish to see military ardor, come here. There are troops of recruits marching through Broadway to the Parade Ground all the time, with no uniform, but with an *expression* on their faces better than any garb, and more imposing.

The boys of a large school, today, I saw being drilled in the Parade Ground. They had a regular drill master.

What a warlike Nation we are becoming, and we need to be, if the *English* papers keep on in the present style.

You will notice one of the London papers suggests the possibility of having to fight for the cotton. It is stated here by high authority that Mr. Adams has power to inform England that cotton shall be exported from or through the middle States. The 'Confederates' say they will *burn* the cotton sooner.

I went this morning to the Cooper Institute to see the operation of an admirably organized society for the relief and aid of the sick and wounded soldiers. This society is in communication with Miss Dolly Dix who informs them of the wants of the Washington Hospital. Several of my particular friends are members of this Society. They have to work very hard, answering notes from people in the country, receiving contributions, etc. This morning while I was there a poor man, belonging to the Middle Classes, came in with two enormous bundles. He said "he was a poor man, but his wife and he wanted to do something," so he brought a donation of *four dozen* sheets, all new and nicely made, three dozen pillow cases, 57 pincushions. Besides lint etc. wasn't that generous?

It gives you some idea of the enthusiasm which pervades all classes. There is much more [enthusiasm] here than in Boston I know. Here *all* the men, who are able bodied, drill every evening, or every other evening, young men and old.

There is a club of elderly men, among them your old friend Mr. Talmadge, who are drilling. And the *babies* drill too. Wil belongs to a company, Lizzie suggested to him to join a new company of Zouaves. Wil said 'Why I belong to a company now. I must stick to my own company.'

It delights me to think that there are many Secessionists here who can see this grand enthusiasm. Isn't it delightful to think that the Massachusetts Sixth are now in possession of Baltimore? Genl. Butler evidently rides around there in great style. I wish I could see him.

. . . believe me your devoted daughter   Charlotte

"The ladies here do nothing but make things for the soldiers. There is an organized body of Nurses, being trained here in the Hospital. One of the first questions asked a woman who is ambitious to become a Nurse is whether she is *over thirty*. None under that age are accepted. It is wonderful how many find it impossible to confess they are *over thirty*" (Charlotte, 5-61).

✳ [CHARLOTTE] New York Friday [May 1861]

My dearest Father,

. . . Dr. Crane came to see us, all, this morning. He enquired particularly for you. He thinks there is going to be an attack on Washington yet.

He says "for three weeks there have been heavy trains pouring into Virginia loaded with troops, and he doesn't doubt there are 50,000 troops there."

The Times communicates the amazement of the Foreign Ministers at the enthusiasm of the North, and it seems they have stated that no Despot in Europe could have raised, in thirty days, such an Army as President Lincoln has done.

Their amazement will produce a good effect on the London Times I trust. It *makes* people here *disgusted* and *mad* to see the *low mercenary* articles in the Times, although, as the writer of one of the articles says himself, "It makes no difference to America what the English advise on the subject. I think the consciousness that seems to be creeping over England that she is slow and stupid is quite amusing. She is so afraid Louis Napoleon will overreach her at one time, and then she fears *we* shall."

I believe, and you know how *valuable* my opinion is, and how *willing* I am to *express* it, that this war is to make us the really strongest and most formidable Nation in the world. If you could hear, as I have several times, two hundred boys voices singing the Star Spangled Banner with . . . enthusiasm that seemed to carry the air way up toward Heaven you would have been impressed, even more than you have been before, with the conviction that the next generation would be patriotic.

Poor Sam has become so tired of hearing the Star Spangled Banner, that When Wil was shouting: "Long may it wave" Sam said, "Why *does* it wave Wil. What's the use of saying all the time 'Long may it wave'?"

Give my love to Annie, and believe me, my dear Father, your devoted daughter Charlotte

I am mortified to acknowledge I am from New Hampshire. I know you feel just so. So write something for some of the papers there.

Here Vermont has sent a splendid Regiment last week. Maine too has sent one. Connecticut too. . . . And what is the use of *saying* New Hampshire is ready? Why don't she *come on*?

If I were Frank I would start for Washington with my men tomorrow. . . . Charlotte

While the war effort continued, the irrepressible Lizzie remained mind-
ful of her own goals. She did not flinch from asking her father (who had
yet to pay the mortgage on the house in Keene) for money to buy a house
for her in New York. Considering poor Annie and Frank's present, eager,
and unanswered claims to the house in Keene, Lizzie's bravado in propos-
ing that her father buy another house for her in Gramercy Park may have
surpassed her request for $15,000 for her dowry.

"I want now to say a few words about a house. John says if I can find a
house which suits me for twelve hundred a year, he will move. Before looking, I ask you to let me know if you feel inclined to buy the house of my
desires in Gramercy Park. John thinks that it may be bought for 19,000–
20,000. down, the rest in bond and mortgage for two and five years.

"If you would, and allow us to be your tenants, until we can pay for it,
you would make me very happy. I don't intend to *ask* for it, but simply as a
matter of business. John has no money just now. . . . If you will give me an
answer as soon as convenient, either yes or no, I shall be much obliged, for
I shall then proceed before the 1st May to make my arrangments. I want
you and Charlotte to come back here for May, and Mr. Sherwood wants
you to come to Delhi" (Lizzie, 1861?).

The answer to her request was evidently a very brusque no.

"You shall not be urged or asked to buy a house or do anything you
don't want to.

"You know you suggested to us to inquire the title of the house in *Fifth
Av*, and said before that you did not know but you should invest in some
N. Y. property.

"Of course you know your own business. I merely spoke on the hint you
gave, knowing you have money to invest and supposing you would like to
invest it here. I did not expect it as a gift, or in any way an investment that
would accrue to my advantage particularly. I shall now go to find a house
that we can hire" (Lizzie, 1861?).

Of course, she may have thought herself justified in asking for help in
buying a new home since Frank's presence did Lizzie out of her usual summers in the house in Keene. Unsettling as it was for the family to admit,
their annual migration had served its purpose. While her father was at home
in Keene, Lizzie herself passed a significant milestone. "You always write
to some of us on your birthday. I must write you on mine, particularly on
so important a one as 'Thirty five.' I am probably more than half through
my life, have reached the hill top, and must now begin to go down, but so

deceptive are human feelings that I do not feel a minute older than I did at sixteen" (Lizzie, 10-27-61). To assuage her nostalgia and homesickness, she asked for mementos of that past to incorporate in her house in New York.

"I very much want a daguerreotype of our old place. Allen of Keene takes them well and now before the leaves are out is just the time, a large sized one from the garden gate, or across the road, as Allen thinks will make the best picture. I want you and Annie to stand on the bank, and Ottie and Paul to be somewhere in the yard and Annie's babies. Annie will group you all nicely. I want you to be leaning on your cane looking at the trees just as I have seen you a hundred times.

"I want the boys to keep in mind the old place where their Mother was '*raised*' and where two of them have been born and where they have passed so many happy hours.

"Will you also send down to me that old picture of me painted by Harding. It is yours, but you don't want it, and we do not like to have it hanging in Frank's house while he has such bitter feelings against me. Annie does not like it, and John does. He thinks it looks as I used to. Please to have Briggs box it. I will repay him for all expenses. Also if agreeable to all I should like one of the pictures of Mother, the old one best. I have nothing of her" (Lizzie, undated).

Despite the widening rift over the house, the relationship among the sisters remained loving and firm. Lizzie never allowed her hard feelings toward Frank or Frank's hard feelings toward her to taint her feelings for Annie. Lizzie worried when Annie became sad and depressed after Frank left for Washington, but presumably the quarrel between her and Frank had gone so far that she could not go to Keene for the summer even to take care of her sister while he was away. Instead, she went reluctantly to Delhi, and Annie was left to fret through Frank's baptism by fire alone in the house in Keene with her baby. With no expression of rancor Lizzie resigned herself to spending the summer in West Point, Delhi, and Long Branch.

"I have this afternoon returned from West Point. I went up yesterday to look for rooms, and staid with a friend of mine Mrs. Bigelow at Buttermilk Falls just below. I found the rooms cheap and agreeable. We shall probably take them for August and Sept. The boys go to Delhi for the summer. We go out to be with them one month, then we have got to come away. . . . I think now we shall spend July in Delhi. I hope you will go out there with us, and also to West Point" (Lizzie, undated).

General Wilson did not return to visit Lizzie in New York despite her pleading, nor did he go with her to West Point. All of the Sherwoods seemed to be particularly eager for him to visit them in Delhi, especially Mr. Sherwood, John's father, who repeatedly requested that Lizzie press him to come. Instead, Wilson, Charlotte, and Mary Sherwood went to Washington, the very place Charlotte had been warned would be attacked, about the same time that Lizzie arrived in Delhi on July 5 with her sons "glorious, brown and strong" and "waving the American flag as we approached" (Lizzie, 7-7-61). The Sherwoods expected the Wilsons to appear in Delhi sometime during the month, and plans were afoot for the Wilsons' comfort.

"Mrs. Sherwood has taken me up to show me Jim's and Charlotte's rooms and to ask if the *bed* is long enough.

"Owing to the uncertainty of the trains, etc, Mr. Sherwood thinks your journey across country would hardly *pay*. However whatever way you come you must write me what day you will arrive at Hancock so I can send a carriage down for you, as the stage carries *eleven* passengers, stops all the time is drawn by poor horses and driven by a disobliging wretch who would not listen to any mercy. It would incommode the ladies and kill you to try and come so, for the roads are very heavy, and bad. A large Rockaway wagon we have sent down for us in which you can stretch your legs, take your time and bring your trunks, for ten dollars for the whole party nearly as cheap as the stage. Write me as soon as you get this, if you please, that I may make this arrangement. You never saw any place *so far off* as Delhi" (Lizzie, 7-7-61).

But all of these arrangements were interrupted. Frank Fiske and Uncle Robert, the only member of the family to remain in the army to the end of the war, had marched off to battle. Frank fought in the first Battle of Manassas, outside of the capital. Now Lieutenant Colonel Frank Fiske, he had departed from Portsmouth with New Hampshire's Second Regiment on June 20, to great fanfare. Once near the nation's capital, they were brigaded under Colonel A. E. Burnside in the first Battle of Manassas, a disastrous defeat for the Union troops. Frank's regiment encountered heavy fire and "lost nine men killed, thirty five wounded—four of them mortally— and sixty-three prisoners taken." (Simon G. Griffin, *A History of the Town of Keene from 1732* [Keene, N.H.: Sentinel Printing Co., 1904], 477). Among those wounded was the commanding officer, which left Lieutenant Colonel Fiske in command of the regiment during the rout that followed.

While the two armies clashed outside Washington, James Wilson, Charlotte, and Mary Sherwood Murray (Mary M.) were in the city, in the path of the stampede of retreating Union soldiers. Wilson may well have been among the crowd of spectators who rode out to see the battle and almost got caught in that stampede. On the very day of the battle Lizzie pouted about their absence.

✳ [LIZZIE]   Delhi, July 21st

My dear Father,

We have been expecting you every day this week. You told me you would probably not stay in Washington more than ten days. So we have been waiting, watching, and hoping. Tell Charlotte I think her conduct has been "heartless in the extreme" not writing to me. That I got her little scratch yesterday and wished for more. Mary M. has been very good about writing to her Mother. We are here quite alone. I, having a lonely desolate time. I would not have come here had I but thought you would be here. I shall leave on the 1st August. So I hope you will be here in this coming week or the first of next. *Private*—Mr. and Mrs. Sherwood feel unpleasantly about Mary's remaining so long in W. . . . so I would if I were you manage to leave soon, if it is, as I suppose that the girls are keeping you there.

Mr. Sherwood will feel greatly disappointed if you do not come. Let me know I beg of you what your future plans are, because I shall bring the boys down to NY to see you before you leave if you do not come here. Otherwise I shall leave the two eldest here most likely.

What stirring news comes with every paper. Our Keene boys are in the thickest of the fight apparantly. Ought not Charlotte to be on her way home, so as to be with poor Annie, who must feel very anxious and lonely. I would go to her if I could.

I am sure you must have enjoyed being at Washington at this time. I long to hear you talk about it. . . .   affectionately your daughter
                                                                              Lizzie

Lizzie's petulance turned into alarm when she heard about the outcome of the battle four days later.

✳ [LIZZIE]   Delhi July 25th [1861]

My dear Father,

Why don't you write to me. Imagine how anxious and distressed I am not to hear from you, through all this trouble and Charlotte too. Pray Heaven you may have left Washington.

Mr. and Mrs. Sherwood increase my claim by saying hourly "Oh now thankful we are *Mary* is out of danger."

As if you and Charlotte were in the jaws of death, which up here and so far away from you, of course increases my natural terror. Write me, do, at least write me, and *do come away*. The Stampede was disgraceful was it not, owing I hope to the officers of the general army. I cannot believe our men are cowards.

Frank I am thankful to see has escaped through his first baptism of fire. I got a very sad letter from Annie today.

I think Charlotte ought to be with Annie. She says herself "It is not well for her to be so much alone."

We can think and talk of nothing but our disgrace. We long to see you here, but I fear we shall not. The boys are very well and very fine. They read the papers and are all alive to this terrible time.

Hoping that you or Charlotte will write to me, and realize how much I suffer from want of knowledge of you. I am always

Lovingly your daughter
Lizzie

Four days later Charlotte and her father, having survived on the fringe of the battle, were on their way back north, but Lizzie missed Wilson once again. While Charlotte went on to Delhi, he stayed in Lizzie's house in New York—but Lizzie was in Delhi. Alarm having subsided, Lizzie wanted to hear the story of his Washington experience.

"Why cannot you and C.[harlotte] accompany [John] to Delhi? Mr. and Mrs. Sherwood still desire very much to see you and it would be a *godsend* to Mr. S. to hear you talk. Do come dear Father. Else I shall lose all your *early impressions of Washington*" (Lizzie, 7-29-61). Not until she had overstayed her visit by more than a week did Lizzie resign herself to her father's failure to visit Delhi, noting meantime one reason she so much disliked being there: her political differences with old Mr. Sherwood, who had been a partner in a law firm with Henry Clay.

"Mr. Sherwood feels disappointed you did not come here. He would have treated you splendidly as he has a great respect for you. He does not treat other people very well much of the time having a hard tyrannical temper. I know he loves the children and has a good deal of affection for me, so I try to bear with his disagreeabilities which are a few because he is John's father and eighty-three years of age. He is also a firm advocate of slavery and Northern non-intervention, so we do not agree at all. He however approves of putting down the rebellion and raising men and money, and does not wish to have the South beat. He says all manner of hateful things to me on account of my abolition principles, and I am not sorry to leave here" (Lizzie, 8-8-61).

While Lizzie endured the last week of her visit to Delhi, in New Hampshire the fallout from Manassas continued. Frank remained in Washington, but rumors began to circulate in New Hampshire about his conduct during the battle. According to his own ardent account and that of Major Stevens, he acquitted himself with courage enough to make himself and any member of his family proud. Maybe. According to rumor reported by Major Stevens and more than one anonymous paragraph in a newspaper, Stevens himself ran away from the battle and Frank was "so dead drunk" that he could not "ride and had to go and lay down to get sober! that Pearl and Patterson ran into the woods and did not get back to Washington for a week." While there must have been many such rumors following the defeat of the Union army, the particular regard the Wilsons had for the military and for a good story and their shifting regard for Frank made the accounts of his behavior especially fascinating. James Wilson made it his business to investigate. In response to his inquiries, on August 6 both Stevens and Frank wrote to Wilson, Stevens from Concord and Frank from Washington. Wilson annotates Stevens's letter "N. B."

"Your letter has just come to hand enclosing the paragraph which was the first time my attention had been called to it. Who is the author, I have not the least idea but I take pleasure in informing you that upon the day of the battle, Lt. Col. Fiske did his duty and his whole duty, and is as brave a man as ever went upon a battlefield. Immediately after Co. Marston fell, Colonel Fiske assumed command and conducted the regiment for a long time! and it was but a short time before leaving the field that he completely exhausted from excessive exertion and extreme heat asked me to take command while he made the best of his way along with us.

"There seems to be an influence exerted in our state by a great many men to whom better things ought to be expected, against the officers and soldiers of our army.

"Upon my return here to my home, I found that the idea was prevalent in circulation that we had run away from the regiment at the commencement of the fight and was in Washington before dark . . . in Concord . . . I found this report was being circulated by men who *knew better*.

"I am exceeding sorry that this report should be put in circulation, and I hope that my presence here has done much to set the matter right, and I have sought opportunity to express my opinion in regard to Col. Fiske, which is that he is as noble brave and generous an officer as ever led a regiment into battle.

"I have just received a dispatch from him ordering me to leave this afternoon. I suppose by this that we shall move again in a few days" (Stevens, 8-2-61).

✳ [FRANK]

Washington D. C.
6th August 1861

My dear Father in law,

I did not fail, "from any cause whatever, in performing my whole duty," at the battle of Bull Run. I was *invariably* at the head of the Reg't when advancing and *invariably* at the rear in retreat. I have reflected, of course, much on the conduct of the regiment and my own during that day but I can not think of a single order under the orders we received, which I would change now.

But I beg you, Dear Sir, not to have any controversy about it. I think Stevens is entirely innocent of those letters and I enclose you one from him which I received yesterday. Please have it preserved carefully.

I feel the slanders less myself because I hear them constantly of officers of other regiments who behaved as well and better than I did.

Of all things I dislike newspaper controversy. I did my duty to the entire satisfaction of my own conscience.

There was not a man in the regiment more exposed than I was and my example had its weight with the men.

Time will make this appear as I can hear of only two men in the Regiment who will say any thing to the contrary.

If any rumors painful to Annie or you should be prevalent, I would suggest that you should write to Col. Burnside and ask him what he can say about me.

I thank you for the active interest you show in it.

I am going through trials now which are worse than Bull Run, and I am overcoming them. If I do carry the Regiment through these, I shall deserve more credit than from any thing I ever did.—This accomplished I *shall resign.* I will not continue with the Reg't on any terms. So that I shall see you before the 1st of Sept unless there should be a prospect of immediate fighting. . . .

Please do not let my darling wife be annoyed by any rumors but tell her that I say I did my duty *perfectly* and it will appear so before long. . . .

always yours
Aff son in law
Frank L. Fiske

While their father was at home in 1861, important family mementos were parceled out, suggesting how near the children were to breaking their ties with home. Among the three sisters one rite of passage remained before they could declare their independence—psychological and material—from the house in Keene. Charlotte needed a husband.

During her father's visit to the East, he acted as a surrogate suitor for Charlotte. He bought her nice things and saw that she had a good time, which Lizzie approved. On November 22, 1861, Lizzie wrote the last letter that we have from her to her father. In this last letter, written when she was thirty-five, the traditional midpoint of a lifetime, she echoed many themes that occupied her, not the least of which was the refrain that haunted all of her letters—"Where is Father?"

✳ [LIZZIE]   Nov 22d

My dear Father,
    I got your kind letter this morning and was quite relieved for Annie wrote us one a day or two since headed "Where is Father?" We did not know but you had made a mysterious disappearance. I was glad you sent Chardie the money. Let us economize on all other subjects before we begin on her. She never until you came home had any fun or real independence. Being the youngest everything had to be sifted by Annie and me and she took the *bran*, so now she is getting furs etc which will be useful to her all her life, and which are cheap now, because as a handsome young lady, as she is, she ought to be well dressed. She is the embodiment of unselfishness and goodness you know, so I think she ought to have a real good time now Father is home. Said she 'He is better than a *dozen* husbands,' which is true. . . .
    We want you to come down and eat Thanksgiving dinner with us next Thursday. Sam says it will be jolly if you'll come. Perhaps Billings will be back. If so I will ask him. Do come dear Papa. Now Frank is home you can leave Annie. John and I, and Charlotte and the boys all desire it so much.
                                                            Affectionately your daughter
                                                                        Lizzie

Playfully, Charlotte repeated the message to her father. "If you ever wish me to be married to anyone, dear Father, you must begin to treat me with severity, for indeed I am only too content with such a protector" (Charlotte, 11-22-61). She need not have imagined that her father would monopolize her for long. As abruptly as his attentions began, so did they end. In September 1862, General Wilson deposited in the bank a note for $2,500 from John Sherwood for 7 percent, along with a note from Levi Chamberlain for $2,000, the interest from both to be paid to Charlotte. Assuming the note from Chamberlain was also for 7 percent, he left Charlotte with an independent income of a little over $300 as he, without a backward glance, returned to California.

"I closed the house, put the silver and your trunk of papers in the bank as my property and Mr. Newell promised to deliver it to no person but me. I sold the old and useless things and they brought me about sixty dollars," Lizzie wrote of packing up the house the first of December 1850 when the children dispersed for that first winter after their father left. Before they left his house forever, his daughters had opened and closed the house in Keene fourteen times, moving into and out of it seasonally in joy, sorrow, regret, dread, anger, relief. In that house Mary Wilson had had seven children and despaired as three of her sons died; Lizzie had had two sons there. For a few years Lizzie's children had made the house at Main and Emerald streets a second home. Annie had got married and had a daughter there, but the quarrel between Frank Fiske and Lizzie ended that idyll. General Wilson came and went.

Two years passed, during which there was another long gap in the correspondence—a gap that is like a breathless pause before the end, the last letter in the correspondence. Annie and Frank remained in Boston and had a son, "a splendid bright fellow" who had a great fondness for music. Lizzie and John bought a house in New York, partially with money Wilson lent them. The war raged on. The slaves were freed.

From entries in Wilson's diaries we learn how Wilson felt about the children who had grown up without much close attention from him. Jamie remained with him in California, taking care of much of Wilson's business, and by and large Wilson was pleased with him. "My son came in and we talked an hour after I went to bed. He told me all about his day's business. . . . He seems to be taking hold of business in earnest and at the right end. I hope he will persevere and I pray God to prosper him. He can do it if he will. His views are elevated and he can now look up and go ahead with no little contemptible pickaune business, no ninepenny yankee grocery or three cent tape 7 needle affair or what is worse two bit professional engagements to cramp and embarrass him" (4-28-64).

About Annie he was even more pleased. "This morning . . . my Son got [a letter] from his Sister Annie. A noble grand letter that of Annie's. *She has more sense than any woman I ever knew* and I must say it if she is my daughter. Her perception is exceedingly penetrating and quick—her judgement always just and unerring. Her Brother thinks there never was such another woman in all respects so grand and noble and *'dats whar I gree wid him'* " (4-28-64).

Meanwhile, Charlotte made herself useful in her sisters' households. She supervised the schooling of Lizzie's children, comforted Annie while Frank was away, explained one faction of the family to another. Of course, none of these activities was as satisfactory as having a household of her own. But Charlotte played the courtship game without any of the passion of Annie or the élan of Lizzie. She remained the coy ingenue long after she weighed 140 pounds and hoped without much hope that some worthy man would find her engaging enough to marry.

November 1864: the Civil War was drawing to a close. Suddenly Charlotte was married; she was twenty-nine. Without hints or innuendos to prepare us for a big event, Charlotte wrote not about her engagement or even her wedding but about returning to Keene from her honeymoon to lock up the house and about the state of the family finances as she, like her sisters before her, gave a last accounting of the chaotic affairs in the eccentric history of the Wilson family as she departed.

Her new husband was Frank Taintor, a banker from New York, and probably a son of the Taintors who, twelve years earlier, had invited Lizzie and Annie to go to hear Jennie Lind, the invitation the sisters refused because they were too busy closing up the house for the winter following their father's departure for California. Probably, but not necessarily, for his name is not listed in the Connecticut census. There are no letters from Lizzie or Annie about Charlotte's marriage to give us a clue about whether Frank Taintor was charming or rich or ambitious or disagreeable or silly or lazy. Whether Charlotte loved and admired him or not she does not say. Whether they had a large wedding or not we can only judge from the accounting she gives of her finances. She spent $1,175. The wedding was already over when we first learn of it.

She gave her father one final accounting, then referred him to Mr. Vose and Mr. Elliot, two Keene bankers, for further details of his affairs. Thus, she relinquished the last claim she had to his support and the last responsibility she had for his property.

Now Charlotte Wilson Taintor put the house at Emerald and Main in order one last time. This time she left it to be rented, perhaps to a stranger. The house the family had held in a death grip as symbolic and actual protection against disintegration had lost its function. The daughters had grown up and created families in other houses. Charlotte's clumsy prose describing her final disposition of her father's personal treasures—his books and even his bedding—betrays her shock at her own lack of interest as she tells him, "Of course, Sir, it is all yours" and "of course, you will decide."

✳ [CHARLOTTE]   Windham Nov. 8th 1864

My dearest Father,

Mr. Taintor and I left Windham a fortnight since, and have made two visits since, a week at Hartford with Mrs. John Taintor, where we had a very pleasant time, and another week we spent with Annie in Boston. We found her and her little covey all well. I suppose you know she expects another addition to her family in December.

While I was there I received your letter about the arrangement you desired made at Keene, so we went up there for a day before we returned here, and having consulted Annie I had every thing arranged as you desired.

I have, of course, not heard yet your decision regarding letting the house, but Annie and I thought the house better be left so that it could be let if you desired.

So I put away every thing nearly in the Hall, marked with your name, and locked up the heavy furniture down stairs in the third bed room over the shed, which you can reserve you know. I had little blocks of wood secured in front of all the book case doors, so they couldn't be opened, and locked up a closet in the Hall all the china left in the closet, with the bedding of your bed. Annie has the key.

With her approval I took some carpets and china.

The silver I have in a trunk locked up. I shall send a list of it to her and to you. Of course, Sir, it is all yours. I only should like to use some, as you say, now, to avoid buying at this dreadful time.

Even if you decide not to let the House it will do no hurt to leave the things as they are. So many people go in and out of the house.

David and Daniel Seward are opposed to having the house let, but we all approve of it. That of course, you will decide however.

About the account at the bank, which you think stands this way,

Col. R.'s note	1,000
Mr. Sherwood	800
check	200
order J. B. E.	100
	2,100

I have had only, from the Bank, this September

Col. R.'s note	200
John Sherwood's note	500
Interest on J. Sherwood's note	175

Check from you   200

J. B. E.   100

                                    1,175

I found Mr. Elliot had not kept any account but in my name, that Uncle Robert had paid all the 2,000 dollars, and that Mr. Elliot had paid out of that a note to Mr. Vose, the interest at the Savings Bank, and other things, so that now there is nothing left.

You will see I have only just had enough to get ready to be married. And I had to keep Mr. Sherwood's money, as I had not enough without it. I told John Sherwood all about it, and he understood it.

I also asked Mr. Elliot to give you an account of the present state of affairs, of your account. I hope he has done so.

John said (in October) he should have about forty dollars of Jamie's to give me. He told me last September that it would be about 125, or so, but I suppose Jamie knows about it.

We are now spending a fortnight here with Mr. and Mrs. Taintor. They are very kind and considerate. I am extremely fond of them already. They would like to know you very much. When you come Home I depend upon your knowing each other. I am sure you will like them.

My Husband sends his regards to you. And with my best love to Jamie, believe me your devoted daughter   Charlotte

I wish you could see Annie's boy. He is a splendid large bright fellow. He doesn't walk yet, but his mind is more developed, and he is very fine. He has discovered a great fondness for music, which the others have not. Theirs is being cultivated however, and, as they are taught to sing at the little school to which they go I suppose they will yet love it.

So the house was closed, and Charlotte looked to the new generation that absorbed so much attention from the family. Even as she, the last daughter, found a husband of her own, "your devoted daughter" seems a more appropriate ending to this correspondence than "they lived happily ever after."

Epilogue

The story of Lizzie, Annie, and Charlotte in Keene and New York and the story of James Wilson, Jr., in California, bridged by the family correspondence, never really merge. For another five years General James Wilson chased the fortune that continued to elude him. Finally in 1867, when he was seventy years old, he left California for the East. He did not follow Lizzie's good advice and settle in New York. Thanks to his daughters' resolution, he still owned the house at the corner of Main and Emerald streets, though he owned almost nothing else, and there he lived for the rest of his life. He sold the rest of his property in California, New Hampshire, and Iowa to appease his creditors. All that remained of his golden dream of finding a fortune in the West was his recollection of the exciting and colorful pursuit. He had years left to feast on those memories, for Wilson was not to die in a timely fashion. In 1871 voters returned him to the legislature in Concord—according to some letters to avoid supporting him in the poorhouse. When he died in 1881 at eighty-four, his will contained a brief list of household possessions to be disposed of to his children. Everything else went to his creditors, and even then debts remained.

Jamie, too, returned to Keene. He never married. Perhaps he too much enjoyed philandering, or perhaps he was leery of being dominated by yet another woman. He, like his father and uncle, took an active part in civic life. Unlike them, Jamie did not live to a ripe old age but died in Keene when he was only two years older than James Wilson had been when he left for California.

About Charlotte's marriage we have only public records, which yield a few sad, cold facts. The public registry tells us that in 1877 or 1878 Charlotte returned to Keene with her three children and began teaching music, and a year or two later her husband joined her. Two thin yellowing forms registered at the Cheshire County Court House record that Frank Taintor became violent and was committed to the state mental hospital in Concord in 1879 and again in 1897. The first is signed by Charlotte, the second by her eldest son, Giles. Charlotte nursed her brother during his last illness. Realizing that he was dying, Jamie made her youngest son, Charles, his heir, with the proviso that his name be changed from Charles Taintor to Charles Wilson Taintor.

Annie and Frank Fiske lived in Boston but maintained a house in Keene as well. Doubtless with Annie's encouragement, Frank abandoned his wandering ways and any serious ambitions to be a writer and became a prosperous lawyer. Though her husband, like her father, tended to be reckless with money, Annie seems never again to have felt the pinch of poverty. Ultimately, Annie also returned to Keene.

However, the lives of Annie and Charlotte remained private. Only Lizzie led a public life and published her memoirs as well as poems, short stories, and a monumentally successful book of etiquette that bore a striking resemblance to the work of her friend Lydia Sigourney. She progressed from social success to social success during the Gilded Age in America and traveled frequently to Europe, where she repeated the process, her career climaxing when Queen Victoria gave her a small diamond pin. Those would be interesting stories, too. The frail Wil died at twelve and was buried in Delhi, but Arthur lived to father the playwright Robert Sherwood—named, perhaps, after Annie's first love.

Unlike their father, brother, and husbands, all three sisters lived to see the twentieth century. Lizzie died in 1903 at age seventy-seven in New York, the only member of the family not buried in Keene. Annie died in 1916 at age eighty-four, and Charlotte died in 1900 at sixty-six. Charlotte and Annie are both buried in the family plot in Keene alongside their father, brother, mother, various children, and their maid Roxana.

The house on Main and Emerald streets was sold and eventually torn down to make way for a service station, since vacated. So the physical treasure of the Wilson family passed like the feelings the daughters wrote about, but the letter remains.

Sources and Acknowledgments

It seems to be impossible to separate our acknowledgments from our bibliography because people led us to books, and books led us to people. The project began with a fortuitous meeting with Carolyn Baldwin, who had cataloged the letters for the New Hampshire Historical Society. There, historian Stephen Cox, now the historian at Connor Prairie Museum in Indiana, gave us access to the material (Wilson, James, 1797–1881: Papers, 1835–1873; in the New Hampshire Historical Society manuscript collections, Concord, N.H.); better yet, with great generosity of spirit he encouraged us and guided us through the early days of the work. The New Hampshire Charitable Trust provided us with a grant for the transcription of the letters. The typist, Deborah Hodges, turned out to be a student of nineteenth-century American history and helped us to date some of the late letters.

In our work with the Wilson letters we have traveled many miles, run down any number of blind alleys, and flipped thousands of pages in pursuit of answers to questions raised by the letters. We have also talked with many historians, amateur and professional, looking for clues. All of those conversations, as well as those with audiences who have come out on icy New Hampshire nights to hear us present the Wilsons' story, have been invaluable to us in shaping our approach to these letters. Nancy Muller, a friend who is curator of the Susan Colby papers at Colby-Sawyer College and Director of the State New Hampshire Historic Preservation Office, took an early interest in our work and unearthed an important cache of letters from the Wilson daughters to Susan Colby.

Perhaps every scholar has one central library that functions as a fount of information for the most important and biggest matters to the smallest and most minute details. For us it was Baker Library at Dartmouth College. The reference staff has shown tireless patience in digging up bits of information for us. Alan Rumrill of the Cheshire County Historical Society has provided us with helpful information about the family, as has the Delaware County (New York) Historical Association. The librarians at the New Hampshire Historical Society, the New England Genealogical Society, the Boston Public Library, the New Hampshire State Library, the Charlestown Historical Society, and the Colby-Sawyer College library were tireless resources. The New Hampshire Council on the Humanities has given us numerous opportunities to present the history of the Wilson family to audiences throughout the state.

Scholars and acquaintances Joan Esch, Mary Kelley, Sarah Woolfolk Wiggins, Jere Daniell, Christine Stansell, Laurel Ulrich, Laurence Davies, the late Tom Biuso, Perry Spiegel, Michelle Seaton, Dr. Stanley Rosenberg, Frances and Bill Rutter, and Elizabeth Hamlin-Morin have given us kind encouragement and information.

For the social and political ambience of the 1850s and 1860s that formed the background for these letters, we relied on George F. Bacon, *Keene and Vicinity: Its Points of Interest and Its Representative Businessmen* (Newark, N.J.: Mercantile Publishing Co., 1891); issues of the *Keene Sentinel* from 1850 to 1860 and *The Patriot* (1845–1854); Thomas C. Rand's, *A Sketch of Keene, The Gem of the Ashuelot Valley* (Keene, N.H.: Sentinel Press, 1895); and Clifford C. Wilbur, *The Story of Central Square, Keene, New Hampshire* (Keene, N.H.: Keene National Bank, 1945). We owe a special debt to S. G. Griffin, *A History of the Town of Keene from 1732* (Keene, N.H.: Sentinel Printing Co., 1904). Though the principal source for information about James Wilson, Jr., and his family remains his collected papers (1835–1873) at the New Hampshire Historical Society, we were able to reconstruct parts of the family's history by searching the collection at the Cheshire County Historical Society in Keene as well as the records of the Clerk of Wills and Deeds at the Cheshire County Court House.

Gravemarkers for all members of the family except Lizzie are in the Keene cemetery. They provided us with death dates for Annie, Roxana, and others.

General histories of the state of New Hampshire (particularly, of course, Nancy Coffey Heffernan and Ann Page Stecker, *New Hampshire: Crosscurrents in Its Development* [Grantham, N.H.: Tompson & Rutter, 1986] provided necessary details about the economic and political life in the state during the Wilson family's lifetime. We also mined nineteenth- and twentieth-century biographical encyclopedias such as Appleton's *Cyclopedia of American Biography* (1898); congressional records covering Wilson's tenure in Washington; U.S. census records; the social registers of New York City, Boston, Washington, and Hartford; and histories of the gold rush (Oscar Lewis, *Sea Routes to the Gold Fields* [New York: Knopf, 1949], and Kevin Starr, *Americans and the California Dream, 1850–1915* [New York: Oxford University Press, 1973]); the Gilded Age (Sean Dennis Cashman, *America in the Gilded Age* [New York: New York University Press, 1984]);

and the Civil War (James M. McPherson, *The Battle Cry of Freedom: The Civil War Era* [New York: Oxford University Press, 1988]).

The rich body of material on the lives and experiences of women in the nineteenth century that has been produced in the past twenty years was invaluable to our research. In spirit, methodology, and content this new work has enabled us to expand our notions of what is "historical" from start to finish. The following were particularly helpful: Martha Banta, *Imaging American Women: Idea and Ideals in Cultural History* (New York: Columbia University Press, 1987); Rachel Brownstein, *Becoming a Heroine: Reading about Women in Novels* (New York: Viking Press, 1982); Nancy F. Cott, *The Bonds of Womanhood: Woman's Sphere in New England, 1780–1835* (New Haven, Conn.: Yale University Press, 1977); Carl N. Degler, *At Odds: Women and the Family in America from the Revolution to the Present* (New York: Oxford University Press, 1980); Ann Douglas, *The Feminization of American Culture* (New York: Anchor Press, 1988), and "Heaven Our Home: Consolation Literature in the Northern United States, 1830–1880" (*American Quarterly* 26 [1974]: 496–515); Jane H. Hunter, "Inscribing the Self in the Heart of the Family: Diaries and Girlhood in Late-Victorian America" (*American Quarterly* 44 [1992]: 53ff); Edward T. James, Janet Wilson, and Paul S. Boyer, *Notable American Women, 1607–1950* (Cambridge, Mass.: Belknap Press, 1971); Joan Kelly, *Women, History, and Theory: The Essays of Joan Kelly* (Chicago: University of Chicago Press, 1984); Linda Kerber, Nancy F. Cott, Robert Gross, Lynn Hunt, Carroll Smith-Rosenberg, and Christine Stansell, "Beyond Roles, Beyond Spheres: Thinking About Gender in the Early Republic—A Symposium" (*William and Mary Quarterly* 46 [1989]: 565–85); Carol Lasser, "Let Us Be Sisters Forever: The Sororal Model of Nineteenth Century Female Friendship" (*Signs* 14 [1988]: 158–81); Mary P. Ryan, *Cradle of the Middle Class: The Family in Oneida County, New York, 1790–1865* (Cambridge, Mass.: Harvard University Press, 1981); Lillian Schlissel, *Women's Diaries of the Westward Journey* (New York: Schocken Books, 1982); Carroll Smith-Rosenberg, "The Female World of Love and Ritual: Relations between Women in Nineteenth-Century America" (*Signs* 1 [1975]: 1–29); Christine Stansell, *City of Women: Work, Sex and Class in New York, 1789–1860* (New York: Knopf, 1987); Laurel Ulrich, *Good Wives: Image and Reality in Northern New England, 1650–1750* (New York: Oxford University Press, 1980), and *A Midwife's Tale: The Life of Martha Ballard Based on Her Diary, 1785–1812* (New York: Oxford University Press, 1990); and Barbara Welter, "The Cult of True Womanhood: 1820–1860" *American Quarterly* 18 [1966]: 151–74).

In a related area of inquiry we pursued demographic studies and histories of the family in America in the nineteenth century. Among the most useful sources we found were the following: Michael Gordon, ed.,

The American Family in Socio-Historical Perspective (New York: St. Martin's Press, 1973); Tamara Hareven, ed., *Transitions: The Family and the Life Cycle in Historical Perspective* (New York: Academic Press, 1978); Tamara Hareven and Maris Vinovskis, eds., *Family and Population in 19th Century America* (Princeton, N.J.: Princeton University Press, 1978); N. Ray Hiner and Joseph M. Hawes, *Growing Up in America: Children in Historical Perspective* (Urbana: University of Illinois Press, 1985); Arlene and Jerome Skolnick, *Family in Transition*, 7th ed. (New York: Harper Collins, 1992); Robert V. Wells, *Revolutions in American Lives: A Demographic Perspective on the History of Americans, Their Families, and Their Society* (Westport, Conn.: Greenwood Press, 1982).

Although it is not hard to find scholarly discussions of the value of the private letters of public figures, finding studies of the letter as a literary genre is more difficult. Janet Altman's *Epistolarity: Approaches to a Form* (Columbus: Ohio State University Press, 1982) introduces this idea with special reference to fiction.

In ways she could never know, Mary Elizabeth Wilson Sherwood (M.E.W.S., Lizzie) also helped us shape our study of her family's letters. Her published writing established her as a popular memoirist, novelist, and arbitrator of manners in her day. This body of writing includes *Amenities of Home* (New York: D. Appleton, 1884), *The Art of Entertaining* (New York: Dodd Mead, 1892), *An Epistle to Posterity* (New York: Harper & Brothers, 1897), *Manners and Social Usage* (New York: Harper & Brothers, 1884), and *The Transplanted Rose* (New York: Harper & Brothers, 1884). They await a biographer's interest, but they never grip the reader with the intensity of one paragraph of a letter to her father. John Mason Brown's biography of Lizzie's grandson, playwright Robert Sherwood (*The Worlds of Robert Sherwood: Mirror of His Times* [New York: Harper & Row, 1965]), contains some interesting observations on Lizzie in her declining years.

We thank our friends for listening to us talk about the Wilsons at innumerable dinner tables. And most of all, of course, we thank our families—our mothers, who saw the beginning of the project but did not live to see it completed; our husbands, Jim and Rick; and our children, Virginia, Andrew, and Hardy.

Index

UNIVERSITY PRESS OF NEW ENGLAND publishes books under its own imprint and is the publisher for Brandeis University Press, Brown University Press, University of Connecticut, Dartmouth College, Middlebury College Press, University of New Hampshire, University of Rhode Island, Tufts University, University of Vermont, and Wesleyan University Press.

Library of Congress Cataloging-in-Publication Data

Heffernan, Nancy Coffey, 1936–
    Sisters of fortune : being the true story of how three motherless sisters saved their home in New England and raised their younger brother while their father went fortune hunting in the California Gold Rush / Nancy Coffey Heffernan and Ann Page Stecker.
    p.   cm.
Includes index.
ISBN 0–87451–650–1. — ISBN 0–87451–651–X (pbk.)
    1. Keene (N.H.) —Biography.   2. Wilson family—Correspondence.   3. Wilson, James, 1797–1881—Correspondence.   4. Women—New Hampshire—Keene—History—19th century.   I. Stecker, Ann Page, 1942–   .   II. Title.
F44.K2H44   1993
974.2'9—dc20
[B]   93–19716
∞